CWTS®

Certified Wireless
Technology Specialist

Official Study Guide

Second Edition

CWTS®

Certified Wireless Technology Specialist

Official Study Guide

Second Edition

Robert J. Bartz

John Wiley & Sons, Inc.

Senior Acquisitions Editor: Jeff Kellum
Development Editor: Jim Compton
Technical Editors: Bryan Harkins and Tom Carpenter
Production Editor: Eric Charbonneau
Copy Editor: Liz Welch
Editorial Manager: Pete Gaughan
Production Manager: Tim Tate
Vice President and Executive Group Publisher: Richard Swadley
Vice President and Publisher: Neil Edde
Media Project Manager 1: Laura Moss-Hollister
Media Associate Producer: Josh Frank
Media Quality Assurance: Doug Kuhn
Book Designer: Judy Fung
Proofreader: Nancy Bell
Indexer: Ted Laux
Project Coordinator, Cover: Katherine Crocker
Cover Designer: Ryan Sneed

Copyright © 2012 by John Wiley & Sons, Inc., Indianapolis, Indiana

Published simultaneously in Canada

ISBN: 978-1-118-35911-2

ISBN: 978-1-118-49487-5 (ebk.)

ISBN: 978-1-118-46131-0 (ebk.)

ISBN: 978-1-118-49484-4 (ebk.)

Dear Reader,

Thank you for choosing *CWTS: Certified Wireless Technology Specialist Official Study Guide, Second Edition*. This book is part of a family of premium-quality Sybex books, all of which are written by outstanding authors who combine practical experience with a gift for teaching.

Sybex was founded in 1976. More than 30 years later, we're still committed to producing consistently exceptional books. With each of our titles, we're working hard to set a new standard for the industry. From the paper we print on to the authors we work with, our goal is to bring you the best books available.

I hope you see all that reflected in these pages. I'd be very interested to hear your comments and get your feedback on how we're doing. Feel free to let me know what you think about this or any other Sybex book by sending me an email at nedde@wiley.com. If you think you've found a technical error in this book, please visit http://sybex.custhelp.com. Customer feedback is critical to our efforts at Sybex.

Best regards,

Neil Edde
Vice President and Publisher
Sybex, an Imprint of Wiley

Acknowledgments

I would like to thank my wife, Jeannie, and two adult children, Ashley and Jason, for their support and patience during the writing of this book. They made completing this project much easier for me.

I would also like to thank everyone at Sybex who helped with the creation of this book, including acquisitions editor Jeff Kellum, production editor Eric Charbonneau, copy editor Liz Welch, editorial assistant Connor O'Brien and editorial manager Pete Gaughan. I owe all these individuals a lot of thanks for their patience while working with me on this book and keeping things on track. Jim Compton is the Development Editor for this edition of the book. Many thanks go to Jim for his time and his work in helping with the flow, organization, and suggestions that allowed me to make this book an easier read. His knowledge and attention to detail were a huge help. Also, thanks to Tom Carpenter the proofread technical editor for this edition of the book.

The Technical Editor for this edition of the book again is Bryan Harkins. I want to thank Bryan for his timely reviews, comments, and great suggestions that helped make this book a valuable reference source. His years of experience as a technical trainer, engineer, security specialist and author were a great contribution in creating a book I hope you will enjoy reading.

I would again like to thank the thousands of students who have taken the time to attend the computer networking classes I was given the opportunity to teach. Educating, mentoring, and entertaining so many of these individuals gave me the inspiration and motivation to author this book and hopefully many more.

Of course, this book would not exist if it were not for the people at CWNP. The CWNP team has realized the need for vendor-neutral wireless LAN training and certification and has done a great job of building a brand over the years that is now known worldwide.

Finally, a thank you to all the manufacturers, vendors, organizations, and individuals that provided the subject matter, allowing me the technology and tools needed to write this book.

Aerohive (www.aerohive.com): Devin Akin and Bryan Harkins

AirMagnet/Fluke Networks (www.flukenetworks.com): Joe Kuo

Aruba Networks (www.arubanetworks.com)

Broadcom Corporation (www.broadcom.com)

Cisco Systems (www.cisco.com)

CompactFlash Association (www.compactflash.org)

CWNP (www.cwnp.com)

Ekahau (www.ekahau.com): Jussi Kiviniemi

EnGenius Technologies (www.engeniustech.com)

HP ProCurve (www.procurve.com)

IEEE (www.ieee.org)

Intel (www.intel.com)

L-com Global Connectivity (www.l-com.com): Jim Corcoran

MetaGeek (www.metageek.net): Mark Jensen, Trent Cutler and Ryan Woodings

Motorola (www.motorola.com)

Netgear (www.netgear.com)

Network Stumbler (www.netstumbler.com)

PCI-SIG (www.pcisig.com)

Proxim Wireless (www.proxim.com)

Psiber Data Systems (www.psiber.com)

SD Association (www.sdcard.org)

TamoSoft (www.tamos.com): Michael Berg

TerraWave Solutions (www.terrawave.com)

USB Implementers Forum, Inc. (www.usb.org)

Wi-Fi Alliance (www.wi-fi.org)

WildPackets (www.wildpackets.com)

Xirrus (www.xirrus.com)

IEEE (www.ieee.org)

Intel (www.intel.com)

L-com Global Connectivity (www.l-com.com): Jim Corcoran

MetaGeek (www.metageek.net): Mark Jensen, Trent Cutler and Ryan Woodings

Motorola (www.motorola.com)

Netgear (www.netgear.com)

Network Stumbler (www.netstumbler.com)

PCI-SIG (www.pcisig.com)

Proxim Wireless (www.proxim.com)

Psiber Data Systems (www.psiber.com)

SD Association (www.sdcard.org)

TamoSoft (www.tamos.com): Michael Berg

TerraWave Solutions (www.terrawave.com)

USB Implementers Forum, Inc. (www.usb.org)

Wi-Fi Alliance (www.wi-fi.org)

WildPackets (www.wildpackets.com)

Xirrus (www.xirrus.com)

Acknowledgments

I would like to thank my wife, Jeannie, and two adult children, Ashley and Jason, for their support and patience during the writing of this book. They made completing this project much easier for me.

I would also like to thank everyone at Sybex who helped with the creation of this book, including acquisitions editor Jeff Kellum, production editor Eric Charbonneau, copy editor Liz Welch, editorial assistant Connor O'Brien and editorial manager Pete Gaughan. I owe all these individuals a lot of thanks for their patience while working with me on this book and keeping things on track. Jim Compton is the Development Editor for this edition of the book. Many thanks go to Jim for his time and his work in helping with the flow, organization, and suggestions that allowed me to make this book an easier read. His knowledge and attention to detail were a huge help. Also, thanks to Tom Carpenter the proofread technical editor for this edition of the book.

The Technical Editor for this edition of the book again is Bryan Harkins. I want to thank Bryan for his timely reviews, comments, and great suggestions that helped make this book a valuable reference source. His years of experience as a technical trainer, engineer, security specialist and author were a great contribution in creating a book I hope you will enjoy reading.

I would again like to thank the thousands of students who have taken the time to attend the computer networking classes I was given the opportunity to teach. Educating, mentoring, and entertaining so many of these individuals gave me the inspiration and motivation to author this book and hopefully many more.

Of course, this book would not exist if it were not for the people at CWNP. The CWNP team has realized the need for vendor-neutral wireless LAN training and certification and has done a great job of building a brand over the years that is now known worldwide.

Finally, a thank you to all the manufacturers, vendors, organizations, and individuals that provided the subject matter, allowing me the technology and tools needed to write this book.

Aerohive (www.aerohive.com): Devin Akin and Bryan Harkins

AirMagnet/Fluke Networks (www.flukenetworks.com): Joe Kuo

Aruba Networks (www.arubanetworks.com)

Broadcom Corporation (www.broadcom.com)

Cisco Systems (www.cisco.com)

CompactFlash Association (www.compactflash.org)

CWNP (www.cwnp.com)

Ekahau (www.ekahau.com): Jussi Kiviniemi

EnGenius Technologies (www.engeniustech.com)

HP ProCurve (www.procurve.com)

About the Author

Robert J. Bartz is a technical trainer and computer networking consultant. He is a graduate of California State University Long Beach, School of Engineering, with a Bachelor of Science degree in Industrial Technology. Prior to becoming a computer networking engineer and technical instructor, Robert was employed as an aerospace test engineer working with radar systems and satellite communications. He has attained many technical certifications over the years, including Master Certified Novell Engineer (MCNE), Master Certified Novell Instructor (MCNI), Microsoft Certified Systems Engineer (MCSE), Microsoft Certified Trainer (MCT), CWNP Certified Wireless Network Administrator (CWNA), Certified Wireless Security Professional (CWSP), and Certified Wireless Network Trainer (CWNT), to name a few. He has over 20 years' experience with computer networking technology and has been involved with the CWNP program since its inception.

Robert attended the first ever CWNA class in 2001 and has taught vendor-neutral IEEE 802.11 wireless LAN technology to thousands of people from various industries and markets across the United States and abroad. Robert is the founder of Eight-O-Two Technology Solutions, LLC, a computer networking technical training and consulting services company providing technical education and services to various organizations local to Colorado and around the country. He spends his spare time learning new technology, having fun outside, and enjoying the beauty of his surroundings at his home in Colorado. Robert is working to one day semi-retire and be the proprietor of a neighborhood eating and drinking establishment in a warm sunny beach community. He can be contacted by e-mail at robert@eightotwo.com.

Contents at a Glance

Contents

Appendix   B   **About the Additional Study Tools**   **519**

Table of Exercises

Foreword

One of the most popular questions that we get through our Forums, customer service email, Twitter account, and phone system is this: "Where do I start in Wi-Fi?" Great question, indeed. So what's the answer? It depends.

It depends on where you are. If the whole subject of Wi-Fi or WLAN or 802.11 is just plain foreign to you, you should start right here: CWTS. We created the CWTS certification for you and people like you. The audience for the CWTS study materials and exam continues to grow, but the groups that make up the audience remain very constant. There are three main groups of people who are actively seeking their CWTS certification: IT Sales Professionals, IT Project Managers, and brand new IT Professionals. Yes, there are people with other titles that don't fall into these buckets, but 80–90% of the CWTS audience falls into one of these three groups. Why? Another good question.

One of the reasons many people never try anything new is fear of the unknown. Even ten years into its life, Wi-Fi is still basically unknown in the IT world. Yes, everyone knows about Wi-Fi, but very few really know Wi-Fi in all its intricate detail. Do you doubt that? Next time you're in the presence of a CWNE or CCIE-Wireless, ask them this question: "What percentage of network engineers really knows Wi-Fi?" The answer will be somewhere south of 50% and more likely lower. Think about that: after 10+ years on the market, astounding market segment growth every one of those years, and near ubiquity in homes and small businesses, your average mainstream network engineer doesn't know Wi-Fi.

So why is that? From our perspective, it's partly that "fear of the unknown" thing, and also the incredible fallacy that Wi-Fi is easy, plug-n-play, anyone can do it, etc. That fallacy was born from the fact that Wi-Fi got its initial growth and market acceptance in the home. You can still get a really good 802.11n home router for less than $100, and have it set up to connect all your household Wi-Fi devices in a few minutes. That is the perception that most IT folks take into their job, and that's what gets them into a lot of trouble.

So this book, and the CWTS certification, serves as one early stepping stone to overcoming the falsehood that, just because you set up your home Wi-Fi network in less than an hour, you can run a mission-critical enterprise Wi-Fi network with no new training or knowledge. This book will enable you, as a fledgling network engineer, project manager, or sales professional, to "get it," meaning you will get the basics of Wi-Fi, RF behavior, and why a home Wi-Fi network is ever so much simpler than an enterprise Wi-Fi network.

Armed with this knowledge, you can "talk the talk," so to speak, when it comes to implementing Wi-Fi. No longer will your Wi-Fi SEs talk over your head or feed you a line of bull just to see if you know what you're talking about. When you understand the fundamentals of Wi-Fi, you are ready to jump with both feet into the amazing world of 802.11 communications. This is your starting point, your first step, your headlong adventure into something new that you need no longer fear.

Wi-Fi is here. Wi-Fi is everywhere. Wi-Fi is no longer a technology we wish we had everywhere all the time. Wi-Fi is everywhere all the time. Unfortunately, sometimes that Wi-Fi service stinks. Why? Why doesn't it work? Why is it so hard to provide Wi-Fi to your customers, guests, employees? Well, you're about to find out that Wi-Fi is not that difficult. It's just that different.

But we must warn you: Wi-Fi is cool. I mean it's way cool. So be careful here. If you're not ready to dive into a technology that may transform your spare time, learning capacity, and maybe even your career, you may not want to read any further.

> Never be afraid to try something new. Remember, amateurs built the ark, professionals built the Titanic. — Unknown

—Kevin Sandlin
CWNP Co-Founder & CEO

Introduction

This book is intended to provide an introduction to the exciting and emerging world of IEEE 802.11 wireless LAN technology. This technology continues to expand at a phenomenal pace, with constant improvements in speed, performance, reliability, and security. Reading this book will teach you the fundamentals of IEEE 802.11 standards-based wireless technology, giving you an overview of the hardware and software components, radio frequency communication principals, terminology overview, and support and maintenance associated with wireless LAN technology, commonly referred to as Wi-Fi™.

In addition to providing an overview of the technology, this book will help you prepare for the Certified Wireless Technology Specialist (CWTS) certification exam available from the Certified Wireless Network Professional (CWNP) program. CWTS is an entry-level enterprise wireless LAN certification, and is recommended as preparation for the Certified Wireless Network Administrator (CWNA) certification. This certification is geared specifically toward wireless local area network (WLAN) support staff, sales and marketing personnel, or anyone who wants to become more familiar with the enterprise WLAN industry.

Not only will this book help you prepare for the CWTS Certification exam, it will give you the fundamental knowledge, tools, and terminology to more effectively sell and support enterprise IEEE 802.11 WLAN technologies. The main goal of this book is for you to learn "what it is," not "how it works." The "how" part comes later, in other CWNP Study Guides and instructor-led courses. After reading this book and completing all the available practice exam tools included, you will have the knowledge needed to take the CWTS certification exam.

For more information about the CWTS and other vendor-neutral wireless LAN certifications from the CWNP program, visit www.cwnp.com.

About CWNP®

CWNP is the abbreviation for Certified Wireless Network Professional and is the industry standard for vendor-neutral, enterprise wireless LAN certifications. The CWNP program develops courseware and certification exams for IEEE 802.11 WLAN technologies in the computer networking industry.

CWNP offers several levels of enterprise WLAN certifications, from novice to expert. The goal of CWNP is to provide educational resources and certifications that are recognized worldwide to information technology (IT) and sales professionals in the field of IEEE 802.11 wireless networking technology. By acquiring this knowledge, these professionals will be able to enter any business and sell, design, install, manage, and support a wireless LAN infrastructure regardless of which manufacturer's solution is used.

In addition to CWTS, there are five other wireless certifications currently offered from CWNP:

CWNA: Certified Wireless Network Administrator   The CWNA (Certified Wireless Network Administrator) certification is the foundation-level enterprise wireless LAN certification for the CWNP program. The CWNA certification will validate one's skills to successfully administer enterprise-class wireless LANs. Passing the CWNA exam will also earn the base certification toward the more advanced CWNP certifications. The CWNA exam measures one's ability to understand all of the features and functions of IEEE 802.11 WLAN technology. Passing the PW0-105 certification exam will satisfy the requirement to become CWNA certified.

CWSP: Certified Wireless Security Professional   The CWSP (Certified Wireless Security Professional) certification is one of the advanced-level WLAN certifications offered by the CWNP program. Acquiring this certification will prove one's ability to successfully apply the most up-to-date IEEE 802.11 WLAN security solutions to an organization's IEEE 802.11 wireless network. This certification will ensure that the successful candidate understands the security weaknesses inherent in IEEE 802.11 WLANs, the solutions available to address those weaknesses, and the steps necessary to implement a secure and manageable WLAN in an enterprise environment. Successfully passing two exams is required to become CWSP certified:

- Exam PW0-105 – Certified Wireless Network Administrator
- Exam PW0-204 – Certified Wireless Security Professional

CWDP: Certified Wireless Design Professional   The CWDP (Certified Wireless Design Professional) certification is a professional-level career certification for those in wireless computer networking who have already obtained the CWNA certification and have a thorough understanding of RF technologies and applications of 802.11 networks. This certification prepares WLAN professionals to properly design an IEEE 802.11 WLAN for various environments and for optimal performance. Successfully passing two exams is required to become CWDP certified:

- Exam PW0-105 – Certified Wireless Network Administrator
- Exam PW0-250 – Certified Wireless Design Professional

CWAP: Certified Wireless Analysis Professional   The CWAP (Certified Wireless Analysis Professional) certification is a professional-level career certification for those in wireless computer networking who have already obtained the CWNA certification and have a thorough understanding of RF technologies and applications of 802.11 wireless networks. This certification provides an in-depth look at 802.11 operations and prepares WLAN professionals to be able to perform, interpret, and understand wireless packet and spectrum analysis. You must successfully pass two exams to become CWAP certified:

- Exam PW0-105 – Certified Wireless Network Administrator
- Exam PW0-270 – Certified Wireless Analysis Professional

CWNE: Certified Wireless Network Expert   The CWNE (Certified Wireless Network Expert) credential is the highest certification offered by the CWNP program. By successfully completing the CWNE requirements, you will have demonstrated that you have the most advanced skills available in today's IEEE 802.11 WLAN market. The CWNE certification ensures that you have mastered all relevant skills to administer, install, configure, troubleshoot, and design wireless network systems. Protocol analysis, intrusion detection and prevention, performance and QoS analysis, spectrum analysis and management, and advanced design are some of the areas of expertise you will need to know. Successfully passing four exams is required to become CWNE certified:

- Exam PW0-105 – Certified Wireless Network Administrator
- Exam PW0-204 – Certified Wireless Security Professional
- Exam PW0-250 – Certified Wireless Design Professional
- Exam PW0-270 – Certified Wireless Analysis Professional

The following criteria must also be met:

- Three years of documented enterprise Wi-Fi implementation experience
- Three professional endorsements
- Two other current, valid professional networking certifications
- Documentation of three enterprise Wi-Fi projects in which you participated or led in the form of 500 word essays
- Re-certification every three years by passing the most current version of either the CWSP, CWAP, or CWDP exam

> For additional information on the details required for CWNE certification, visit www.cwnp.com.

CWNT: Certified Wireless Network Trainer   Certified Wireless Network Trainers (CWNT) are qualified instructors certified by the CWNP program to deliver CWNP training courses to IT professionals. CWNTs are technical and instructional experts in wireless technologies, products, and solutions. CWNP Training Partners are required to use CWNTs when delivering training using Official CWNP Courseware.

> Keep in mind that the certification exam numbers listed in this book are as of this writing. When CWNP updates an exam, the exam reference number will change. For the most current information regarding all certifications and exams, visit www.cwnp.com.

CWNP Learning Resources

There are a variety of resources available from CWNP to help learn vendor-neutral wireless LAN technology. Listed are some of these resources:

- Self-study materials
- Official study guides from Sybex
- Online practice exams from www.cwnp.com

- Instructor-led classroom training
- Online live training
- Computer-based training (CBT)
- CWNP website
- CWNP forums
- CWNP blog
- CWNP learning center, offering 1,000+ white papers

How to Become a CWTS

To become a CWTS, you must complete the following two steps:

- Agree that you have read and will abide by the terms and conditions of the CWNP confidentiality agreement.
- Pass the CWTS PW0-071 certification exam.

 A copy of the CWNP confidentiality agreement can be found online at the CWNP website.

When you take the CWTS certification exam, you will be required to accept the confidentiality agreement before you can continue to complete the exam. After you have agreed, you will be able to continue with the exam. When you pass the exam with a score of 70 percent or higher, you will have met the requirements to become CWTS certified.

The information for the CWTS exam is as follows:

- Exam name: Certified Wireless Technology Specialist
- Exam number: PW0-071
- Cost: $125.00 (USD)
- Duration: 90 minutes
- Questions: 60
- Question types: Multiple choice/multiple answer
- Passing score: 70 percent
- Available languages: English
- Renewal: None—lifetime certification. Recommended prior to CWNA.
- Availability: Register at Pearson VUE (www.vue.com/cwnp)

When you schedule the exam, you will receive instructions regarding appointment and cancellation procedures, ID requirements, and information about the testing center location. In addition, you will receive a registration and payment confirmation e-mail. Exams can be scheduled weeks in advance or, in some cases, even as late as the same day.

After you have successfully passed the CWTS exam, the CWNP program will award you the lifetime certification. If the e-mail contact information you provided the testing center is correct, you will receive an e-mail from CWNP recognizing your accomplishment and providing you with a CWNP certification number. After you earn any CWNP certification, you can request a certification kit from CWNP. You will need to log in to the CWNP tracking system, verify your contact information, and request your certification kit.

Who Should Buy This Book?

Reading this book will provide you with an overview of IEEE 802.11 WLAN technology. This book is written with the CWTS exam objectives in mind and "what it is," not "how it works." The exam objectives were designed based on the skill set the intended audience should need in order to perform their job functions or roles in an organization. One thing to keep in mind is that this book will introduce and teach you a technology, a combination of computer local area networking and radio frequency.

If you follow the exam objectives, perform the hands-on exercises, and utilize all the available exam questions and practice exams at the book's companion website (`www.sybex.com/go/cwts2e`) and at `www.cwnp.com`, this book should be enough to effectively prepare you to pass the CWTS certification exam. It will also serve as a stepping-stone to more advanced books that teach the technology in more depth as well as a reference guide for the technology.

How to Use This Book and the Companion Website

Several testing features are in this book, and an exam engine that contains flashcards and additional practice exams is available on the book's companion website (`www.sybex.com/go/cwts2e`). These are designed to test your knowledge of the information you have learned from reading the book and performing the exercises. Although there is no guarantee you will pass the certification exam if you use this book and the additional online material, you will have all the tools necessary that effectively prepare you to do so.

Before you begin   At the beginning of the book (right after this introduction) is an assessment test you can use to check your readiness for the certification exam. Take this test before you start reading the book; it will help you determine the areas you may need to brush up on. The answers to the assessment test appear on a separate page after the last question of the test. Each answer includes an explanation, shows a chapter reference, and describes why the other options are incorrect.

Chapter review questions   To test your knowledge as you progress through this book, there are review questions at the end of each chapter. As you finish each chapter, answer the review questions and then check your answers—the correct answers appear on the page following the last review question. You can go back and revisit the section that deals with each question you answered wrong to ensure that you understand the material and answer correctly the next time you are tested on that topic.

Electronic flashcards   You will find flashcard questions on the book's companion website (www.sybex.com/go/cwts2e). These are short questions and answers, just like other flashcards you may be familiar with and have used in the past. You can answer them on your PC or download them onto a tablet, smart phone, or other client device for quick and convenient reviewing.

Test engine   The book's companion website (www.sybex.com/go/cwts2e) also contains the Sybex Test Engine. With this custom test engine, you can identify weak areas up front and then develop a solid studying strategy that includes each of the robust testing features described previously. The readme file will walk you through the quick, easy installation process.

In addition to the assessment test and the chapter review questions, you will find two bonus exams. Use the test engine to take these practice exams just as if you were taking the actual exam (without any reference material). When you have finished the first exam, move on to the next one to solidify your test-taking skills. After you get a high percentage of the answers correct, it is an indication you are ready to take the actual certification exam.

Labs and exercises   Several chapters in this book have lab exercises that use evaluation software that is downloadable from the manufacturer's website, which can be linked from the book's companion website (www.sybex.com/go/cwts2e). These exercises will provide you with a broader learning experience by providing hands-on experience and step-by-step problem solving.

White papers   Several wireless networking white papers and case studies are also provided on the book's companion website (www.sybex.com/go/cwts2e) or available for download from other sources or the manufacturer's websites. These white papers serve as additional reference material for preparing for the CWTS or other CWNP certification exams.

The CWTS Certification Exam (PW0-071) Is Based on the CWTS Exam Objectives

It is important to note that in order to pass the certification exam you should study from the currently posted exam objectives. Use this book as a learning aid to understand the CWTS exam objectives. For the most up-to-date certification exam objectives, visit the CWNP website at www.cwnp.com.

CWNP Exam Terminology

The CWNP program uses specific terminology when phrasing the questions on any of the CWNP exams. The terminology used most often mirrors the language that is used in the IEEE 802.11 standard. While technically correct, the terminology used in the exam questions often is not the same as the marketing terminology that is used by the Wi-Fi Alliance or the manufacturers of WLAN equipment.

As of this writing the most current IEEE version of the 802.11 standard is the IEEE 802.11-2012 document, which includes all the amendments that have been ratified since the

IEEE 802.11-2007 standard. Standards bodies such as the IEEE often create several amendments to a standard before "rolling up" the ratified amendments (finalized or approved versions) into a new standard.

For example, you might already be familiar with the term *802.11g*, which is a ratified amendment that has now been integrated into the IEEE 802.11-2012 standard. The technology that was originally defined by the 802.11g amendment is called Extended Rate Physical (ERP). Although the name 802.11g effectively remains the more commonly used marketing terminology, exam questions may use the technical term ERP instead of 802.11g. A document with exam terms is available from the CWNP website. At the time of this writing, the URL to access this document is `www.cwnp.com/exams/exam_terms.html`.

CWTS Exam Objectives

The Certified Wireless Technology Specialist (CWTS) certification, covering the current objectives, will certify that successful candidates know the fundamentals of RF behavior, can describe the features and functions of wireless components, and have the skills needed to install and configure wireless network hardware components. A typical candidate should have a basic understanding of data networking concepts.

The skills and knowledge measured by this examination are derived from a survey of wireless networking experts and professionals. The results of this survey were used in weighing the subject areas and ensuring that the weighting is representative of the relative importance of the content.

CWTS: Certified Wireless Technology Specialist Official Study Guide has been written to cover every CWTS exam objective at a level appropriate to its exam weighting. The following tables provide a breakdown of this book's exam coverage, showing you the weight of each section and the chapter where each objective or subobjective is covered.

Subject Area	Percent of Exam
Wi-Fi Technology, Standards, and Certifications	25%
Hardware and Software	20%
Radio Frequency (RF) Fundamentals	20%
Site Surveying and Installation	10%
Applications, Support, and Troubleshooting	15%
Security and Monitoring	10%
Total	100%

Exam Objective	Chapter
802.11n	2
Wi-Fi Multimedia (WMM) certification	2
WMM Power Save (WMM-PS) certification	2
Wi-Fi Protected Access (WPA/WPA2) certification	2
Enterprise	2
Personal	2
1.4 Explain the role of Wi-Fi as a network access technology.	
WPAN, WLAN, WMAN, WWAN	2
The OSI reference model	1

Hardware and Software—20%

2.1 Identify the purpose, features, and functions of the following wireless network components. Choose the appropriate implementation or configuration steps in a given scenario.

Access points	3
Controller-based	3
Autonomous	3
Cooperative	3
Mesh	3
Wireless LAN routers	3
Wireless bridges	3
Wireless repeaters	3
WLAN controller	3
Distributed and centralized data forwarding	3
Power over Ethernet (PoE) devices	3

Applications, Support, and Troubleshooting—15%

5.1 Identify deployment scenarios for common WLAN network types and suggest best practices for these scenarios.

Exam Objective	Chapter
Small Office/Home Office (SOHO)	2
Extension of existing networks into remote locations	2
Building-to-building connectivity	2
Public wireless hotspots	2
Carpeted office, education, industrial, and healthcare	2
Last-mile data delivery – wireless ISP	2
High density environments	2

5.2 Recognize common problems associated with wireless networks and their symptoms, and identify steps to isolate and troubleshoot the problem. Given a problem situation, interpret the symptoms and the most likely cause.

Throughput problems	12
Connectivity problems	12
Interference from Wi-Fi or non-Wi-Fi sources	12
Application performance problems	12
RF performance problems, such as multipath and hidden nodes	12

5.3 Identify procedures to optimize wireless networks.

Infrastructure hardware selection and placement	12
Identifying, locating, and removing sources of interference	12
Client load-balancing and infrastructure redundancy	12
Analyzing infrastructure capacity and utilization	12

Security and Monitoring—10%

6.1 Identify and describe the following legacy WLAN security technologies.

SSID hiding	9

Exam domains and objectives are subject to change at any time without prior notice and at CWNP's sole discretion. Please visit their website (www.cwnp.com) for the most current information.

Assessment Test

1. What two software items must be installed on a notebook computer prior to connecting to a wireless network? (Choose 2.)

    A. Site survey software

    B. Device driver software ✓

    C. Signal strength software

    D. Client utility software ✓

    E. AutoConfig software

2. IP addresses are considered part of which layer of the OSI model?

    A. Physical

    B. Data Link

    C. Network

    D. Transport ✓

    E. Application

3. The amount of output power and usable frequency ranges for wireless devices is determined by which organization?

    A. Wireless Ethernet Compatibility Alliance

    B. Wi-Fi Alliance

    C. Institute of Electrical and Electronics Engineers ✓

    D. Local regulatory authorities

4. Which statement is accurate regarding mesh access points and mesh technology?

    A. Mesh is a legacy technology and the priority should be to select an appropriate upgrade path.

    B. In a full mesh network, all nodes connect together with at least two paths for every node.

    C. Mesh access points are unreliable communications and represent a single point of failure.

  ✓ **D.** Mesh access points require a separate radio for communications and therefore can be costly to implement.

5. Wireless repeaters are devices in wireless networking that are _____.

    A. Used to extend the radio frequency cell

  ✓ **B.** Used to repeat and strengthen the RF signal for better performance

    C. Used as a backup solution in the event of an access point failure

    D. Used to increase the bandwidth of the WLAN

6. Some common wireless personal network (WPAN) devices such as Bluetooth use a commu-
    nication technology that has the potential to interfere with IEEE 802.11g wireless LANs.
    What is the name for this technology?

    A. FHSS

    B. DSSS

    C. HR/DSSS

    D. HR/FHSS

    E. ERP-OFDM

7. The manual site survey process allows the site surveyor to perform the survey in one of two
    modes. What are these two modes? (Choose two.)

    A. Passive

    B. Visual

    C. Predictive

    D. Active

    E. Placement

8. A third-party client utility such as Microsoft Windows Wireless Zero Configuration can be
    used with _____.

    A. SOHO implementations

    B. Enterprise implementations

    C. Both A and B

    D. Neither A nor B

9. Which of the following options are required components of the gathering of technical infor-
    mation for an IEEE 802.11n wireless LAN site survey in a new installation? (Choose 3.)

    A. Number of users

    B. Applications in use

    C. Other IEEE 802.11 wireless networks

    D. Cost of equipment

10. Manufacturers' client software utilities for wireless LAN adapters _____.

    A. Allow for additional configuration

    B. Are required in order for the adapter to operate

    C. Are usually available at an additional fee

    D. Are generic regardless of the manufacturer

11. An independent basic service set requires a minimum of how many access points?

    A. 0

    B. 1

    C. 2

    D. 3

12. What is the horizontal angle of measurement in degrees of an omnidirectional antenna with a gain of 2.2 dBi?

    A. 0

    B. 90

    C. 180

    D. 270

    E. 360

13. Which IEEE 802.11 standard or amendment can use three radio chains per band and multiple input/multiple output (MIMO) to transmit data?

    A. 802.11

    B. 802.11a

    C. 802.11g

    D. 802.11h

    E. 802.11n

14. Which amendment to the standard operates in the 2.4 GHz ISM band and supports data rates up to 54 Mbps?

    A. 802.11a

    B. 802.11b

    C. 802.11g

    D. 802.11n

15. An HR/DSSS channel used to transmit data an IEEE 802.11g wireless LAN is _____ wide.

    A. 2.412 GHz

    B. 5.160 GHz

    C. 11 MHz

    D. 22 MHz

16. IEEE 802.11g wireless networks can operate in which unlicensed RF band?

    A. 902 – 928 MHz ISM

    B. 2.400 – 2.500 GHz ISM

    C. 5.725 – 5.825 GHZ UNII

    D. 5.250 – 5.350 GHz UNII

    E. 5.725 – 5.875 GHz ISM

17. What network type is usually contained in the same physical area and usually is bounded by the perimeter of a building?

    A. Local area network (LAN)

    B. Campus area network (CAN)

C. Wide area network (WAN)

D. Metropolitan area network (MAN)

18. What Data Link layer (Layer 2) security methods are weak and should not be used to secure a IEEE 802.11 wireless LAN? (Choose three.)

  A. SSID hiding

  B. WPA

  C. VPN

  D. WEP

  E. WPA 2.0

  F. RBAC

  G. MAC filter

19. Which RF channels are considered non-overlapping for an IEEE 802.11g network using HR/DSSS modulation? (Choose 2.)

  A. 1 and 4

  B. 6 and 9

  C. 1 and 6

  D. 3 and 7

  E. 11 and 13

  F. 2 and 7

20. What can have a negative effect on the capacity of an IEEE 802.11g wireless LAN access point?

  A. Reflections caused by furnishings

  B. Frequency range in use

  C. Number of associated users

  D. Output power of access point

21. What could cause low throughput in an 802.11a/b/g/n wireless network?

  A. Access point output power is too high.

  B. Too many associated client devices.

  C. Load-balancing features are moving clients.

  D. The clients are too close to the access points and are overpowered.

22. What can contribute to voltage standing wave ratio (VSWR) in an IEEE 802.11g wireless LAN circuit?

  A. Output power of the access point

  B. Impedance mismatch

    C. Gain of an antenna

    D. Attenuation value of cable

23. Open system authentication is _____ in an IEEE 802.11-2012 wireless network.

    A. Flawed

    B. Optional

    C. Secure

    D. Required

24. The Service Set Identifier (SSID) in an IEEE 802.11 wireless LAN is also known as what?

    A. The name of the wireless network

    B. The media access control address of the radio

    C. The name of the access point

    D. The wireless medium identifier

25. What does the term *authenticator* identify in an IEEE 802.1X secure network?

    A. The RADIUS server

    B. The access point

    C. The client device

    D. The RAS server

26. A virtual private network (VPN) most commonly operates at what layer of the OSI model?

    A. Physical, Layer 1

    B. Data Link, Layer 2

    C. Network, Layer 3

    D. Transport, Layer 4

    E. Application, Layer 7

27. You are a wireless LAN engineer hired to perform a predictive analysis site survey for a 150,000-square-foot office building. This space includes walled offices as well as cubicles. What is an advantage of a predictive modeling site survey over a manual survey in this specific application?

    A. A predictive site survey is the most accurate survey type available.

    B. The amount of time required for accurate results is much less than a complete manual walkthrough.

    C. Because of an extensive attenuation database, a predictive modeling site survey will be able to determine the interference values of any obstacles.

    D. A predictive modeling site survey will allow you to experiment with different access point criteria, including power settings, channels, and locations, without the need for a physical visit.

28. What are some of the main factors in determining the number of access points that will be required for an IEEE 802.11n wireless LAN deployment? (Choose 2.)

    A. Type of client devices in use

    B. Number of client devices

    C. Manufacturer of client devices

    D. Applications to be used

29. What will a protocol analyzer do during a manual site survey?

    A. Perform an RF analysis of the proposed area.

    B. Help locate sources of RF interference.

    C. Identify existing wireless networks.

    D. Describe security requirements of the wireless LAN.

30. What could be the cause of intermittent connectivity for a wireless client device in an IEEE 802.11a/b/g/n wireless network?

    A. A weak received signal strength on the client.

    B. A signal-to-noise ratio of 35 dB.

    C. The access point power is set too high and overpowering the client device.

    D. The radio in the client device is disabled.

31. Which layers of the OSI model *do not* specify wireless LANs technology? (Choose 3.)

    A. Session

    B. Network

    C. Physical

    D. Application

    E. Data Link

32. The signal to noise ratio (SNR) is the difference between the _____ and the _____ (Choose 2.)

    A. Noise floor

    B. RF channel

    C. Fresnel zone

    D. RF line of sight

    E. Received signal

33. If an autonomous access point is set to what is commonly referred to as root mode, it will be able to perform which function?

    A. Connect to a distribution system and allow client devices to send information to other devices.

    B. Connect to a distribution system as a root bridge and allow two or more LANs to connect wirelessly.

   C. Connect to a distribution system but is seldom used as this mode requires extensive configuration.

   D. Connect to a distribution system as a repeater which allows the RF cell to be extended.

34. Wi-Fi Protected Access 2 (WPA 2.0) requires _____ for the encryption mechanism and _____ for the cipher.

   A. TKIP, RC4

   B. TKIP, RC5

   C. WEP, RC4

   D. CCMP, RC4

   E. CCMP, AES

35. The access method that an IEEE 802.11a wireless network would use to get control of the wireless medium in order to transmit data is called what?

   A. CSMA/CD

   B. FHSS

   C. HR/DSSS

   D. CSMA/CA

   E. CSMA/DSSS

36. An antenna will propagate RF energy in specific radiation patterns, both horizontally and vertically. How do antenna manufacturers identify the horizontal radiation patterns?

   A. Elevation

   B. Azimuth

   C. Dipole

   C. Longitude

37. A beacon is an example of what type of frame used in an IEEE 802.11 wireless LAN?

   A. Control

   B. Management

   C. Data

   D. Null function

Answers to Assessment Test

1. **B, D.** A device driver allows the computer operating system to control the wireless network adapter and must be installed in order for the adapter to function. Client utility software allows a user to configure the adapter with network specific settings such as the SSID and security settings. Client utility software may be part of the computer operating system or third-party software provided by the manufacturer of the adapter. Site survey software and signal strength software may be part of the client utility software. AutoConfig is a service that runs on a Microsoft Windows 7 computer. See Chapter 4 for more information.

2. **C.** The Network layer is responsible for addressing and routing of frames and is where IP addresses are used. The Data Link layer of the OSI model is responsible for compiling or packaging bits into frames. The Physical layer allows frames to be sent and received across a medium. The Transport layer is responsible for connection-oriented or connectionless protocols, and the Application layer is the "interface to the user." For more information, see Chapter 1.

3. **D.** Local regulatory authorities manage the RF spectrum used in both unlicensed and licensed applications. The IEEE creates standards and the Wi-Fi Alliance certifies devices for interoperability. Wireless Ethernet Compatibility Alliance is the former name of the Wi-Fi Alliance. For more information, see Chapter 2.

4. **B.** In a full mesh network, all nodes connect together with at least two paths for every node. This technology is on the increase in outdoor installations and starting to appear in indoor installations as well. It is common in metropolitan area networks and campus area networks. Many access points and wireless LAN switches/controllers have the capability built in. For more information, see Chapter 3.

5. **A.** A wireless repeater—which in most cases is a function of an access point—will extend the RF cell to allow users at a greater distance to connect. This will have an impact on throughput for users connected to the repeater and this solution is recommended only when necessary. For more information, see Chapter 3.

6. **A.** Some wireless personal networks (WPANs), such as Bluetooth, use FHSS for communications. This will potentially interfere with IEEE 802.11 wireless networks. DSSS, HR/DSSS, and ERP-OFDM are all used in wireless LANs. HR/FHSS does not exist. For more information, see Chapter 5.

7. **A, D.** Passive and active are the two modes in which a manual site survey can be performed. Passive mode monitors all RF, and active mode requires a client association. For more information, see Chapter 11.

8. **C.** Third-party client utilities such as Microsoft's WZC can be used in either SOHO or enterprise implementations. Because this utility is built into the Microsoft Windows operating system, it is very common in both types of installations. See Chapter 4 for more information.

9. **A, B, C.** The number of users, applications both hardware and software, and other IEEE 802.11 wireless networks are technical areas that must be known for a new IEEE 802.11 wireless LAN installation. The cost of the equipment does not fall under the technical category. For more information, see Chapter 10.

10. A. Most manufacturers that offer utilities for wireless LAN adapters allow for additional configuration above and beyond the settings that are included with an operating system. Manufacturer utilities are not required for the adapter to operate, because some settings can be made in the device driver or a third-party client utility. Unless it is specialty client software, the utility is usually included with the adapter and is not subject to additional fee. Manufacturers' client software utilities are unique to only those adapters and will not work across manufacturers. See Chapter 4 for more information.

11. A. An independent basic service set (IBSS) is an ad hoc network that is used for peer-to-peer communications. No access points are used in an IBSS implementation. For more information, see Chapter 8.

12. E. An omnidirectional antenna has a horizontal radiation pattern of 360 degrees. The vertical radiation pattern will vary based on the gain of the antenna. This measurement is known as the beamwidth and is used for both horizontal and vertical radiation patterns. Beamwidth is measured at the −3dB or half-power point. For more information, see Chapter 7.

13. E. 802.11n and MIMO commonly use up to three radios in either the 2.4 GHz ISM or the 5 GHz UNII band. 802.11a/g uses one radio per band but can use two antennas for diversity. 802.11h is for spectrum management. For more information, see Chapter 5.

14. C. The IEEE 802.11g amendment to the standard and the 802.11a amendment both support up to 54 Mbps maximum data rates. However, of the two, only 802.11g operates in the 2.4 GHz ISM band. 802.11b also operates in the 2.4 GHz ISM band but only supports a maximum data rate of 11 Mbps. The IEEE 802.11n amendment allows support of up to 600 Mbps. For more information, see Chapter 2.

15. D. Both DSSS and HR/DSSS channels are 22 MHz wide. 2.412 GHz and 5.160 GHz is the center frequency of some channels used. For more information, see Chapter 5.

16. B. IEEE 802.11g networks operate in the 2.4 GHz ISM band. 802.11a networks operate in the 5 GHz UNII bands and in the United States the 5.725–5.875 GHz ISM band. IEEE standards-based wireless networks do not use the 900 MHz ISM band. For more information, see Chapter 6.

17. A. A local area network (LAN) is usually contained in the same physical area and usually is bounded by the perimeter of a building. A campus area network (CAN) includes a set of interconnected LANs within an office or school campus and is usually within a limited geographical area. A wide area network (WAN) mostly consists of point-to-point or point-to-multipoint connections between two or more LANs and a metropolitan area network (MAN) consists of networks that may span from several blocks of buildings to entire cities. For more information, see Chapter 1.

18. A, D, G. SSID hiding, WEP, and MAC filtering are legacy security mechanisms for IEEE 802.11 wireless networks and should not be used. WPA and WPA 2.0 are Wi-Fi certifications and are more advanced. Virtual private network (VPN) is a Layer 3 security solution typically used for remote access. RBAC is role-based access control. For more information, see Chapter 9.

19. C, F. In the 2.4 GHz ISM band, 25 MHz or 5 channels of separation is considered non-overlapping. Based on the IEEE 802.11-2012 Standard Clause 18, HR/DSSS channels must be separated by 25 MHz or greater in order to be considered non-overlapping. For more information, see Chapter 6.

20. C. The number of associated users will affect the capacity of an access point. The frequency range will affect the propagation as well as the output power. Reflections will cause multipath. For more information, see Chapter 6.

21. B. Low throughput may occur when too many client devices are associated to an access point and cause overloading. Load balancing would help to solve this problem. Because of DRS, the closer the client device is to an access point, the better the throughput. For more information, see Chapter 12.

22. B. An impedance mismatch between connections in a WLAN system will cause VSWR. The gain of an antenna is a relative value that has to do with the size or shape of the RF pattern emitted. Attenuation of cable adds to the overall loss of the system. For more information, see Chapter 7.

23. D. Open system authentication is addressed in the IEEE original 802.11 standard and allows a wireless client device to 802.11 authenticate to an access point in order to 802.11 associate. Shared key authentication is legacy and flawed and either cannot or should not be used. Open system authentication is a "null" authentication, is automatic and not secure. For more information, see Chapter 8.

24. A. The SSID is the name that identifies a wireless network. The MAC address of the access point radio is the BSSID. For more information, see Chapter 8.

25. B. 802.1X is for port-based access control and the terminology for the access point is *authenticator*. The RADIUS server is the authentication server and the client device is a supplicant. The RAS server is the predecessor to RADIUS. For more information, see Chapter 9.

26. C. A virtual private network (VPN) solution is a Layer 3 (Network) VPN security solution and is commonly used for remote access connectivity from unsecured networks such as hotspots. For more information, see Chapter 9.

27. B. A predictive analysis site survey will minimize the time required on-site for testing and analysis. This site survey will be accurate if the information about the location input is accurate. A manual site survey requires a walkthrough of the area and can be time consuming. For more information, see Chapter 11.

28. B, D. The number of devices is an important determining factor in the number of access points required for a wireless LAN deployment as well as the software and hardware applications that may be used. The type and manufacturer of devices are not concerns. For more information, see Chapter 10.

29. C. A protocol analyzer will help identify existing wireless networks in an area and provide other information about these networks that can be used in the site survey/design process. An RF analysis is performed by a spectrum analyzer, which will also help locate sources of

RF interference. A protocol analyzer can help identify security-related issues from existing wireless networks but will not describe security requirements of a new wireless LAN. For more information, see Chapter 11.

30. A. The received signal strength represents how much of a transmitted signal is being received. If this signal is weak, the difference between the signal and noise may not be high enough to recover the data. If the power on an access point is high, it would provide more received signal. A signal-to-noise ratio of 35 dB is more than adequate. If the radio on the client was disabled, it would not be able to connect at all. For more information, see Chapter 12.

31. A, B, D. Wireless LAN technology operates and is specified at layers 1 (Physical) and 2 (Data Link) of the OSI model. The Session layer opens, closes, and manages sessions between end-user application processes. The Network layer is responsible for addressing and routing functions of data and the Application layer is the interface to the user. For more information, see Chapter 1.

32. A, E. The signal to noise ratio is the difference between the received signal and the noise floor. The common noise floor value is –95 dBm, and an acceptable receive signal is –65 dBm. Therefore the signal to noise ratio is 30 dBm. The RF channel is a specified frequency a WLAN operates in. The Fresnel zone consists of a number of concentric ellipsoidal volumes that surround the direct, RF line of sight between two points such as an RF transmitter and receiver. For more information, see Chapter 6.

33. A. Most enterprise-level autonomous access points have the capability to operate in root, repeater, or bridge modes. Root mode is the most common. Root mode allows devices to authenticate, associate, and access network resources and services. For more information, see Chapter 3.

34. E. Wi-Fi Protected Access 2 (WPA 2.0) requires CCMP/AES. TKIP/RC4 is optional. WEP/RC4 is legacy and should not be used. It cannot be used with a robust secure network. RC5 is a stream cipher and not used with IEEE 802.11 wireless LANs. CCMP uses AES, not RC4. For more information, see Chapter 2.

35. D. CSMA/CA stands for Carrier Sense Multiple Access/Collision Avoidance and is used as an access method for wireless LANs to share the communication medium, which is the air. CSMA/CD is Carrier Sense Multiple Access Collision/Detection Avoidance and is used with Ethernet networks. FHSS and HR/DSSS are spread-spectrum technologies used with some standards or amendments. CSMA/DSSS does not exist. For more information, see Chapter 5.

36. B. The technical term for the horizontal radiation pattern is azimuth. The elevation is the vertical radiation pattern. For more information, see Chapter 7.

37. B. A beacon frame is a management frame and is used to advertise information about the wireless LAN. For more information, see Chapter 8.

CWTS®
Certified Wireless
Technology Specialist
Official Study Guide
Second Edition

Chapter

1

Introduction to Computer Networking

THE FOLLOWING CWTS EXAM OBJECTIVE IS COVERED IN THIS CHAPTER:

✓ **1.4 Explain the role of Wi-Fi as a network access technology**

  ▪ The OSI reference model

It is important to have an understanding of basic computer networking concepts before you begin exploring the world of wireless networking technology and its terminology. This chapter looks at various topics surrounding computer networking including network types (LAN and WAN), topologies, the OSI model, and device addressing. The chapter is intended to provide an overview of basic networking concepts as an introduction for those who need to gain a basic understanding or for those who want a review of the concepts.

You will look at the various types of wireless networks—including wireless personal area networks (WPANs), wireless local area networks (WLANs), wireless metropolitan area networks (WMANs), and wireless wide area networks (WWANs)—in Chapter 2, "Introduction to Wireless Local Area Networking."

Network Types

Personal computer networking technology has evolved at a tremendous pace over the past couple of decades, and many people across the world now have some type of exposure to the technology. Initially, personal computers were connected, or "networked" together, to share files and printers. This type of network was usually confined to a few rooms or within a single building. As the need for this technology continued to grow, so did the types of networks. Networking started with the *local area network* (LAN) and grew on to bigger and better types, including wide area networks (WANs) and metropolitan area networks (MANs). The following are some of the common networking types in use today:

- Local area networks (LANs)
- Wide area networks (WANs)
- Metropolitan area networks (MANs)
- Campus area networks (CANs)
- Personal area networks (PANs)

The Local Area Network

A local area network (LAN) can be defined as a group of computers connected by a physical medium in a specific arrangement called a topology. The *topology* used depends on the location where the network is installed. Some common topologies such as bus, ring, and star are discussed later in this chapter. Local area networks are contained in the same physical area and usually are bounded by the perimeter of a building. However, in some cases a LAN may span a group of buildings in close proximity that are on the same subnet.

Common uses of early LANs were mostly for file and print services. This allowed users to store data securely and provided a centralized location of data for accessibility when the user was physically away from the LAN. This central storage of data also provided the ability for a network administrator to back up and archive all the saved data for disaster recovery purposes. As for print services, it was not cost effective to have a printer at every desk, so LANs allowed the use of shared printers for any user on the local area network. Figure 1.1 illustrates a local area network that includes both wired and wireless devices.

FIGURE 1.1   A local area network (LAN)

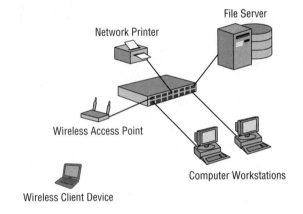

The Wide Area Network

As computer networking continued to evolve, many businesses and organizations that used this type of technology needed to expand the LAN beyond the physical limits of a single area or building. The local area networks began to expand into the *wide area network* (WAN). As illustrated in Figure 1.2, a WAN mostly consists of point-to-point or point-to-multipoint connections between two or more LANs and may span a relatively large geographical area. The WAN has allowed users and organizations to share data files and other resources with a much larger audience.

WANs can use leased lines from telecommunication providers (commonly known as "telcos"), fiber connections, and even wireless connections. The use of wireless for bridging local area networks is growing at a fast pace, because it can often be a cost-effective solution for connecting LANs together.

FIGURE 1.2   Wide area network (WAN) connecting three LANs

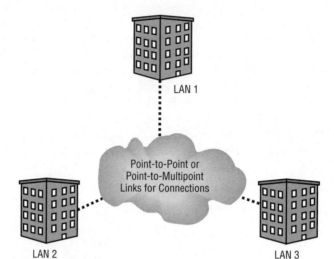

Point-to-Point Connections

Connecting at least two LANs together is known as a *point-to-point connection* or link (see Figure 1.3). The connection can be made using either wired or wireless network infrastructure devices and can include bridges, wireless access points, and routers. Wireless LAN (WLAN) point-to-point links can sometimes extend very long distances depending on terrain and other local conditions. These links can serve both wired and wireless users on the connected local area networks.

Wired point-to-point links consist of fiber-optic connections or leased lines from local telecommunication providers. Wireless point-to-point links typically call for semidirectional or highly directional antennas. With some regulatory domains such as the Federal Communications Commission (FCC), when an omnidirectional antenna is used in this configuration it is considered a special case, called a point-to-multipoint link. Wireless point-to-point links include directional antennas and encryption to protect the wireless data as it propagates through the air.

Point-to-Multipoint Connections

A network infrastructure connecting more than two LANs together is known as a *point-to-multipoint connection* or link (see Figure 1.4). When used with wireless, this configuration usually consists of one omnidirectional antenna and multiple semidirectional or highly directional antennas. Point-to-multipoint links are often used in campus-style deployments, where connections to multiple buildings or locations may be required. Point-to-multipoint WANs are often called "clouds." Like point-to-point connections, wired point-to-multipoint connections can use either direct wired connections such as fiber-optic cables or leased line connectivity available from telecommunication providers.

FIGURE 1.3   Point-to-point connections using either wired or wireless

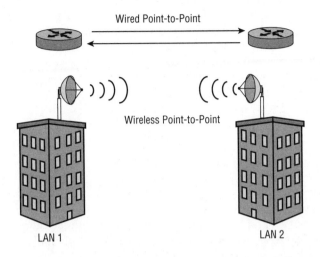

FIGURE 1.4   Point-to-multipoint connections using either wired or wireless

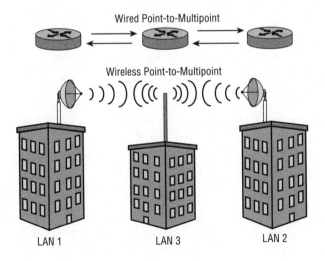

The Metropolitan Area Network

The *metropolitan area network* (MAN) consists of networks that can span from several blocks of buildings to entire cities and interconnect devices for access to computer resources in a region or area larger than that covered by local area networks (LANs) but yet smaller than the areas covered by wide area networks (WANs). The MAN is growing in popularity as the need for access in this type of environment also increases. MANs also include fast connectivity between local networks and may include fiber optics or other wired connectivity that is capable of longer distances and higher capacity than those in a LAN.

MANs also allow for connections to outside larger networks such as the Internet. They may include services such as cable TV, streaming video, and telephone. Devices and connectivity used with metropolitan area networks may be owned by a town, county, or other locality and may also include the property of individual companies. Wireless MANs are also becoming a common way to connect the same type of areas. Wireless MANs will be discussed further in Chapter 2.

Campus Area Networks

A *campus area network* (CAN) includes a set of interconnected LANs, is basically a smaller version of a wide area network (WAN) within an office or school campus, and is usually within a limited geographical area. Each building within the campus would have a separate LAN, and the LANs are often connected using fiber-optic cable, which provides a greater distance than copper wiring using IEEE 802.3 Ethernet technology. Wireless connections between the buildings used with CANs are now a common way to connect the individual LANs. These wireless connections or wireless bridges provide a quick, cost-effective way to connect buildings together in a university campus.

In a university campus environment, a CAN may link many buildings, including all of the various schools—School of Business, School of Law, School of Engineering, and so on—as well as the university library, administration buildings, and even residence halls. Wireless LAN deployments are becoming commonplace in university residence halls. With the number of mobile wireless devices increasing at a very fast pace in places like university campus residence halls, the number of wireless access points and the capacity of each need to be considered.

As in the university campus environment, a corporate office CAN may connect together all the various building LANs that are part of the organization. This type of network will have the same characteristics of a WAN but confined to the internal resources of the corporation or organization. Many organizations are deploying wireless networks within the corporate CAN as a way to connect various parts of the business together. Like the university CAN, in the corporate world wireless can be a quick, cost-effective way to provide connectivity between buildings and departments. All of the physical connection mediums and devices are the property of the office or school campus, and responsibility for the maintenance of the equipment lies with the office or campus as well.

Personal Area Networks

Personal area networks (PANs) are networks that connect devices within the immediate area of individual people. PANs may consist of either wired or wireless connections or both. On the wired side, this includes universal serial bus (USB) devices such as printers, keyboards, and computer mice that may be connected with a USB hub. With wireless technology, PANs are short-range computer networks and in many cases use Bluetooth wireless technology. Wireless Bluetooth technology is specified by the IEEE 802.15 standard and is not IEEE 802.11 wireless local area technology. Bluetooth will be discussed in more detail in Chapter 5, "Physical Layer Access Methods and Spread Spectrum Technology."

Like wired PANs, wireless PANs are commonly used in connecting an individual's wireless personal communication accessories such as phones, headsets, computer mice, keyboards tablets, and printers and are centered on the individual personal workspace without the need for physical cabling. Figure 1.5 illustrates a typical wireless PAN configuration.

FIGURE 1.5   Bluetooth network connecting several personal devices together

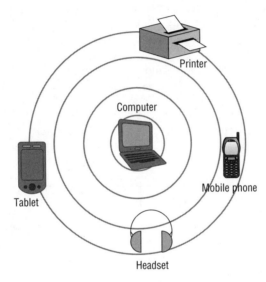

Network Topologies

A computer physical network topology is the actual layout or physical design and interconnection of a computer network. A topology includes the cabling and devices that are part of the network. In this section you will look at several network topologies:

- Bus
- Ring
- Star
- Mesh

Bus

A *bus topology* consists of multiple devices connected along a single shared medium with two defined endpoints. It is sometimes referred to as a high-speed linear bus and is a single broadcast domain in which all devices on the bus network receive all messages. Both endpoints of a bus topology have a 50 ohm termination device, usually a Bayonet Neill–Concelman (BNC) connector with a 50 ohm resistor. The bus topology is now considered a legacy design and was commonly used with early local area networking.

One disadvantage to the bus topology is that if any point along the cable is damaged or broken, the entire LAN goes down. Troubleshooting a bus network is performed by something known as the half-split method. A network engineer "breaks" or separates the link at about the halfway point and measures the resistance on both ends. If the segment measures 50 ohms, there is a good chance that side of the LAN segment is functioning correctly. If the resistance measurement is not 50 ohms, it signals a problem with that part of the LAN segment. The engineer continues with this method until the exact location of the problem is identified. Figure 1.6 illustrates an example of the bus topology.

FIGURE 1.6   Example of the bus topology

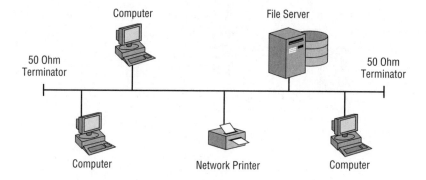

Ring

The *ring topology* is rarely used with LANs today, but it is still widely used by Internet service providers (ISPs) for high-speed, resilient backhaul connections over fiber-optic links. In the ring topology, each device connects to two other devices, forming a ring pattern. Ring topologies in LANs may use a token-passing access method, in which data travels around the ring in one direction. Only one device at a time will have the opportunity to transmit data. Because this access method does not use collision detection, it will commonly outperform the bus topology, achieving higher data rates than are possible using a collision detection access method. Each computer on the ring topology can act as a repeater, a capacity that allows for a much stronger signal. Figure 1.7 shows an example of the ring topology.

Troubleshooting the Bus Topology

I remember many years ago I was called to troubleshoot a problem on a small local area network using a bus topology. The network consisted of a network file server, about 20 client stations, and a few network printers. The users complained of intermittent problems with the network. After spending some time looking over the network, I decided to test the bus using the half-split method and checked to verify that the cable was reporting the correct resistance using a volt-ohm-milliamp (VoM) meter. Sure enough, one side of the network cable reported the correct resistance reading, but the other side was giving intermittent results.

After spending some time repeating the troubleshooting method, I was able to determine the problem. It turns out that someone had run the coax (bus) cable underneath a heavy plastic office chair mat and one of the little pegs used to protect the flooring was causing the intermittent connection as it struck the cable when the user moved their chair around the mat. I quickly replaced and rerouted the section of cable in question. It is a good thing I was there during the normal business operating hours when the person was moving around in the chair or I might have never found the problem. Ah, the joys of troubleshooting a bus topology.

FIGURE 1.7   An example of the ring topology

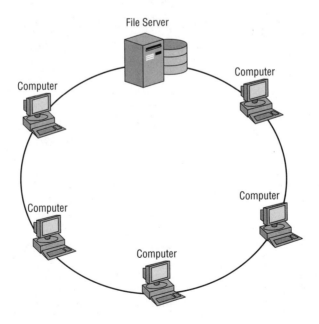

Star

The *star topology*, as shown in Figure 1.8, is the most commonly used method of connecting devices together on a LAN today. It consists of multiple devices connected by a central connection device. Common central connection devices include hubs, switches, and wireless access points, although hubs are rarely used today. The hub provides a single broadcast domain similar to a bus topology. However, the switch and wireless access point both have intelligence—the ability to decide which port specific network traffic can be sent to. A big advantage over the bus and ring topologies is that if a connection is broken or damaged the entire network is not down; only a single device in the star topology is affected. However, the central connection device such as a switch or wireless access point can be considered a potential central point of failure.

FIGURE 1.8 A common star topology using either wired or wireless devices

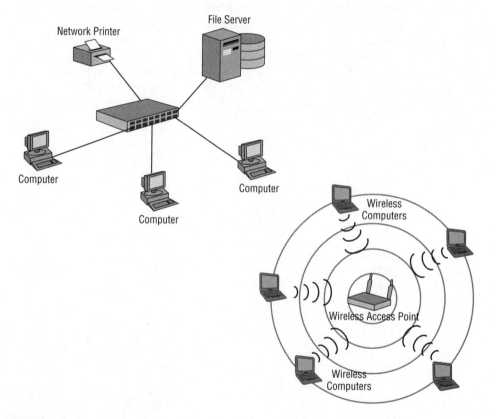

Mesh

Each device in a *mesh topology* (Figure 1.9) has one or more connections to other devices that are part of the mesh. This approach provides both network resilience in case of link or device failure and a cost savings compared to full redundancy. Mesh technology can operate with both wired and wireless infrastructure network devices. The amendment to the IEEE 802.11 standard for mesh networking is 802.11s. This amendment was ratified in 2011 and is now part of the IEEE 802.11-2012 standard.

Manufacturers currently are using proprietary Layer 2 routing protocols, forming a self-healing wireless infrastructure (mesh) in which edge devices can communicate. Manufacturers of enterprise wireless networking infrastructure devices provide support for mesh access points (APs) such that the mesh APs connect back to APs that are directly wired into the network backbone infrastructure. This is a form of wireless distribution system (WDS) deployment. The APs or wireless controllers in this case are used to configure both the wired and mesh APs.

FIGURE 1.9   Mesh networks can be either wired or wireless devices.

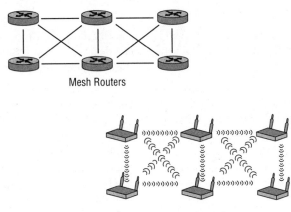

Mesh Routers

Wireless Mesh Routers

The OSI Model

Before we continue with wireless LAN technology, you should have some background on computer networking theory. The basics of a computer networking discussion start with the OSI model. The *Open Systems Interconnection (OSI) model* has been around for several decades. It describes the basic concept of communications in the computer network environment.

There are seven layers to the OSI model. Each layer is made up of many protocols and serves a specific function. You will take a quick look at all seven layers of the OSI but only layers that pertain to wireless networking will be discussed in depth in this book. Figure 1.10 illustrates the seven layers of the OSI model.

FIGURE 1.10 The OSI model

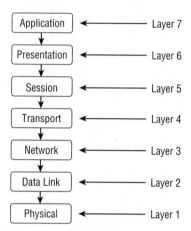

Wireless networking functions at the two lowest layers of the OSI model, Layer 1 (Physical) and Layer 2 (Data Link). However, to some degree Layer 3 (Network) plays a role as well, generally for the TCP/IP protocol capabilities. Here's how each layer is used:

- Layer 1 (*PHY*, the *Physical layer*) consists of bit-level data streams and computer network hardware connecting the devices together. This hardware includes network interface cards, cables, switches, wireless access points, and bridges. In the case of wireless networking, radio frequency (RF) uses air as the medium for wireless communications. The Physical layer consists of two sublayers: the Physical Layer Convergence Protocol (PLCP) and Physical Medium Dependent (PMD). The PLCP, the higher of the two layers, is the interface between the PMD and Media Access Control (MAC) sublayer. The PMD is the lower sublayer at the bottom of the protocol stack and is responsible for transmitting the data onto the wireless medium.

- Layer 2 (*Data Link layer*) is responsible for organizing the bit-level data for communication between devices on a network and detecting and correcting Physical layer errors. The Data Link layer consists of two sublayers: the Logical Link Control (LLC) sublayer and Media Access Control (MAC) sublayer. The bit-level communication is accomplished through Media Access Control (MAC) addressing. A *MAC address* is a unique identifier of each device on the computer network and is known as the physical address.

- Layer 3 (*Network layer*) is where the Internet Protocol (IP) protocol resides and is responsible for addressing and routing data. An IP address is defined as a numerical identifier or logical address assigned to a network device. The IP address can be static, manually assigned by a user, or it can be dynamically assigned from a server.

- Layer 4 (*Transport layer*) Transmission Control Protocol (TCP) is a connection-oriented protocol and is used for communications requiring reliability and is analogous to a circuit-switched phone call. User Datagram Protocol (UDP) is a connectionless protocol and is used for simple communications requiring efficiency. UDP is analogous to sending a postcard through a mail service. You would not know if the postcard was received. UDP and TCP port numbers are assigned to applications for flow control and error recovery.

- Layer 5 (*Session layer*) opens, closes, and manages sessions between end-user application processes.
- Layer 6 (*Presentation layer*) provides delivery and formatting of information for processing and display.
- Layer 7 (*Application layer*) "Application" is another term for a "program" that runs on a computer or other networking device. Examples of Application layer protocols are File Transfer Protocol (FTP), Hypertext Transfer Protocol (HTTP), and Post Office Protocol v3 (POP3).

In order for computers and other network devices to communicate with one another using the OSI model, a communication infrastructure of some type is necessary. In a wired network, such an infrastructure consists of cables, repeaters, bridges, and Layer 2 switches. In a wireless network, these devices are access points, bridges, repeaters, radio frequency, and the open air. All will be discussed in more detail in Chapter 3, "Wireless LAN Infrastructure Devices."

 Real World Scenario

OSI Model Memorization Tip

One common method you can use to remember the seven layers of the OSI model from top to bottom is to memorize the following sentence: "All people seem to need data processing." Take the first letter from each word and that will give you an easy way to remember the first letter that pertains to each layer of the OSI model.

- All (Application)
- People (Presentation)
- Seem (Session)
- To (Transport)
- Need (Network)
- Data (Data Link)
- Processing (Physical)

Peer Communication

Peer layers communicate with other peer layers, and the layers underneath are their support systems. Peer layer communication is the "horizontal" link between devices on the network. Figure 1.11 shows only three examples of *peer communication*. Keep in mind, however, that this principle applies to all seven layers of the OSI model. This allows for the layers to communicate with the corresponding layer to which a device is sending or receiving information.

FIGURE 1.11   Peer communication between three of the seven layers

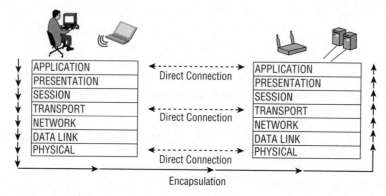

Encapsulation

The purpose of *encapsulation* is to allow Application layer data communication between two stations on a network using the lower layers as a support system. As data moves down the OSI model from the source to the destination, it is encapsulated. As data moves back up the OSI model from the source to the destination, it is decapsulated. Each layer adds a header and/or trailer when information is being transmitted and removes them when information is being received. Encapsulation is the method in which lower layers support upper layers. Figure 1.12 illustrates the process.

FIGURE 1.12   Information is added at each layer of the OSI model as data moves between devices.

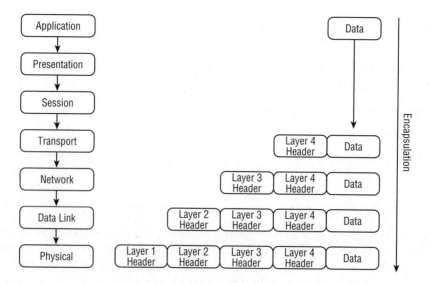

Device Addressing

Every device on a network requires unique identification. This can be accomplished in a couple of ways:

- Physical addresses
- Logical addresses

The *physical address* of a network adapter is also known as the media access control (MAC) address. As shown in Figure 1.13, every device on a network (like every street address in a city) must have a unique address.

The *logical address* is also known as the Internet Protocol (IP) address. Every device on a Layer 3 network (like every city's zip code) must have a unique IP address.

FIGURE 1.13   The MAC address is analogous to the address of buildings on a street.

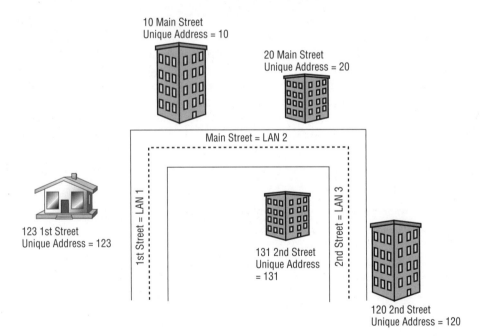

The streets shown in Figure 1.13—1st, Main, and 2nd—represent Local Area Networks. The unique street addresses—10, 20, and so on—represent a unique address of each structure on a street as a MAC address would a device on a LAN.

Physical Addressing

The physical address of a network device is called a MAC address because the *MAC sub-layer* of the Data Link layer handles media access control. The MAC address is a 6-byte (12-character) hexadecimal address in the format AB:CD:EF:12:34:56. The first 3 bytes (or octets) of a MAC address are called the organizationally unique identifier (OUI). Some manufacturers produce many network devices and therefore require several OUIs. A table of all OUIs is freely available from the IEEE Standards Association website at `http://standards.ieee.org/develop/regauth/oui/oui.txt`. MAC addresses are globally unique; an example is shown in Figure 1.14. The first 3 bytes or octets (6 characters) are issued to manufacturers by the IEEE. The last 3 bytes or octets (6 characters) are incrementally assigned to devices by the manufacturer.

FIGURE 1.14   Example of a Layer 2 MAC address

The MAC address of a device is usually stamped or printed somewhere on the device. This allows the device to be physically identified by the MAC address. By typing the simple command **ipconfig /all** in the command-line interface of some operating systems, you can view the physical address of the network adapter. Figure 1.15 shows an example of the information displayed by using this command-line utility in the Microsoft Windows operating system.

FIGURE 1.15   The ipconfig command-line utility displaying a physical/MAC address in Microsoft Windows XP

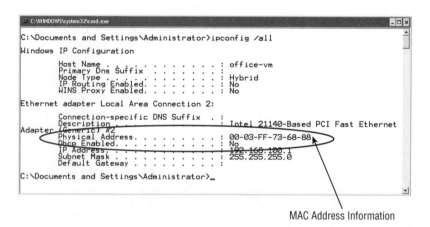

Logical Addressing

Network devices can also be identified by a logical address, known as the Internet Protocol (IP) address. The Layer 3 IP protocol works with a Layer 4 transport protocol, either User Datagram Protocol (UDP) or Transport Layer Protocol (TCP). UDP is a connectionless protocol analogous to a postcard being sent through the mail. The sender has no way of knowing if the card was received by the intended recipient. TCP is a connection-oriented protocol analogous to a telephone call and provides guaranteed delivery of data. During a telephone conversation, communication between two people will be confirmed to be intact, with the users acknowledging the conversation. Routable logical addresses such as TCP/IP addresses became more popular with the evolution of the Internet and the Hypertext Transfer Protocol (HTTP) that is used with the World Wide Web (WWW) service. IP moves data through an internetwork such as the Internet one router (or hop) at a time. Each router makes a decision where to send the data based on the logical IP address. Figure 1.16 shows a basic network utilizing both Layer 2 and Layer 3 data traffic.

FIGURE 1.16   A network with Layer 3 network device logical addressing

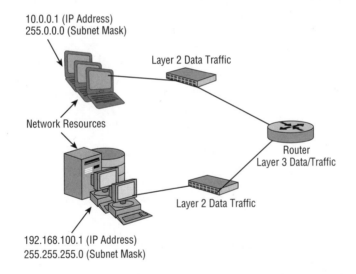

Logical addresses (IP addresses) are 32-bit dotted decimal addresses usually written in the form www.xxx.yyy.zzz. Figure 1.17 illustrates an example of a logical Class C, 32-bit IP address. Each of the four parts is a byte, or 8 digital bits. There are two main IP address types: public addresses and private addresses. Private addresses are unique to an internal network, and public addresses are unique to the Internet. These addresses consist of two main parts: the network (subnet) and the host (device). Logical addresses also require a subnet mask and may have a gateway address depending on whether the network is routed. IP addresses fall under three classes: Class A addresses, Class B addresses, and Class C addresses.

FIGURE 1.17 Example of a Class C logical IP address

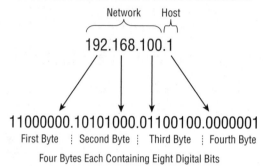

A 32-bit Class C Address Shown in Dotted Decimal Notation

Network Host

192.168.100.1

11000000.10101000.01100100.0000001

First Byte ⋮ Second Byte ⋮ Third Byte ⋮ Fourth Byte

Four Bytes Each Containing Eight Digital Bits

Unlike a MAC address, an *IP address* is logical and can be either specified as a static address assigned to the device by the user or dynamically assigned by a server. However, the same command-line utility used to identify the physical address of a device can be used to identify the logical address of a device.

Typing `ipconfig` at a command prompt displays the logical address, including the IP address, subnet mask and default gateway (router) of the device. The `ipconfig /all` command illustrated earlier in the chapter will yield additional information, including the physical or MAC address of the devices network adapter. This command is for a computer using the Microsoft Windows operating system. For some Apple and Linux devices, the `ifconfig` command will yield similar information. Figure 1.18 shows the ipconfig utility displaying the logical address information, including the IP address and subnet mask.

FIGURE 1.18 The ipconfig command-line utility showing logical address information in Microsoft Windows XP

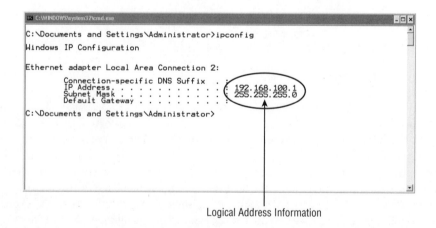

```
C:\WINDOWS\system32\cmd.exe

C:\Documents and Settings\Administrator>ipconfig

Windows IP Configuration

Ethernet adapter Local Area Connection 2:

        Connection-specific DNS Suffix  . :
        IP Address. . . . . . . . . . . . : 192.168.100.1
        Subnet Mask . . . . . . . . . . . : 255.255.255.0
        Default Gateway . . . . . . . . . :

C:\Documents and Settings\Administrator>
```

Logical Address Information

In Exercise 1.1, you will use the ipconfig utility from a command prompt on a computer using the Microsoft Windows operating system.

NOTE   This exercise was written using a computer with the Microsoft Windows 7 operating system. If you're using another version of the operating system, the steps may vary slightly.

EXERCISE 1.1

Viewing Device Address Information on a Computer

1. Click the Start button.

2. Mouse over the All Programs arrow. The All Programs window will appear in the left pane.

3. Navigate to and click on the Accessories folder. The accessories programs will appear.

4. Click the Command Prompt icon. The command window will appear.

5. In the command window, type **ipconfig /all**.

6. View the results in the command window. Notice the physical address of the network adapter as well as other information. The results should look similar to that shown here for the Microsoft Windows XP but may vary slightly based on the OS version in use.

```
C:\WINDOWS\system32\cmd.exe                                              _ □ X

C:\Documents and Settings\Administrator>ipconfig /all

Windows IP Configuration

        Host Name . . . . . . . . . . . . : office-vm
        Primary Dns Suffix  . . . . . . . :
        Node Type . . . . . . . . . . . . : Hybrid
        IP Routing Enabled. . . . . . . . : No
        WINS Proxy Enabled. . . . . . . . : No

Ethernet adapter Local Area Connection 2:

        Connection-specific DNS Suffix  . :
        Description . . . . . . . . . . . : Intel 21140-Based PCI Fast Ethernet
Adapter (Generic) #2
        Physical Address. . . . . . . . . : 00-03-FF-73-68-88
        Dhcp Enabled. . . . . . . . . . . : No
        IP Address. . . . . . . . . . . . : 192.168.100.1
        Subnet Mask . . . . . . . . . . . : 255.255.255.0
        Default Gateway . . . . . . . . . :

C:\Documents and Settings\Administrator>_
```

Summary

This chapter provided a survey of networking topics to help you understand where wireless LANs fit into the larger networking picture. We began with an outline of the common network technology types:

- Local area networks (LANs)
- Wide area networks (WANs)

- Metropolitan area networks (MANs)
- Campus area networks (CANs)
- Personal area networks (PANs)

The next fundamental networking concept we discussed was topology, and we examined network topologies ranging from the legacy high-speed linear bus and ring to the current star topology, the most common topology used today with both wired and wireless networks. Although still in IEEE draft form, mesh networking is growing in popularity with wireless networking and is used in proprietary forms.

We then reviewed the basics of the OSI model, with the understanding that wireless networking technology operates at Layers 1 and 2 of the OSI model. Then we discussed the basics of peer communications and data encapsulation.

The chapter's final topic was physical addressing. We explored the concepts of MAC and the logical addressing, including the IP address and subnet mask. A simple exercise using a computer with the Microsoft Windows operating system showed how to view device addressing information.

Exam Essentials

Understand the components of a local area network (LAN).   A local area network is a group of computers connected by a physical medium in a specific arrangement called a topology.

Know the different types of networks.   Networks types are LAN, WAN, PAN, CAN, and MAN.

Understand point-to-point and point-to-multipoint connections.   These can consist of both wired and wireless connections and will connect two or more LANs together.

Become familiar with various networking topologies.   Bus, star, ring, and mesh are some of the topologies used in computer networking. Bus is considered legacy, and the star topology is one of the most common in use today.

Remember the lower two layers of the OSI model.   The Physical layer and Data Link layer are the two lowest layers in the OSI model. Wireless networking technology operates at these layers. The Data Link layer consists of two sublayers: the Logical Link Control (LLC) sublayer and the Media Access Control (MAC) sublayer.

Understand the OSI model basics.   Each of the seven layers of the OSI model serves a specific function. An overview of all seven layers is beneficial to know.

Understand device addressing.   Devices are assigned a unique physical address by the manufacturer. This address is known as the MAC address. Devices may also be assigned a logical address to identify devices on different internetworks.

Review Questions

1. At which two layers of the OSI model do wireless LANs operate? (Choose 2.)
   A. Session
   B. Network
   C. Physical
   D. Application
   E. Data Link

2. A high-speed linear topology is defined as a _____?
   A. Ring
   B. Mesh
   C. Bus
   D. Star

3. The lower three layers of the OSI model are _____, _____, and _____.
   A. Data link, Physical, Transport
   B. Physical, Data Link, Network
   C. Session, Physical, Application
   D. Application, Presentation, Session

4. The IP address of a network adapter is also known as which address?
   A. MAC address
   B. Logical address
   C. Layer 4 address
   D. Mesh address

5. Which layer of the OSI model is responsible for organizing bit-level data for communication between devices on a network and detecting and correcting Physical layer errors?
   A. Application
   B. Transport
   C. Network
   D. Data Link
   E. Physical

6. Which layer of the OSI model is responsible for addressing and routing?
   A. Physical
   B. Network

    C. Transport

    D. Application

7. _____ allows for Application layer data communication between two stations using lower layers as a support system.

    A. Logical addressing

    B. Physical addressing

    C. Data encapsulation

    D. Data encryption

    E. Point-to-point

8. Which topology may use a token passing access method?

    A. Ring

    B. Mesh

    C. Bus

    D. Star

9. Which layer of the OSI model provides an interface to the user?

    A. Physical

    B. Network

    C. Transport

    D. Application

    E. Data Link

    F. Presentation

10. The physical address of a network adapter is the _____.

    A. MAC address

    B. Logical address

    C. Layer 3 address

    D. Mesh address

11. The term encapsulation means to _____.

    A. Add an IP address to a network adapter

    B. Add a MAC address to a network adapter

    C. Add topology information to a frame

    D. Add layer header and trailer information to a payload

12. Which of the following is an accurate description of peer communication (Choose 2)?

    A. The horizontal link between devices on the network

    B. The vertical link between devices on the network

   C. The logical link between devices on the network

   D. The physical link between devices on the network

13. Physical addresses on a network device are responsible for which of the following?

   A. To identify the logical location on the network

   B. To identify which device should receive the information

   C. To identify the routing information on the network

   D. To identify the protocol in use on the network

14. At which layer of the OSI model are bits compiled into frames?

   A. Physical

   B. Data Link

   C. Network

   D. Transport

   E. Application

15. Which protocol is used to guarantee delivery?

   A. UDP

   B. IP

   C. ARP

   D. TCP

   E. HTTP

16. Which protocol is responsible for addressing and routing?

   A. IP

   B. TCP

   C. UDP

   D. ARP

17. Which layer of the OSI model allows physical addresses to be converted to logical addresses?

   A. Application

   B. Session

   C. Transport

   D. Network

   E. Data Link

18. The Data Link layer of the OSI model is divided into which two sublayers?

   A. PLCP, PMD

   B. LLC, MAC

    C. TCP, UDP

    D. HTTP, FTP

19. Which layer of the OSI model uses physical addresses to deliver data to the destination?

    A. Physical

    B. Data Link

    C. Network

    D. Transport

20. Which is a valid logical IP address?

    A. 255.255.0.0

    B. 192.168.200.1

    C. AB.CD.EF12.34.56

    D. 12.34.56.AB.CD.EF

Chapter

2

Introduction to Wireless Local Area Networking

THE FOLLOWING CWTS EXAM OBJECTIVES ARE COVERED IN THIS CHAPTER:

✓ **1.1 Define the roles of the following organizations in providing direction and accountability within the wireless networking industry**

- IEEE
- Wi-Fi Alliance
- Local regulatory authorities

✓ **1.3 Summarize the basic attributes of the following WLAN standards, amendments, and product certifications**

- 802.11a
- 802.11b
- 802.11g
- 802.11n
- Wi-Fi Multimedia (WMM) certification
- WMM Power Save (WMM-PS) certification
- Wi-Fi Protected Access (WPA/WPA2) certification
- Enterprise Mode
- Personal Mode

✓ **1.4 Explain the role of Wi-Fi as a wireless network access technology**

✓ **WPAN, WLAN, WMAN, WWAN**

✓ **5.1 Identify deployment scenarios for common WLAN network types and suggest best practices for these scenarios**

- Small office/home office (SOHO)

- Extension of existing networks into remote locations

- Building-to-building connectivity

- Public wireless hotspots

- Carpeted office, education, industrial, and healthcare

- Last-mile data delivery: wireless ISP

- High density environments

IEEE 802.11 wireless computer networking continues to take computer communication to a new level. This communication technology is the combination of computer local area networking (LAN) and radio frequency (RF) technology. By combining these two technologies, computer users have the opportunity to access and share information in ways that would seem unattainable not too many years ago.

This chapter will examine various ways in which wireless local networks are used and deployed. We will also cover organizations that determine the use of radio frequency and those responsible for creating and managing wireless LAN standards. We'll look in detail at the IEEE 802.11 standard and its amendments, illustrating the communications and functional aspects. Finally, we will discuss interoperability certifications for IEEE 802.11 wireless networks for communications, quality of service, and security that are available from the Wi-Fi Alliance.

The Wireless Computer Network

The main objective of this book is to provide an introduction to IEEE 802.11–based wireless computer networking, following the "what it is not how it works" philosophy. However, it is important to understand the various ways in which wireless fits with computer networking in general and the various physical applications. In this section, we will take a look at how wireless technology allows users to connect to and use resources in a wireless networking environment. Wireless networks come in a variety of types and sizes and include the following wireless topologies:

- Wireless personal area network (WPAN)
- Wireless local area network (WLAN)
- Wireless metropolitan area network (WMAN)
- Wireless wide area network (WWAN)

In Chapter 1, "Introduction to Computer Networking," you learned about the different types of computer networks. You will now look at some of these network types from a wireless perspective.

The Wireless Personal Area Network

The personal area network (PAN) is a network that connects devices within the immediate area of individual people, as you saw in Chapter 1. With the use of wireless technology, PANs have evolved into the wireless personal area network (WPAN). This type of network allows users to connect various devices wirelessly to their own personal area network, including but not limited to computer keyboards, mice, and headsets.

Bluetooth technology is becoming the most popular type of WPAN and uses frequency hopping spread spectrum (FHSS) for communications. Bluetooth falls under the IEEE 802.15 standard, which specifies the WPAN standards. Bluetooth devices operate in the unlicensed 2.4 GHz Industrial, Scientific and Medical (ISM) band, as do wireless local area networks. The effects of FHSS and Bluetooth on a WLAN will be discussed further in Chapter 5, "Physical Layer Access Methods and Spread Spectrum Technology."

WPANs may also use infrared technology, which uses near-visible light in the 850 nm to 950 nm range for communications. Infrared technology was specified in the original 802.11 standard, but according to the latest version of the standard is now considered obsolete. Regarding the Infrared (IR) specification, the IEEE 802.11-2012 Standard states that "The mechanisms described in this clause are obsolete. Consequently, this clause may be removed in a later revision of the standard. This clause is no longer maintained and may not be compatible with all features of this standard."

The Wireless Local Area Network

As you learned in Chapter 1, local area networks (LANs) can be defined as a group of computers connected by a physical medium in a specific arrangement called a topology. LANs are contained in the same physical area and usually are bounded by the perimeter of a building or a group of buildings. Wireless local area networks (WLANs) fall under the same description as a LAN but no longer require a physical wire to connect devices together. Wireless LANs have been in existence for many years, even prior to IEEE 802.11 standards-based technology, and mostly included proprietary technology or government deployments.

Since the IEEE released the 802.11 standard in 1997, WLAN technology has continued to excel and is becoming a major component of every computer network. WLANs may operate in either the licensed or unlicensed radio frequency spectrum. The most commonly used frequency spectra for WLANs are the unlicensed 2.4 GHz ISM band and the unlicensed 5 GHz Unlicensed National Information Infrastructure (UNII) band. The frequency bands used with IEEE 802.11 wireless networking are discussed later in this chapter in the "Radio Frequency Regulatory Domain Governing Bodies and Local Regulatory Authorities" section.

The Wireless Metropolitan Area Network

Metropolitan area networks consists of networks that may span from several blocks of buildings to entire cities and interconnect devices for access to computer resources in a region or area larger than that covered by LANs but smaller than the areas covered by WANs. You learned about this network type in Chapter 1. You can expand on this technology and add much flexibility to MANs by incorporating wireless technology and creating the wireless metropolitan area network (WMAN). The IEEE 802.16 Standard was developed to address this type of wireless network. This technology may fall under the Worldwide Interoperability for Microwave Access (WiMAX) category and addresses different technologies. The WMAN may include a combination of public and private entities that encompass town services such as police, fire, and public utility access.

The Wireless Wide Area Network   *cellular*

You know from Chapter 1 that a WAN consists of point-to-point or point-to-multipoint connections between two or more LANs. WANS have the capability of extending very long distances through the use of fiber-optic connections or leased lines from telecommunications providers. When it comes to the wireless wide area network (WWAN), this extends beyond the point of connecting LANs together. The WWAN will encompass very large geographical areas and may include different wireless technologies, including cellular.

The WWAN also provides wireless broadband communications for Internet access through the use of special external adapters or even adapters built into notebook computers or other mobile devices, including smart phone technology. Because of the technology used, performance such as data rates will be lower than that expected and realized with IEEE 802.11 wireless networking.

Common WLAN Deployment Scenarios

The availability and technology enhancements of IEEE 802.11 wireless networking have increased while the cost continues to decrease, making wireless LANs a viable solution for many business models, including personal use, home offices, small offices, and enterprise organizations. This section will look at various scenarios in which this type of wireless networking is used. We'll explore the following common deployment scenarios that utilize wireless local area networks (WLANs):

- Small office/home office (SOHO)
- Enterprise deployments: corporate data access and end-user mobility
- Extension of existing networks into remote locations
- Public wireless hotspots
- Carpeted office deployments
- Educational institution deployments
- Industrial deployments
- Healthcare deployments
- Last-Mile data delivery: wireless ISP
- High-density deployments
- Other deployments, including municipal, law enforcement, and transportation networks

Small Office/Home Office

Many small office/home office (SOHO) businesses have the same needs as those of larger businesses with regard to technology, computer networking, and communication. These common needs regardless of the network size include access to a common infrastructure for resources such as computer data (files), printers, databases, other networks, and the Internet. Computer networking technology is common regardless of the size of the business. Whether there are 1 or 100 employees, many are categorized as small businesses. Wireless LANs now play a major role in small businesses. Many of these locations have a high-speed Internet connection such as DSL (digital subscriber line) or cable modem for access outside the local area network.

With the number of work-at-home professionals continuing to grow at a very high rate, the need for wireless networking in this environment is also continuing to grow. The same goes for the small office environment. Deployments such as these typically involve a smaller number of users. Therefore, the equipment used may be consumer models sold in consumer electronics department stores and online retailers.

In addition, many companies or organizations now allow for employees to work remotely part or full time. In these cases the company network is now extended to the remote location, which, whether it is a home office or other location, may be considered a branch office of the company's corporate network. When wireless LAN technology is used at a remote location, new concerns arise, such as data security and network availability. Depending on the size of the small office/home office and the number of potential users and devices, a WLAN RF site survey may be required. A site survey will help determine areas of radio frequency (RF) coverage and interference as well as the number and placement of access points. Even if the small office/home office will only require a single access point, it is still beneficial to know what other wireless networks or devices are in the same coverage area that may cause radio frequency interference.

Figure 2.1 shows a SOHO configuration with a wireless LAN router connected to an Internet service provider allowing access to the necessary network/Internet resources.

FIGURE 2.1   Example of a SOHO wireless LAN configuration

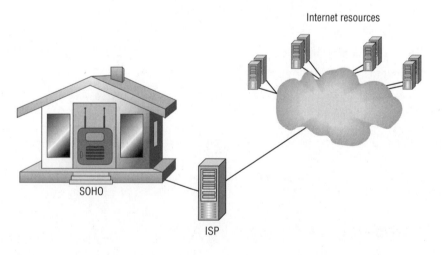

Internet resources

SOHO

ISP

Enterprise Deployments: Corporate Data Access and End-User Mobility

Enterprise organizations have used wired local area networking technology for decades. With the increased need for mobility, wireless LANs within enterprise organizations have also increased in popularity. In earlier years, due to lack of interoperability and security features, many enterprise organizations limited wireless LAN deployments to extensions of networks where wired connectivity was either not feasible or too costly. Because of advancements in wireless LAN technology over the recent years, IEEE 802.11 deployments in enterprise organizations are continuing to grow at a rapid pace.

Wireless LANs in the enterprise are used with—but not limited to—client workstation connectivity (desktop, notebook and tablet devices), printers, barcode scanners, voice handsets, and location services. The cost of this technology has decreased whereas capabilities, performance, speed, and security have increased, making wireless an attractive solution for many enterprise organizations. The cost savings over hardwired solutions such as Ethernet are enormous, adding to the attractiveness. Finally, wireless connectivity is the only option in some cases, such as mobile Voice over Wi-Fi handsets for voice communications.

Figure 2.2 shows a floor plan drawing of an office area that may include a wireless deployment. Each individual or shared office would contain one or two networked desktop computers and phones, and many would also have laptops. Printers might be located in centrally located common areas accessible to the individuals who have permissions to use them. The conference room might contain a videoconferencing system and an access point depending on the number of available seats, and the reception area might have wireless guest access for vendors or other visitors not belonging to the company or organization. Connecting all these networked devices to each other and the outside world are the wireless access point and other WLAN infrastructure discussed in Chapter 3, "Wireless LAN Infrastructure Devices"; these will be located throughout the facility based on the wireless network design to provide coverage and capacity for all wireless devices.

Extension of Existing Networks into Remote Locations

In its early days, wireless networking technology was typically deployed as an extension of an existing wired network infrastructure. For example, some users who required access to the computer network were farther than the physical limit of 100 meters that the IEEE 802.3 Ethernet standard allows for a copper-wired connection, so other solutions were needed to provide this connectivity. Other wired technology, such as fiber optics and leased lines, was sometimes cost-prohibitive or not logistically feasible. Wireless local area networks were an excellent alternative.

Now IEEE 802.11 wireless LANs are a major part of every network, including home, corporate, and branch/remote locations. Remote network locations may include the SOHO, branch office locations, public wireless hotspots, and wireless Internet service providers

(WISPs). When a user connects to a corporate office network from any of these scenarios, the network is basically being extended to a remote location. This extension should be treated as such with regard to network, security, availability, and performance. This chapter discusses each of these deployment scenarios in more detail.

FIGURE 2.2   Floor plan of a typical office area that may use IEEE 802.11 wireless LAN technology

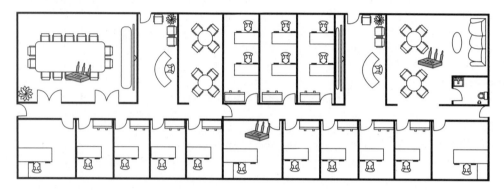

Public Wireless Hotspots

Portability and mobility are major benefits of wireless networking. Portability allows users to access information from a variety of locations, either public or private. Mobility allows the continuous connection to a wireless network while a device is on the move. One example of portability is the wireless hotspot. In today's world, it is rare to visit any public location, whether a restaurant, hotel, coffee shop, or airport, and not be able to find a public wireless hotspot.

A *wireless hotspot* is defined as a location that offers wireless network connectivity for free or for-profit public or patron services. It allows a variety of mobile devices (computers, tablets, smart phones, and so on) to connect to and access public Internet and private network resources. As mentioned earlier in this chapter, many users work from remote locations and require Internet access as part of their job. This can include access from a wireless hotspot.

A typical wireless hotspot will be configured with at least one wireless LAN router connected to an ISP. In some cases, this setup could be as simple as a location offering free Wi-Fi Internet access for its customers. More sophisticated hotspots will have several wireless access points or a complete wireless infrastructure and will be connected to a remote billing server that is responsible for collecting revenue from the user.

In many cases, when a user connects to the hotspot router, they will be prompted with a web page for authentication. At this point they might be asked to enter information such as an account number, username and password, or a credit card number to allow usage for a limited period of time. In the case of a free hotspot, typically this web page lists terms and conditions the user agrees to prior to accessing the Internet. This type of web page configuration is known as a *captive portal*. Captive portals are discussed in more detail in Chapter 9, "Wireless LAN Security Basics."

Wireless hotspots can raise security concerns for the user. Without a secure connection, all information is passed in clear text through the air via radio frequency, potentially allowing an intruder to capture usernames, passwords, credit card numbers, or other information that could lead to identity theft. Most hotspots do not have the capability to provide a secure wireless connection from the user's computer or wireless device to the wireless router or network. The secure connection then becomes the responsibility of the user. Since many corporations do allow employees to work remotely from wireless hotspot connections, extra security measures need to be explored and implemented. In this case, usually a *virtual private network* (VPN) is used to ensure security. A VPN creates a secure tunnel between the user and the corporate network, allowing for a secure encrypted connection for the user from the wireless hotspot to their corporate network over the Internet or public network.

For users who connect to wireless hotspots, it is very important for their wireless devices to be secured with the appropriate antivirus software, firewall software, and up-to-date operating system patches or service packs. Following these guidelines can help protect the user from attacks when they are connected to and using a wireless hotspot.

Figure 2.3 shows a simple wireless hotspot implementation.

FIGURE 2.3 Wireless hotspot allows users to connect to the Internet from remote locations.

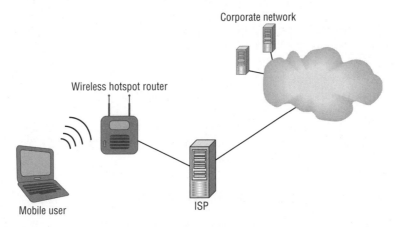

Carpeted Office Deployments

Computer networking in traditional office space, or "carpeted offices," now rely on wireless technology to a large extent. This is for several reasons:

- Cost
- Portability
- Mobility
- Convenience

Many offices do have an existing wired network infrastructure, and I do not expect that to go away any time soon. In most cases copper wire for Ethernet connectivity is already in place and is adequate for the intended use. However, the cost to upgrade the copper wiring or install new wired network drops can be expensive. Therefore, wireless LAN technology is an attractive alternative to wired networks in many office deployment scenarios. What we are now seeing in the enterprise is a new era of wireless networks by default and wired networks only as required. Depending on the use of the network—that is, the types of software applications and the number of devices requiring connectivity—wireless may be the best solution simply because of the cost.

Without trying to set firm limits, it is common to connect as many as 20–25 users/devices to a single wireless access point. However, the maximum size does depend on the software applications and the number of devices connected, as mentioned earlier. A major benefit of IEEE 802.11 wireless LAN technology is that an access point will require only a single Ethernet drop to support all the devices or users. Of course, don't forget that an access point is part of a shared medium for everything that connects, and performance and throughput can be an issue if proper design practices are not used.

Again, remember the difference between portability and mobility. Portability allows users to access information from a variety of set locations, and mobility allows a continuous connection to a wireless network while the device is moving. Carpeted space offices may have a need to provide support for both portability and mobility. For the user who moves from an office cubicle to a conference room to attend a meeting, portability will be sufficient. In this situation they will probably shut down their mobile device, such as a laptop computer, and carry it to a conference room for the meeting. Restarting the computer will then require the device to reconnect to the wireless network, hence, portability.

Devices such as mobile phones using voice over IP (VoIP) or tablet devices usually require continuous connectivity to the wireless network while the user/device is in motion. This mobility feature allows uninterrupted communications and a pleasant experience for the user. Both portability and mobility provide the convenience network that people desire. Figure 2.4 shows a common office scenario.

Educational Institution Deployments

Educational institutions can benefit from wireless networking in many ways. Wireless LAN deployments are common in elementary and high schools both public and private. Universities deploy campus-wide wireless LANs amounting to thousands of access points servicing tens of thousands of users on a single campus.

Wireless LAN technology allows for increased mobility in the educational environment, providing huge cost savings when technology needs to be refreshed. Mobile carts with notebook computers are one example. A high school can deploy wireless infrastructure devices such as access points in classrooms and purchase several mobile carts with notebook or tablet computers to be used when and where needed. This is beneficial since it will save on supplying many classrooms with computers when continuous need for the computers or devices may be low. Some school buildings may be older or historic buildings and installing cabling is impossible or cost-prohibitive. Wireless provides the solution. The architecture of many school buildings may also pose concerns that need to be addressed with many wireless network deployments. These include building materials, such as these:

- Brick and concrete walls
- Lath and plaster walls
- Inconsistent materials due to building additions

FIGURE 2.4   Office with conference area and cubicle offices

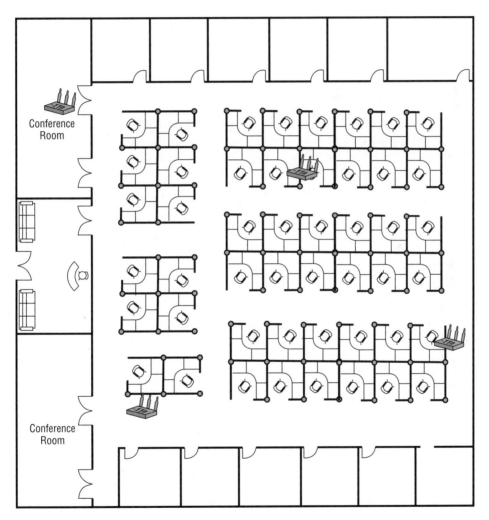

These materials may cause issues because the radio frequency may not propagate well depending on the density and composition of the building materials. This means potentially additional wireless access points and extra design considerations.

In addition, there may be modular or temporary classrooms; the issue with these is the density of devices and users, which will affect the wireless network capacity and may result in performance issues. Also, the location and distance from the main building should be taken into consideration because this equates to a point-to-multipoint connection and line of sight needs be taken into account.

Some educational institutions are implementing a "one-to-one" initiative—in other words, the goal is to have one Internet-accessible device for every one student. This type of initiative will introduce density concerns, because of the potentially high number of students in a single classroom. Educational institutions, whether an elementary school, a high school, or a college campus, should always consider starting with an RF wireless site survey and follow best practices from the equipment manufacturer to ensure a successful deployment. Figure 2.5 shows a typical small school environment.

Industrial Deployments

Some industrial organizations have been using wireless LAN technology for many years, even prior to the development of IEEE 802.11 wireless standards-based solutions. Examples of these deployments include barcode and scanning solutions for manufacturing, warehousing, inventory, and retail. Although this type of deployment may not be very dense, coverage is very important. Many businesses of this type include the following building characteristics:

- High ceilings
- Tall storage racks
- Large inventory of product
- Forklifts

These building characteristics can cause issues with wireless networks because of the way radio frequency propagates. With high ceilings, various antennas will need to be tested and coverage verified throughout the facility. Tall storage racks may have varying levels of inventory or product, resulting in poor propagation. Depending on what the products are made of, this will have a direct impact on the radio frequency behavior. For example, a high density of water products and paper products will absorb radio frequency. In many cases, forklifts will be outfitted with wireless barcode scanners or other mobile devices that require the ability for fast secure transition capabilities.

In this type of environment, it is important to understand that radio frequency will behave in ways that could impact the performance of the wireless network. Chapter 6, "Radio Frequency Fundamentals for Wireless LAN Technology," will explain the behaviors of radio frequency in more detail. These behaviors can lead to coverage issues for the devices in use. Careful evaluation of this type of environment is essential, and an RF site survey is highly recommended to ensure proper RF coverage.

The physical characteristics of this type of environment are fairly static, although additional racks or shelving may occasionally be added. However, product inventory is dynamic and may change constantly. Moreover, forklifts and other product-moving equipment are constantly moving and in different locations. These are some of the factors that must be taken into consideration when deploying wireless networking in an industrial environment. Figure 2.6 shows a typical warehouse facility with 35-foot-high ceilings.

FIGURE 2.5   Classrooms for wireless LAN deployment

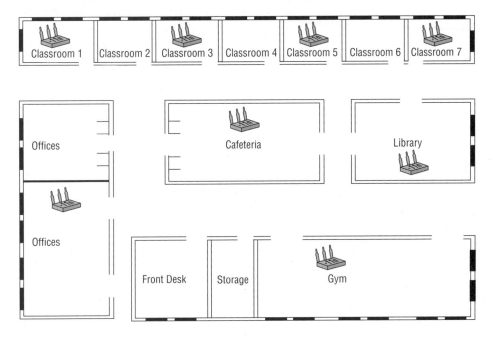

FIGURE 2.6   Warehouse facility with high ceilings and storage shelving inside

Healthcare Deployments

The growth of wireless LAN deployments in the healthcare industry is quite impressive. Today, healthcare is one of the fastest-growing sectors of the U.S. economy. Healthcare environments pose many challenges for the design, deployment, and support of wireless networking.

Hospitals in most cases run 24 × 7 × 365 days a year. Wireless LANs have numerous applications in hospitals, including these:

- Patient registration
- Patient charting
- Prescription automation
- Treatment verification
- Inventory tracking
- Electronic medical records
- Location services
- Electronic imaging

One of the obstacles to take into consideration for wireless networking is interference. Hospitals use many devices that operate in the unlicensed ISM RF band. This can create challenges for design and reliability of the wireless network. Licensed and unlicensed RF bands are discussed later in this chapter. Other potential issues for healthcare deployments to be aware of include:

- Building materials that can hinder RF propagation, such as lead-lined walls used in radiology areas to protect people from X-rays
- Identical floor layouts above and below, which leads to stacking access point issues
- Limited accessibility to areas such as surgery and patient care rooms
- Aesthetics of the installed equipment

Compliance with legislation such as the Health Insurance Portability and Accountability Act of 1996 (HIPAA) also needs to be taken into consideration when designing wireless installations for healthcare. Security concerns and different legislations will be discussed in Chapter 9. Figure 2.7 illustrates a common medical office that uses wireless LAN technology.

Last-Mile Data Delivery: Wireless ISP

Last-mile data delivery is a term commonly used in telecommunications to describe the connection from a provider to an endpoint such as a home or business. (Last-mile is not necessarily a mile in distance.) This can be a costly solution in many applications, since each endpoint needs a separate physical connection. Wireless technology provides a more cost-effective solution for last-mile data delivery.

Some communication technologies, such as DSL, have physical limitations that prohibit connections in some cases. It may not be cost-effective for telecommunication service providers to supply connections in rural or semi-rural areas. Wireless LANs can service areas that may not be part of a last-mile run. Providing Internet access from a wireless ISP is one application. Things to consider for feasibility are line of sight, obstacles, and RF interference. Figure 2.8 shows an example of wireless last-mile data delivery.

FIGURE 2.7 Medical offices often use wireless LAN technology.

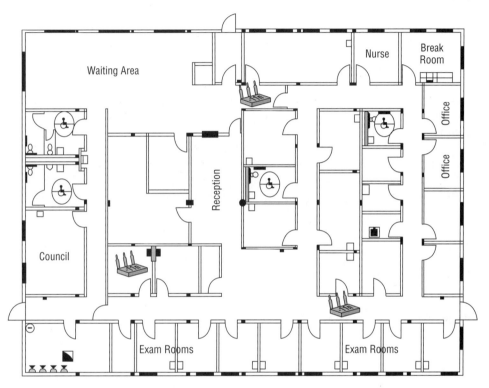

FIGURE 2.8 Wireless last-mile data delivery

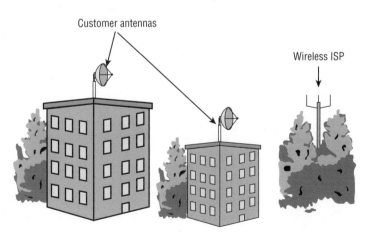

In December 2009 the 802.11 task group TGaf was formed to define the 802.11af amendment (not to be confused with IEEE 802.3af for Power over Ethernet). This amendment to the 802.11 standard addresses the use of "TV White Space" frequency bands for use with wireless networking technology. These lower frequencies propagate well over longer distances and may be ideal to provide Internet connectivity for rural or semi-rural areas as well as other types of wireless technology innovation.

High-Density Deployments

What does the term "high-density Wi-Fi deployment" really mean? People have differing opinions on this, as it can be subjective. Some industry experts claim that in the next few years the number of installed wireless devices will exceed the number of installed wired devices. When you think about it, this projection may be realistic. Take a moment and count the number of wireless devices that you have in your possession, at your home, the classroom, and the office. This includes notebook computers, smart phones, tablets, and broadband Internet devices. The average person may have between one and five separate wireless devices, many of which include IEEE 802.11 wireless technology. This gives an idea of how the density of wireless LAN devices in all environments—home, office, education, and industrial—will continue to increase in the coming years.

Some high-density deployments have been discussed in this chapter and include educational institutions and medical such as hospital environments. Issues to consider in this type of environment are the frequency band to use, co-channel interference, cell sizing, and access point capacity.

Municipal, Law Enforcement, and Transportation Networks

Wireless LANs are valuable technology in the industrial, municipal, and law enforcement fields, and in transportation networks.

Federal and local law enforcement agencies frequently maintain state-of-the-art technology utilizing computer forensics and wireless LAN technology. Technologies that use 19.2 Kbps connectivity are becoming obsolete because of their slower data transfer rates. Municipal deployments that include police, fire, utilities, and city or town services are often all connected to a common wireless LAN.

Transportation networks are no exception. Wireless LAN installations are becoming more common in places like commuter buses, trains, airplanes and automobiles. Users can connect for free or by paying a nominal fee. This type of connectivity now allows a user to better employ idle time. This is especially helpful to the mobile user or "road warrior" who needs to make the best use of available time.

Building-to-Building Connectivity Using Wireless LAN Technology

Connecting two or more wired LANs together over some distance is often necessary in computer networking. Depending on the topology, this can be an expensive and time-consuming task. Wireless LAN technology is often used as an alternative to copper cable, fiber optics, or leased line connectivity between buildings. Whether connecting two or multiple locations together, point-to-point or point-to-multipoint links can be a quick and cost-effective solution for building-to-building connectivity.

Antenna selection plays an important role in this type of connectivity and will be discussed further in Chapter 7, "WLAN Antennas and Accessories." Other factors to consider in either point-to-point or point-to-multipoint connections are the radio frequency band used and the distance, both of which will determine whether a link is feasible for a wireless connection.

Wireless Point-to-Point Connections

As discussed in Chapter 1, connecting at least two wired LANs together is known as a *point-to-point connection*. Wireless point-to-point connections can provide long-range coverage depending on terrain and other local conditions. These links can serve both wired and wireless users on the connected local area networks. Wireless point-to-point connections typically call for semidirectional or highly directional antennas. With some regulatory agencies, when an omnidirectional antenna is used in this configuration, it is considered a special case, called a *point-to-multipoint connection*. Correct antenna selection is important and will be discussed in more detail in Chapter 7. Figure 2.9 shows a wireless point-to-point connection.

FIGURE 2.9 A wireless point-to-point connection using directional antennas

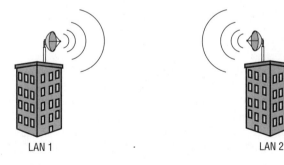

LAN 1   LAN 2

Wireless Point-to-Multipoint Connections

As you learned in Chapter 1, a network connecting more than two LANs together is known as a point-to-multipoint connection. With wireless networking, this configuration usually consists of one omnidirectional antenna and multiple semi- or highly directional antennas (see Figure 2.10). Point-to-multipoint connections are often used in campus-style deployments where connections to multiple buildings or locations may be required.

FIGURE 2.10   A typical point-to-multipoint connection using omnidirectional and directional antennas

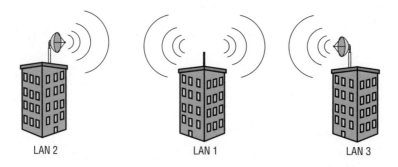

Wireless point-to-point and point-to-multipoint connections are becoming more common with many IEEE 802.11 wireless LAN deployments, thanks to the low cost of the equipment and the ease of installation. The installation time for a wireless point-to-point connection can be as little as a few hours.

RF Regulatory Domain Governing Bodies and Local Regulatory Authorities

Wireless networks use radio frequency (RF) to communicate. The RF spectrum needs to be regulated in order to ensure correct use of the allocated frequency bands. At the global level, the International Telecommunication Union–Radiocommunication Sector (ITU-R) is responsible for global management of RF spectrum, in addition to satellite orbits. This organization currently has 191 member states and over 700 sector members. It manages five regions, one of which is Region A, North and South America, Inter-American Telecommunication Commission (CITEL).

Figure 2.11 shows all five regions and the geographic area they encompass.

FIGURE 2.11   ITU-R region map

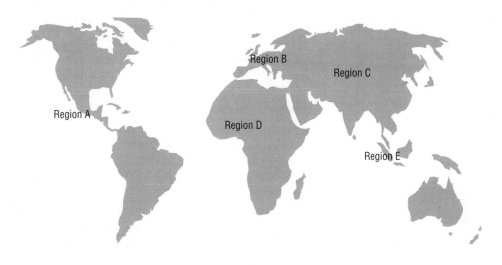

      For additional information, visit www.itu.int/ITU-R.

Table 2.1 shows the five regions, the geographic areas they cover, and the URL address for each region's website.

TABLE 2.1   ITU-R regions, geographic locations, and URLs

Region	Location	URL
Region A	America	www.citel.oas.org
Region B	Western Europe	www.cept.org
Region C	Eastern Europe and Northern Asia	www.en.rcc.org.ru/
Region D	Africa	www.atu-uat.org
Region E	Asia and Australia	www.aptsec.org

United States: Federal Communications Commission

The *local regulatory authority* that manages RF spectrum for the United States is the Federal Communications Commission (FCC). The FCC, founded in 1934, is (along with other local regulatory authorities) responsible for regulating the licensed and unlicensed radio frequency spectrum. IEEE 802.11 wireless networks may use licensed or unlicensed frequencies for communication between devices. A benefit of using unlicensed radio spectrum is no cost to the end user. The IEEE commonly uses two of three unlicensed RF bands allowed by the FCC:

- 2.4 GHz ISM
- 5 GHz UNII

Later in this chapter we will further discuss this and other details of standards-based wireless communications.

The unlicensed 900 MHz ISM band is not used with IEEE 802.11 wireless networking.

Licensed RF Bands Used with IEEE 802.11

Two additional licensed bands can be used with IEEE 802.11 networking:

- 3.650–3.700 GHz band
- 4.940–4.990 GHz public safety band

In 2008 the IEEE ratified the IEEE 802.11y amendment to the standard. This amendment allows for the use of high-powered wireless LAN equipment to operate in the 3.650–3.700 GHz band. Within the United States this is a licensed band that requires the user to pay some type of licensing fees.

The IEEE 802.11-2012 standard also specifies the use of the 4.940–4.990 GHz public safety band for use within the United States, consisting of 5 MHz, 10 MHz, and 20 MHz wide channels with both high and low power limits.

For additional information regarding radio frequency use in the United States, visit www.fcc.gov.

Europe: European Telecommunications Standards Institute

The European Telecommunications Standards Institute (ETSI) is responsible for producing standards for information and communications technologies, including fixed, mobile, radio, converged, broadcast, and Internet technologies in Europe.

ETSI was created by the European Conference of Postal and Telecommunications Administrations (CEPT) in 1988.

In Europe, radio frequency use is managed by CEPT, which develops guidelines and provides national administrations with tools for coordinated European radio frequency spectrum management.

IEEE and Wireless LAN Standards

The *IEEE* (originally known as the Institute of Electrical and Electronics Engineers), pronounced "eye triple E," is a nonprofit organization responsible for generating a variety of technology standards, including those related to information technology. The IEEE is the world's largest technical professional society. Since 1997 the IEEE has released a series of standards related to wireless local area networking.

This section describes the IEEE wireless networking standard and the amendments in the order in which they were ratified and released. They define what some call the power, range, and speed of the radio frequency and WLAN technology. This is because the IEEE 802.11 standard specifies the maximum amount of radio frequency (RF) transmit power, the allowed radio frequency spectrum (which is related to the range), and the allowed data rates or speed.

For additional information about the IEEE, visit www.ieee.org.

The IEEE 802.11 Standard

The *IEEE 802.11* standard, released in 1997, is what initially defined the wireless LAN communication standards. The data rates used in this original standard (1 and 2 Mbps) are considered slow compared to today's technology.

As of this writing, the IEEE 802.11-2012 standard is the most current ratified IEEE 802.11 standard. This latest version includes the IEEE 802.11-2007 standard and outstanding amendments at the time of ratification, such as IEEE 802.11k/n/p/r/s/u/v/w/y/z, into one document. However, many in the industry still refer to the original names of the amendments: 802.11b, 802.11a, 802.11g, 802.11n, and so on. The IEEE considers all of the previously published amendments and revisions retired as a result of the release of the new IEEE 802.11-2012 Standard.

Device and application requirements for IEEE 802.11 are discussed in Chapter 6.

Here are the frequency range, spread spectrum technology, and data rates for the IEEE 802.11-1997 standard:

- 2.4 GHz ISM band

- Frequency hopping spread spectrum (FHSS)

- Direct sequence spread spectrum (DSSS)

- Infrared (IR)

- 1 and 2 Mbps

Frequency hopping spread spectrum is considered legacy technology with regard to IEEE 802.11 wireless networking. However, it is still used in other wireless technologies, such as IEEE 802.15 Bluetooth devices, and wireless cordless public switched telephone network (PSTN) telephones.

 To see the most up-to-date status of the IEEE 802.11 standard and amendments, visit the Official IEEE 802.11 Working Group Project Timelines web page at www.ieee802.org/11/Reports/802.11_Timelines.htm.

The IEEE 802.11b Amendment

The IEEE 802.11b amendment to the 802.11 standard works in the 2.4–2.5 GHz ISM band. This amendment, released in 1999, specifies high rate DSSS (HR/DSSS) for 5.5 and 11 Mbps.

 The IEEE 802.11b amendment was released before the IEEE 802.11a amendment.

Here are the frequency range, Physical layer (PHY) technology, spread spectrum technology, and data rates for the *IEEE 802.11b* amendment:

- 2.4 GHz ISM band

- 2.4 GHz–2.4835 GHz in North America, China, and Europe (excluding Spain and France)

- Direct sequence spread spectrum (DSSS)

- High rate–direct sequence spread spectrum (HR/DSSS)

- 5.5 and 11 Mbps

- Backward compatible to 802.11 DSSS for 1 and 2 Mbps

With the release of the IEEE 802.11b amendment, wireless LAN technology became more affordable and mainstream. This amendment introduced two higher-rate data speeds,

5.5 and 11 Mbps, making the technology more desirable. Today wireless infrastructure device manufacturers still support IEEE 802.11b wireless technology; however, it is unlikely you would be able to purchase any "new" devices that support only IEEE 802.11b technology. Devices sold today that operate in the 2.4 GHz ISM band will support IEEE 802.11b/g/n and may be marketed as such or as IEEE 802.11g/n, which implies support for IEEE 802.11b.

The acronyms described in following section such as FHSS, DSSS, HR/DSSS, OFDM, ERP, and HT are shown and defined to help explain the details of each amendment to the standard. You will learn more about each of these Physical layer technologies in Chapter 5.

The IEEE 802.11a Amendment

This amendment to the IEEE 802.11 standard defined operation in the 5 GHz UNII band. Released in 1999, this amendment originally defined three frequency ranges in three bands—UNII-1, UNII-2, and UNII-3. The UNII-1 band is intended for indoor use only, the UNII-2 band is for indoor or outdoor use, and the UNII-3 band may be used indoors or outdoors but was most commonly used outdoors. The data rates for IEEE 802.11a are up to 54 Mbps using orthogonal frequency division multiplexing (OFDM). OFDM and other Physical layer technologies will be discussed in Chapter 5. Although this amendment was released in 1999, devices were not widely available until 2001.

Here are the frequency range, PHY technology, and data rates as specified in the original *IEEE 802.11a* amendment.

- 5GHz UNII band
  - 5.150–5.250 GHz UNII-1
  - 5.250–5.350 GHz UNII-2
  - 5.725–5.825 GHz UNII-3

- Orthogonal frequency division multiplexing (OFDM)
- 6, 12, 24 Mbps OFDM required data rates
- 9, 18, 36, 48, and 54 Mbps OFDM data rates supported but not required

A benefit to using the 5 GHz UNII band is less interference, because not all wireless devices support operation in this band. Currently, many fewer devices use the 5 GHz UNII license-free band than use the 2.4 GHz ISM license-free band, including non-802.11 devices. However, the number of wireless devices that operate in the 5 GHz band is always increasing. If there are fewer devices that utilize the band it means less interference, which allows for increased performance and reliability.

Since the IEEE 802.11a amendment was ratified, some changes have been implemented and are now addressed in the IEEE 802.11-2012 standard and previously the 802.11-2007 standard. They include a new frequency range (5.470–5.725 GHz) that is allowed by some local regulatory agencies and is known as the UNII-2e band. This extra frequency space allows for 11 additional 20 MHz–wide nonoverlapping channels. Also, based on the IEEE 802.11-2012 standard, in the United States, one channel (channel 165 in the 5 GHz ISM) band is allowed to be used with IEEE 802.11 wireless LAN technology.

The IEEE 802.11g Amendment

This amendment to the IEEE 802.11 standard was released in 2003. Like 802.11 and 802.11b, it operates in the 2.4 GHz ISM band. This amendment addresses extended data rates with OFDM technology and is backward-compatible to 802.11 and 802.11b.

Here are the frequency range, PHY technology, spread spectrum technology, and data rates for the *IEEE 802.11g* amendment:

- 2.4 GHz ISM band
- 2.4 GHz–2.4835 GHz in North America, China, and Europe (excluding Spain and France)
- Direct sequence spread spectrum (DSSS)
- High rate–direct sequence spread spectrum (HR/DSSS)
- Extended rate physical–orthogonal frequency division multiplexing (ERP-OFDM)
- Packet binary convolutional code (PBCC; optional)
- 1 and 2 Mbps (compatible with DSSS)
- 5.5 and 11 Mbps complementary code keying (CCK; compatible with HR/DSSS)
- 6, 12, 24 Mbps OFDM required data rates
- 9, 18, 36, 48, and 54 Mbps OFDM data rates supported but not required

IEEE 802.11g is backward-compatible to 802.11 and 802.11b because it operates in the same 2.4 GHz ISM license-free band and supports the same access methods or technology as 802.11b. One benefit of IEEE 802.11g compatibility is that many established network infrastructures and devices have used 802.11 and 802.11b for years. This allows them to continue to operate as normal with upgrades or replacement as appropriate or necessary.

To allow the slower DSSS and HR/DSSS data rates of 1, 2, 5.5, and 11 Mbps to operate in an IEEE 802.11g network, the amendment addresses the use of protection mechanisms. These protection mechanisms will degrade the performance of IEEE 802.11g clients to some degree when IEEE 802.11b radios are present in the basic service area (BSA).

Some organizations are moving to drop support for IEEE 802.11b devices. This is accomplished by disabling the 802.11b data rates on the infrastructure devices—access points, controllers, and so on. They do this to minimize performance issues such as throughput when IEEE 802.11b devices are present in the IEEE 802.11g BSA. In some deployment scenarios, such as public wireless hotspots or areas with wireless guest networks, it would be difficult to disallow the use of IEEE 802.11b devices. However, this is strictly a decision to be made by the organization and information technology staff.

 Real World Scenario

Maximizing Throughput in an IEEE 802.11g Network

In certain cases the only way to maximize the throughput of an 802.11g network is to set the data rates of the access points to support 802.11g data rates only. The trade-off is that 802.11b devices will not be able to connect to the network, because the access point will not recognize the 802.11b data rates. This would work well where backward compatibility to 802.11b is not required and all equipment in use supports 802.11g. An analogy would be a group of individuals all speaking one language. They all understand the same language, so they have no need to accommodate a second language.

Because of protection mechanisms defined in the 802.11g amendment, throughput will degrade in an 802.11b/g mixed mode environment when 802.11b devices are present. The 802.11b devices have a maximum data rate of 11 Mbps (HR/DSSS), and they share the medium with the 802.11g devices that have a maximum data rate of 54 Mbps (ERP-OFDM). Think of the language analogy. If a group of individuals are speaking two different languages, a translator may be required for complete communication. A discussion among the group would take longer, because the translator would need to translate the languages. Likewise, protection mechanisms will have an impact on the throughput for the 802.11g devices, since the 2.4 GHz medium is shared. If there are no 802.11b devices in the radio range of an access point in an 802.11b/g mixed mode environment, protection mechanisms should not affect throughput since the access point will not have to share the medium with the two different technologies, ERP-OFDM and HR/DSSS.

If you do not have any 802.11b devices on your network, you can set your access point to 802.11g-only mode by disabling the 802.11b data rates. In this configuration, your 802.11g devices will perform better, because protection mechanisms will not be enabled. However, if there are any 802.11b devices that don't belong to your network in the "listening" range of the access point, data collisions will increase at the access point. This is because 802.11b and 802.11g operate in the same RF range, and the 802.11g (ERP-OFDM) access point would stop listening to the 802.11b (HR/DSSS) transmissions. (It would simply see them as RF noise.) In this configuration, overall throughput will still exceed that of an access point set to 802.11b/g mixed mode in the presence of 802.11b devices. The access point will hear the 802.11b transmissions, but they will not be serviced since they are only seen as RF noise. Thus they will have less impact on throughput.

The IEEE 802.11n Amendment

After several years of drafts, the *IEEE 802.11n* amendment was finally approved in September 2009. The release of this document opened the doors for manufacturers of IEEE 802.11 wireless LAN equipment, giving them the opportunity to move forward with new technology that allows for better performance, higher throughput, and several other benefits. Wi-Fi certified devices under 802.11n draft 2.0 were available for several years prior to the ratification of IEEE 802.11n. Most if not all enterprise manufacturers had at least one wireless infrastructure device certified under draft 2.0 by the Wi-Fi Alliance prior to the release of the new amendment.

Here are the frequency range, PHY technology, data rates, and other details for the IEEE 802.11n amendment:

- 2.4 GHz ISM band

- 5 GHz UNII band

- Multiple-input multiple-output technology (MIMO)

- HT-OFDM

- Physical layer (PHY) layer enhancements

- Data Link layer (MAC) layer enhancements

- Data rates up to 600 Mbps

IEEE 802.11n devices are capable of operating in both unlicensed frequency bands, the 2.4 GHz ISM band, and the 5 GHz UNII band. This means that they must be backward-compatible with previous technologies, such as IEEE 802.11b/g devices that operate in the 2.4 GHz ISM band and IEEE 802.11a devices that operate in the 5 GHz UNII band.

Multiple-input multiple-output (MIMO) is a big part of what makes IEEE 802.11n such an amazing technology. Prior to 802.11n, IEEE 802.11a/b/g devices used a single radio to transmit and receive radio signals. This is known as single-input single-output (SISO) technology. MIMO uses multiple radios or "radio chains" to transmit and receive radio signals. SISO systems were subject to a phenomenon called multipath, in which several wavefronts of a signal would be received out of phase because of reflections. This is a problem for IEEE 802.11a/b/g systems, whereas MIMO actually uses the reflections to help enhance the performance and throughput using several radio chains in 802.11n. Multipath is discussed in more detail in Chapter 7. MIMO consists of several types of new technologies that include the following among others:

- Transmit beamforming (TxBF)

- Maximal ratio combining (MRC)

- Spatial multiplexing (SM)

- Space time block coding (STBC)

It is best to check with the specific manufacturers of the wireless equipment to determine how they implement MIMO technology. The details of the types of MIMO technologies listed here are beyond the scope of the objectives of the *CWTS Study Guide* but can be found in other CWNP Study Guides and training materials.

IEEE 802.11n provides many enhancements to the physical layer 1, including the following, among others:

- 40 MHz channels through the use of channel bonding
- More subcarriers for higher data rates
- Optional short guard intervals to provide more potential throughput
- Varying modulation types for data rates of up to 600 Mbps

The Media Access Control (MAC) sublayer of the Data Link layer also provides enhancements to improve performance and throughput with IEEE 802.11n. These include but are not limited to the following:

- Frame aggregation for less 802.11 overhead
- Block acknowledgments (block ACKs)
- Reduced interframe spacing (RIFS)
- Spatial multiplexing power save (SMPS) to help conserve battery life
- Power save multi-poll (PSMP) for devices enabled for quality of service (QoS)

It is beneficial to understand all the frequencies, PHY technology, spread spectrum technologies, and data rates for all the IEEE 802.11 standards and amendments mentioned in this chapter. This will help for certification exam purposes as well as for basic knowledge of the technology. Table 2.2 provides a summary and comparison of the currently released IEEE 802.11 communication standards and amendments.

TABLE 2.2 Summary of 802.11 communication standards and amendments

Details	802.11	802.11a	802.11b	802.11g	802.11n
2.4 GHz ISM band	x		x	x	x
5 GHz UNII bands		x			x
FHSS	x				
DSSS	x		x	x	x
HR/DSSS			x	x	x
OFDM		x			x
ERP-OFDM				x	x
HT-OFDM					x
1 and 2 Mbps	x		x	x	x

TABLE 2.2 Summary of 802.11 communication standards and amendments *(continued)*

Details	802.11	802.11a	802.11b	802.11g	802.11n
5.5 and 11 Mbps			x	x	x
6, 9, 12, 18, 24, 36, 48, 54 Mbps		x		x	x
Up to 600 Mbps					X

Additional IEEE 802.11 Amendments

In addition to communications, the IEEE creates amendments defining specific functionality, including QoS and security. We will look at those functions next.

 Although the following IEEE 802.11 amendments are not included in the exam objectives, it is important to understand this information as it pertains to the technology.

The IEEE 802.11e Amendment

The original IEEE 802.11 standard lacked QoS functionality features. In the original IEEE 802.11 standard, Point Coordination Function (PCF) mode provided some level of QoS. PCF mode is a function of the access point and allows for polling of connected client devices. This creates a contention-free period for data transmissions and provides QoS-like functionality. However, few if any vendors implemented this mode of operation.

The IEEE 802.11e amendment defines enhancements for QoS in wireless LANs. 802.11e introduced a new coordination function, the hybrid coordination function (HCF). HCF defines traffic classes and assigns a priority to the information to be transmitted. For example, voice traffic is given a higher priority than data traffic, such as information being sent to a printer. The IEEE 802.11e amendment was incorporated into the IEEE 802.11-2007 standard and is now part of the IEEE 802.11-2012 Standard. The Wi-Fi Alliance created a proactive interoperability certification for 802.11e called Wi-Fi Multimedia (WMM). The Wi-Fi Alliance and interoperability certifications are discussed later in this chapter.

The IEEE 802.11i Amendment

The IEEE 802.11i amendment addresses advanced security solutions for wireless LANs, since the original IEEE 802.11 standard was known for security weaknesses. Manufacturers of IEEE 802.11 WLAN equipment addressed the following:

- Wired Equivalent Privacy (WEP)
- Service set identifier (SSID) hiding
- Media access control (MAC) address filtering

Wired Equivalent Privacy (WEP) was defined by the IEEE 802.11 standard intended to prevent casual eavesdropping. WEP was compromised early on, making wireless LANs vulnerable to intrusion and providing little if any security. This issue was addressed by stronger security mechanisms (mainly CCMP/AES – Counter Mode with Cipher-Block Chaining Message Authentication Code Protocol /Advanced Encryption Standard) that became available with the introduction of the IEEE 802.11i amendment to the standard.

Service set identifier (SSID) hiding and media access control (MAC) address filtering are both manufacturer-implemented features that may be used by some for "pseudo" security. It is important to understand that neither of these provides any kind of security for an IEEE 802.11 wireless network.

WEP, SSID hiding, and MAC filtering all have known security vulnerabilities, allowing for security weaknesses in IEEE 802.11 wireless LANs. The IEEE 802.11i amendment addressed security weaknesses with wireless LANS by including several enhancements, all of which will be discussed in Chapter 9. The IEEE 802.11i amendment was incorporated into the IEEE 802.11-2007 standard and is now part of the IEEE 802.11-2012 Standard.

The IEEE 802.11r Amendment

The IEEE 802.11r amendment was approved in May 2008. The 802.11r amendment specifies fast secure roaming or fast transition (FT) technology. The IEEE 802.11 standard did not address standards-based transition (roaming) mechanisms, so manufacturers used proprietary methods. The IEEE attempted to standardize transition techniques for wireless LAN technology with the ratification of a recommended practice, IEEE 802.11F. This recommended practice was never implemented by many (if any) manufacturers and was eventually withdrawn by the IEEE.

The main goal of IEEE 802.11r was to provide fast transition for voice over IP (VoIP) with wireless LAN technology. Although this amendment has been ratified for some time and most enterprise equipment manufacturers support it, they still rely on the use of proprietary methods for fast transition. This is partly because there was no interoperability certification until the formation of the Wi-Fi Alliance. The IEEE 802.11r amendment was incorporated into the IEEE 802.11-2012 Standard.

The IEEE 802.11k Amendment

IEEE 802.11k is the amendment to the IEEE 802.11 standard that addresses radio resource management. This amendment was approved in May 2008, the same day as the IEEE 802.11r amendment. 802.11k and 802.11r work together to form fast, secure basic service set transition for mobile devices. IEEE 802.11k aids the wireless device in locating the best access point to transition to, by defining the technology to be used to manage the radio frequency. The IEEE 802.11k amendment was incorporated into the IEEE 802.11-2012 Standard.

The IEEE 802.11w Amendment

Wireless LAN management frames, such as the 802.11 authentication frames and 802.11 association frames used in IEEE 802.11 wireless LANs, are susceptible to intrusion and can cause security issues. This is because the IEEE 802.11 standard did not provide any protection for management frame information that traverses the air. With some basic knowledge of the technology and the correct software tools, an intruder can perform a denial-of-service (DoS) or hijacking attack. When implemented, technology specified in the IEEE 802.11w amendment helps to mitigate these types of attacks or security issues. This is still considered newer technology and is not yet implemented by all manufacturers of wireless LAN equipment. The IEEE 802.11w amendment was incorporated into the IEEE 802.11-2012 Standard.

The IEEE 802.11s Amendment

The IEEE 802.11s amendment specifies wireless mesh networking. Mesh networking with wired networking has been available for many years. Wireless mesh networking started with military deployments but has evolved into the public sector. Mesh networking allows infrastructure devices such as wireless access points or mesh routers to create a self-forming, self-healing and intelligent network infrastructure. A wireless mesh network is sometimes referred to as a wireless distribution system (WDS). Most manufacturers of enterprise wireless equipment have been using mesh technology for years with proprietary protocols. Although the IEEE has ratified the standard for this technology, most manufacturers still use proprietary methods. Mesh technology will be discussed further in Chapter 3. The IEEE 802.11s amendment was incorporated into the IEEE 802.11-2012 Standard.

Interoperability Certifications

By creating standards, the IEEE is encouraging technological progress. Manufacturers often implement wireless devices and networks in a proprietary manner, within or outside the standard. The proprietary approach often leads to a lack of interoperability among devices. In the wireless community, such practices are not widely accepted. Users want all of their devices to function well together. The combination of proprietary implementations and user dissatisfaction fostered the creation of interoperability testing and certifications.

This section will discuss vendor interoperability certifications related to IEEE 802.11 standards-based wireless LAN equipment. These certifications address communications, QoS, and security.

Wi-Fi Alliance

As mentioned in the previous section, the IEEE is responsible for creating the standards for wireless networking. However, equipment manufacturers are not required to provide proof that their equipment is compliant with the standards. Starting with the release of the IEEE 802.11b amendment, several early WLAN equipment manufacturers—including Symbol Systems, Aironet, and Lucent—formed an organization known as Wireless Ethernet Compatibility Alliance (WECA) to promote the technology and to provide interoperability testing of wireless LAN equipment manufactured by these and other companies. In 2000, WECA was renamed the *Wi-Fi Alliance*. The term *Wi-Fi* represents a certification and is often misused by people in the industry. Wi-Fi is a registered trademark, originally registered in 1999 by WECA and now registered to the Wi-Fi Alliance. People often use the term Wi-Fi synonymously with wireless LAN technology; in fact it means wireless technology certified to be interoperable.

 For additional information about the Wi-Fi Alliance, visit www.wi-fi.org.

Figure 2.12 shows an example of a Wi-Fi certified logo, showing the device has met the interoperability testing criteria.

FIGURE 2.12   Wi-Fi Certified logo for devices that are Wi-Fi certified

(Logo used with permission from the Wi-Fi Alliance)

Wi-Fi Protected Access Certification

The *Wi-Fi Protected Access (WPA)* certification was developed because security in the original IEEE 802.11 standard was weak and had many security vulnerabilities. This certification was designed as an interim solution until an amendment to the IEEE 802.11 standard addressing security improvements was released. The IEEE 802.11i amendment addressed security for the IEEE 802.11 family of standards. The bottom line is that WPA is a pre-802.11i certification, introducing more advanced security solutions such as Temporal Key Integrity Protocol (TKIP), passphrase, and 802.1X/EAP.

This pre-802.11i certification addressed two options for wireless LAN security: personal mode and enterprise mode. Personal mode is intended for small office/home office (SOHO) and home users. Enterprise mode is intended for larger deployments. Personal mode allowed for a user to enter an 8- to 63-character passphrase (password) on both the access point and all of the devices that connected to the access point. Enterprise mode provides user-based authentication utilizing 802.1X/EAP. Both personal and enterprise modes are discussed in more detail in Chapter 9.

Wi-Fi Protected Access 2 Certification

The WPA certification by the Wi-Fi Alliance worked out so well that the alliance decided to certify wireless LAN hardware after the IEEE 802.11i amendment was released. This new certification, known as *Wi-Fi Protected Access 2 (WPA 2.0)*, is a post-802.11i certification. Like WPA, WPA 2.0 addresses two options for wireless LAN security: personal mode and enterprise mode. This certification addresses more advanced security solutions and is backward-compatible with WPA. The following is a preview of its key points; we will look at both WPA and WPA 2.0 in more detail in Chapter 9.

- The personal mode security mechanism uses a passphrase for authentication, which is intended for SOHO and personal use. The use of a passphrase to generate a 256-bit pre-shared key provides strong security. Personal mode may also be identified as pre-shared key (PSK).

- The enterprise mode security mechanism uses 802.1X/EAP for user-based authentication, which is port-based authentication and is designed for enterprise implementations. 802.1X/EAP provides strong security using external authentication and Extensible Authentication Protocol (EAP). 802.1X/EAP uses an authentication server for the user authentication. Remote Authentication Dial-In User Service (RADIUS) is a common authentication server. This works well as a replacement for legacy IEEE 802.11 security solutions.

Table 2.3 provides a high-level description of the WPA and WPA 2.0 certifications.

TABLE 2.3   Details of the WPA and WPA 2.0 certifications

Wi-Fi Alliance security mechanism	Authentication mechanism	Encryption mechanism/cipher
WPA – Personal	Passphrase	TKIP/RC4
WPA – Enterprise	802.1X/EAP	TKIP/RC4
WPA 2.0 – Personal	Passphrase	CCMP/AES or TKIP/RC4
WPA 2.0 – Enterprise	802.1X/EAP	CCMP/AES or TKIP/RC4

Temporal Key Integrity Protocol (TKIP)
Rivest Cipher 4 (RC4) named after Ron Rivest of RSA Security
Counter Mode with Cipher-Block Chaining Message Authentication Code Protocol (CCMP)
Advanced Encryption Standard (AES)

    Encryption mechanisms and ciphers will be discussed further in Chapter 9.

Wi-Fi Multimedia Certification

The *Wi-Fi Multimedia (WMM)* certification was designed as a proactive certification for the IEEE 802.11e amendment to the 802.11 standard. As mentioned earlier in this chapter, the 802.11e amendment addresses QoS in wireless LANs. The WMM certification verifies the validity of features of the 802.11e amendment and allows for a vendor-neutral approach to quality of service.

Quality of service is needed to ensure delivery of information for time-sensitive, time-bounded applications such as voice and streaming video. If a wireless network user were to send a file to a printer or save a file to a server, it is unlikely they would notice any minor delay, or latency. However, in an application that is tuned to the human senses such as hearing or eyesight, latency would more likely be noticeable.

Wi-Fi Multimedia Power Save Certification

Wi-Fi Multimedia Power Save (WMM-PS) is designed for mobile devices and specific uses of wireless LAN technology that require advanced power-save mechanisms for extended battery life. Here are some of these devices and technology that benefit from WMM-PS:

- Voice over IP (VoIP) phones
- Notebook computers
- Tablet devices

Power-save mechanisms allow devices to conserve battery power by "dozing" for short periods of time. Depending on the application, performance could suffer to some degree with power-save features enabled. WMM Power Save consumes less power by allowing devices to spend more time in a "dozing" state—an improvement over legacy power save mode that at the same time improves performance by minimizing transmission latency.

Wi-Fi Protected Setup Certification Overview

Wi-Fi Protected Setup (WPS) was defined because SOHO users wanted a simple way to provide the best security possible for their installations without the need for extensive technical knowledge of wireless networking. Wi-Fi Protected Setup provides strong out-of-the-box setup adequate for many SOHO implementations.

The Wi-Fi Protected Setup certification requires support for two types of authentication that enable users to automatically configure network names and strong WPA2 data encryption and authentication:

- Push-button configuration (PBC)
- PIN-based configuration, based on a personal identification number

Support for both PIN and PBC configurations are required for access points; client devices at a minimum must support PIN. A third, optional method, near field communication (NFC) tokens, is also supported.

Security Hole with WPS

In December 2011 a security flaw was reported with WPS. This allegedly allowed an intruder to recover the personal identification number (PIN) used to create the 256-bit pre-shared key. Acquiring the PIN would allow access to the wireless network. Wherever possible, it is recommended that users disable certain features in the wireless router or access point that allow this to happen. A firmware update may also be available to provide adequate protection. Keep in mind that this solution to the issue may only be possible with newer-model wireless routers. You should check with the manufacturer to determine if a solution (either a software setting or firmware upgrade) is available for a specific device. Otherwise, consider a different method such as WPA or WPA2.0 to secure the wireless router. Upgrading to a newer wireless router is another possible solution.

Summary

This chapter discussed many applications in which wireless LANs are currently used, from small office/home office to corporate deployments and last-mile connectivity. Standards-based wireless deployments continue to grow at a fast pace, adding new installations or replacing proprietary and legacy-based implementations.

The IEEE is an organization that creates standards and amendments used for IEEE 802.11 wireless LAN technology. This chapter described the released communication standards, including:

- IEEE 802.11a
- IEEE 802.11b
- IEEE 802.11g
- IEEE 802.11n

Amendments that addressed quality of service, security, fast transition, radio resource management, and management frame protection were also discussed. The IEEE creates standards based on radio frequency regulations. We also looked at radio frequency regulatory domain governing bodies and their role in regulation of the RF spectrum used for IEEE 802.11 wireless networking.

As discussed in this chapter, the Wi-Fi Alliance is an organization addressing interoperability testing for equipment manufactured to the IEEE standards. This testing results in a variety of certifications for

- Communication
- Quality of service
- Security

Exam Essentials

Understand details of common WLAN applications. These common WLAN applications can include small office/home office (SOHO), corporate data access, end-user mobility, and building-to-building connectivity.

Understand the function and roles of organizations that are responsible for the regulation and development of WLAN technology.   The IEEE, FCC, ETSI, ITU-R, and Wi-Fi Alliance play important roles with wireless technology. Know the function and role of each organization.

Know the frequency ranges, data rates, spread spectrum, and PHY technologies for IEEE 802.11 communication standards.   Understand the details of the 802.11, 802.11b, 802.11a, 802.11g, and 802.11n standard and amendments. It is important to know the supported data rates and operating radio frequency of each.

Know the purpose of IEEE specific-function amendments.   Be familiar with the details of 802.11e and 802.11i specific function amendments. Know that 802.11e is for quality of service and 802.11i addresses security.

Understand the differences among interoperability certifications by the Wi-Fi Alliance.   Know the purpose of the WPA, WPA 2.0, WMM, and WMM-PS, Wi-Fi Alliance certifications. Understand which address security, quality of service, and power-save features.

Review Questions

1. Point-to-point links typically use which antenna types? (Choose 2.)

   A. Semidirectional

   B. Omnidirectional

   C. Highly directional

   D. Long-range omnidirectional

2. Point-to-multipoint links consist of _____ or more connections.

   A. Two

   B. Three

   C. Four

   D. Five

3. IEEE 802.11n devices use an enhanced radio technology known as multiple-input multiple-output (MIMO). Which statement correctly describes a benefit of MIMO?

   A. MIMO uses reflections to allow for increased throughput.

   B. MIMO rejects reflections to allow for increased throughput.

   C. MIMO uses a single radio with diversity technology for increased throughput.

   D. MIMO rejects data rates less than 54 Mbps for increased throughput.

4. What organization is responsible for unlicensed frequency band regulation in the United States?

   A. ETSI

   B. Wi-Fi Alliance

   C. IEEE

   D. FCC

   E. WPA

5. IEEE 802.11g WLANs operate in what frequency range?

   A. 900 MHz

   B. 5.15–5.25 GHz

   C. 5.25–5.35 GHz

   D. 2.4–2.5 GHz

6. Which of the following organizations is responsible for standards compliance?

   A. FCC

   B. ETSI

   C. IEEE

   D. WPA2

   E. Wi-Fi Alliance

7. IEEE 802.11a uses which PHY technology?

   A. ERP-OFDM

   B. HR/DSSS

   C. OFDM

   D. FHSS

8. 802.11b is capable of which of the following data rates? (Choose 3.)

   A. 1 Mbps

   B. 6 Mbps

   C. 5.5 Mbps

   D. 11 Mbps

   E. 12 Mbps

9. 802.11g is backward-compatible with which of the following IEEE wireless LAN standards? (Choose 2.)

   A. 802.11 DSSS

   B. 802.11a OFDM

   C. 802.11a ERP-OFDM

   D. 802.11b HR/DSSS

   E. 802.3af

10. In the 802.11a amendment, the UNII-3 band can be used for which of the following WLAN applications?

   A. Indoor and outdoor

   B. Outdoor only

   C. Indoor only

   D. The UNII-3 band cannot be used for WLANs.

11. The 802.11i amendment to the standard addresses which of the following technologies?

   A. Quality of service

   B. DSSS

   C. Security

   D. MIMO

12. Which of the following best describes the Wi-Fi Alliance?

   A. U.S.-based standards organization

   B. Interoperability testing organization

   C. Works with the FCC to verify compliance

   D. Local regulatory body for Europe

13. Which of the following is addressed by the Wi-Fi Multimedia (WMM) certification?
    A. Security/encryption
    B. Fast transition
    C. Management frame protection
    D. Quality of service

14. Wi-Fi Protected Setup was designed for which of the following wireless applications?
    A. Small office/home office (SOHO) organizations
    B. Enterprise organizations
    C. FCC interoperability
    D. Security organizations

15. The 802.11g standard uses which two Physical layer technologies? (Choose 2.)
    A. FHSS
    B. OFDM
    C. ERP-OFDM
    D. DSSS
    E. MIMO

16. WPA was developed as an interim solution for which amendment to the 802.11 standard?
    A. 802.11a
    B. 802.11n
    C. 802.11e
    D. 802.11i
    E. 802.11g

17. Which of the following is correct regarding 802.11e?
    A. Only operates in the 5 GHz frequency range
    B. Only operates at 1, 2, 5.5, and 11Mbps
    C. Addresses wireless security
    D. Addresses wireless quality of service

18. According to the 802.11a amendment, which of the following data rates are mandatory?
    A. 1, 2, 5.5, and 11 Mbps
    B. 6, 24, and 54 Mbps
    C. 6, 9, 12, 18, 24, 36, 48, and 54 Mbps
    D. 6, 12, and 24 Mbps
    E. 1, 6, 12, and 24 Mbps

19. You support a wireless network for an office of five employees. The installation consists of one access point, three notebook computers, and two desktop computers. The access point and computers in the office have wireless adapters that are Wi-Fi WPA 2.0 Certified. You want to use the highest level security possible without additional cost or administration. Which of the following solutions would be best for this deployment? (Choose 2.)

    A. WEP

    B. WPA 2.0 personal

    C. WPS

    D. WMM

    E. WPA 2.0 enterprise

20. Which two of the following options are available for Wi-Fi Protected Access 2 (WPA 2.0)?

    A. Personal mode

    B. Protection mode

    C. Professional mode

    D. Enterprise mode

    E. WPA 2 mode

Chapter

3

Wireless LAN Infrastructure Devices

THE FOLLOWING CWTS EXAM OBJECTIVES ARE COVERED IN THIS CHAPTER:

✓ **2.1: Identify the purpose, features, and functions of the following wireless network components. Choose the appropriate installation or configuration steps in a given scenario.**

- Access Points
  - Controller-based
  - Autonomous
  - Cooperative
- Mesh
- Wireless LAN Routers
- Wireless Bridges
- Wireless Repeaters
- WLAN Controllers
  - Distributed and centralized data forwarding
- Power over Ethernet (PoE) Devices
  - 802.3af and 802.3at
  - Midspan
  - Endpoint

Choosing the correct wireless LAN infrastructure devices to be installed as part of a computer network is a critical element of a successful wireless LAN deployment. In this chapter, we will look at a variety of infrastructure devices, including wireless access points, wireless mesh devices, wireless bridges, wireless repeaters, and wireless LAN controllers. This chapter will describe some of the features, benefits, and advantages of these and other infrastructure devices. Power over Ethernet (PoE) is an extension to the IEEE 802.3 Ethernet standard that allows direct current voltage to be supplied over Ethernet cable to any PoE-capable device. Power over Ethernet now consists of two ratified amendments and is commonly used in enterprise wireless LAN deployments. This chapter will discuss the concepts involved in PoE, including both of its amendments to the IEEE 802.3 standard.

The Wireless Access Point

The wireless *access point* (AP) is an integral component of a wireless LAN infrastructure. Wireless access points are what allow a variety of wireless devices access to any network resources that the device or user may have permissions for. Wireless access points are available in three common types—autonomous, controller-based, and cooperative. Autonomous access points are self-contained units and can function as independent network infrastructure devices. Controller-based access points, by contrast, function in conjunction with the wireless LAN controller. Cooperative access points provide a wireless infrastructure without the use of a hardware controller. This chapter discusses all three types of access points—autonomous, controller-based, and cooperative. The AP provides computers, voice over Wi-Fi phones, tablets, and other wireless devices access to a local area network using radio frequency (RF) as the communication mechanism through free space (air) as the communication medium.

When a wireless device is connected to an access point, it is said to be in *infrastructure mode*. In this operation mode, all wireless data traffic is passed through the access point to the intended destination, whether that is a file server, a printer, the Internet, or anything else. An access point can operate as a standalone network device, in which it is configured independently to allow wireless devices to connect. It can also operate as part of a larger wireless network by sharing some of the same configurations, such as the service set identifier (SSID). The SSID is the logical name or identifier that all devices connected to the access point will share. Figure 3.1 shows an example of an access point connected to an Ethernet network.

FIGURE 3.1   Access point connected to an Ethernet network

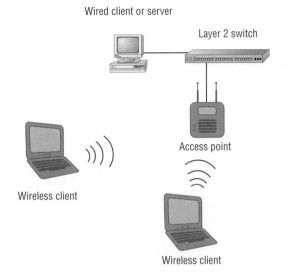

In addition to providing access through a shared medium, access points are *half-duplex* devices. Half duplex in computer terminology is defined as two-way communication that occurs in only one direction at a time. (By contrast, full duplex, the other communication method used in computer networking, allows two-way communication to occur between devices simultaneously.) Communication only one way at a time means less data throughput for the connected device. An access point is a network infrastructure device that can connect to a distribution system (DS)—typically an Ethernet segment or Ethernet cable—and allow wireless users to access network resources. According to the IEEE 802.11 standards, access points are considered stations (abbreviated STA). In a completely Ethernet-switched network, devices will communicate directly with the Ethernet switch. Figure 3.2 illustrates half-duplex communication in a wireless network.

The CWNP program uses the terms autonomous AP, cooperative AP, and controller-based AP to describe the following devices. In the industry, they are also known as intelligent AP, split MAC architecture, and thin AP, or various other terms manufacturers use to identify them.

Autonomous Access Points   *Layer 3*

Autonomous access points are self-contained units with all the intelligence necessary to provide devices with wireless access to a wired network infrastructure and access to the resources the devices have permission to use. There are two popular types of autonomous access points—small-office home-office (SOHO) and enterprise. Not surprisingly, the enterprise type offers generally more robust features.

FIGURE 3.2   Half duplex—communication one direction at a time

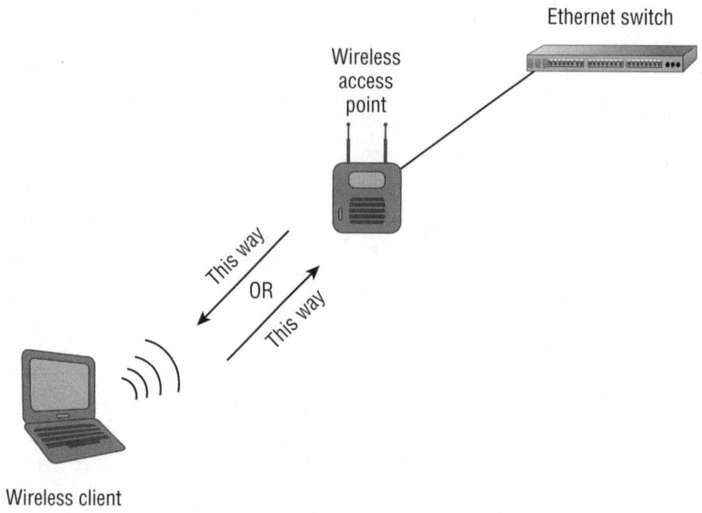

The SOHO Access Point

Although they are very powerful devices, SOHO-grade access points usually have a less extensive feature set than enterprise-grade access points. However, most consumer (SOHO)-grade and enterprise-grade access points now support the highest standards-based security options available, including Wi-Fi Protected Access 2.0 (WPA 2.0) certifications. *SOHO* or consumer-grade access points are best used in the SOHO or home environment and usually have a limited number of connections for computers and devices. SOHO-grade access points have the following features:

- IEEE 802.11 standards support
- Wi-Fi Alliance certifications
- Removable antennas
- Static output transmit power
- Advanced security options
- Wireless bridge functionality
- Wireless repeater functionality
- Dynamic Host Configuration Protocol (DHCP) server
- Configuration and settings options

Figure 3.3 shows an example of a SOHO access point.

FIGURE 3.3   DLink DAP-2553 AirPremier N dual-band PoE SOHO access point

IEEE 802.11 Standards Support

Most later-model SOHO access points support the current IEEE 802.11 standards, whereas others require firmware updates for standards compliance. Some older devices have no firmware update available, which can cause implementation challenges where interoperability between newer and legacy devices is required. The 802.11 standards supported will vary based on several factors, including the cost and complexity of the unit. The most common SOHO access points support the IEEE 802.11b, IEEE 802.11g, and IEEE 802.11n communication amendments. Dual-band access points (which support both IEEE 802.11a/n and IEEE 802.11b/g/n) are not as common in the SOHO market. Most equipment manufacturers do make dual-band models, but the cost is normally higher than single-band (IEEE 802.11b/g/n) consumer-grade access points. The wireless residential wireless gateway or broadband router is another popular device in the SOHO environment. We will learn more about wireless residential gateways later in this chapter. See Chapter 2, "Introduction to Wireless Local Area Networking," if you need to review these 802.11 amendments.

Wi-Fi Alliance Certifications

Certifications from the Wi-Fi Alliance are a common feature of SOHO access points. As mentioned in Chapter 2, these certifications include WPA/WPA 2.0 and WPS for security, and WMM and WMM-PS for QoS. Selecting a SOHO access point that is Wi-Fi certified ensures compliance with IEEE standards and interoperability with other devices.

Removable Antennas

Some SOHO access points are equipped with removable antennas. This allows the end user to change to a larger (higher-gain) antenna, thereby allowing a radio frequency to cover a wider area. Conversely, connecting a smaller (lower-gain) antenna will decrease the coverage area. Antennas and radio frequency radiation patterns are discussed in Chapter 7, "WLAN Antennas and Accessories." Many SOHO access points have fixed or nonremovable antennas, so you cannot add a higher-gain antenna.

 RF coverage of an access point can be increased by adding a higher-gain antenna to an access point. For more information, see Chapter 7.

Static Output Transmit Power

Occasionally an end user will have the ability to adjust the transmit output power in a SOHO access point. If this is available, the settings are usually very basic, such as low, medium, and high. With enterprise access points you can change the power in increments of mW or dBm. The transmit output power will determine in part the area of radio frequency coverage, also known as the *cell*. The typical transmit output power of a SOHO model access point is about 15 dBm or 32 mW; however, this will vary with the manufacturer. An access point model with static output power cannot be adjusted, which will limit your ability to decrease or increase the size of the radio frequency cell. Changing the cell size will allow the user to cover a larger area in the home or small office where the access point is installed. In this case, the only way to change the cell size is to change the gain of the antenna in models that have the removable antenna feature. Note that replacing the antenna will also change the vertical and horizontal beamwidths or radiation pattern that propagates away from it.

Advanced Security Options

All newer-model SOHO access points support the highest security features, including IEEE 802.11i, and WPA 2.0 personal and enterprise modes. These security features give users with limited technical knowledge the ability to provide the most up-to-date security for their wireless network. For those users who have greater technical know-how, SOHO access points also provide more advanced security features, such as 802.1X/EAP or virtual private network (VPN) pass-through. Users can find more information about these advanced features in most user guides provided with the access point or online at the manufacturers' website.

Wireless Bridge Functionality

SOHO access points occasionally can be configured in wireless bridge mode. Both point-to-point and point-to-multipoint settings are available, enabling administrators to connect two or more wired LANs together wirelessly.

Wireless Repeater Functionality

Some SOHO access points can be configured to function as wireless repeaters. Configuring an access point as a repeater enables administrators to extend the size of the radio frequency cell, so that devices not in hearing range of an access point can connect to the wireless network. However, the cost is reduced throughput for other devices accessing the network through a wireless repeater.

Dynamic Host Configuration Protocol (DHCP) Server

It's also common for SOHO access points to be able to act as Dynamic Host Configuration Protocol (DHCP) servers. A DHCP server will automatically issue an Internet Protocol (IP) address (logical address) to allow upper-layer communication between devices on the network. IP addresses are a function of Layer 3 of the OSI model, as outlined in Chapter 1, "Introduction to Computer Networking."

Configuration and Settings Options

SOHO access points are configured via a web browser, using either HTTP (Hypertext Transfer Protocol) or HTTPS (Hypertext Transfer Protocol Secure). This type of browser-based configuration is an easy way for the novice administrator to make all the necessary settings based on the application in which the access point will be used. SOHO access points rarely offer configuration from the command line interface (CLI). Figure 3.4 shows a sample of a configuration page from a SOHO access point.

FIGURE 3.4   SOHO access point configuration page in a web browser

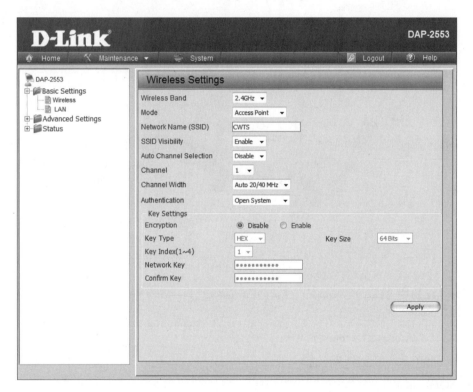

For security, however, it is best practice to configure the access point from the wired side of the network whenever possible. Configuration should only be done wirelessly if absolutely necessary. If configuring the access point from the wireless side is the only option, a secure connection should be in place to prevent unauthorized access.

Some manufacturers of SOHO wireless equipment have online emulators that allow customers to view a sample of the configuration process for a device. This allows a user to go through the configuration of the device before making a purchase.

The Enterprise Access Point

Enterprise access points typically have a much more extensive feature set than the previously mentioned SOHO access points. This section will look at some of the more advanced features available in enterprise-grade access points.

Figure 3.5 shows an enterprise-grade access point.

FIGURE 3.5   The Motorola AP 7131 IEEE 802.11n dual-band access point

Enterprise-grade access points can include the following features:

- IEEE 802.11 standards support
- Wi-Fi Alliance certifications
- Removable or expandable antennas
- Adjustable output transmit power
- Advanced security options
- Multiple operation modes, including root access point, wireless bridge, and wireless repeater capabilities
- Graphical user interface (GUI) configuration
- Command-line interface configuration

In addition to the items listed here, enterprise-grade access points have various other features that make them stand above the SOHO-grade access point. Some of these features include outdoor use, plenum ratings, industrial environment ratings, more memory, and faster processors to help handle the load and various environmental conditions.

IEEE 802.11 Standards Support

Like SOHO access points, enterprise access points also support IEEE standards. Enterprise access points have a more extensive feature set than SOHO access points, and depending on the manufacturer and model, they will support all communication standards by utilizing IEEE 802.11a/n and IEEE 802.11b/g/n dual-band radios. Enterprise-grade access points can include support for some amendments to the standard not supported by SOHO-grade access points. Examples include support for IEEE 802.11e QoS, Wi-Fi multimedia, IEEE 802.11r fast BSS transition (FT), and IEEE 802.11w for the security of management frames, to name a few.

Wi-Fi Alliance Certifications

Certifications by the Wi-Fi Alliance are an important feature of enterprise-grade access points. These certifications include WPA/WPA 2.0 for Security, WMM, and WMM-PS for QoS. Selecting an enterprise-grade access point that is Wi-Fi certified ensures compliance with IEEE standards and interoperability with other IEEE 802.11–compliant devices.

Removable or Expandable Antennas

Many enterprise access points have removable or expandable antenna capabilities. These antenna configurations provide a lot of flexibility, as an installer can choose the appropriate antenna based on the deployment scenario. Omnidirectional, semidirectional, and highly directional antennas are all types of antennas commonly used in the enterprise environment. Enterprise-quality access points that use internal antennas can offer options for connecting external antennas should they be required. Antennas will be discussed in more detail in Chapter 7.

Adjustable Output Transmit Power

Unlike some SOHO-grade access points, enterprise-grade access points have the capability to adjust output transmit power. This feature allows an installer to select the correct amount of transmit power based on the installation needs of the access point. One benefit of having adjustable output power is that an installer can adapt to the environment in which the access point is installed. If the radio frequency dynamics of an area change, the ability to change access point settings, such as output transmit power, without physical intervention is beneficial.

Advanced Security Options

Compared to access points used in the SOHO environment, enterprise access points typically have more advanced security features. In addition to IEEE 802.11i, WPA/WPA 2.0, passphrase, and IEEE 802.1X, features such as a built-in user database for local *Remote Authentication Dial-In User Service (RADIUS)* authentication are also included. As discussed later in this chapter, local RADIUS authentication allows small to medium-sized businesses to provide their own advanced authentication features without the need of external RADIUS authentication services. This reduces costs and lowers administration overhead.

RADIUS is just one example of the more advanced security features available in enterprise-level access points. Another advanced security feature that may be available is some level of a wireless intrusion prevention system (WIPS). A WIPS will help determine and have the potential to mitigate certain levels of wireless intrusions or attacks on the network. One example is the detection of a rogue (unknown) access point. Advanced security features are discussed in more detail in Chapter 9, "Wireless LAN Security Basics."

Some other configuration options available for one model of enterprise access point are shown in Figure 3.6.

FIGURE 3.6 Motorola AP-7131 Enterprise-grade access point configuration page in a web browser

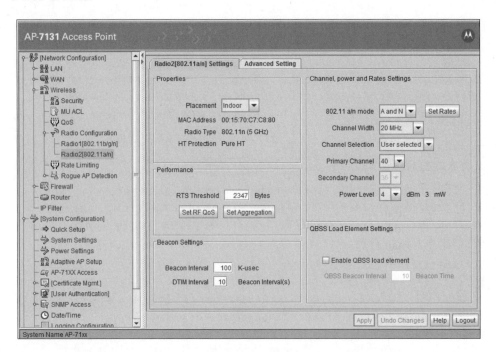

Multiple Operation Modes

In addition to the features we've just discussed, enterprise access points typically have several operation modes. These modes are:

Root Access Point Mode—the most common configuration   What some refer to as *root access point mode* is typically the default operation mode in which an enterprise-grade access point is set. Root access point mode involves connecting the access point to a distribution system (DS) such as an Ethernet segment, wireless distribution system (WDS), or network infrastructure. This allows computers and other devices to connect to the access point and use network resources based on the assigned permissions of the user, computer, or device.

Wireless Bridge Mode—for connecting LANs together   This configuration allows an access point to be set in *bridge mode* for wireless point-to-point or point-to-multipoint configurations connecting two or more LANs together. Benefits of using wireless access points to bridge LANs together include cost savings and high data transfer rates compared to some other connectivity options.

Wireless Repeater Mode—to extend the radio frequency cell   An access point configured in wireless *repeater mode* can act to extend the radio frequency cell. This allows computers and devices outside the radio hearing range to connect to the network and access network resources via the wireless repeater.

Access point configuration methods

Enterprise access points can commonly be configured or "staged" two different ways:

Graphical User Interface (GUI) Configuration   Enterprise access points can be configured using a GUI configuration from a web browser using Hypertext Transfer Protocol (HTTP) or Hypertext Transfer Protocol Secure (HTTPS). This is a convenient way to configure and change settings on the access point using a common graphical interface tool. If the access point is configured using a wireless connection, using the HTTPS protocol is recommended for security at a minimum.

Command-Line Interface (CLI) Configuration   Most enterprise-grade access points have *command-line interface (CLI)* capabilities to allow extensive and detailed configuration of the device. In some cases, the CLI command set provides higher-level commands that allow an administrator to perform additional configuration tasks that aren't available using the browser method. This allows consistency in configuring other network infrastructure devices because many manufacturers share common commands among devices. CLI capabilities vary depending on the manufacturer, but most enterprise models have an extensive set of commands.

Controller-Based Access Points

Controller-based access points differ from autonomous access points in that they are used with wireless LAN controllers and not as standalone devices. (As discussed in the previous section, an autonomous access point is a self-contained unit that has all the intelligence needed to provide computer and device access to a wireless network.) Controller-based access points have shifted much of the intelligence to the wireless LAN controller. Since a controller-based access point contains less intelligence than an autonomous access point, the cost of a controller-based access point can be significantly lower.

Controller-based access points are centrally managed from the wireless LAN controller. Depending on the manufacturer, they may have a more extensive feature set than autonomous access points, while also including many of the features of those devices. One of these features is Layer 3 VPN connectivity for computers and other devices. Figure 3.7 shows a typical controller-based access point.

FIGURE 3.7   Aruba Dual-Radio 802.11a/n + 802.11b/g/n using three antennas

Cooperative Access Points

Cooperative access point technology provides an alternative for deploying wireless local area network infrastructures. Cooperative networks are sometimes referred to as a "controllerless architecture," because the intelligence has been pushed back out to or distributed to the access point edge, similar to that of the autonomous access point but with much more intelligence and capabilities. The access points are managed through a "cloud" software configuration tool, eliminating the need for a hardware controller. This software control can be accessed from any computer with an Internet connection, assuming the user has appropriate permissions. Some manufacturers also have "software appliances," eliminating the reliance on the cloud server. Many if not all of the benefits, features, and advantages available with the wireless LAN controller architecture are also available in the cooperative or controllerless architecture and are explained later in this chapter. Figure 3.8 shows an example of *cooperative access points*.

Cooperative access points provide all the benefits and features of a wireless LAN controller solution without the need and extra expense of a hardware controller. This technology is scalable and performs well without relying on a "tunnel" to be built from the access point to a controller. This distributed intelligence allows the cooperative access point to make decisions about how frames traverse both the wired and wireless network.

Some manufacturers of controller-based solutions provide a variant of the cooperative technology by allowing autonomous access points to be "adoptable" by a controller in a large enterprise environment. These access points are then site survivable, meaning they will still be able to function standalone should connectivity with the controller be temporarily lost. The description of this technology includes the term "adaptive access point."

FIGURE 3.8 The Aerohive family of cooperative-control access points

Wireless Mesh

Wireless mesh networking continues to grow at a steady pace. The concept of mesh networking has been in existence for many years. In a full mesh network, all nodes connect together with at least two paths for every node. This allows for reliable communication in the event of a device or path failure.

Wireless mesh networking is popular in the outdoor market. Some examples where wireless mesh networks are currently utilized are:

- Metropolitan
- University campuses
- Public safety
- Transportation
- Government
- Amphitheaters

Most outdoor mesh infrastructure devices provide the highest levels of wireless security and are usually inside a rugged weatherproof enclosure for protection from the elements.

Currently many wireless LAN manufacturers use proprietary mechanisms and protocols for wireless mesh networking. IEEE 802.11s is an amendment to the IEEE 802.11 standard to include wireless mesh networking that was ratified in 2011. Many enterprise-grade access points have the ability to operate in mesh mode, whereas others have a dedicated mesh function.

Wireless mesh networking for indoor deployments is still in the testing phase. Some manufacturers recommend using both unlicensed bands for mesh operation. One common solution is to use the 2.4 GHz ISM band for device access and the 5 GHz UNII band for mesh device connectivity. The use of a third radio may be an option in some cases. Mesh can also be used in the event of Ethernet loss to an access point. Some cooperative access points are able to automatically mesh together when they suffer an Ethernet loss. They typically by default support clients in both bands but can mesh in 5 GHz if an Ethernet connection fails. Figure 3.9 illustrates mesh access points connected to a wired infrastructure.

FIGURE 3.9   Mesh access points/routers connected to a common infrastructure and to the Internet

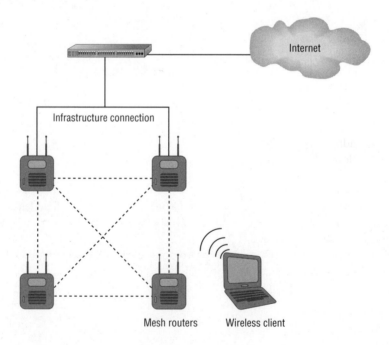

Wireless LAN Routers

Wireless LAN routers can be defined differently depending on the application. In the SOHO or home market, a wireless LAN router is also known as a wireless broadband router. The CWNP program and associated material refer to these devices as wireless residential gateways. In the enterprise environment, a wireless LAN router has similar functionality plus extended features and is known as a wireless VPN router.

Wireless Residential Gateway

SOHO or home broadband routers (also known as wireless residential gateways) are usually equipped with an Internet port, several ports for Ethernet switches, and a wireless access point. These routers are configured through a web browser using either the HTTP or HTTPS protocols. Configuration of the devices is fairly simple for the novice user using a web browser via a built-in web server. In most cases, a broadband wireless router connects to either a cable modem or a digital subscriber line (DSL) connection available from an Internet service provider (ISP). In this configuration, a router is able to accept wired and wireless connections for computers and other devices, providing them access to the LAN or the Internet. Some of the features of a broadband router include:

- Network Address Translation (NAT)
- Dynamic Host Configuration Protocol (DHCP) server
- IP routing
- Domain Name System (DNS) services
- Firewall

A wireless broadband router has many of the same features as a SOHO access point. An example of a wireless broadband router is shown in Figure 3.10.

FIGURE 3.10 Netgear WNDR3300 RangeMax dual-band wireless-N router

Wireless Branch Router

A *wireless branch router* can be used to extend a corporate network to a remote location such as a home, conference room, or branch office through a secure connection using a WAN or the Internet. This type of device typically has three interfaces available:

- Ethernet port(s) to connect to a LAN

- Internet port to connect to the WAN or to an Internet connection

- Wireless port to allow IEEE 802.11 computers and devices to connect to a network through a wireless connection

Wireless branch routers are usually compact and lightweight, making them easy for sales representatives and other corporate employees to travel with. They also have a more extensive feature set than wireless broadband routers, including Layer 3 VPN tunnels between devices and the router on each side that acts as a VPN endpoint or pass-through. Other features include:

- Point-to-Point Tunneling Protocol (PPTP)

- Layer 2 Tunneling Protocol/Internet Protocol Security (L2TP/IPSec)

- SSH2

- Advanced IP networking services

- Edge router capability

Figure 3.11 shows an example of a wireless branch router.

FIGURE 3.11   Aerohive BR200 wireless branch router

Wireless Bridges

Wireless bridges connect two or more wired LANs together. As discussed in Chapter 2, typically there are two configurations for wireless bridges: point-to-point or point-to-multipoint. A wireless bridge is a dedicated device that functions in much the same way as an access point in bridge mode. Wireless bridges have many of the same features as enterprise access points, including removable antennas and selectable power levels.

Connecting locations together using wireless bridging has many benefits, including fast installation, cost savings, and high data transfer rates. Depending on the circumstances, a wireless bridge can be installed in as little as one day. Cost savings can be enormous compared to installing and maintaining a physical wired connection between locations, whether it is copper, fiber optics, or a leased line from a service provider.

Wireless bridges can work in either the 2.4 GHz ISM or 5 GHz UNII band. The connection can span long distances, so it is important to take security and environmental conditions into consideration as well as the proper antenna selection.

Figure 3.12 illustrates wireless bridges connecting two LANs.

FIGURE 3.12   Wireless bridges connecting two LANs

LAN 1   LAN 2

When LANs are connected using wireless bridges, the bridges must be set to the same RF channel and have the same SSID.

Wireless Repeaters

Wireless repeaters are used to extend the radio frequency cell. In a wired Ethernet network, repeaters function at Layer 1 of the OSI model to extend the Ethernet segment. An Ethernet repeater lacks intelligence—that is, it cannot determine data traffic types and simply passes all data traffic across the device. Since wireless infrastructure devices including repeaters are Layer 2 devices, they have more intelligence than Ethernet repeaters.

Just as an Ethernet segment has a maximum distance for successful data transmission, wireless LANs do as well. This distance depends on several factors, including the transmit power of the access point and the gain of the antenna. Like an access point, the wireless client device is also a transmitter and a receiver and will have a radio frequency range limited by the transmit power and gain of the antenna. A wireless repeater provides the capability for computers and other devices to connect to a wireless LAN even when outside the normal hearing range of the access point connected to the network. Figure 3.13 illustrates how a wireless repeater can extend the range of a wireless network.

FIGURE 3.13   A wireless repeater extends the range of a wireless network.

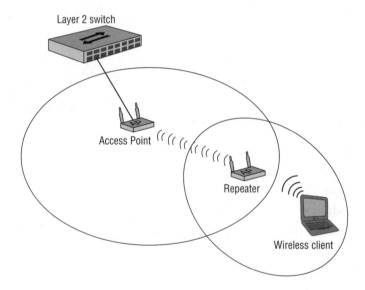

As illustrated, the wireless client is not within hearing range of the access point, so adequate communication is not possible between these devices. In order for wireless LAN devices to communicate effectively with an access point, the transmitter must be able to hear the receiver, and the receiver must be able to hear the transmitter. A wireless repeater will allow this communication to occur in the case where the wireless client is outside the radio frequency cell or basic service area (BSA) of the access point. The wireless client will send information or frames to the repeater and the repeater will forward them to the access point, and vice versa. The downside of this configuration is that it will reduce the overall throughput as described. The wireless repeater may be named differently by the manufacturer and include the term wireless *range extender*.

> ### 🌐 Real World Scenario
>
> #### Using Wireless Repeaters Reduces Throughput
>
> Before using a wireless repeater, consider whether it would be the best solution. Since wireless LANs are half duplex (two-way communication but only one way at a time), data throughput will suffer when using repeaters. Every time the data traverses a wireless link using the same frequency, the data throughput is reduced by about 50 percent. If a physical wired connection is available, it should be used for an access point connection rather than a wireless repeater. For security purposes, the Ethernet port on a wireless repeater should be disabled since it is not connected to an infrastructure.

Wireless LAN Controllers

Wireless LAN controllers are a main component in many wireless LAN deployments. Wireless LAN controllers range from branch office models with a few controller-based access points to large-scale enterprise devices with hundreds or even thousands of controller-based access points. The branch office models are typically used in remote office installations or small/medium business (SMB) applications with a limited number of access points. This section discusses some of the many benefits, features, and advantages available on wireless LAN controllers:

- Centralized administration
- Controller-based access points
- Virtual LAN (VLAN)
- Power over Ethernet (PoE) capability
- Improved device roaming
- Wireless profiles
- Advanced security features
- Captive portal
- Built-in RADIUS services
- Site survey tools
- Radio frequency spectrum management
- Firewall
- Quality of service

- Redundancy
- Wireless intrusion prevention system (WIPS)
- Direct or distributed AP connectivity
- Layer 2 and Layer 3 AP connectivity

Centralized Administration

A wireless LAN controller with *centralized administration* gives an administrator complete control over the wireless network from a single location. Unlike autonomous access points that require intervention at each device for configuration, a wireless LAN controller can be a "one-stop shop" for configuration and management of the wireless network. A wireless network management system (WNMS) can be used as a centralized tool to manage autonomous access points. A WNMS be used to help scale the autonomous access point architecture but is not required.

Controller-Based Access Points

The benefits of controller-based access points are similar to those of autonomous access points, including radio frequency management, security, and quality of service. But controller-based access points can cost less than autonomous access points, and very little or no information is contained within the devices. Controller-based access points are PoE-capable for ease of deployment in either mid-sized or large organizations.

Virtual LAN

According to the IEEE 802.1Q standard, *virtual local area networks (VLANs)* define broadcast domains in a Layer 2 network by inserting VLAN membership information into Ethernet frames. Layer 2 Ethernet switches can create broadcast domains based on how the switch is configured by using VLAN technology. This allows an administrator to separate physical ports into logical networks to organize traffic according to the use of the VLAN for security profiles, QoS, or other applications. The concept of a Layer 2 wired VLAN is extended to IEEE 802.11 wireless LANs. Wireless LAN controllers have the ability to configure broadcast domains and segregate broadcast and multicast traffic between VLANs.

Power over Ethernet Capability

Wireless LAN controllers support Power over Ethernet (PoE), allowing direct current voltage and computer data to be sent over the same cable. Details of PoE are discussed later in this chapter in the section "Power over Ethernet."

Improved Device Roaming

Fast seamless Layer 2 and Layer 3 *roaming* between access points is another common feature of wireless LAN controllers. This feature is beneficial in order for computers and other wireless devices connected to the wireless LAN to maintain a connection while physically moving throughout the wireless network. As you learned in Chapter 2, the IEEE 802.11r amendment specifies fast transition (FT) and the IEEE 802.11k helps with this functionality. Roaming is more often than not an enterprise requirement and exists in very few SOHO deployments.

Wireless Profiles

A wireless LAN controller can give network administrators the ability to create a variety of configuration profiles. These profiles can work in conjunction with VLANs to allow or deny access based on requirements for the computer, device, or user access. Profiles can be configured for various situations, including different SSIDs for guest, corporate, and voice networks, security configurations, and QoS support. This can also be accomplished with a WNMS for controllerless or cooperative deployments.

Using profiles, you can allow legacy devices that may be limited to Wired Equivalent Privacy (WEP) to be located on a separate VLAN without compromising the security of the entire network.

Advanced Security Features

Like autonomous access points, wireless LAN controllers will also provide advanced security options. Wireless LAN controllers will include security options based on IEEE 802.11i and WPA/WPA 2.0, with both passphrase and enterprise configuration capabilities.

Captive Portal

Captive portal capability is a common feature in wireless LAN controllers and cooperative-based systems. A *captive portal* will intercept a user's attempt to access the network by redirecting them to a web page for authorization. This web page may request account credentials, payment information from a user, or a simple agreement to terms and conditions before granting access to the wireless network. One common example where you will see a captive portal is in a paid or free wireless hotspot. The captive portal can be hosted by an outside service provider, an autonomous access point, or a wireless controller, and in a cooperative system on the access point.

Built-in RADIUS Services

Another common feature of wireless LAN controllers and cooperative-based systems is RADIUS services for 802.1X/EAP authentication, which is supported by WPA and WPA 2.0. Built-in RADIUS allows a network administrator to utilize the most advanced security features available today to secure the wireless network. Built-in RADIUS server databases typically have a limited number of users that can be created in the user database, which means that built-in RADIUS is a good solution for SMB or remote office locations but not for very large organizations. Larger networks can use external RADIUS services for scalability. See `www.gnu.org/software/radius` for more about this server.

Site Survey Tools

Predictive site survey tools assist in placement of access points and other infrastructure devices. These tools are sometimes a feature of a wireless LAN controller. Performing a predictive site survey will assist in planning to determine coverage and capacity for data and voice for both indoor and outdoor deployments.

Aerohive provides a free online wireless network planning tool with an auto-placement feature. See `www.aerohive.com/planner` for more information and to access this free tool.

Radio Frequency Spectrum Management

Keeping an eye on the radio frequency (RF) environment is another responsibility of the wireless network administrator. RF spectrum management consists of adjusting RF parameters such as the channel (frequency) and the RF transmit power after deployment. This allows the network to adapt to changes in the environment and assist in the event of hardware failures.

Firewall

An integrated stateful firewall feature helps protect a network from unauthorized Internet traffic but still allows authorized traffic. Firewalls can be hardware based, software based, or a combination of the two. Stateful firewalls, which keep records of all connections passing through the firewall, help protect against broadcast storms, rogue DHCP server attacks, Address Resolution Protocol (ARP) poisoning, and other potential attacks against the wireless LAN.

Quality of Service

Quality of service features help time-critical applications such as voice and video communications minimize latency and allow for traffic prioritization. With the continual expansion of voice and video technology in the wireless LAN arena, QoS is becoming an increasingly important component in the wireless network.

Redundancy

Redundancy allows for fault-tolerant deployments and provides uninterrupted access in the event an access point or wireless LAN controller fails. Complete redundancy will prevent a major outage caused by hardware failure for mission-critical or other deployments. Coverage is maintained by alternating access points between the redundant devices, minimizing interruption for user access in the event of a hardware failure.

Wireless Intrusion Prevention System

A wireless intrusion prevention system (WIPS) monitors all activity across the wireless network for potential intrusion and malicious activities. A WIPS can take appropriate action to mitigate an attack based on the type of intrusion.

Direct and Distributed AP Connectivity

Connecting access points that are not directly plugged into a port on the wireless LAN controller is a feature known as distributed AP connectivity and is beneficial in large-scale deployments. Most manufacturers support distributed AP connectivity. Direct AP connectivity is defined as a direct connection to ports on the switch. A typical device with distributed connectivity is shown in Figure 3.14.

FIGURE 3.14   Meru MC 5000 large-scale enterprise wireless LAN controller

Layer 2 and Layer 3 AP Connectivity

Early wireless network implementations were built with dedicated Layer 2 connectivity, which meant limited wireless mobility. Layer 2 roaming occurs when a computer or other wireless device moves out of the radio cell of the currently connected access point and connects to a different AP maintaining Layer 2 connectivity.

As wireless networking technology evolved, so did the need for Layer 3 connectivity and roaming. IP addresses are logical Layer 3 addresses that identify devices on a network. All IP devices on the same network or subnet are considered to be in the same IP boundary. Layer 3 roaming occurs when a client moves to an AP that covers a different IP subnet. After roaming, the client will no longer have a valid IP address from the original subnet and the device will be issued an IP address from the new subnet while maintaining Layer 3 connectivity. Figure 3.15 illustrates Layer 2 and Layer 3 connectivity.

FIGURE 3.15   Wireless client device roaming across Layer 2 and Layer 3 boundaries

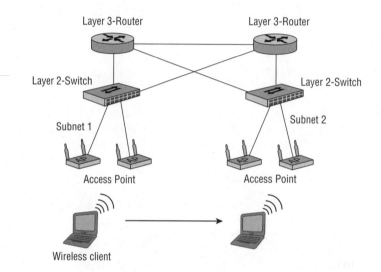

Distributed and Centralized Data Forwarding

Wireless LAN controller solutions consist of two common types of architectures: centralized and distributed. Early WLAN controller solutions supported the centralized architecture, which is also known as split-MAC architecture. This design separated the intelligence from the access point and placed it into the wireless controller to allow for centralized management and control of the wireless network. The access point for the most part was just a radio and antenna, and traffic decisions were sent to the controller through an Ethernet cable. This technique is also known as *centralized data forwarding*. Depending on where the controller was placed, it could cause bottlenecks and other issues in the case of an overloaded or poorly designed network infrastructure. With the data rates possible with IEEE 802.11n, the aggregate throughput could be too much for the network to handle, resulting in poor performance.

Distributed data forwarding reduces the amount of infrastructure traffic because the controller-based access point is able to make more decisions, taking some of the load away from the wireless controller. Moving some of the intelligence back to the edge (the wireless access point) minimizes the bottlenecks and other potential issues such as latency. This is also true in a cooperative or controllerless architecture, thus eliminating the need for the data to be sent to the controller for handling. Many wireless LAN equipment manufacturers now support both the centralized and distributed WLAN architectures.

Power over Ethernet

Power over Ethernet (PoE) sends direct current (DC) voltage and computer data over the same Ethernet cable, enabling a device to receive DC power and computer data simultaneously. This eliminates the need for an external alternating current (AC) power source to be near the Ethernet device. Power over Ethernet now consists of two ratified amendments to the IEEE 802.3 standard. It is defined in *802.3-2005 Clause 33*, also known as *IEEE 802.3af*, and *IEEE 802.3at*, sometimes called PoE+. These amendments define the specifications for devices used in wired or wireless networking to receive DC power from the Ethernet connection without the need for an external DC power source.

An Ethernet cable has four copper wire pairs or eight copper wires. Depending on the technology in use, either two or all four wired pairs may be used to carry data traffic. Figure 3.16 shows an example of a standard Ethernet cable pin assignment.

The PoE amendments to the Ethernet standard allow electrical power to be supplied in one of two ways, either over the same wired pairs that carry computer data or over the pairs that do not carry data. 10BASE-T and 100BASE-T (Fast Ethernet) implementations use only two wired pairs (four wires) to carry data. 1000BASE-T (Gigabit Ethernet) may use all four pairs (eight wires) to carry computer data. The standard defines which wire pairs are allowed to carry the DC power based on whether the network is 10BASE-T, 100BASE-T, or 1000BASE-T and whether the power is sourced from an endpoint or midspan injector. Both midspan and endpoint are explained later in this chapter.

FIGURE 3.16   Standard Ethernet pin assignment

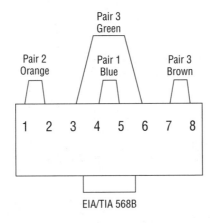

EIA/TIA 568B

The nominal voltage for PoE is *48 VDC*, but the amendments allow for a range of 44 to 57 VDC at the power source. The PoE amendments address two types of devices: power sourcing equipment (PSE), the source of the DC power, and the powered device (PD), the receiver of the DC power.

 Before PoE was standardized, some manufacturers used proprietary implementations. These solutions used various voltages, polarities, and pin assignments and may still be in the market today. I recommend that you verify PoE standard compliance before using this technology to prevent potential hardware or device failures.

The IEEE 802.3-2005 Clause 33 (802.3af) amendment was released in 2003 and allocates 15.4 watts (W) of power per port maximum. This amendment has been incorporated into the IEEE 802.3-2008 standard. The IEEE 802.3at amendment, also known as PoE+, was released in 2009 and includes changes to add to the capabilities of the IEEE 802.3-2008 standard with higher power levels and improved power management information. IEEE 802.3at allows for 25.5 W of power per port maximum, a 60 percent increase over IEEE 802.3af. IEEE 802.3af PoE will work with access points from all manufacturers of enterprise-grade IEEE 802.11n access points. Using IEEE 802.3af will make it easier for organizations to transition from older model access points to the newer 802.11n technology, which will improve their client service and provide overall better performance without having to immediately upgrade their PoE infrastructure to IEEE 802.3at.

Power Sourcing Equipment

The *power sourcing equipment (PSE)* is the device that supplies the DC voltage to the end devices that receive the DC power. The DC voltage (power) can be delivered to the device in one of two ways:

- An *endpoint* device (usually a wireless LAN controller or an Ethernet switch) delivers DC power directly over the same wire pairs that carry data or over the unused wire pairs.

- A *midspan* device (usually a single port or multiple port injector) injects DC power into the Ethernet cable over the unused wire pairs or over the data pairs, depending on the version of the standard.

Powered Device

The *powered device (PD)* is defined as the device receiving DC power, such as a wireless access point, wireless bridge, IP camera, IP phone, and so on. The IEEE 802.3 standard defines the maximum cable length of an Ethernet cable to be 328' or 100 m. Because of line loss, the standard specifies less maximum power than what is available at the port. Table 3.1 shows the maximum power allowed for both the PSE and the PD.

TABLE 3.1 Maximum power supplied by PSE and drawn by PD for both amendments to the IEEE 802.3 Ethernet Standard

Specification	802.3-2005 clause 33	802.3at
PSE power maximum	15.4 W	25.5 W
PD power maximum	12.95 W	24.0 W

Powered Device Classifications

Equipment manufacturers have the option of defining a *classification signature*. This classification signature determines the maximum amount of power a device requires, thereby allowing the PSE to better manage the amount of power delivered to a specific port. The PoE standard makes five classes of powered device available (class 0 through class 4). Table 3.2 shows the available classes and the amount power in watts for each class for IEEE 802.3-2005 clause 33 (802.3af) devices.

TABLE 3.2 Classes of powered device described in the PoE amendment to the Ethernet standard, 802.3-2005 clause 33 (802.3af)

Class	Use	PSE power output in watts	PD max levels in watts
0	Default	15.4 W	0.44 W to 12.95 W
1	Optional	4.0 W	0.44 W to 3.84 W
2	Optional	7.0 W	3.84 W to 6.49 W
3	Optional	15.4 W	6.49 W to 12.95 W
4	Reserved for future use. If class 4 is detected it will be treated as class 0.	n/a	n/a

Figure 3.17 shows an example of PSE and a PD.

FIGURE 3.17   Motorola PSE single-port injector and PD Motorola access port

Single port injector

Powered device/controller-based
access point

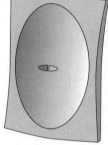

Benefits of PoE

There are many benefits to using devices that support PoE, including cost savings and convenience. As mentioned in the previous section, the IEEE 802.3 Standard (Ethernet) specifies a maximum distance of 100 m or 328' for unshielded twisted pair (UTP) Category 5 (CAT5) Ethernet cable. Power over Ethernet enables a PoE device to receive DC power and computer data at this distance without the need for electrical power at the point where the device is installed or located. This can amount to a large cost savings if a voltage source is not available where the device is located, because there is no need to install electrical power at that point.

Midspan Devices

Midspan devices inject the required DC voltage (48V nominal) into the Ethernet cable allowing the AP, bridge, or other powered device to receive electrical power and computer data. There are two types of midspan device—single-port injectors and multiport injectors. A single-port injector supplies power to a single device. This is useful in an implementation that may have only a few PoE devices. A single-port injector is an in-line device that adds DC power to the Ethernet cable. A multiport injector can supply DC power to many devices simultaneously. A multiport injector is an in-line device that functions like a patch panel. Two ports on this device are required to supply both DC power and computer data to a single powered device such as an access point, bridge, or IP camera. Therefore, a 24-port injector will allow connectivity for only 12 devices.

Endpoint Devices

Endpoint devices supply DC power and computer data directly at the Ethernet port rather than relying on an intermediate device to supply the power. Wireless LAN controllers and Ethernet switches are examples of endpoint devices. A benefit of endpoint PoE is that no intermediate adapter to inject power is necessary. Figure 3.18 shows an example of an endpoint PoE device.

FIGURE 3.18   Cisco wireless controller with PoE endpoint capability

Courtesy of Cisco Systems, Inc. Unauthorized use not permitted.

Summary

This chapter discussed wireless LAN infrastructure devices, which are commonly used to provide wireless connectivity to a network for computers and other wireless devices. These devices include the access point—an integral part of the wireless LAN—available as a self-contained intelligent (autonomous) device, a controller-based device for use with wireless LAN controllers, or a cooperative AP providing user access to network resources. Other infrastructure devices include wireless LAN routers for SOHO or home use, wireless bridges for connecting LANs together, and wireless repeaters for extending the RF cell. This chapter explained some of the features, benefits, and applications of these infrastructure devices. Finally, the chapter covered the two Power over Ethernet (PoE) amendments (IEEE 802.3-2005 Clause 33, also referred to as 802.3af and IEEE 802.3at), components, the DC voltage and amount of DC power supplied (in watts), and how the power may be delivered to an end device.

Exam Essentials

Remember the function and features of the three access point technologies.   Compare and contrast the differences and features between autonomous, controller-based, and cooperative access points. Know that autonomous access points are self-contained units and controller-based access points work with wireless LAN controllers. Cooperative access points do not require a hardware controller but use software for configuration and management.

Understand differences in various infrastructure devices.   Identify the features and applications of wireless access points, wireless bridges, wireless repeaters, and the wireless LAN controller.

Explain the function of other infrastructure devices.   Understand the different modes in which wireless infrastructure devices operate as well as the uses for specific devices such as wireless bridges and wireless repeaters.

Explain the differences regarding Power over Ethernet devices.   Know the differences between power sourcing equipment (PSE) and powered devices (PD), and know their use in wireless networking.

Know details of the IEEE 802.3-2005 Clause 33 (802.3af) and 802.3at Power over Ethernet (PoE) amendments to the Ethernet standard.   Know that PoE uses 48 volts nominal. Identify the different classifications. Understand the difference between midspan and endpoint PoE solutions. Remember IEEE 802.3at allows 25.5 W maximum power per port where IEEE 802.3-2005 clause 33 (802.3af) allows for 15.4 W of power maximum.

Review Questions

1. In computer network terminology, the definition of half duplex is closest to which of the following?

   A. One-way communication only

   B. One-way communication one way at a time

   C. Two-way communication both directions simultaneously

   D. Two-way communication one way at a time

2. A self-contained intelligent access point is:

   A. Controller-based

   B. Heavyweight

   C. Autonomous

   D. Thin

3. SOHO access points commonly support which of the following features? (Choose 3.)

   A. WPA 2.0 support

   B. CLI configuration

   C. Static output power

   D. Wi-Fi certifications

4. Wireless bridges must be configured with _____ and _____. (Choose 2.)

   A. A null SSID

   B. The same SSID

   C. The same RF channel

   D. Channel scanning

   E. Wired Equivalent Privacy

5. Which of the following is a benefit of a wireless repeater? (Choose 2.)

   A. Higher data transfer rate

   B. Larger cell size allows more devices to access the medium.

   C. Smaller cell size allows fewer devices to access the medium.

   D. Less data throughput

   E. Extends cell size

6. True or false: A benefit of a wireless LAN controller is distributed administration.

   A. True

   B. False

7. Static output transmit power of a SOHO access point is typically:

    A. 32 dBm

    B. 15 dBm

    C. 23 mW

    D. 15 mW

8. The 802.3-2005 Clause 33 standard specifies _____ VDC as the nominal voltage.

    A. 32

    B. 57

    C. 48

    D. 12

9. Which of the following devices is an in-line device that will inject DC voltage into the Ethernet cable?

    A. Midspan

    B. Midpoint

    C. Endspan

    D. Endpoint

10. Which layer of the OSI model is responsible for delivering data to a unique hardware address?

    A. Layer 1

    B. Layer 2

    C. Layer 3

    D. Layer 4

    E. Layer 5

    F. Layer 6

    G. Layer 7

11. SOHO access points are typically configured by using _____ and _____. (Choose 2.)

    A. HTTP

    B. FTP

    C. HTTPS

    D. CLI

    E. SMTP

12. True or false: An administrator should always configure an access point from the wireless network.

    A. True

    B. False

13. Access points work at which layers of the OSI model? (Choose 2.)

   A. Layer 1

   B. Layer 2

   C. Layer 3

   D. Layer 4

   E. Layer 5

   F. Layer 6

   G. Layer 7

14. Enterprise access points may contain which of the following features? (Choose 3.)

   A. WPA 2.0 support

   B. RADIUS server

   C. Static output power

   D. Repeater mode

   E. Power sourcing equipment

15. Which of the following statements is true regarding a wireless LAN controller?

   A. Virtual local area networks (VLANs) involve physical separation of ports.

   B. Virtual local area networks (VLANs) involve a logical separation of ports.

   C. Virtual local area network (VLAN) is another name for a repeater.

   D. Virtual local area networks (VLANs) require Power over Ethernet (PoE).

16. A controller-based access point connected to a port on the wireless LAN controller and not to an intermediate device is considered to have which of the following?

   A. Direct connectivity

   B. Distributed connectivity

   C. Decentralized connectivity

   D. Centralized connectivity

17. Power sourcing equipment delivers which of the following?

   A. RF power to the access point

   B. DC power to the end device

   C. RF power to an antenna

   D. DC power to an antenna

18. Which access point mode involves connecting the access point to a distribution system for user access to the LAN?

   A. Bridge only mode

   B. Repeater only mode

   C. Root access point mode

   D. Access mode

19. Which of the following are midspan PoE devices? (Choose 2.)

    A. Single-port injectors

    B. Multiport injectors

    C. Endpoint injectors

    D. Endspan injectors

20. Wireless LAN controllers may contain which of the following features? (Choose 3)

    A. Centralized administration

    B. Captive portal

    C. Network Address Translation (NAT)

    D. Built-in RADIUS services

    E. IP routing

Chapter

4

Wireless LAN Client Devices

THE FOLLOWING CWTS EXAM OBJECTIVES ARE COVERED IN THIS CHAPTER:

✓ **2.2 Identify the purpose, features, and functions of the following client device types. Choose the appropriate installation or configuration steps in a given scenario.**

- PC Cards (ExpressCard, CardBus, and PCMCIA)

- USB2

- PCI, Mini-PCI, Mini-PCIe, and Half Mini PCIe cards

- Workgroup Bridges

- Client utility software and drivers

Client devices are often thought of as computers—either desktop or notebook—connected to a computer network. However, there are many other devices, both wired and wireless, that can connect to a network. Wireless LAN client devices include various types of computers, tablets, smart phones, scanners, print servers, cameras, and other devices that are used to send data across the network. This chapter will look at the features of various wireless LAN client adapter types and the software for configuration and management of these devices.

Devices that connect to wireless networks use various types of adapters. Which adapter is used depends on the device that it connects to. You can connect wireless adapters to such devices as a notebook computer, tablet, desktop computer, or barcode scanner. Wireless LAN adapters are available in various types, both external and internal to the device. External adapters will connect to an available interface in the device such as a USB port or card slot. Examples of external adapter types are PCMCIA, ExpressCard, USB, and CompactFlash (CF).

Some devices use internal adapters that may require some level of disassembly or removal of a cover panel prior to the installation. Examples of internal adapter types are PCI, Mini-PCI, Full Mini-PCIe, and Half Mini PCIe.

Wireless LAN client adapters differ from other networking adapters (such as Ethernet adapters) because they contain radio hardware and use radio frequency (RF) to send the computer data over the air. Chapter 6, "Radio Frequency Fundamentals for Wireless LAN Technology," will discuss RF fundamentals in more detail. A wireless LAN design should be partly based on the needs of the client applications, client device types to be supported, and the environment where they will be used.

Radio Hardware Used with Wireless LAN Technology

Wireless LAN client devices require some type of radio hardware or chipset to send the digital data (all the ones and zeros) across the air using radio frequency. It is important to understand that based on the IEEE 802.11 standard, every addressable unit used in a wireless LAN is considered a station (STA). This includes both client devices that connect to the network and wireless access points that allow devices to connect to and use network resources.

Another point to consider is that with the recent advancements in wireless LAN technology, including the release of the IEEE 802.11n amendment, client device selection will need to be carefully considered. Although it is beneficial to use 802.11n-capable client devices along with the newer 802.11n multiple-input multiple-output (MIMO) access points, radio technology used in 802.11a/b/g devices may benefit from MIMO technology as well. Selecting the correct wireless adapter will allow a user to take advantage of the newest wireless LAN technology available.

Many organizations now have to deal with the Bring Your Own Device (BYOD) issue. This is a trend in which employees bring their own personal electronic wireless devices such as tablets and Wi-Fi–enabled smart phones to the office or place of business. These devices will then have access to company resources, including email services, file servers, computer data, and printers. This may create problems for technical support and security issues. BYOD is forcing organizations to address this in corporate policies.

PCMCIA

PCMCIA technology was developed in the early 1990s because the portable computer industry demanded smaller, lighter, and more mobile technology. The international standards organization developed to promote the growth of such technology is the Personal Computer Memory Card International Association (PCMCIA). With the advancements in computer device technology, PCMCIA adapters are becoming less popular. In the early days of standards-based wireless LAN technology, it was common for a device such as a notebook computer to have an interface or a "slot" that allowed for the use of a PCMCIA adapter. With the advancements in technology, it is much less common to find a computer or device that supports this type of adapter than it was a few years ago. Most portable devices now use either a built-in wireless networking adapter or a USB adapter; both are discussed in this chapter.

Features of PCMCIA Cards

The PCMCIA standard addressed three types of cards—Type I, Type II, and Type III. These cards are named after the PCMCIA organization that promoted this card technology and was responsible for the standards. You might also see the term *PC Card* used to describe these cards; this refers to the physical card or peripheral. All three types are the same width and length and have a 68-pin connector.

Figure 4.1 shows an example of a PCMCIA card that allows a computer to connect to a wireless network.

The only difference among the three types of cards is their thickness. Table 4.1 lists the different thicknesses and common uses of the card types.

FIGURE 4.1   Netgear WN511T Wireless PCMCIA adapter

TABLE 4.1   Features of the three types of PCMCIA card

Card Type	Thickness	Common use
Type I	3.3 millimeters	RAM, flash, OTP, and SRAM memory cards
Type II	5.0 millimeters	LANs, data/fax modems, and mass storage I/O devices
Type III	10.5 millimeters	Rotating mass storage devices

There are five versions of the PCMCIA standard. The release numbers are 1.0, 2.0, 2.1, 5.0, and 8.0. Releases 1.0 through 2.1 support 16-bit applications; releases 5.0 and up address a 32-bit interface.

According to the ExpressCard website, "the PCMCIA Association has been dissolved and the San Jose office closed. All activities and Standards, including the ExpressCard Standard and PC Card Standard, will be managed going forward by the USB Implementer's Forum." For additional information on this and other details, visit the USB Implementers Forum, Inc. website at www.usb.org.

Even with the advancements in this technology, there are still some devices in the marketplace that support PCMCIA adapters, and PCMCIA is included in the CWTS exam objectives. For that reason we'll next look at some details of its configuration.

Some older wireless access points used PCMCIA cards as their radios before radios were integrated into the access point and before the Mini-PCI card was used in access points.

Installation and Configuration of PCMCIA Cards

Installation of a PCMCIA card is a fairly simple process. The first consideration is to verify the physical characteristics of the card, such as the type (Type I, II, or III) and device in which it will be used—a notebook computer, for example. The card and the host device must be physically compatible with each other to ensure correct operation.

Another consideration is the device driver. A *device driver* is software required for a component such as a PCMCIA card to communicate with the computer or device operating system. The installer should have the latest version of the device driver accessible. The adapter usually comes with an installation CD that contains the device driver. It is best to follow the manufacturer's installation recommendations for the installation process, which may involve updating the driver from the manufacturer's website.

It is important to verify compatibility and minimum system requirements prior to installing any wireless network adapter in a device. Refer to the owner's manual or manufacturer's website for this information.

Configuration Using Installer Software

In many cases, a user will be required to first install a setup software program from the card manufacturer. This software will usually load the device driver within the computer operating system and install the configuration utility for the card.

Configuration Using a Wizard

In some cases, when the PCMCIA card is inserted into the correct interface, the computer operating system will automatically install the required device driver. If the operating system cannot find the correct driver, the user will be prompted to search the Internet or insert a CD or other data source from the manufacturer with the software device driver. Figure 4.2 shows a wizard that the Microsoft Windows 7 Professional operating system will display to help load the device driver.

FIGURE 4.2   Microsoft Windows 7 Professional Add A Device Wizard

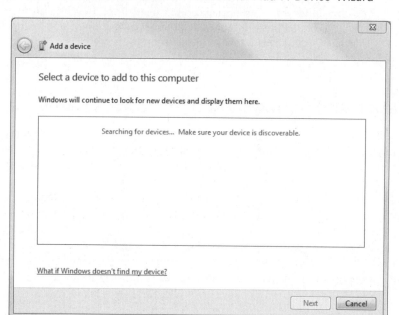

Exercise 4.1 illustrates how a common PCMCIA wireless LAN card will be installed. Do not insert the adapter until instructed to do so by the installation program. The manual device driver installation process described in Exercise 4.1 for PCMCIA is also applicable for other types of adapters explained in this chapter.

EXERCISE 4.1

Installing a PCMCIA Card

The following general steps are typical for installation of a PCMCIA wireless LAN card. Exact installation steps are specific to the manufacturer, and I recommend that you follow the manufacturer's installation instructions. Always read the manufacturer's manual regarding setup and safety before attempting installation.

1. Insert the Setup CD into the CD-ROM drive. The program should start automatically, and a welcome screen may appear.

    The graphic shows the welcome screen for the Linksys Wireless-G Notebook Adapter Setup Wizard.

2. After reading and accepting the license agreement, click to continue the installation and the program will begin copying the files onto your computer.

3. The setup program will now prompt the installer to install the adapter into the PC. The next image illustrates inserting the adapter into a notebook computer.

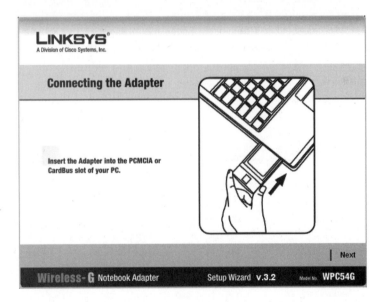

4. After the card has been identified, the program will copy the driver files to the computer.

5. The setup program will display the available wireless networks in the area or mode for connecting. Create a profile by selecting or typing in the desired wireless network. The following image shows the Linksys Setup Wizard's Wireless Mode connection screen.

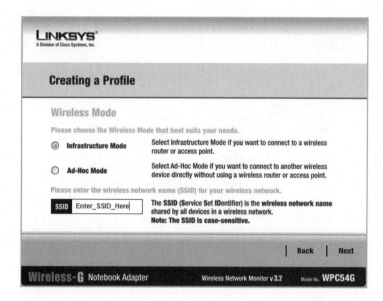

6. On the Wireless Security screen of the wizard, select the appropriate security settings—in this case, WPA2-personal. Enter the preshared key of the wireless network. The key must be 8 to 63 characters and must match the network key.

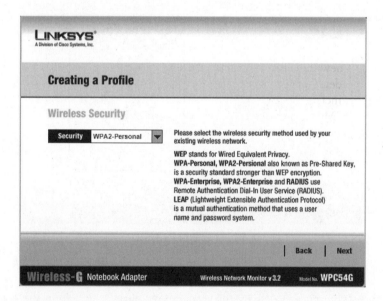

7. Connect to the wireless network using the created profile. The wizard summary screen shows the results of the installation.

8.   Setup is complete. Remove the Setup CD from the drive.

ExpressCard

ExpressCard is a newer generation of PC Card technology. This type of adapter is narrower than its predecessor (the PCMCIA adapter) and is available for newer wireless LAN technology, including IEEE 802.11n. Hewlett-Packard, Dell, Intel, and Microsoft are some of the PCMCIA member companies responsible for creating the ExpressCard standard. This technology is used in a large percentage of notebook computers to add new hardware capabilities. The ExpressCard is also used on some wireless LAN controllers and wireless access points to allow the addition of another radio, most often an Evolution-Data Optimized (EVDO) card to provide a backhaul for emergency use in high-availability roles.

Lower cost, smaller size, and higher performance were the driving forces behind ExpressCard technology. Applications include wired and wireless networking and communications, multimedia, and additional memory storage.

Features of the ExpressCard

The ExpressCard standard is built on the 16-bit and 32-bit PC Card standards. ExpressCard modules are available in four types: 34mm, 34mm extended, 54mm, and

54mm extended. The extended modules can be used for external connectors, television tuners, and wireless broadband, whereas standard modules will have specific functionality such as a wireless network adapter. Figure 4.3 shows the four types of available ExpressCards.

FIGURE 4.3   The four types of ExpressCard module

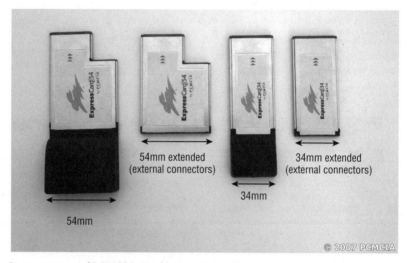

Image courtesy of PCMCIA. Used by permission.

Users can install or remove an ExpressCard without having to power down the computer or device. This technology is known as *hot-plug*. Hot-plug technology is also commonly supported by USB and other adapters.

 According to the ExpressCard website, "the PCMCIA Association has been dissolved and the San Jose office closed. All activities and Standards, including the ExpressCard Standard and PC Card Standard, will be managed going forward by the USB Implementer's Forum." For additional information on this and other details, visit the USB Implementers Forum, Inc. website at www.usb.org.

Installation and Configuration of an ExpressCard

The installation and configuration steps for an ExpressCard are similar to those for installing a PCMCIA card. (See the earlier section, "Installation and Configuration of PCMCIA Cards.") Figure 4.4 shows an ExpressCard plugged into a notebook computer.

FIGURE 4.4   ExpressCard installed in a notebook computer

Image courtesy of PCMCIA. Used by permission.

USB 1.0, USB 1.1, USB 2.0, and USB 3.0

Introduced in 1995, the *Universal Serial Bus* (USB 1.0) standard was designed as a replacement for legacy serial and parallel connections.

Serial communication is the process of transmitting one data bit at a time. *Parallel communication* has the capability of transmitting several data bits at a time. Imagine a single-lane road compared to a four-lane highway. On a single-lane road, only one car at a time can travel, whereas on a four-lane highway, many cars can traverse the same path at the same time.

USB allows connectivity for various devices that once used serial and parallel data connection ports. These devices include but are not limited to:

- Keyboard
- Mouse
- Digital camera
- Printer
- Computer networking adapter

USB 1.0 specified data rates from 1.5 Mbps to 12 and was replaced by USB 1.1 in 1998. Devices using this version of the standard were more common in the market.

USB standards are implemented by the USB Implementers Forum (USB-IF). This organization consists of companies from the computer and electronics industries, including Intel, Microsoft, NEC, and HP.

The *USB 2.0* specification was released in April 2000. The first revision appeared in December 2000, and the standard has been revised several times since. USB 2.0 incorporates several changes, including connector types. Data rates now allow for a maximum speed of up to 480 Mbps (USB 1.0 supported a maximum of 12 Mbps).

Figure 4.5 shows an example of a USB 2.0 port.

FIGURE 4.5   USB 2.0 port on notebook computer panel

USB 2.0 port

USB 3.0 technology was introduced in early 2010 and is commonly available to the point of being included on newer system boards. USB 3.0 devices have faster transfer rates and use a wider bandwidth, and they allow multiple logical streams and improved bus use with asynchronous readiness notification without polling. USB 3.0 greatly increases the transmission speed from the 480 Mbps of USB 2.0 up to 4.8 Gbps. This is more than 10 times that of the earlier standard, and as a result USB 3.0 is known as "SuperSpeed." In addition to speed, the new USB 3.0 specification addresses improvements to the technology, including bandwidth, by using bidirectional data paths, power management, and improved bus utilization.

Features of USB

USB uses a standard connector that replaces 9-pin serial, 25-pin parallel, and various other connector types. External configuration allows the user to plug in the USB device and power it with a single USB port. The computer operating system will guide the user through the device driver installation process. External installation minimizes the need to open up a computer case and make adjustments within the computer such as switch or jumper settings. USB also supports hot-swapping of devices, allowing connection and disconnection without the need to power down the device or the computer. In some cases, USB allows for power to be delivered to the peripheral device, eliminating the need for an external power supply. Fewer and fewer devices are being built with PC card or ExpressCard interfaces and most use only USB ports for adding peripheral devices.

> For additional information and specifications regarding the USB standards, visit the USB Implementers Forum (USB-IF) at www.usb.org.

Installation and Configuration of USB Devices

Exercise 4.2 walks you through the steps for installation of the D-Link Wireless N USB 2.0 adapter. Many USB wireless LAN adapters use installation procedures similar to this one.

Installation steps are specific to the manufacturer, and I recommend that you follow the manufacturer's installation instructions. Always read the manufacturer's manual regarding installation and safety before attempting installation.

EXERCISE 4.2

Installing a USB 2.0 Wireless LAN Adapter

To install the D-Link Wireless N USB 2.0 Adapter on a computer running Microsoft Windows, follow these steps:

1. Insert the Setup CD into the CD-ROM drive. The program should start automatically and an Autorun screen will appear. Click to start the installation, and the Installation Wizard window will appear.

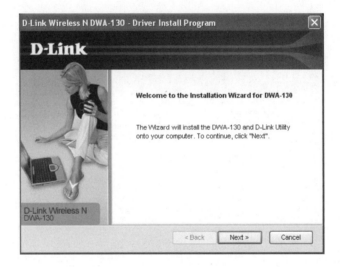

2. Accept the default location to install the files or browse for an alternate file location.

3. When prompted, insert the USB adapter into an available USB port on your computer.

4. When prompted, enter the network name (SSID) manually. If you don't know the SSID, click Scan to see the site survey page.

    The site survey page will also appear if the SSID is entered incorrectly. Click on the network name (SSID) and click Next.

5. Click Finish to continue. If prompted to restart the computer, select Yes, Restart The Computer Now.

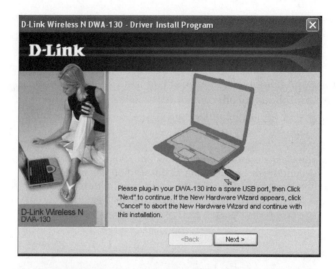

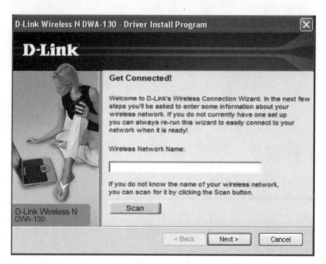

Peripheral Component Interconnect

PCI is the acronym for *Peripheral Component Interconnect*, a standard for computer interface cards that was developed by Intel. A PCI card is inserted into a slot in the main board
or motherboard of a desktop computer, allowing for the attachment of peripheral devices.
Installing a PCI card may require basic tools such as a screwdriver, and the installer usually will need to remove the cover from the desktop computer case. Figure 4.6 shows an
example of an IEEE 802.11 wireless PCI card.

FIGURE 4.6   Netgear WG311T IEEE 802.11g wireless PCI adapter

Features of PCI

A PCI adapter connects to what is known as a *data bus* in a desktop computer. In basic terms, a data bus allows connection of devices to the computer's processor or "brain." In the early days of personal computers, many devices used a data bus. These devices included video, hard disks, serial ports, Ethernet adapters, and parallel ports for printers. These interfaces connected to what is known as an *Industry Standard Architecture* (ISA) bus.

Modern computers have integrated many of these interfaces directly into the motherboard, system board, or main board. As PC technology evolved, so did the data bus architecture, going to 32-bit and now 64-bit bus. Wireless networks are no stranger to PCI. Even though wireless is often thought of as portable or mobile, in many cases stationary desktop computers can utilize wireless LAN connectivity through the use of wireless PCI interface cards.

 PCI-SIG (Peripheral Component Interconnect–Special Interest Group) is the industry organization for development and management of the PCI standards. For additional information, visit www.pcisig.com.

Installation and Configuration of PCI Cards

Back in 1995, Microsoft introduced a feature in the Windows 95 operating system called Plug and Play (PnP). This new feature accelerated the interest in PCI. PnP made installing a PCI card a snap. All that was required was for the installer to plug the card into the motherboard and it would be recognized and automatically work with the operating system. However, this process still required user intervention to open the case in order to physically install the card. Exercise 4.3 describes the steps for installing a PCI card in a desktop computer.

EXERCISE 4.3

Installing a PCI Card

The following steps are typical for installation of a PCI wireless LAN card. Exact installation steps are specific to the manufacturer, and I recommend that you follow the manufacturer's setup instructions. Always read the manufacturer's manual regarding setup and safety before attempting installation.

1. Insert the Setup CD into the CD-ROM drive. The program should start automatically, and a welcome or Autorun screen may appear. When the screen appears, click Next to continue and follow the instructions to install and configure the wireless PCI adapter. The installation wizard will appear on the screen.

2. The setup program will copy the required files to the desktop computer.

    Turn off the computer to install the card. Once the computer is turned off, unplug the power cord from the wall jack.

3. Open the case and identify an available PCI slot in the motherboard. Using the appropriate tool, remove the cover over the slot. Insert the wireless PCI adapter into the available PCI slot and securely fasten in place. The following image shows an available PCI slot in a desktop computer.

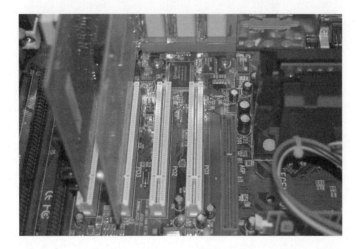

4. Once the card is securely mounted, close the case and insert the power cable into the wall jack. Turn on the computer.

5. The setup program will appear on the screen. Follow the onscreen instructions to complete the installation.

In some cases, the installation and setup may require the computer to be restarted in order for the adapter to operate correctly. Follow the manufacturer's recommendations.

Mini-PCI, Mini-PCIe, and Half Mini-PCIe

Mini-PCI is a variation of the PCI standard, designed for laptops and other small-footprint computer systems. One common example of a Mini-PCI card is the IEEE 802.11 Mini-PCI adapter shown in Figure 4.7.

FIGURE 4.7   IEEE 802.11 Mini-PCI adapter

Mini-PCI cards are common in many devices, such as Fast Ethernet networks, Bluetooth, modems, hard drive controllers, and wireless LANs. In the wireless world, Mini-PCI cards are used in access points and client devices such as laptop or notebook computers.

Mini-PCI Express (*Mini-PCIe*) cards are a replacement for the Mini-PCI card and are based on PCI Express.

 Many notebook and portable computers with built-in wireless LAN use either Mini-PCI or Mini-PCIe or now Half Mini-PCIe cards for wireless IEEE 802.11 wireless LAN connectivity.

Features of Mini-PCI, Mini-PCIe, and Half Mini-PCIe Cards

Mini-PCI cards are available in three types; Type I, Type II, and Type III. Types I and II use a 100-pin stacking connector. Type III cards use a 124-pin edge connector. Type II cards have RJ11 and RJ45 connectors for telephone and Ethernet network connections. These cards are commonly located at the edge of the computer or docking station so that the connectors can be mounted for external access, such as to a modem or computer network.

Mini-PCIe cards are 30mm × 56mm and have a 52-pin edge connector, consisting of two staggered rows on a 0.8mm pitch. These cards are 1.0mm thick excluding components. Table 4.2 summarizes the features of Mini-PCI and Mini-PCIe cards.

The *Half Mini-PCIe* cards are 30mm × 31.90mm. The main difference between this card and the Mini-PCIe card mentioned earlier is the length. The length of this new form factor is about half of the Mini-PCIe card.

With the introduction of the Half Mini-PCIe card form factor, the Mini-PCIe card is now called the *Full Mini-PCIe* card.

TABLE 4.2 Features of Mini-PCI, Full Mini-PCIe, and Half Mini-PCIe cards

Card type	Connectors	Size
Mini-PCI Type IA	100-pin stacking	7.5mm × 70mm × 45mm
Mini-PCI Type IB	100-pin stacking	5.5mm × 70mm × 45mm
Mini-PCI Type IIA	100-pin stacking, RJ11, RJ45	17.44mm × 70mm × 45mm
Mini-PCI Type IIB	100-pin stacking, RJ11, RJ45	5.5mm × 78mm × 45mm
Mini-PCI Type IIIA	124-pin edge	5mm × 59.75mm × 50.95mm
Mini-PCI Type IIIB	124-pin edge	5mm × 59.75mm × 44.6mm
Full Mini-PCIe	52-pin edge, two staggered rows on 0.8mm pitch	30mm × 31.90mm × 1mm (excluding components)
Half Mini-PCIe	52-pin edge, two staggered rows on 0.8mm pitch	30mm × 56mm × 1mm (excluding components)

Figure 4.8 shows a Mini-PCIe adapter.

FIGURE 4.8   Intel 3945 IEEE 802.11a/b/g Full Mini-PCIe adapter

Installation and Configuration of Mini-PCI, Full Mini-PCIe, and Half Mini-PCIe Cards

As with the PCI card installation process, Mini-PCI and Mini-PCIe installation may require the user to physically install hardware in the computer. Location of the Mini-PCI or Mini-PCIe interface varies depending on the computer manufacturer. On some computers you just have to remove a cover panel on the bottom of the notebook. On others you need to disassemble the computer case. Exercise 4.4 describes the typical installation steps.

EXERCISE 4.4

Installing Mini-PCI and Mini-PCIe Cards

The following steps are typical for installation of a Mini-PCI and Mini-PCIe wireless LAN card on a notebook computer. Exact installation steps are specific to the manufacturer, and I recommend that you follow the manufacturer's setup instructions.

1. Shut down the computer. Verify that the computer is not in Hibernation mode. If it is, turn on the computer and perform a complete shutdown.

2. Disconnect the AC power cord from the wall jack.

3. Disconnect all connected peripherals and remove the battery pack.

4. Remove the panel covering the Mini-PCI–Mini-PCIe compartment (details of this step will depend on the computer model).

5. Insert the Mini PCI or Mini-PCIe card into the correct slot. Note the correct pin orientation.

6. Connect the wireless antenna cables to the Mini PCI or Mini-PCIe card.

7. Replace the panel for the Mini-PCI–Mini-PCIe compartment.

8. Replace all peripheral devices and battery pack. Plug in the AC power cord to the wall jack.

9. Power on the computer and insert the Setup CD-ROM into the CD-ROM drive. The program should start automatically, and a welcome or Autorun screen may appear. When the screen appears, click Install Drivers and follow the onscreen instructions to install and configure the wireless Mini PCI or Mini-PCIe card.

Always read the manufacturer's manual regarding installation and safety before attempting installation.

 Real World Scenario

Replacing a Full Mini-PCIe with Half Mini-PCIe Adapter

Upgrading an IEEE 802.11g wireless Full Mini-PCIe card to a newer IEEE 802.11n Half-Mini PCIe card may require the use of a special adapter or bracket. Keep in mind that the Half Mini-PCIe card is about half the length of the full card, and you may not be able to install the card securely. Therefore, you may need to purchase a special bracket in order for the new Half Mini-PCIe card to be securely mounted in the notebook computer or other device where the card is to be installed.

Additional Adapter Types

The following section describes some additional wireless radios and adapters. These adapters are not as common as some of the others mentioned earlier in this chapter but are still available for purchase and are used with networking devices. The following adapters were originally designed as memory storage cards but had a wireless network technology added to them:

- CompactFlash (CF) devices
- Secure Digital (SD)

CompactFlash Devices

CompactFlash (CF) was originally designed as a mass storage device format used in portable electronic devices. SanDisk introduced this format in 1994. The CF format is now used for a variety of devices and technologies, including Ethernet networks, Bluetooth, digital cameras, RFID, and wireless LANs.

Features of CF Cards

CF cards are available in two types: Type I and Type II. Both types have the same length and width, 36mm × 43mm. The only difference is the thickness.

Table 4.3 lists physical characteristics and typical uses of CompactFlash cards.

TABLE 4.3   Characteristics and uses of CF cards

Card type	Thickness	Common use
Type I	3.3 millimeters	RAM, flash memory cards
Type II	5.0 millimeters	Wireless LANs, microdrives

Figure 4.9 shows the front and back of a CompactFlash wireless LAN card supporting IEEE 802.11a/b/g wireless connectivity.

FIGURE 4.9   Motorola LA-5137 IEEE 802.11a/b/g CompactFlash card

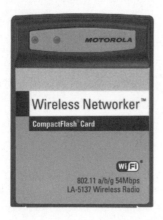

 For additional information regarding this technology, visit the CompactFlash organization at www.compactflash.org.

Installation and Configuration of a CF Card

Installing a CF IEEE 802.11 wireless LAN card differs from some of the previous installation examples. For example, you may need to connect a handheld personal computer running a Microsoft operating system (Pocket PC) or personal digital assistant (PDA) to another computer in order to complete the installation process. Always follow the manufacturer's setup instructions for installing the specific card.

Secure Digital

Like the CompactFlash card, Secure Digital (SD) was designed as a flash memory storage device with storage capacities from 8 MB to 4 GB. The SD memory card was a joint venture among SanDisk, Toshiba, and Panasonic in 1999.

Even though the SD card was designed as to provide flash memory, the slot will allow for connection of other devices such as cameras, global positioning system (GPS) units, FM radios, TV tuners, Ethernet networks, and of course wireless LANs. In this format the SD card is known as *Secure Digital Input Output (SDIO)*. This card is designed to provide high-speed data I/O with low power consumption for mobile electronic devices. Figure 4.10 is an example of an SDIO wireless LAN adapter.

FIGURE 4.10   SanDisk SDIO Wi-Fi card

Features of SDIO Cards

SDIO cards are available in two sizes:

- The full-size SDIO card is 24mm × 32mm × 2.1mm—approximately the size of a postage stamp. This SDIO card is intended for portable and stationary applications.

- The mini-SDIO is 27mm × 20mm × 1.4mm in size and used with wireless LAN and Bluetooth adapters.

For additional information regarding SD and SDIO technology, visit the SD Association at www.sdcard.org.

Installation and Configuration of SDIO Cards

Installing an SDIO 802.11 wireless LAN card is similar to installing a CompactFlash card, and differs from the installation of PCMCIA and ExpressCard. These differences may include connecting a Pocket PC or PDA to another host PC running ActiveSync in order to complete the installation process. I recommend that you follow the manufacturer's setup instructions for installing a specific card. Here are the typical steps for installing an SDIO wireless LAN card:

1. Connect the Pocket PC or PDA to the host PC running ActiveSync.
2. Install the software using the host PC.
3. Insert the SDIO Wireless LAN card.
4. Start the program on the Pocket PC or PDA.
5. Find a wireless LAN to connect and create a profile.
6. Connect to the wireless LAN.

Always read the manufacturer's manual regarding installation and safety before attempting installation.

Wireless Workgroup Bridges

A wireless workgroup or client bridge is a wireless device acting as a client device that will allow potentially several Ethernet devices on an Ethernet segment (devices connected to a common physical layer boundary) to connect to an infrastructure through a wireless access point. This is accomplished without the need to upgrade each wired device on the Ethernet segment to wireless. Figure 4.11 illustrates an application of a wireless workgroup bridge.

Features of Workgroup/Client Bridges

The *wireless workgroup bridge* (WWB), also known as a *wireless client bridge,* can be used in a variety of business or SOHO applications, including enterprise, medical, retail, education, and warehouse. Supported devices include computers, printers, scales, medical equipment, barcode readers, and point-of-sale machines such as cash registers. Although the workgroup/client bridge may have the appearance and features of an infrastructure device such as a wireless access point, it is considered a client device. A workgroup bridge will allow for a limited number of wired client devices to connect to and use network resources. A wireless access point sees a wireless workgroup bridge as a single station even if several wired stations are connected, because the wireless workgroup bridge multiplexes the signal to a single wireless connection. In other words, it is basically a multiplex device.

FIGURE 4.11   Typical application for an enterprise wireless workgroup bridge

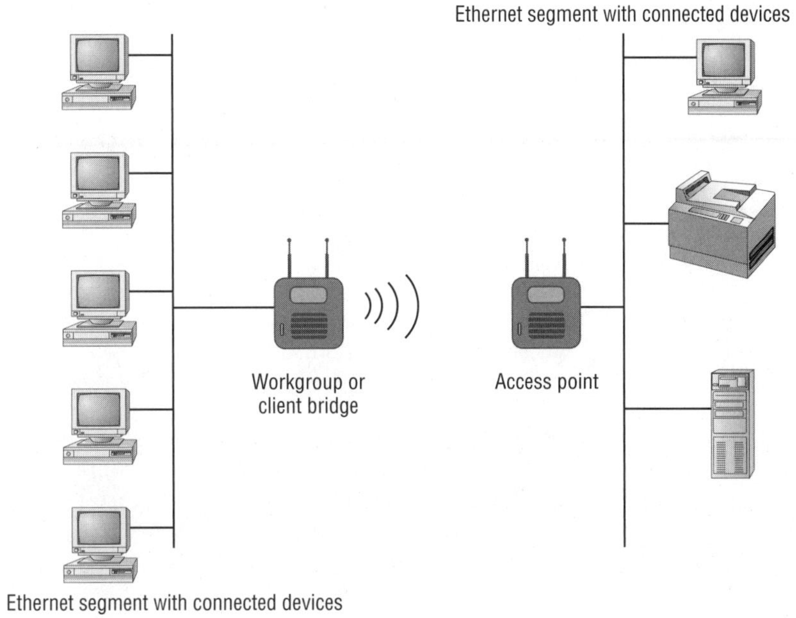

Wireless workgroup/client bridges may include these features:

- Fixed or detachable antennas
- Security features such as WEP, WPA, or WPA 2.0
- Web browser and/or command-line interface management utilities
- MAC filtering options
- Multiple connectivity modes
- Power over Ethernet
- Support for connection of a limited number of client devices

Installation and Configuration of Workgroup/ Client Bridges

The following are the steps usually necessary for installing and configuring a workgroup or client bridge:

1. Connect the workgroup or client bridge to the Ethernet segment that needs to have a wireless connection.

2. If Power over Ethernet (PoE) is not a feature of the device, connect the bridge power adapter to the wall jack.

3. Using a web browser, connect to the assigned IP address. In some cases it may be necessary to assign an IP address to the workgroup or client bridge from a CLI prior to configuring the bridge.

4. From the web management interface, assign the correct service set identifier (SSID) and RF channel in order to associate to the correct access point.

5. Configure the correct security settings, either WPA or WPA2 and Personal or Enterprise mode.

6. Verify association of the workgroup/client bridge to the desired access point.

Always read the manufacturer's manual regarding installation and safety before attempting installation.

Another form of wireless client bridge is one that is designed to allow a variety of single Ethernet devices, not just computers, to connect to and use wireless networks. These devices will have an Ethernet port but are not wireless-capable. This type of client bridge also has characteristics similar to some infrastructure devices, such as wireless access points. One benefit is that in most cases no software is required; that is, you will not have to install device driver or client utility software on the client Ethernet device. These devices are seen by the access point as a single wireless client. Devices that can benefit from this type of client bridge are printers, DVD/media players, and game consoles. Figure 4.12 shows a wireless client bridge.

FIGURE 4.12   EnGenius Technologies ECB3500 802.11g High Power 600mW wireless access point/bridge/repeater/router

Client Device Drivers

All devices connected to a computer require a device driver. Components requiring drivers include keyboards, mice, video cards, USB ports, printers, wired network interface cards, IEEE 802.11 wireless LAN cards, and many others. The device driver is software that allows the installed device to communicate with or take instructions from the computer operating system in order to provide correct functionality.

It is important to verify the latest revision of the device driver from the client device manufacturer. Having the latest revision installed will ensure correct operation and sometimes add additional features. Figure 4.13 shows a device listing in the Windows 7 Professional operating system.

FIGURE 4.13   Microsoft Windows 7 Professional Device Manager utility

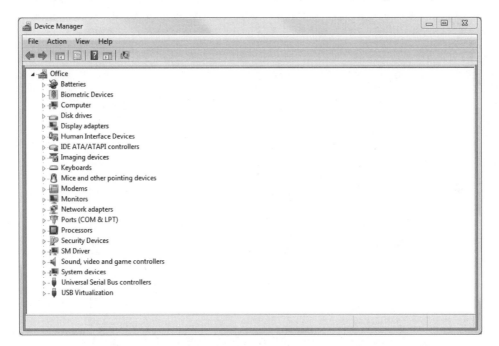

Client Utility Software

All IEEE 802.11 wireless LAN cards require configuration in order to connect to a wireless network. The configuration capabilities of device drivers are usually very limited. Therefore, a user needs additional configuration software. The user can choose from either manufacturer-specific utilities or third-party client utilities built into some operating systems. When IEEE 802.1X port-based authentication is used, the client device is known as the supplicant. The supplicant will provide authentication credentials to the authenticator, which in wireless networking is the access point. 802.1X authentication will be discussed in more detail in Chapter 9, "Wireless LAN Security Basics." Regardless of the client utility installed, a user has the capability to create a profile that will retain the connection/session parameters. A profile will contain information regarding a specific connection, including network name or SSID and security settings.

Manufacturer-Specific Client Utilities

Most manufacturers of wireless LAN adapters provide a software client utility for the wireless adapter. The features of the utility depend on whether the client is SOHO grade or enterprise grade. SOHO grade client utilities have basic connection and security parameters. The client software installation usually is part of the adapter install process and is typically performed through a setup wizard. Figure 4.14 shows a screenshot from a SOHO client utility.

FIGURE 4.14   Linksys Dual-Band Wireless-N USB client utility

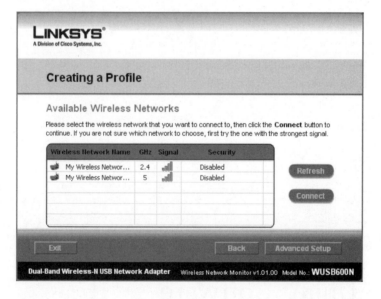

Enterprise-grade client utilities may have a more advanced feature set, including connection statistics and site survey. Typically, a user can install the device driver and client utility simultaneously or will be able to choose separate installation procedures. In most enterprise-grade client utilities, profile setup is a manual process requiring a user to have a basic understanding of the adapter's capabilities as well as the network configuration. Figure 4.15 shows an enterprise-grade client utility.

FIGURE 4.15   Proxim Client Utility for 8494-US 802.11a/b/g/n USB adapter

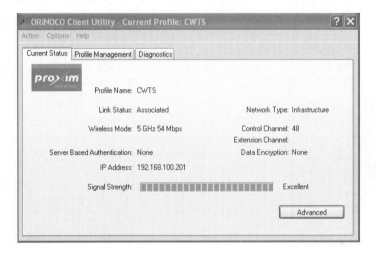

Third-Party Client Utilities

Another option for a wireless LAN adapter client utility is a third-party utility built into a computer operating system. Recent versions of the Microsoft Windows operating system—Windows XP Vista and Windows 7, for example—have a client utility built in and running as a service. In Windows XP this client utility is available from the *Wireless Zero Configuration (WZC) service*. Figure 4.16 shows the Windows XP WZC client utility.

In later versions such as Windows 7, the service is now called the WLAN AutoConfig. After the wireless adapter is installed, a user may select a wireless network to connect to and supply security parameters if required. Figure 4.17 shows the Windows 7 Professional client utility using the Microsoft *AutoConfig service*.

FIGURE 4.16   Microsoft Windows XP WZC client utility

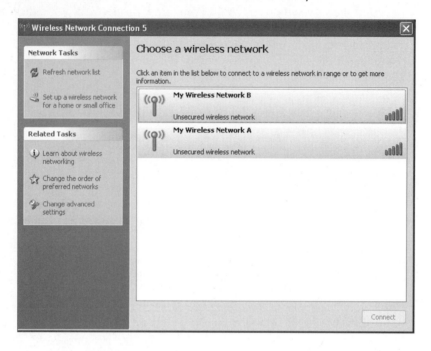

FIGURE 4.17   Microsoft Windows 7 Professional operating system client utility

Summary

There are many types of wireless LAN client devices used in various applications. These device types include desktop and notebook computers, printers, and barcode scanners, to name a few. A wireless client adapter uses radio hardware or chipset to send the digital data (all the ones and zeros) across the air using radio frequency. This chapter looked at some of the various IEEE 802.11 wireless LAN adapter types, explaining the features, common hardware, software, and configuration procedures. External adapters with wireless LAN functionality include:

- PCMCIA
- ExpressCard
- USB 2.0
- CompactFlash (CF)

PCMCIA adapters, although still available for purchase and used in many installations, are becoming less popular. Finding a newer notebook computer that has an interface to support a PCMCIA adapter is not as common. The PCMCIA Association has been dissolved and the San Jose office closed. This specification is now handled by the USB Implementers Forum.

Wireless LAN adapters are also available as internal adapters. These adapters may require some disassembly or removal of a panel for installation. Internal adapter types include these:

- PCI
- Mini-PCI
- Full Mini-PCIe
- Half Mini-PCIe

Wireless LAN adapters require a device driver in order to communicate with the operating system, and in most cases software utilities may be installed and/or configured in order to connect the wireless network. This chapter described several installation scenarios for various types of wireless LAN adapters, including PCMCIA, USB, and PCI. We also looked at how a wireless workgroup bridge can be used to connect computers and other devices on an Ethernet segment to a network by connecting to an access point.

Finally, this chapter showed how wireless LAN client utilities simplify the process of connecting to a wireless network. Client utilities are sometimes supplied by the manufacturer of the adapter or may part of the operating system. Windows Wireless Zero Configuration (WZC) or WLAN AutoConfig (Windows 7) is a commonly used operating system client utility.

Exam Essentials

Know the various types and features of external client adapters used in wireless LAN clients.   Understand the features and function of external client adapters, including PCMCIA, ExpressCard, and USB 2.0.

Know the various types and features of internal client adapters used in wireless LAN clients.   Be familiar with internal adapter cards used with 802.11 wireless LAN technology, including PCI, Mini-PCI, Full Mini-PCIe, and Half Mini-PCIe cards. Understand the installation factors involved with internal network adapters.

Understand the installation process of client adapters and client software.   PCMCIA, ExpressCard, USB2, CompactFlash (CF), SDIO, PCI, Mini-PCI, and Full and Half Mini-PCIe cards require software components such as a device driver and client utility software to be installed in order to function correctly.

Explain the function and features of specialty client devices.   Specialty client devices such as a wireless workgroup or client bridge can be used to connect devices on a common physical layer cable to a wireless network.

Know the differences among software components of wireless client adapters.   Device drivers, client utility software, and third-party client software all play important roles in the successful installation of a wireless client adapter. Understand the details of software components used in wireless networking.

Review Questions

1. You have a notebook computer and wish to connect to an IEEE 802.11n wireless network. The computer does not have a built-in wireless LAN card or a PC card interface. You do not want any peripherals connected to the notebook that use wires and do not want to disassemble the computer. Which wireless adapter would be the best solution?

    A. Wireless PCI

    B. Wireless PCMCIA

    C. Wireless Full Mini-PCIe

    D. Wireless USB 2.0

2. You need to select a wireless LAN card for a notebook computer to connect to an IEEE 802.11n network. The notebook has an interface or slot on the side that will accept one of three physical types of adapter. Which card would work best in this case?

    A. PCI

    B. Half Mini-PCIe

    C. PCMCIA

    D. ISA

3. In addition to wireless networking, which adapter was designed for flash memory storage and can be used in a digital camera?

    A. PCI

    B. PCMCIA

    C. ISA

    D. SDIO

4. A _____ computer requires the user to disassemble the computer case to install a wireless PCI network adapter. Which computer would be the best candidate in this situation?

    A. Notebook

    B. Desktop

    C. Tablet

    D. Barcode scanner

5. Which component is required for a successful installation and operation of an 802.11n wireless USB adapter?

    A. Device driver

    B. Client utility

    C. Profile software

    D. Windows WZC

6. You want to connect a desktop computer to an IEEE 802.11n wireless network. Which wireless LAN adapter would be the best solution if you do not want to disassemble the computer?

    A. Mini-PCI

    B. USB 2.0

    C. Half Mini-PCIe

    D. PCMCIA

7. Which client device will allow a user to connect several Ethernet devices on a common segment to an access point?

    A. PCMCIA

    B. PCI bridge

    C. Wireless workgroup bridge

    D. Ethernet bridge

8. USB was designed as a replacement for which two legacy communication connections?

    A. Serial and PCI

    B. Serial and parallel

    C. Parallel and ISA

    D. Parallel and EISA

9. How many data bits does serial communication transmit at a time?

    A. 1

    B. 3

    C. 4

    D. 8

10. Which wireless adapter may require some disassembly of a notebook computer to install?

    A. PCI

    B. PCMCIA

    C. PC Card

    D. Mini-PCI

11. Most manufacturers recommend installing a wireless IEEE 802.11n USB adapter at what point?

    A. When the computer is not powered on

    B. When instructed by the setup utility

    C. After calling technical support

    D. Before starting the setup process

12. Enterprise-grade IEEE 802.11g client utilities typically contain which advanced feature?

    A. PCI configuration

    B. Spectrum analyzer

    C. Setup wizard

    D. Site survey

13. Which item is required for an IEEE 802.11g PCI card to communicate with a computer connected to an unsecured wireless LAN?

    A. Mini-PCI card

    B. Device driver

    C. Third-party utility

    D. Enterprise utility

14. A wireless workgroup bridge will allow you to do which of the following?

    A. Connect two wireless LAN NICs together.

    B. Connect a wired LAN to an AP.

    C. Connect a PCI card to a WLAN.

    D. Connect two client bridges.

15. CompactFlash (CF) cards are available in two types. What is the main difference between the two types?

    A. Length

    B. Width

    C. Thickness

    D. Height

16. Which two wireless LAN adapters can be installed in a computer without the need to disassemble the computer in any way? (Choose 2.)

    A. PCI

    B. PCMCIA

    C. USB 2.0

    D. PCIe

    E. Mini-PCI

17. Of all the devices listed, Secure Digital Input Output (SDIO) cards are most likely to be installed in which?

    A. Desktop computer

    B. Access point

    C. Notebook computer

    D. Pocket PC

18. A device driver can be used in wireless networking. Which is an example of a device driver?

    A. Software to control a wireless NIC

    B. Software to control the OS

    C. Hardware to install a PCI card

    D. Hardware to install a client bridge

19. Six wired clients can connect to a wireless LAN by using which device?

    A. Workgroup bridge

    B. PCI bridge

    C. Mini-PCI adapter

    D. PCI adapter

20. Which is required in order to successfully install an IEEE 802.11n wireless LAN adapter?

    A. Security profile

    B. Device driver

    C. Third-party client utility

    D. SOHO utility

Chapter

5

Physical Layer Access Methods and Spread-Spectrum Technology

THE FOLLOWING CWTS EXAM OBJECTIVES ARE COVERED IN THIS CHAPTER:

✓ **3.4 Define and differentiate between the following physical layer wireless technologies**

- 802.11b HR/DSSS

- 802.11g ERP

- 802.11a OFDM

- 802.11n HT

✓ **3.5 Define concepts which make up the functionality of RF and spread-spectrum communication**

- 802.11 channels

- Co-location of 802.11a/b/g/n systems

- Adjacent-channel and co-channel interference

- WLAN/WPAN coexistence

- CSMA/CA operation

- Half duplex communications

It is important to understand how digital data is sent from one device to another. Whether on a wired network or a wireless network, an access method is used to transfer this type of electronic information. Two common access methods are CSMA/CD and CSMA/CA. The type of medium in use—wired or wireless—will determine which of these two access methods is best suited for the application. You saw in previous chapters that wireless LANs use radio frequencies with air as the communication medium. This chapter will discuss the various techniques and methods used to get digital computer data from one device to another using spread-spectrum and other physical layer modulation technologies.

It is important to understand that different spread-spectrum technologies such as FHSS, DSSS, and HR/DSSS will allow for various data rates. The spread-spectrum or other physical layer technology used will determine the maximum amount of data transfer as well as the resilience to noise and other interfering sources. We will look at the 802.11 channels, the number of channels available, channel spacing, and the frequencies of the unlicensed radio frequency bands used with wireless networking. We will also discuss the implications of overlapping channels and interference. Finally, this chapter will discuss co-location of different technologies used in various amendments to the standard as well as interference from wireless LANs and other sources, including WPANs.

The IEEE 802.11-2012 standard has been officially released. This standard includes all communication amendments that were outstanding or part of the IEEE 802.11-2007 standard, including IEEE 802.11a/b/g/n. Even though these amendments are now incorporated into the newest version of the standard, we will discuss the technology using the original amendment names, 802.11b, 802.11a, and so on, because these names are still commonly used in the industry.

Network Access Methods

Network access methods allow devices connected to a common infrastructure to communicate and transmit data across a network medium from one device to another. Several different types of network access methods are used in computer networks. The two types we will discuss in this chapter are:

- Carrier Sense Multiple Access/Collision Detection (CSMA/CD)
- Carrier Sense Multiple Access/Collision Avoidance (CSMA/CA)

Because Ethernet networks have the capability to detect collisions, 802.3 Ethernet networks use *CSMA/CD* as the access method. Devices on a wireless LAN do not have the capability to detect collisions; therefore 802.11 wireless LANs use *CSMA/CA* for the access method. Since multiple wireless devices can use an access point at the same time, wireless devices that connect to an access point are competing to share the medium; therefore, it is important to control the medium in order to minimize collisions. The CSMA/CA process provides this control.

Detecting Network Traffic Collisions with CSMA/CD

802.3 Ethernet networks use CSMA/CD to share the medium. The name of this access method describes how it functions.

The abbreviation CSMA/CD is broken down as follows:

- Carrier Sense—Devices sense the medium (in this case, Ethernet cable) to see if it is clear (no data being transmitted).
- Multiple Access—Many devices accessing the medium at the same time.
- Collision Detection—Detecting collisions that occur on the medium during the transmission of data.

CSMA/CD is a contention-based media access control method that Ethernet devices use to share the medium. This method allows only one device to transmit at any one time.

In computing terminology, contention is defined as multiple devices competing for a chance to send data on the network. CSMA/CD functions like this:

1. A device with data to transmit checks whether any data is being transmitted on the Ethernet cable (sensing).

2. If the device senses that the medium is clear and no data is being transmitted, it transmits its own data.

3. If more than one device transmits simultaneously, a collision occurs and the data is lost. The devices detect the collision and each will back off for a random amount of time.

4. After the random amount of time expires, the device checks the cable and attempts to send the data again.

This contention of the Ethernet segment is one reason for decreased data throughput of the transmitting devices. Figure 5.1 demonstrates CSMA/CD with desktop computers connected to an Ethernet segment.

FIGURE 5.1   Computers connected to Ethernet cable using CSMA/CD

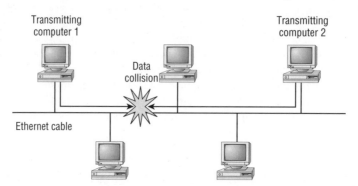

Conversation as a Form of CSMA/CD

An analogy for CSMA/CD is conversation among a group of people in which all the individuals in the group would like a chance to speak. Everyone is listening to each other (sensing the medium). Only one person at a time gets a chance to say something. This is an example of a multiple access shared medium (MA). If there is a pause in the conversation, two or more people listening may notice the opportunity and may say something at the exact same time, in which case neither may be heard by the rest of the group. This is an example of a collision. At this point, the collision is detected (CD) and those involved in the failed communication wait a few seconds and attempt to speak again later—hence, CSMA/CD.

Avoiding Network Traffic Collisions with CSMA/CA

Wireless LANs use CSMA/CA to share the medium. The main difference from CSMA/CD is the CA—collision avoidance. Just as in CSMA/CD, the abbreviation CSMA/CA gives an idea of how it functions:

- Carrier Sense—Sensing the medium, in this case the air

- Multiple Access—Many devices accessing the medium at the same time

- Collision Avoidance—Avoiding collisions that may occur on the medium during transmission

Because wireless LAN devices have no way to detect collisions, the CSMA/CD access method is not an adequate solution for wireless LAN communications. If wireless LANs were to use CSMA/CD, collisions would occur at the wireless access point and all data would be lost. At this point, a transmitting device would not know that it should retransmit the information, because the receiving device would be unaware that a collision occurred; the result would be very poor performance.

Instead of detecting transmission collisions, CSMA/CA uses mechanisms that attempt to avoid collisions. Although these mechanisms impose some overhead, the overall benefit is better data throughput because data collisions are minimized. This overhead occurs because devices use "countdown timers" that require them to wait for periods of time before they are able to transmit again. This helps to avoid data collisions.

Lecture Q&A as a Form of CSMA/CA

An analogy for CSMA/CA is the question-and-answer period following a lecture. The lecture hall is filled with many people (multiple access). A presenter has finished giving a speech and it is now question-and-answer time. The presenter shouts out, "Does anyone have a question?" An attendee by the name of Marvin listens (sensing the carrier). He does not hear anyone speaking, so he yells out a question. Although many people are in the room (again, multiple access), they can hear that Marvin has the floor and this time is dedicated to him. So they defer and do not ask their question until Marvin's question has been answered by the speaker (collision avoidance); hence, CSMA/CA.

Reserving Time for Data Transmission Using Distributed Coordination Function

One of the access methods wireless LAN devices use to communicate is known as *distributed coordinated function (DCF)*. This method of access employs a contention period for devices competing to send data on the network. This collision avoidance mechanism is part of a detailed process requiring certain criteria to be met in order for a frame (a Layer 2 digital transmission unit) to be transmitted across the medium. In the case of wireless LAN technology, this medium is the air, using radio frequencies (RF).

To avoid collisions, the devices are required to:

- Detect the RF energy of other devices transmitting, a technique known as Clear Channel Assessment (CCA).

- Announce how much time is required for the frame exchange to occur allowing other stations read the duration field and set their Network Allocation Vector (NAV).

- Wait for a predetermined period of time between frames, a technique known as interframe spacing.

- Back off and retry if the medium is busy, a technique known as the random backoff timer via the contention window.

In short, these devices are reserving the medium so that transmissions can take place and avoid collisions. Figure 5.2 illustrates wireless LAN devices using CSMA/CA for an access method.

FIGURE 5.2   Wireless LAN devices using CSMA/CA and DCF

 The 802.11 standard also specifies two other access methods used with wireless networking. Point Coordination Function (PCF) mode is a contention-free mode that works by polling stations and giving them an opportunity to send information without contending with other devices. PCF mode was optional and never implemented by any manufacturers. Another access method, Hybrid Coordination Function (HCF) mode, was introduced with 802.11e for quality of service (QoS) technology.

Effects of Half Duplex on Wireless Throughput

As discussed in Chapter 3, "Wireless LAN Infrastructure Devices," wireless LANs use half duplex communication. To review, *half duplex* in computer terminology is defined as two-way communication that occurs in only one direction at a time. Communication only one way at a time means less data throughput for the connected device(s). Half-duplex communication is part of the reason why in wireless LANs the amount of data being transferred is sometimes less than half of the advertised data rate; collisions and additional overhead are other factors to consider. An 802.11b device may only get 5.5 Mbps or less data transfer even though this technology is rated at 11 Mbps. On a good day, 802.11a or 802.11g devices will also average less than half of the advertised data rates. Figure 5.3 shows the half-duplex communication method and some of the effect it has on throughput. The data rate in this example is 54 Mbps, but the throughput is less than half of that, about 22 Mbps. The newest IEEE amendment, 802.11n, uses MIMO technology and has a potential maximum data rate of up to 600 Mbps. However, many of the client devices available today have a maximum of about 300–450 Mbps. The actual throughput can be as low as 30 Mbps.

FIGURE 5.3   Half-duplex operation has some effect on overall data throughput.

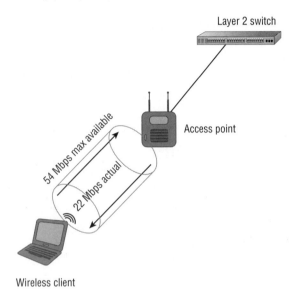

Narrowband vs. Spread-Spectrum Communication

Narrowband and spread-spectrum are two examples of how devices can communicate using radio frequency.

One example of narrowband communication is an FM radio station. FM radio stations use licensed frequency ranges that are tuned to a specific radio frequency in the FM band. A radio station can transmit a signal at a high power of tens of thousands of watts in a very narrow frequency. Depending on the conditions, a receiver can hear the station for tens or even possibly hundreds of miles.

Figure 5.4 shows the high amount of output power over a narrowband frequency of a potential FM radio station.

In contrast, spread-spectrum technology uses low power over a wider range of frequency. Figure 5.5 illustrates how a spread spectrum–capable access point uses low power over a wide frequency range.

FIGURE 5.4   Narrowband frequency—high power, narrow frequency

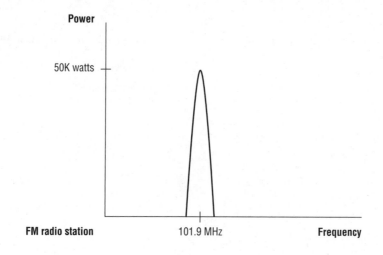

FIGURE 5.5   Spread-spectrum technology—low power, wide frequency

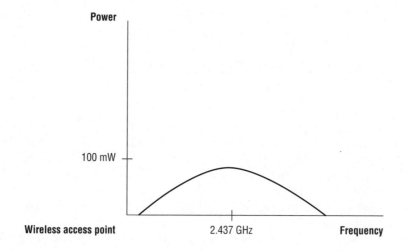

Lecturer vs. Breakout Discussions

Narrowband communication is similar to a lecture presented in a large room filled with several hundred attendees. The presenter may have a microphone connected to an amplifier or PA system to address the large audience. All attendees at this event will pay attention to the presenter, who will get the message across to the entire audience in this very large venue.

Spread-spectrum communication is similar to what happens when the same audience breaks out into small groups in which each member is communicating only with other members of that group. These groups of individuals will be speaking at a much lower volume without the help of a high-power microphone, and the conversation volume will not exceed the area in which this group is contained.

Spread-Spectrum Technology

Two types of *spread-spectrum* technology were specified in the original IEEE 802.11 wireless LAN standard ratified in 1997:

- Frequency-hopping spread spectrum (FHSS)
- Direct-sequence spread spectrum (DSSS)

These spread-spectrum technologies communicate in the 2.4 GHz ISM frequency range. There are advantages and disadvantages to each of these spread-spectrum types.

Spread-spectrum technologies take the digital information generated by a computer (ones and zeros) and, through the use of modulation technologies, send it across the air between devices using radio frequency (RF).

In order for devices to communicate effectively and understand one another, they must be using the same spread-spectrum and modulation technology. This would be analogous to two people trying to talk with each other. If the two people don't know the same language, they will not be able to understand each other and a conversation could not take place.

Frequency-Hopping Spread Spectrum

Frequency-hopping spread spectrum (FHSS) is used in a variety of devices in computer technology and communications. FHSS was used by many early adopters of wireless networking, including computers, barcode scanners, and other handheld or portable devices. Although defined in the original IEEE 802.11 standard, this technology is considered "legacy" (out of date) in IEEE 802.11 wireless networking. However, FHSS is still common today in many devices such as cordless telephones and IEEE 802.15 wireless personal area networks (WPANs), including Bluetooth mice, cameras, phones, wireless headsets, and some older wireless LAN technology devices. Bluetooth technology using FHSS is comparatively slower than newer IEEE 802.11 wireless communications.

FHSS operates by sending small amounts of information such as digital data across the entire 2.4 GHz ISM band. As the name implies, this technology changes the frequency ("hops") constantly in a specific sequence or hopping pattern and remains on a frequency for a specified amount of time known as the dwell time. The dwell time value will depend on the local regulatory domain where the device is used. In the United States, for example, the Federal Communications Commission allows a maximum dwell time of 400 milliseconds. A transmitter and receiver will be synchronized with the same hopping sequence, therefore allowing the devices to communicate.

The data rate for IEEE 802.11 FHSS is only 1 and 2 Mbps, which is considered slow by modern computer applications. However, the data rate is more than adequate for some applications. For example, various wireless devices in retail and manufacturing used FHSS in handheld scanners and other portable technology for many years. The cost of upgrading these devices to support higher data rates was prohibitive and unnecessary in many cases, and so until recently they were still used in such environments. Figure 5.6 illustrates what FHSS would look like if you could see the RF hopping through the band.

FIGURE 5.6   FHSS hops the entire 2.4 GHz ISM band.

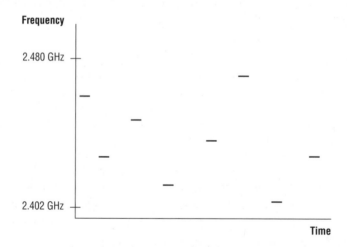

For Sales Personnel

FHSS use in IEEE 802.11 wireless networking is considered legacy and is rarely if at all supported. Therefore, if a customer wishes to purchase any FHSS wireless LAN equipment, they should be directed to the proper upgrade path for a more current and supported solution.

> **For Technical Support Personnel**
>
> There may be some legacy IEEE 802.11 wireless networking FHSS devices in operation in various industries today. For whatever reason these are still in use, it is important to understand that replacement devices will be very difficult to find, if they can be found at all. It is best to consider the appropriate upgrade path for a more current and supported solution.

802.11 Direct-Sequence Spread Spectrum

Direct-sequence spread spectrum (DSSS) is a spread-spectrum technology used with wireless LANs and defined by the original IEEE 802.11 standard. Like FHSS, DSSS supports data rates of 1 and 2 Mbps and is considered slow by today's computer networking requirements.

DSSS uses special techniques to transmit digital data (ones and zeros) across the air using radio frequency (RF). This is accomplished by modulating or modifying the radio frequency characteristics such as phase, amplitude, and frequency (see Chapter 6, "Radio Frequency Fundamentals for Wireless LAN Technology").

In addition to modulation, DSSS uses technology known as a *spreading code* to provide redundancy of the digital data as it traverses through the air. The spreading code transmits information on multiple *subcarriers*, and the redundancy helps the receiver detect transmission errors due to interference. Subcarriers are smaller segments of the radio frequency channel that is in use. This spreading of information across the 22 MHz–wide channel is what helps makes DSSS resilient to interference. This spreading code technology allows the receiver to determine if a single bit of digital data (symbol) received is a binary 0 or binary 1. Depending on the data rate, the transmitter and receiver understand the spreading code in use and therefore are able to communicate.

An example of a coding technique is Barker code. Barker code is used as the spreading code for DSSS at the data rates of 1 and 2 Mbps. IEEE 802.11 wireless LANs can use this 11 "chip" spreading code for communications. Each digital data bit (binary 1 or 0) is combined with the set Barker code through what is called an exclusive OR (XOR) process. XOR is a way of combining binary data bits in digital electronics. The result then spreads the binary 0 or 1 over a 22 MHz wide channel, helping to make it resilient to radio frequency interference. Since both the transmitter and receiver understand the same code, they would be able to determine the information that was sent across the air.

DSSS operates within a range of RF frequency also known as a *channel*. The channel is defined by its center frequency; that is, Channel 1 is 2.412 GHz on center, Channel 2 is 2.417 GHz on center, and so on. Each channel in the 2.4 GHz ISM band is separated by 5 MHz on center. Unlike narrowband communication, which operates on a single narrow frequency, a DSSS channel is 22 MHz wide and is one of 14 channels in the 2.4 GHz to 2.5 GHz ISM band. The country and location of the device will determine which of the 14 channels are available for use in that specific area.

Figure 5.7 shows that channel 6 is 22 MHz wide in the ISM unlicensed RF band.

FIGURE 5.7   DSSS is limited to a 22 MHz–wide channel in the 2.4 GHz ISM band. Each channel for DSSS is 5 MHz on center.

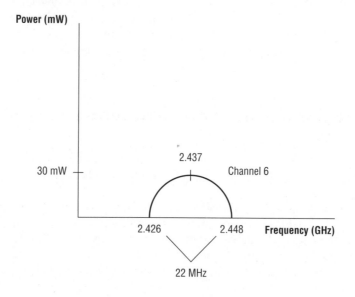

 FHSS and DSSS both operate in the same frequency range. If devices that use both technologies are occupying the same physical area, the devices may encounter some interference. Therefore, RF interference may occur from either IEEE 802.11 wireless LAN devices using the same channel or non-IEEE 802.11 wireless LAN devices that are using the same RF channel. This includes anything wireless that does not use IEEE 802.11 technology but is operating in the same frequency range, such as 2.4 GHz wireless cameras, 2-way radios or radio monitors, and even microwave ovens.

802.11b High Rate/Direct-Sequence Spread Spectrum

High rate/direct-sequence spread spectrum (HR/DSSS) is defined in the IEEE *802.11b* amendment to the IEEE 802.11 standard. HR/DSSS (802.11b) introduced higher data rates of 5.5 and 11 Mbps. At the time this amendment was released, because of the higher data rates this technology helped fuel the acceleration of IEEE standards based on wireless LAN technology. The desire for 802.11 technology grew as the availability became greater and the cost decreased.

Like DSSS, HR/DSSS uses one of fourteen 22 MHz wide channels to transmit and receive digital computer data. The main difference between these two technologies is that HR/DSSS supports higher data rates of 5.5 Mbps and 11 Mbps.

HR/DSSS (802.11b) also uses a different spreading code or an encoding technique than DSSS. HR/DSSS uses complementary code keying (CCK) for transmitting data at 5.5 and 11 Mbps. The detailed operation of CCK is beyond the scope of this book.

IEEE 802.11 DSSS and HR/DSSS Channels

DSSS and HR/DSSS operate in the 2.4 GHz industrial, scientific, and medical (ISM) license free band. This band has 14 available channels. Depending on the country and location, all 14 channels may not be available. Table 5.1 shows the 14 available channels in the 2.4 GHz ISM band for a few different countries.

TABLE 5.1   14 available channels in 2.4 GHz ISM band

Channel	Frequency (GHz)	Americas	EMEA	Israel*	China	Japan
1	2.412	✓	✓	✓	✓	✓
2	2.417	✓	✓	✓	✓	✓
3	2.422	✓	✓	✓	✓	✓
4	2.427	✓	✓	✓	✓	✓
5	2.432	✓	✓	✓	✓	✓
6	2.437	✓	✓	✓	✓	✓
7	2.442	✓	✓	✓	✓	✓
8	2.447	✓	✓	✓	✓	✓
9	2.452	✓	✓	✓	✓	✓
10	2.457	✓	✓	✓	✓	✓
11	2.462	✓	✓	✓	✓	✓
12	2.467		✓	✓		✓
13	2.472		✓	✓		✓
14	2.484					✓

* Israel allows channels 1–13 indoors, but outdoors only 5–13.

Figure 5.8 shows the 14 available channels and the amount of overlap in the 2.4 GHz ISM band.

FIGURE 5.8   The 2.4 GHz ISM band allows 14 channels.

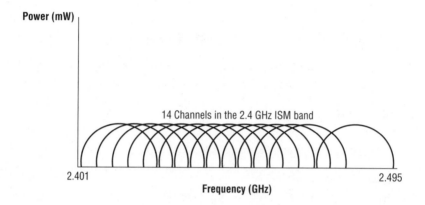

Of these 14 channels, mathematically there are only 3 adjacent nonoverlapping channels, with the exception of channel 14. According to the IEEE 802.11-2012 standard, "Channel 14 shall be designated specifically for operation in Japan." Channel 14 is separated by 12 MHz on center from Channel 13, whereas Channels 1–13 are separated by 5 MHz on center of each channel. There are 3 MHz of separation where the radio frequency of one channel ends and the next adjacent nonoverlapping channel begins. For example, Channel 1 and Channel 6 are adjacent nonoverlapping channels. Channel 1 ends at 2.423 GHz and Channel 6 begins at 2.426 GHz. Mathematically this is a separation of 3 MHz. This means that three access points can be co-located in the same physical space without overlapping channel interference. However, there is still theoretically a small amount of overlapping RF or harmonics between these two channels. This small level of overlap is not large enough to cause any real interference issues. Figure 5.9 illustrates 3 of the first 14 channels that do not overlap in the 2.4 GHz ISM band.

Each DSSS channel is 22 MHz wide. Using spread-spectrum technology, a 22 MHz–wide channel helps add resiliency to interference for data transmissions and gives the capability to move large amounts of data with a small amount of power. Some early IEEE 802.11 devices included barcode scanners, and they worked with limited battery life. Using a spreading technology instead of narrowband technology helped to conserve battery life and increased the use of IEEE 802.11 devices as a whole.

FIGURE 5.9   3 Nonoverlapping channels possible in the 2.4 GHz ISM band

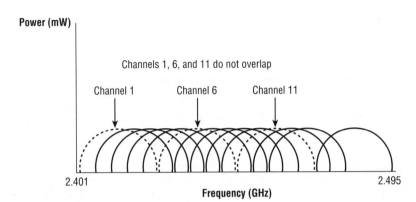

IEEE 802.11g Extended Rate Physical

The IEEE 802.11g amendment was released in 2003 and introduced technology that allowed for higher data rates for devices and operation in the 2.4 GHz ISM band. The objective of this amendment was to allow for these higher data rates (up to 54 Mbps) using orthogonal frequency division multiplexing (OFDM) and still maintain backward compatibility with existing 802.11b technology and devices. This technology, known as Extended Rate Physical (ERP), builds on the data rates of 1, 2 Mbps DSSS (802.11) and 5.5, 11 Mbps HR/DSSS (802.11b). The 802.11g amendment addresses several compatibility operation modes:

- ERP-DSSS/CCK

- ERP-OFDM

- ERP-PBCC (Optional)

- DSSS-OFDM (Optional)

The *802.11g* amendment required support for ERP-DSSS/CCK and ERP-OFDM. This allowed for both the 802.11b data rates of 1, 2, 5.5, and 11 Mbps and the new OFDM data rates of 6, 9 ,12, 18, 24, 36, 48, and 54 Mbps. Manufacturers of wireless LAN equipment implement this in various ways. In a graphical user interface, there may be a drop-down menu that allows a user to select a specific operation mode such as mixed mode, b/g mode, b-only mode, and so on. Another possibility is to select the individual data rates using radio buttons. For manufacturers that provide a command-line interface (CLI) option, the appropriate commands would need to be executed in order to enable or disable the desired data rates. Figure 5.10 illustrates an example of how manufacturers allow a user to select the ERP operation mode on an access point.

FIGURE 5.10   Selecting an operation mode on an IEEE 802.11b/g Cisco/Linksys access point

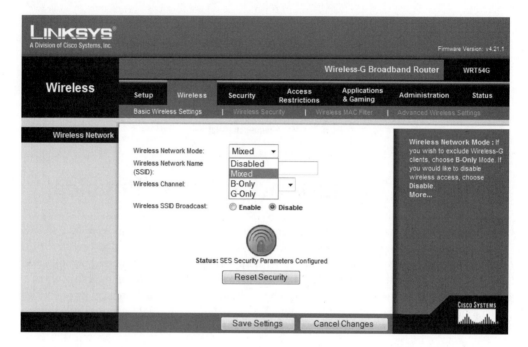

IEEE 802.11n High Throughput

The IEEE 802.11n amendment was ratified in September 2009. This new high throughput (HT) physical layer (PHY) technology is based on the OFDM (PHY) in Clause 17 (802.11a) PHY. 802.11n HT allows extensibility of up to four spatial streams, using a channel width of 20 MHz. Also, transmission using one to four spatial streams is defined for operation in 20/40 MHz channel width mode. This technology is capable of supporting data rates up to 600 Mbps using four spatial streams with a 20/40 MHz channel. IEEE 802.11n HT provides features that can support a throughput of 100 Mbps and greater. Other optional features on both the transmit and receive sides include:

- HT-greenfield format
- Short guard interval (GI), 400 ns

- Transmit beamforming (TxBF)
- Space–time block coding (STBC)

The *802.11n* amendment allows for operation in both the 2.4 GHz ISM and 5 GHz UNII bands with either 20 MHz or 40 MHz wide channels. Although 40 MHz wide channels are allowed in the 2.4 GHz ISM band, best practices recommend against it. Using a 40 MHz channel in this band would only equate to a single channel without any channel overlap.

It is important to understand the difference between data rate and throughput. Data rates are what a station is capable of exchanging information, whereas throughput is the rate at which the information is actually moving. Data rate and throughput are compared in more detail in Chapter 8, "WLAN Terminology and Technology."

IEEE 802.11a, 802.11g and 802.11n Orthogonal Frequency Division Multiplexing

OFDM is used by the IEEE 802.11a (OFDM), IEEE 802.11g Extended Rate Physical Orthogonal Frequency Division Multiplexing (ERP-OFDM), and IEEE 802.11n High Throughput (HT-OFDM) amendments to the IEEE 802.11 standard. OFDM allows for much higher data rate transfers than DSSS and HR/DSSS, up to 54 Mbps for 802.11a and 802.11g and potentially up to 600 Mbps for 802.11n.

Orthogonal frequency division multiplexing (OFDM) is a technology designed to transmit many signals simultaneously over one transmission path in a shared medium and is used in wireless and other transmission systems. Every signal travels within its own unique frequency subcarrier (a separate signal carried on a main RF transmission). *802.11a* and 802.11g OFDM distributes computer data over 52 subcarriers equally spaced apart, and 4 of the 52 subcarriers do not carry data and are used as pilot channels. 802.11n allows for 56 subcarriers of which 52 are usable for data with a 20 MHz wide channel and 114 subcarriers, of which 108 are usable for data with a 40 MHz wide channel. Having many subcarriers allows for high data rates in wireless LAN IEEE 802.11a and IEEE 802.11g devices. 802.11n devices (HT-OFDM) may use a MIMO technology known as spatial multiplexing (SM), which uses several radio chains to transmit different pieces of the same information simultaneously, greatly increasing throughput. In addition to high data rates, OFDM helps provide resiliency to interference from other wireless devices.

IEEE 802.11a, 802.11g, and 802.11n OFDM Channels

OFDM functions in either the 2.4 GHz ISM or the 5 GHz UNII bands. The channel width is smaller than DSSS or HR/DSSS. The width of an OFDM channel is only 20 MHz compared to 22 MHz for DSSS. Figure 5.11 shows a representation of a 20 MHz–wide OFDM channel.

FIGURE 5.11   OFDM transmit spectral mask for 20 MHz transmission

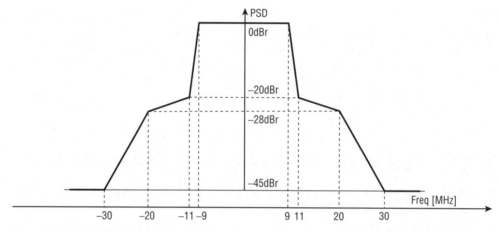

Image provided by IEEE Std 802.11™-2012

Like DSSS, when OFDM is used in the 2.4 GHz ISM band there are only three non-overlapping adjacent channels for use. This will limit the use of bonded channels (20/40 MHz wide channels) in IEEE 802.11n (HT-OFDM) deployments that are located in the same radio frequency physical area. In the 5 GHz Unlicensed National Information Infrastructure (UNII) bands, the channel spacing is such that there is no overlap. The frequency range used will determine how many nonoverlapping channels are available for use. In the lower and upper UNII bands, 4 non-overlapping channels are available. The middle UNII band has 15 nonoverlapping channels available. All UNII band channels are 20 MHz wide and separated by 20 MHz from the center frequencies of each channel. Certain regulatory domains, including the United States Federal Communication Commission (FCC) and the European Telecommunications Standards Institute (ETSI), require the use of dynamic frequency selection (DFS) support for wireless devices such as access points that operate in the middle 5 GHz (5.250 GHz–5.725 GHz) UNII band. DFS will allow an access point to change the radio frequency channel it is operating on in order to avoid interfering with certain type of radar systems. Table 5.2 shows the 23 available channels, center frequency, and channel number in the 5 GHz UNII band. Also displayed is a single 5 GHz ISM channel that is available by some regulatory agencies for use with wireless networking.

TABLE 5.2   5 GHz UNII Band Channels

Regulatory domain	Frequency band (GHz)	Frequency center (GHz)	Channel number
Americas/EMEA (4 channels)	5.150–5.250	5.180	36
		5.200	40
		5.220	44
		5.240	48
Americas/EMEA (4 channels)	5.250–5.350	5.260	52
		5.280	56
		5.300	60
		5.320	64
Americas/EMEA (11 channels)	5.470–5.725	5.500	100
		5.520	104
		5.540	108
		5.560	112
		5.580	116
		5.600	120
		5.620	124
		5.640	128
		5.660	132
		5.680	136
		5.700	140
Americas/EMEA (4 channels)	5.725–5.825	5.745	149
		5.765	153
		5.785	157
		5.805	161
ISM	5.725–5.850	5.825	165

Some regulatory agencies allow the use of a 5.8GHz ISM band (5.725–5.850 GHz) for wireless networking. This frequency range is specified in the IEEE 802.11-2012 Standard. This channel does not overlap the upper UNII band channels. The use of this ISM frequency range is regulated separately with some similarities to the 2.4 GHz ISM band and allows for the use of more devices such as cordless telephones.

IEEE 802.11n Multiple Input/Multiple Output Technology

Multiple input/multiple output (MIMO) is a technology used by IEEE 802.11n devices. MIMO technology potentially has data rates up to 600 Mbps. Currently, devices using MIMO technology are capable of data rates of up to 300–450 Mbps. MIMO provides users with a better overall experience for data, voice, and video communications with throughput up to five times more than current 802.11 a/g, *single input/single output (SISO)* networks.

SISO is the most basic wireless antenna technology used in a wireless LAN system. One antenna is used at the transmitter to transmit data, and one antenna is used at the receiver to receive the data. Some SISO systems support a technology known as diversity, which uses two antennas with a single radio. Diversity technology will help to lessen the effects of multipath, which is caused by reflections. Diversity and multipath are discussed in more detail in Chapter 7, "WLAN Antennas and Accessories." Coverage is more predictable and consistent with MIMO networks because devices using this technology are able to utilize reflected signals, which are a problem for wireless networks using other WLAN technologies.

MIMO also allows 802.11n networks better throughput than DSSS or OFDM-based networks at the same distance. IEEE 802.11n MIMO-based networks offer backward compatibility with 802.11a/b/g networks and devices in both the 2.4 GHz ISM and the 5 GHz UNII bands, allowing for deployments to continue using their existing hardware.

Some of the benefits of 802.11n MIMO networks include throughput, reliability, and predictability:

- Five times more throughput

  Enhanced file transfer and download speeds for large files

- Twice as reliable

  Lower latency for mobile communications

- Twice as predictable

- More consistent coverage and throughput for mobile applications

Unlike IEEE 802.11b (HR/DSSS) and IEEE 802.11a/g (OFDM) access points, MIMO access points use multiple radios with multiple antennas. The multiple radio chains and some additional intelligence are what give 802.11n MIMO access points the capability to process reflected signals. Since MIMO works with both the 2.4 GHz ISM and the 5 GHZ UNII bands, a dual-band IEEE 802.11n MIMO access point will have up to six radio chains—three for 2.4 GHz and three for 5 GHz—and six antennas (one for each radio) for data rates of up to 450 Mbps. Figure 5.12 shows that MIMO uses multiple radio chains and multiple antennas to transmit and receive data.

802.11n systems use MIMO technology; they have more receivers and are much more sensitive than the average 802.11a or 802.11g radio. The following techniques are what allow for better performance and much higher data rates (currently up to 450 Mbps with $3 \times 3 \times 3$ MIMO and eventually up to 600 Mbps with $4 \times 4 \times 4$ MIMO):

- Maximal ratio combining (MRC)

- Transmit beam forming (sometimes abbreviated TxBF)
- Spatial multiplexing (sometimes abbreviated SM)

FIGURE 5.12   MIMO hardware uses separate radio chains for each band and one antenna for each radio.

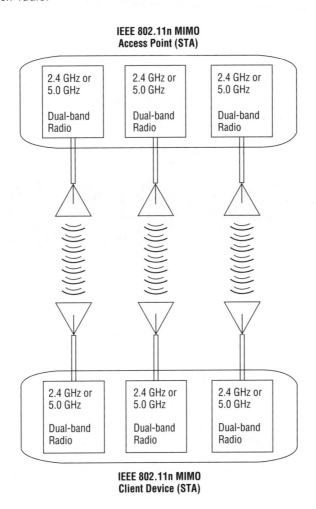

802.11a/b/g networks are known as single input/single output (SISO) systems, which means that performance can degrade as a result of multipath, poor reception because of obstacles, and RF interference sources. 802.11n MIMO networks can take advantage of multipath to help increase throughput at a given range, providing much higher throughput at the same range.

MIMO Channels

As mentioned earlier in this chapter, IEEE 802.11n MIMO networks can operate in both the 2.4 GHz ISM and 5 GHz UNII bands and are capable of either 20 or 20/40 MHz–wide channels. Even while operating in 20/40 MHz channel width mode, many frames are still transmitted with a 20 MHz channel width. The 20 and 20/40 MHz channel widths are defined by the IEEE for transmission of OFDM modulated data. As you would expect, wider channels mean more data can be transmitted over the RF medium simultaneously. Therefore, wider channels allow higher data throughput. Think of this like cars traveling on a two-lane or a four-lane highway. A 20 MHz–wide channel can be looked at as the two-lane highway and a 40 MHz wide channel the four-lane highway. More cars can pass through four lanes in the same amount of time than can pass through two lanes. Figure 5.13 illustrates this point.

FIGURE 5.13   More lanes, more cars—wider channels, more data

A 40 MHz wide channel is like moving from 2 to 4 lanes.

Image provided www.cwnp.com

The 20 MHz or 20/40 MHz channels can be used in either the 2.4 GHz or 5 GHz frequency ranges. Because of the limited amount of frequency space in the 2.4 GHz ISM band, there is only one 20/40 MHz–wide channel without any adjacent-channel overlap. Figure 5.14 shows a 40 MHz wide channel as specified in the 802.11n amendment.

Although most enterprise-grade access points support bonded (20/40 MHz wide) channels, there are still some wireless client devices, both new and legacy, that do not support this technology. To achieve the higher data rates that IEEE 802.11n offers, the client and the access point must both support the newer technologies. If the wireless client device does not support the bonded channels, the access point will be able to adapt, allowing for coexistence.

FIGURE 5.14   OFDM transmit spectral mask for 40 MHz transmission

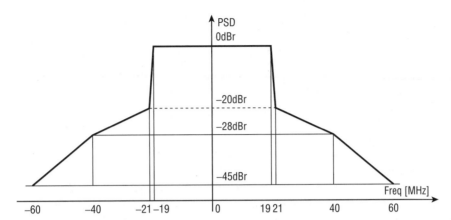

Co-location of IEEE 802.11b HR/DSSS and IEEE 802.11a/g/n OFDM Systems

Now we will look at the co-location of different 802.11a/b/g/n devices. One thing to understand is that some consider 802.11b systems to be legacy devices that are on the verge of becoming obsolete. However, this may not be the case in all installations. Mostly because of legacy hardware and depending on the type of WLAN installation (typically public guest networks and the retail environment), support for 802.11b networks may still be required. Additionally, the latest revision of the 802.11 standard (IEEE 802.11-2012) still addresses this technology, and therefore it is important to understand the implications of co-location of 802.11b devices.

All IEEE-based wireless LANs can be *co-located*—that is, they can function in the same RF space. The technologies that the devices use determine how well they work together. Both HR/DSSS (802.11b) and ERP-OFDM (802.11g/n) networks operate in the 2.4 GHz frequency range ISM band. 802.11g-compliant devices are backward-compatible with 802.11b-compliant devices. However, this backward compatibility comes at a price: reduced data throughput. Because of protection mechanisms, ERP-OFDM devices used in 802.11g will suffer in performance when an HR/DSSS device is in the same radio or hearing range of the ERP-OFDM device.

HR/DSSS and ERP-OFDM systems have many common features:

- Both operate in the 2.4 GHz ISM band.

- Both have three nonoverlapping channels.

- Both are subject to interference from other devices operating in the same frequency range.

HR/DSSS and ERP-OFDM (802.11b-compliant and 802.11g-compliant) devices are backward-compatible. ERP-OFDM is rated at 6, 9, 12, 18, 24, 36, 48, and 54 Mbps. Actual throughput in an environment relatively free of interference will be about 15 to 20 Mbps. If a DSSS or HR/DSSS device is introduced in the radio range of the ERP-OFDM device, the throughput will decrease significantly because of protection mechanisms. How much of an impact this makes depends on many factors in the environment. Typically, the decrease in throughput is about 25 percent to 30 percent. It is important to understand that this is not just limited to a single wireless access point or the basic service area. If an 802.11g access point can "hear" another 802.11g access point on the same radio frequency channel that is in ERP protection mode, that access point will also enter a protection mode state. This is known as what some call the "ripple effect."

Just as co-location of 802.11b/g/n EPR-OFDM systems needs to be taken into consideration, the same holds true with 802.11a/n OFDM systems. The real difference is the frequency band that 802.11a/n systems operate in. As mentioned earlier in this chapter, 802.11 devices operate in the 5 GHz UNII band. The IEEE 802.11n High Throughput (HT) amendment to the standard addresses different protection mechanisms. This is because 802.11n devices can operate in both the 2.4 GHz ISM and 5 GHZ UNII bands. Therefore, an 802.11n access point will need to allow 802.11a devices to utilize the network along with 802.11n devices, both types in the 5 GHz UNII band.

802.11a OFDM and 802.11n HT-OFDM systems have several common features:

- Both operate in the 5 GHz UNII band.

- Both have up to 23 nonoverlapping channels (depending on the regulatory agency).

- Both are subject to interference from other devices operating in the same frequency range.

802.11n HT networks offer various protection mechanisms to ensure interoperability and co-location.

OFDM and HT-OFDM (802.11n-compliant and 802.11a-compliant) devices are backward-compatible. OFDM is rated at 6, 9, 12, 18, 24, 36, 48, and 54 Mbps. Actual throughput in an environment relatively free of interference may be a little higher than an 802.11g environment, about 18 to 22 Mbps. Networks that operate in the 5 GHz UNII band are not subject to co-location issues with DSSS or HR/DSSS, because they operate in different frequency ranges. The 802.11n amendment introduced a new concept called the *modulation and coding scheme* (MCS). This is a different way to represent the data rates that are available with 802.11n technology. Previously, the IEEE 802.11 standard and amendments specified data rates as individual values—1 Mbps, 2 Mbps, 5.5 Mbps, and 11 Mbps in IEEE 802.11b technology, for example. The IEEE 802.11n amendment to the standard now refers to this as the modulation and coding scheme (MCS). This is because depending on the technology enabled or used, a single MCS may support multiple data rates. For example an MCS Index 7 will support either 65.0 Mbps or 72.2 Mbps, depending on whether short guard interval is enabled.

As mentioned earlier in this chapter, 802.11n devices have a maximum data rate or MCS of up to 600 Mbps. However, most technologies available at the time of this writing offer maximum data rates of 300–450 Mbps. Just as devices that operate in the 2.4 GHz ISM band must be able to coexist, devices that operate in the 5 GHz band must be able to coexist as well. Co-location of 802.11a/n devices is possible through the use of additional protection mechanisms. ERP and HT protection mechanisms will be discussed in more detail in Chapter 8. Figure 5.15 illustrates co-location of various 802.11 technologies.

FIGURE 5.15   Co-location of various IEEE 802.11 devices/technologies

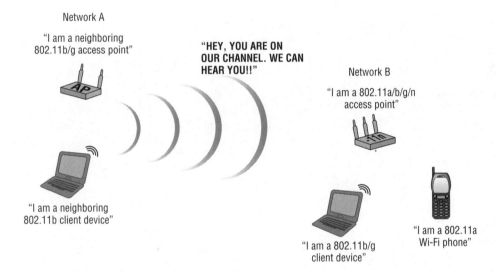

Adjacent-Channel and Co-channel Interference

Adjacent-channel and *co-channel* interference (two or more RF signals interacting with each other and causing a degradation of performance) is a concern in the design, development, and deployment of IEEE 802.11-based wireless networks. Another term used for this type of interference is "co-channel cooperation." This is because the wireless devices are contending to use the medium rather than just being seen as radio frequency noise to each other. This type of interference will have an impact on the amount of actual throughput between devices over a wireless network. As mentioned earlier, the 2.4 GHz ISM band has only three non-overlapping channels. Careful channel planning is required when designing or implementing a wireless network. This type of planning will minimize issues such as poor throughput as a result of adjacent and co-channel interference. *Channel planning* involves designing wireless networks so that overlapping RF cells are on different (nonoverlapping) channels—for example, channels 1, 6, and 11 in the 2.4 GHz ISM band. This will help optimize performance and minimize degradation of throughput because of adjacent and co-channel *interference*.

With the advancements in 802.11 technologies, channel planning is more "automated" by the use of spectrum management technology and the IEEE 802.11 standard. However, it is still important to understand the concept of channel planning. RF energy propagates in several directions simultaneously. A well-designed wireless network will account for a three-dimensional propagation. In other words, in a three-story building, the RF from an access point on the second floor building may pass through to the first and third floors; therefore, interference could be an issue if the network is not planned properly. Figure 5.16 illustrates overlapping channel interference with two access points in the 2.4 GHz ISM band.

FIGURE 5.16 Two access points on overlapping channels as seen in MetaGeeks Chanalyzer Pro. The "Data" access point is on channel 5 and the "Guest" access point is on channel 8 in the 2.4 GHz ISM band.

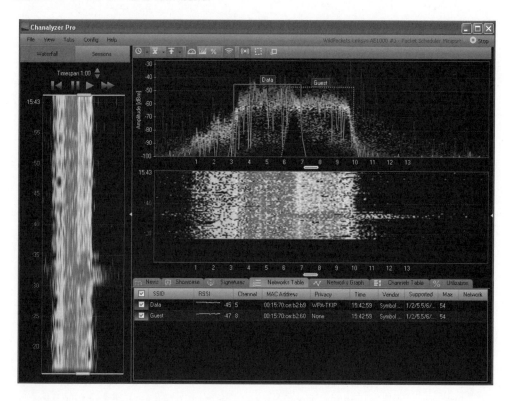

WLAN/WPAN Coexistence

Wireless personal networks (WPANs) typically consist of portable devices such as personal digital assistants (PDAs), cell phones, headsets, computer keyboards, mice, and now tablet devices. In Chapter 6, we will discuss how the performance of IEEE 802.11 wireless LANs can be affected when co-located with WPAN devices. The IEEE 802.15 standard addresses WPANs and includes Bluetooth and Zigbee networks. Bluetooth is one of the most popular

WPAN network technologies and operates in the 2.4 GHz ISM band using frequency hopping spread spectrum (FHSS) technology.

Early Bluetooth devices can cause significant interference while operating in close proximity to IEEE 802.11 wireless LANs. Bluetooth was designed to hop at a rate of 1,600 times per second across the entire 2.4 GHz band, potentially causing significant interference with 802.11 wireless networks. Newer versions of Bluetooth use adaptive frequency hopping (AFH) and thus are less likely to interfere with IEEE 802.11 wireless networks, even though they still operate in the 2.4 GHz ISM band. Devices that use adaptive frequency hopping will try to avoid using the same frequencies, decreasing the chance of interference. Since these devices operate at low power, most WPANs communicate in small, close-range, peer-to-peer networks.

 Real World Scenario

Taking Adjacent-Channel and Co-channel Interference into Consideration When Planning a New Wireless Network

As a wireless network engineer, you are tasked with deploying a new wireless network in a multi-tenant building. The area to be covered is approximately 50,000 square feet.

Your first task, prior to the procurement and deployment of the wireless network, should be to perform a spectrum analysis and site survey. This will help determine the best frequency and channels to be used in the new deployment.

A survey reveals that tenants on the floors above and below where the new deployment is to be installed are also using IEEE 802.11b/g/n networks, with many access points on channels across the entire 2.4 GHz ISM band. A situation such as this may make the deployment difficult. There is an increased possibility of adjacent-channel and co-channel interference.

Upon further evaluation, it is determined that the lower band of the 5 GHz UNII band is not being utilized to any large extent. Since this is a new deployment, you have the opportunity to purchase equipment that will utilize the 5 GHz UNII band as well as the 2.4 GHz ISM band. Some of the questions that need to be evaluated include:

- Are any devices limited to 802.11b/g/n capability only?

- Does the network require backward compatibility to 802.11b/g/n?

- Does the network need to support guest access?

- What impact would a network using only 5 GHz 802.11a/n have on the business?

- Is it possible to utilize both frequency bands in this deployment to maximize throughput while limiting interference?

These are just some questions that need to be considered prior to making any final decisions on the network to be installed and the equipment to be purchased.

Summary

In this chapter, we looked at access methods used to get data from one device to another when multiple users share the medium. These access methods consist of collision avoidance and collision detection:

- CSMA/CD—Carrier Sense Multiple Access/Collision Detection
- CSMA/CA—Carrier Sense Multiple Access/Collision Avoidance

WLANs have no way of detecting collisions; therefore they must use collision avoidance or CSMA/CA. Wireless LANs use half-duplex communication, which decreases the performance of the communication data transfer.

This chapter also looked at the spread-spectrum and physical layer (PHY) technologies used with WLANs and the differences among them. The IEEE standard and various amendments use different spread-spectrum and PHY technologies and unlicensed radio spectrum allowing for data rates up to 450 Mbps. These physical layer (PHY) technologies include:

- FHSS—For data rates of 1 and 2 Mbps
- DSSS—For data rates of 1 and 2 Mbps
- HR/DSSS—For data rates of 5.5 and 11 Mbps
- OFDM—For data rates up to 54 Mbps
- HT-OFDM—Currently for data rates of up to 450 Mbps, eventually may be up to 600 Mbps

Even though FHSS is considered legacy technology for WLANs, it is still important to understand some of the basics of this technology since it is still in use today in many industries in various types of wireless technologies, including IEEE 802.15 personal area networking (PAN), Bluetooth, and cordless telephones.

We looked at the different channel sets used with 802.11 wireless networks and some of the co-location considerations.

Some of the physical layer technologies discussed in this chapter are more susceptible to interference than others. This can make installations in some industries challenging. We also looked at co-location of HR/DSSS and ERP-OFDM systems and some of the challenges it can pose. Finally, this chapter discussed the coexistence of WPANs and WLANs and the various devices and technology that can cause interference when working in the same RF space.

Exam Essentials

Know the frequencies and channels HR/DSSS and OFDM use.   Understand that HR/DSSS operates in the 2.4 GHz ISM band and can use 14 channels depending on the country/location used. Know that ERP-OFDM is used for the 2.4 GHz band, OFDM is used for the 5 GHz band, and HT-OFDM in either band. Know the four UNII bands OFDM uses for the 802.11a and 802.11n amendments. Understand that MIMO systems may use HT-OFDM and can operate in either the 2.4 GHz ISM band or the 5 GHz UNII band.

Understand the difference between CSMA/CD and CSMA/CA.   Know the differences between access methods and that they can either detect or attempt to avoid collisions. Also understand that IEEE 802.11 wireless networks use distributed coordination function (DCF) mode as a contention method to send data.

Know the differences among various physical layer wireless technologies, such as FHSS, DSSS, HR/DSSS, OFDM, ERP-OFDM, and MIMO.   The uses of physical layer technologies vary depending on radio frequency, applications, and desired data rates. Understand the standard or amendment each physical layer technology uses as well as advantages and disadvantages of each, including co-location and interference.

Understand that co-location of WPAN and WLAN devices may cause interference and affect performance.   WPAN and WLAN devices might be co-located in the same RF space. Know the potential impact of co-location on performance and other factors. Some WPAN and WLAN devices use the same frequency and spread-spectrum technology. Understand that this can cause interference.

Review Questions

1. IEEE 802.11a/b/g/n devices use what type of communication?

    A. Half diplex

    B. Full diplex

    C. Half duplex

    D. Full duplex

2. HR/DSSS devices operate in which frequency range?

    A. 2.400 GHz ISM

    B. 5.250 GHz UNII

    C. 5.350 GHz UNII

    D. 5.750 GHz UNII

    E. 5.725 GHz ISM

3. How many access points can be co-located without channel reuse in the same radio frequency area to maximize total system throughput while minimizing RF interference in an IEEE 802.11g network?

    A. Two

    B. Three

    C. Four

    D. Six

4. Devices compliant with which amendment to the IEEE standard use multiple radio chains and multiple antennas?

    A. 802.11a

    B. 802.11b

    C. 802.11g

    D. 802.11n

5. What technology is used to send WLAN data over a wireless medium using many subcarrier frequencies?

    A. Wireless broadband

    B. Narrowband

    C. Spread-spectrum

    D. Spectral masking

    E. Wideband

6. Which two channels could be used so that the access points do not interfere with each other in an 802.11b wireless network? (Choose three.)

    A. Channel 1 and channel 5

    B. Channel 3 and channel 9

    C. Channel 6 and channel 11

    D. Channel 2 and channel 8

    E. Channel 4 and channel 7

7. Which network access method attempts to avoid collisions?

    A. CSMA/CA

    B. CSMA/CD

    C. CSMA/CR

    D. CSMA/DSSS

8. DSSS uses which spreading code at 1 Mbps?

    A. Barker

    B. CCK

    C. DBPSK

    D. DQPSK

9. FM radio stations use what type of RF communication?

    A. High power, narrow bandwidth

    B. High power, wide bandwidth

    C. Low power, narrow bandwidth

    D. Low power, wide bandwidth

10. An HR/DSSS channel is how wide?

    A. 1 MHz

    B. 20 MHz

    C. 22 MHz

    D. 40 MHz

11. Bluetooth devices use _____, which can potentially cause interference with WLANs.

    A. Bluetooth spread spectrum (BTSS)

    B. Orthogonal frequency division multiplexing (OFDM)

    C. Direct-sequence spread spectrum (DSSS)

    D. Frequency hopping spread spectrum (FHSS)

12. OFDM that is used with 802.11a and 802.11g stations (STA) supports a maximum data rate of _____ Mbps.

    A. 11

    B. 22

    C. 33

    D. 54

13. Which wireless LAN technology can be used to obtain the highest data transfer rate possible?

    A. DSSS

    B. Ethernet

    C. HT-OFDM

    D. OFDM

14. Which frequency ranges are used in an IEEE 802.11a-compliant wireless LAN? (Choose two.)

    A. 900 MHz ISM range

    B. 2.40 GHz ISM range

    C. 5.25 GHz UNII range

    D. 5.35 GHz UNII range

15. Stations (STA) operating in which two IEEE 802.11 amendments are interoperable?

    A. 802.11 and 802.11a

    B. 802.11a and 802.11b

    C. 802.11a and 802.11g

    D. 802.11b and 802.11g

16. Without any regulatory domain taken into consideration, the 2.4 GHz frequency range allows for how many channels using 802.11b?

    A. 3

    B. 6

    C. 11

    D. 14

17. FHSS uses which communication method to exchange data?

    A. 1 MHz–wide subcarriers

    B. 20 MHz–wide subcarriers

    C. 22 MHz–wide subcarriers

    D. 40 MHz–wide subcarriers

18. What is the maximum data rate of HR/DSSS 802.11b devices?

    A. 5.5 Mbps

    B. 11 Mbps

    C. 24 Mbps

    D. 54 Mbps

19. What IEEE 802.11 PHY technology specifies that frequencies change regularly while transmitting and receiving data?

    A. DSSS

    B. OFDM

    C. FHSS

    D. ERP-OFDM

20. Which wireless LAN technology in wireless networking uses the effects of multipath to provide data rates of 600 Mbps?

    A. OFDM

    B. HR/DSSS

    C. HT/DSSS

    D. MIMO

Chapter 6

Radio Frequency Fundamentals for Wireless LAN Technology

THE FOLLOWING CWTS EXAM OBJECTIVES ARE COVERED IN THIS CHAPTER:

✓ **1.2 Define basic characteristics of and concepts relating to Wi-Fi technology**

- Range, coverage, and capacity
- Frequencies/channels used
- Channel reuse and co-location

✓ **3.1 Define the basic concepts and units of RF measurements, identify when they are used, and perform basic unit conversion**

- Watt (W) and milliwatt (mW)
- Decibel (dB)
- dBm
- dBi
- RSSI
- SNR

✓ **3.2 Identify and explain RF signal characteristics**

- Frequency
- Wavelength
- Amplitude
- Phase

✓ **3.3 Identify factors which affect the range and rate of RF transmissions**

- Line-of-sight requirements
- Interference (Wi-Fi and non-Wi-Fi)
- Environmental factors, including building materials
- Free space path loss

Radio frequency (RF) plays an essential role in wireless LAN technology. Radio waves are passed through the air (which is the medium) and are used to get information from one wireless device to another. Technically speaking, with respect to wireless LANs, RF consists of high-frequency alternating current (AC) signals passing over a copper cable connected to an antenna. The antenna then transforms the signal into radio waves that propagate through the air from a transmitter to a receiver.

Unlike wired devices, which use physical cable to communicate, wireless LANs use the radio waves and the air to communicate. This chapter will discuss the characteristics of RF and explain how far a radio signal will travel depending on various factors, the area covered by the radio frequency propagation, and some of the factors determining how many clients or devices can use the RF signals for data communications. This chapter will also explain the range and speed of RF transmissions. Range (how far radio waves will travel) and speed can be affected by several environmental conditions or behaviors, such as reflection and refraction. Additionally, this chapter will examine some of the conditions that affect the transmission of information across the air, including interference.

Understanding RF units of measure such as watts (W), milliwatts (mW), and decibels (dB) is important to RF work, just as understanding denominations of money such as U.S. dollars and British pounds is an important part of daily life. We will discuss RF signal measurements, including received signal strength indicator (RSSI) and signal-to-noise ratio (SNR).

Understanding Radio Frequency

Radio frequency (RF) waves are used in a wide range of communications, including radio, television, cordless phones, wireless LANs, and satellite communications. RF is around everyone and everything, and comes in many forms. RF energy is emitted from the numerous devices that use it for various types of communications. For the most part, it is invisible to humans. There is so much of it around, that if you could actually see RF, it would probably scare you. Don't let it scare you, however, because the amount of regulated RF power transmitted from the devices used in daily lives is harmless. Figure 6.1 shows some of the many ways RF is used. Studies have shown that the amount of power emitted from many of these devices, such as cordless telephones or wireless network adapters, will not cause any physical harm if the devices are manufactured not to exceed the maximum regulated power allowed for the device.

FIGURE 6.1 Radio frequency is used in many different devices to provide wireless communications.

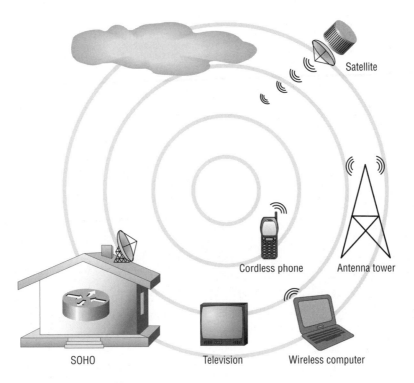

Remember, RF consists of high-frequency alternating current (AC) signals passing over a copper cable connected to an antenna. This antenna will then transform the received signal into radio waves that propagate through the air. The most basic AC signal is a sine wave. This wave is the result of an electrical current varying uniformly in voltage over a period of time. This sine wave cycle will repeat a specific number of times (cycles) over a period of one second. The number of cycles per second will result in different frequencies. Frequency is discussed later in this section. Figure 6.2 shows a basic sine wave.

Successful radio transmissions consist of a minimum of two components, a *transmitter* and *receiver* (see Figure 6.3). With IEEE 802.11 wireless networking, a wireless station can transmit and receive and is known as a transceiver. These two components work together: For every radio transmitter there must be one or more radio receivers. It is important to understand the basic characteristics of radio frequency transmissions. These characteristics work together to form alternating current signals and include the wavelength, frequency, amplitude, and phase. The antenna will transform these signals into radio waves that travel through the air carrying information from the transmitter to the receiver. This is accomplished in different ways depending on the wireless technology in use. This theory will be discussed more in Chapter 7, "WLAN Antennas and Accessories."

FIGURE 6.2 A basic sine wave, one complete cycle varying voltage at a point in time

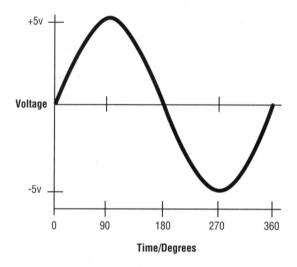

FIGURE 6.3 RF transmitter and receiver. In a wireless LAN, the transmitter and receiver could be an access point and client device.

Wavelength in Wireless LANs

The *wavelength* is the distance of one complete cycle or one oscillation of an AC signal. Wavelength is typically identified by the Greek symbol lambda (λ), which is used in formulas for calculations. This distance is usually measured in centimeters or inches. Figure 6.4 shows an example of a wavelength.

IEEE 802.11 wireless LANs use both the 2.4 GHz and 5 GHz unlicensed frequency ranges for transmission. The IEEE 802.11-2012 Standard also specifies some additional frequency ranges in which wireless LANs can operate. Although these do not fall under the "unlicensed" category, 4.9 GHz public safety and 3.650 GHz (IEEE 802.11y amendment) can also be used for IEEE 802.11 wireless LAN communications. Table 6.1 lists some examples of wavelengths for IEEE 802.11 wireless LANs using unlicensed frequencies.

FIGURE 6.4 The wavelength is the distance of one complete cycle, measured in centimeters or inches.

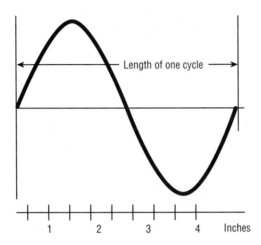

2.437 GHz channel 6 ISM band, approximately 4.85 inches

TABLE 6.1 Typical radio transmission wavelengths for WLANs

RF Channel	Frequency (GHz)	Length (in)	Length (cm)
6	2.437 GHz	4.85 in	12.31 cm
40	5.200 GHz	2.27 in	5.77 cm
153	5.765 GHz	2.05 in	5.20 cm

Frequency in Wireless LANs

Frequency is defined as the number of complete cycles in one second. Low frequencies correspond to long waves and high frequencies to short waves, so the higher the frequency, the shorter the wavelength (range). In formulas, frequency is typically identified by the lower-case letter *f*.

Figure 6.5 shows an example of frequency.

FIGURE 6.5   Frequency is the number of complete cycles in 1 second.

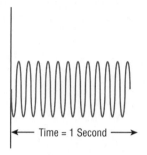

← Time = 1 Second →

How Far Can a Signal Travel?

A few years back, 900 MHz cordless telephones were very popular. Cordless telephones were introduced in the 1970s, and in 1990 the FCC opened the 900 MHz range for these telephones. With a 900 MHz phone you could hypothetically go up to 500 feet away from the cordless phone's base station before losing the signal and no longer being able to make a phone call. In the past few years, higher-frequency phones have increased in popularity. After upgrading to a 2.4 GHz phone, you may have noticed you can only get about 250 feet away (half the distance compared to a 900 MHz phone) in the same environment before losing the signal. This is because the 2.4 GHz wavelength is about half the distance of a 900 MHz wavelength, assuming both phones are operating at the same output power. With 5.8 GHz cordless telephones now becoming available, the range will be still less, assuming the same amount of transmit power.

IEEE 802.11 wireless LANs work in several unlicensed frequency ranges. The unlicensed ranges used for WLANs are 2.4 GHz to 2.5 GHz and 5.15 GHz to 5.875 GHz. There are some areas in the 5.15 GHz to 5.875 GHz range that are not used for standards-based wireless networking.

Amplitude in Wireless LANs

From a wireless LAN perspective, the *amplitude* is the strength or the amount of power of an RF signal. This is calculated from the height (in a two-dimensional view), on the Y axis of the sine wave, representing the voltage. As mentioned earlier, a basic sine wave is a change in voltage over a period of time. Using a formula, the voltage at the peak of the signal can be used to calculate the amount of RF power. So an increase in amplitude is equal to an increase in RF power. An increase in power is also known as *gain*. Conversely, any decrease in amplitude will be a decrease in power. A decrease in power is also known as *loss*. If a transmitter outputs a certain amount of RF power—for example, 100 mW—it has a specific amplitude of some value. As this signal travels through an RF cable, it will have a specific level of loss based on the cable in use, resulting in attenuation. Therefore the result will be less amplitude at the end of the cable due to the loss value of the cable.

Figure 6.6 shows two signals operating at the same frequency with different amplitudes. The signal with the higher amplitude (Signal A) is more powerful than the signal with the lower amplitude (Signal B).

FIGURE 6.6   Two signals at the same frequency with different amplitudes

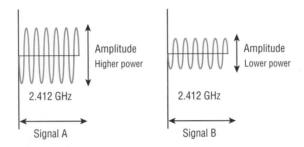

Phase in Wireless LANs

Phase is the difference in degrees at a particular point in the time of a cycle, measured from some arbitrary zero and expressed as an angle. For example, if a second sine wave starts a quarter of a wavelength after the first sine wave, it is considered to be 90° out of phase with the first sine wave. Figure 6.7 shows an example of the phase relationship between two AC signals. Two radio waves that have the same frequency but start at different times are known to have a phase difference and are considered out of phase with one another. The amount of the phase difference is typically measured in degrees ranging from 0° to 360°.

Waves that arrive at a receiver out of phase will experience some level of distortion, which will cause corruption. This is known as multipath. The difference in time of arrival of the main signal and a reflected signal that causes the multipath problem is called the delay spread. If two waves arrive at a receiver 180° out of phase, this will usually result in a cancellation effect or nullify the two signals. Conversely, two waves that arrive in phase are additive, and this will result in an increase in signal strength known as upfade. Keep in mind, however, that the amplitude of the waves that experience the upfade effect will never be higher than the wave transmitted.

Radio Frequency Used in Wireless LANs

As discussed in Chapter 2, "Introduction to Wireless Local Area Networking," RF *spectrum* is governed by local regulatory agencies. The country where the RF is used determines the regulations, such as frequency use and maximum power. Table 6.2 illustrates examples of local RF regulations.

FIGURE 6.7 Phase is the difference in degrees between two signals.

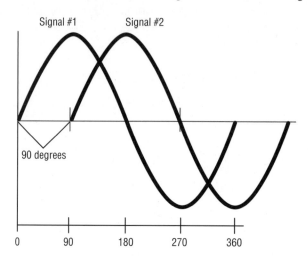

TABLE 6.2 Local RF regulations

Location	Regulation
Canada	ISC RSS-210
China	RRL/MIC Notice 2003-13
Europe (ETSI)	ETS 300.328ETS 301.893
Israel	MOC
Japan (MKK)	TELEC 33BTELEC ARIB STD-T71
Singapore	IDA/TS SSS Issue 1
Taiwan	PDT
United States	FCC (47 CFR) Part 15C, Section 15.247FCC (47 CFR) Part 15C, Section 15.407

U.S. (FCC) Unlicensed Frequency Bands

In the United States, the Federal Communications Commission (FCC) is the local regulatory agency responsible for regulating licensed and unlicensed radio spectrum. Listed are the unlicensed RF bands available in the United States for use with wireless communications:

- *ISM*: Industrial, Scientific, and Medical

- 902–928 MHz (not specified for use with standards-based IEEE 802.11 wireless networks)

- 2.400–2.4835 GHz

- 5.725–5.875 GHz

> The 5.725–5.875 GHz ISM band is used in the United States for a single channel (Channel 165). The IEEE 802.11-2012 Standard reads "The OFDM PHY shall not operate in frequency bands not allocated by a regulatory body in its operational region. Regulatory requirements for a given frequency band are set by the regulatory authority responsible for spectrum management in a given geographic region or domain." The FCC in the United States allows this frequency for IEEE 802.11 wireless networking.

- *UNII*: Unlicensed National Information Infrastructure

  - 5.15–5.25 GHz: UNII-1, lower

  - 5.25–5.35 GHz: UNII-2, lower middle

  - 5.470–5.725 GHz: UNII-2e, upper middle

  - 5.725–5.825 GHz: UNII-3, upper

The IEEE 802.11 standard addresses the 2.4 GHz ISM band and the 5 GHz UNII bands. In the United States, the 2.4 GHz ISM band allows for 11 of 14 total channels to be used for wireless LAN communications. The 5 GHz UNII band consists of four bands utilizing four frequency ranges: UNII-1, the lower band; UNII-2 and UNII-2e, the middle bands; and UNII-3, the upper band. Table 6.3 shows unlicensed frequency bands and channels used by IEEE 802.11 wireless LAN technology. Keep in mind that the 5.725-5.875 GHz ISM band is used where allowed by the regulatory agency.

TABLE 6.3   IEEE 802.11 frequency and channel allocations

Band	Frequency	Number of channels
ISM	2.400–2.4835 GHz	14
UNII-1	5.150–5.250 GHz	4
UNII-2	5.250–5.350 GHz	4
UNII-2e	5.470–5.725 GHz	11
UNII-3	5.725–5.825 GHz	4
ISM	5.725–5.8750 GHz	1

A chart of the United States frequency allocations is available from the National Telecommunications and Information Administration. To view this chart, visit www.ntia.doc.gov/osmhome/allochrt.pdf.

Radio Frequency Channels

As you have seen, radio frequency is divided into bands. These bands can be further separated into *channels*. A channel is a smaller allocation of the radio frequency band. One familiar application in which this is accomplished is television. Until over-the-air television became available in digital format, television was allocated certain frequency ranges. Common television channels operated in the very high frequency (VHF) band—for example, channels 2 through 13 operated from 54 through 216 MHz. This frequency range was divided into 12 channels, allowing optimal use of the frequency range for the application, in this case television signals.

A viewer can change channels on a television to watch different programs running simultaneously. However, only one program can be viewed at any one time depending on which channel is currently selected. (Picture-in-picture televisions can show two or more channels at once on the screen, but each picture is still being received on a different channel.)

Wireless LANs use channels in the same way. Certain unlicensed frequency ranges are allocated for wireless networking, and those frequency ranges are subdivided into channels. In order for a transmitter and receiver to communicate with one another, they must be on the same channel. The 2.4 GHz ISM band has a total of 14 channels available for wireless networking. The locale where they are used will determine which of the 14 channels can be legally used for wireless networking. In the United States, IEEE 802.11b/g/n wireless networks use 11 of the 14 channels available in the 2.4 GHz ISM band. Each of these 11 channels for DSSS or HR/DSSS is 22 MHz wide, and for OFDM it is 20 MHz wide. Understand that these channels are further defined by their center frequency; for example, Channel 1 in the 2.4 GHz ISM band has the center frequency at 2.412 GHz. Simple mathematics show there will be overlap in order to accommodate all of the 20 MHz or 22 MHz wide channels in this frequency range. Table 6.4 shows the 14 available channels in the 2.4 GHz range.

TABLE 6.4 Channels in the 2.4 GHz ISM band

Channel Number	Frequency in Hz	United States	Europe	Israel*	China	Japan
1	2.412	✓	✓	✓	✓	✓
2	2.417	✓	✓	✓	✓	✓
3	2.422	✓	✓	✓	✓	✓

Channel Number	Frequency in Hz	United States	Europe	Israel*	China	Japan
4	2.427	✓	✓	✓	✓	✓
5	2.432	✓	✓	✓	✓	✓
6	2.437	✓	✓	✓	✓	✓
7	2.442	✓	✓	✓	✓	✓
8	2.447	✓	✓	✓	✓	✓
9	2.452	✓	✓	✓	✓	✓
10	2.457	✓	✓	✓	✓	✓
11	2.462	✓	✓	✓	✓	✓
12	2.467		✓	✓		✓
13	2.472		✓	✓		✓
14	2.484					✓

*Israel allows only channels 5–13 outdoors, but 1–13 indoors.

The 5 GHz UNII band is also divided into channels. This band consists of four bands—lower, lower middle, upper middle, and upper. These four bands consist of four different frequency ranges. Since there are fewer channels in the same amount of space, channels in the UNII band do not overlap. In the 5 GHz UNII band, channels are 20 MHz wide. Table 6.5 shows the 5 GHz UNII band for the FCC and ETSI locales.

TABLE 6.5   Channels in the 5 GHz bands

Locale	Frequency	Number of channels
Americas/EMEA	UNII-1 band (5.15–5.25)	4
Americas/EMEA	UNII-2 band (5.25–5.35)	4
Americas/EMEA	UNII-2e band (5.470–5.725)	11
Americas/EMEA (with restrictions)	UNII-3 band (5.725–5.825)	4
Americas	ISM (5.725–5.850)	1

Radio Frequency Range

Range for wireless LANs is based on the wavelength or distance of a single cycle. The higher the frequency, the shorter the range of the signal and the lower the frequency, the longer the range of the signal. At the same output power level, a 2.4 GHz signal will travel almost twice as far as a 5 GHz signal. If a network design is planning to use dual-band access points, range will need to be considered to ensure proper coverage for both the 2.4 GHz ISM and 5 GHz UNII bands. A wireless site survey will help determine the usable range an access point will produce. A survey can involve physically walking around the proposed space and/or predictive modeling using one of many software programs. This process is discussed further in Chapter 11, "Performing an RF Wireless LAN Site Survey."

Wireless LAN Coverage and Capacity

Coverage and capacity are two key factors to take into consideration when designing and implementing an IEEE 802.11 wireless LAN. During the design phase of an IEEE 802.3 wired network, the design engineer will take capacity into account, verifying and validating that there are enough capacity switches, ports, and so on for the user base of the network. The same is true for a wireless network. The number of devices/users connected to an access point is something that needs to be carefully considered. The fact that wireless networks use a shared medium is an issue because the more devices that are connected to an access point, the lower the performance may be, depending on what the devices are doing. This capacity consideration will ensure satisfied end users and excellent network performance—proof of a successful wireless network design and deployment.

In wireless networks, coverage also needs to be considered. Coverage is determined by the RF cell size. In IEEE 802.11 wireless networks, a cell is the area of RF coverage of the transmitter, in most cases an access point. Depending on implementation, wide coverage or large cell size may not be the best solution. A large space covered by a single access point could result in less than adequate network performance based on factors such as the users' distance from the access point. The farther away from an access point, the less throughput a device or user will experience. If users will be scattered throughout a large space, it may be best to have several access points covering the space to allow for optimal performance.

 The term *cell* has several different meanings depending on the context. In the world of IEEE 802.11 wireless networks, a cell is the radio coverage area for a transmitter such as an access point or a client device.

Wireless LAN Coverage

The term *coverage* has different meanings depending on the context in which it used. For example, if you buy a gallon of paint, the label will specify the approximate coverage area in square feet. If one gallon of paint covers 300 sq ft and the room you wish to paint is 900 sq ft, simple math shows at least three gallons of paint would be needed to effectively cover the room.

The concept is similar in IEEE 802.11 wireless networking. However, unlike with paint, there is no simple rule that determines how much space an access point will cover with the RF energy it is transmitting. This coverage will depend on many factors, some of which include:

- Physical size of the area
- Bandwidth-intensive software applications in use or hardware applications may negatively impact the performance therefore requiring smaller RF coverage cells
- Obstacles, including building materials and propagation (the way radio waves spread through an area)
- Radio frequency range
- WLAN hardware in use (this affects coverage because higher frequencies, such as 5 GHz, do not travel as far as lower frequencies, such as 2.4 GHz)
- Transmitter output power

You might initially assume that you want the RF signal to propagate over the largest area possible. But this may not be the best solution. A very large cell may allow too many devices to connect to a single access point, causing a decrease in overall performance. For those client devices connected at a greater distance, the performance will be lower than for stations closer to the access point. Figure 6.8 shows a large coverage area, approximately 11,250 sq ft (1,046 sq m) covered with a single access point. This is an example of too large an area for a single access point.

FIGURE 6.8 Wide coverage with only a single access point is not recommended.

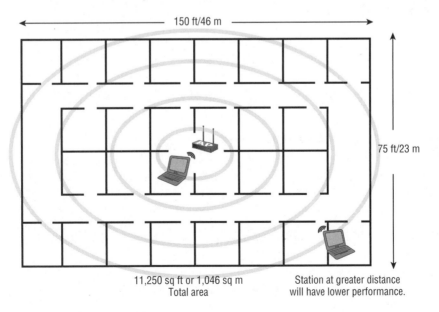

150 ft/46 m

75 ft/23 m

11,250 sq ft or 1,046 sq m
Total area

Station at greater distance
will have lower performance.

Physical Size of the Area

Rarely, if at all, will a manufacturer of enterprise-grade IEEE 802.11 wireless LAN hardware commit to the amount of area an access point will cover. There are too many variables to take into consideration, which makes it difficult to specify an exact number. However, some manufacturers may estimate the effective range of the device or access point. A site survey of the area will help determine the coverage area of an access point. A manual survey will allow for testing to verify the distance a signal will travel. A predictive site survey will model the environment and determine the signal propagation. This concept will be discussed further in Chapter 11.

Applications in Use

The application types in use—either software or hardware—can affect the bandwidth of an access point. If the devices connected to an access point use bandwidth-intensive applications such as a computer-aided design/computer-aided manufacturing (CAD/CAM) application, it could result in poor throughput for all devices or users connected to that access point. This is another example where more access points, with each covering a smaller area, could be a better solution than a single access point covering a large area. Multiple access points could allow the high-bandwidth users to be separated from other parts of the network, increasing overall performance of the network.

Obstacles, Building Materials, Propagation, and RF Range

Obstacles in an area, including building materials such as walls, doors, windows, and furnishings, as well as the physical properties of these obstacles—thickness of the walls and doors, density of the windows, and type of furnishings—can also affect coverage. The radio frequency used—either 2.4 GHz or 5 GHz—will determine how well a signal will propagate and handle an obstacle.

For example, a wall made from sheetrock or drywall materials may have an attenuation value of about 3 dB to 4 dB, whereas a wall made of concrete may have an attenuation value of about 12 dB. Therefore the sheetrock wall would have less impact on the RF propagation than the concrete wall. Partitions, walls, and other obstacles will also determine the coverage pattern of an access point because of the way RF behaves as it travels through the air. Behaviors of RF will be discussed later in this chapter in the section "Environment: RF Behavior."

WLAN Hardware and Output Power

The wireless LAN hardware in use can also have an impact on the coverage area. Examples include the antenna type, antenna orientation, and gain of the antenna. The higher the gain of an antenna, the greater the coverage area; conversely, the lower the gain of an antenna, the smaller the coverage area. The polarization of an antenna (horizontal vs. vertical) will also have an effect on the coverage area because of the different shapes of the radiation patterns. The output power of the transmitter or access point will also have an effect on coverage. The higher the output power, the greater distance a signal will propagate. A higher power signal will provide more coverage. Most enterprise-grade access points provide the capability to control or adjust the output power.

Wireless LAN Capacity

One definition of *capacity* is the maximum amount that can be received or contained. An example of this would be an elevator in a building. Typically an elevator will have a maximum number of people or amount of weight it can hold; this is usually stated on a panel within the elevator. To ensure safety, the elevator may have a safety mechanism to prevent overloading. Likewise, a restaurant has a certain number of chairs to hold customers; therefore, they would have a maximum capacity of customers who can be served at any one time. Does this mean that when a restaurant fills its seats to capacity, the doors close and no other customers can enter the building? Not necessarily. In some cases, a restaurant could have customers standing and waiting to be seated.

Just as an elevator or a restaurant has a limited number of people they can accommodate comfortably, wireless access points also have a limited number of devices they can handle, known as capacity. The capacity of an access point is how many devices or users the AP can service effectively, offering the best performance. This capacity depends on several factors, including:

- Software and hardware applications in use
- Desired throughput or performance
- Number of devices/users

The following sections discuss how these factors affect the capacity of an access point.

 Real World Scenario

What Happens When an Access Point Is Overloaded?

If the capacity of a single access point has exceeded the maximum number of users or devices based on the performance metrics, access points may need to be added. If a wireless network is installed correctly, an access point will not be overloaded with an excessive number of users. An overloaded access point will result in poor performance and therefore unhappy users.

To understand why, look back at the restaurant example. If a restaurant seats 20 customers and all 20 seats are taken, the restaurant has reached its capacity. Let's say the restaurant is short-staffed because two servers did not show up for work. The servers who did show up will have to work extra hard to handle the customers. This may cause delays in service because the servers need to handle more than their normal number of tables. The delays may result in unhappy customers.

The same is true for wireless access points. If a wireless access point has reached its capacity, it could get overloaded. This would result in its taking longer to handle any individual request for access. The delays may result in unhappy users. Therefore this situation could justify adding another access point in the area to handle the additional users. Just as a restaurant will not close its doors when all seats are taken, an access point will continue to accept users to connect unless restrictions such as load balancing are implemented.

Software and Hardware Applications in Use

The software and hardware applications in use may affect the capacity of an access point. Some applications are more bandwidth-intensive than others. For example, word processing applications may not require much bandwidth whereas database or CAD/CAM applications may require much more bandwidth than other applications. If high-bandwidth applications are in use, the contention among the connected users will increase because they are using a shared medium (air and RF). Therefore performance will potentially be reduced for all users connected to the access point. The access point is providing the same amount of bandwidth, but the overall performance has been decreased for the connected users because the software applications are all using a lot of bandwidth.

The use of Voice over Wireless LAN (VoWLAN) technology is also increasing steadily in many wireless network deployments. This is an example of a hardware application. Voice technology on wireless networks is subject to latency. Therefore, depending on the number of voice client devices connecting to an access point, the network must be carefully planned. Capacity planning and quality of service (QoS) features are important when it comes to deploying voice technology on wireless networks.

Desired Throughput or Performance

The desired *throughput* or performance can also affect capacity. A large number of users connected to an access point using a bandwidth-intensive application will cause poor performance. Therefore, it may be necessary to limit the capacity to a certain number of users to give the connected users the best performance possible. Any software application that is bandwidth-intensive, such as CAD/CAM, streaming video, or File Transfer Protocol (FTP) downloads, can have an effect on overall performance. One way to help resolve this would be to use load balancing to limit the number of users that can connect to an access point. Another way would be to create RF cells with smaller coverage and add more access points.

Number of Devices/Users

The number of devices or users in an area will also affect the access point capacity. A single access point covering a large area will potentially allow for a large number of devices connecting to the access point. For example, an office of 8,000 sq ft may consist of 100 people, each with their own wireless device. This is an example of wide coverage and large capacity. The software applications in use on the wireless network will have an impact on the overall performance. If all 100 devices connected are using a CAD/CAM application, which is a bandwidth-intensive application, the overall performance will be poor because this type of application requires a lot of resources. Therefore more access points, each covering less space and less capacity, would parlay into better overall performance for all of the users.

Wide coverage in a densely populated area may allow too many devices to connect to a single access point, resulting in poor performance overall. As you learned earlier, wireless LANs use what is known as a shared medium. In other words, all devices users connected to an access point will share the available bandwidth. Too many devices using powerful applications will overload the access point, adding to the poor performance issues. This scenario is considered a capacity issue. In this situation more access points with each AP covering a smaller area and a lower number of devices or less capacity would be a better solution. As you learned in Chapter 4, "Wireless LAN Client Devices," many organizations now have to deal with the "Bring Your Own Device (BYOD)" issue.

In addition to potential problems with technical support and security, wireless LAN capacity is also a major concern. The BYOD expansion of Wi-Fi capable devices is causing a wireless client device density issue within the enterprise market. If a company's corporate policy allows employees to bring their own wireless capable devices, then wireless LAN capacity needs to be carefully evaluated to address this potential issue.

Radio Frequency Channel Reuse and Device Co-location

Earlier in this chapter, it was noted that the 2.4 GHz ISM band has a total of three non-overlapping channels. In the U.S. FCC implementation of this band, the three *nonoverlapping channels* are 1, 6, and 11. This means there must be a separation of five channels in order for them to be considered nonoverlapping. In the 2.4 GHz ISM band, channels are separated by 5 MHz on center. Taking this into consideration, channels must be separated by 25 MHz or greater in order to be considered nonoverlapping (IEEE 802.11-2012, Clause 18). This is calculated from five channels of separation multiplied by 5 MHz on center ($5 \times 5 = 25$). With deployments larger than a few access points, a channel plan may be necessary. A channel plan will minimize the chance of interference caused by two transmitters (access points) set to the same or adjacent overlapping channels.

The IEEE 802.11-2012 Clause 16 (formerly Clause 15 in the IEEE 802.11-1007 Standard) specifies 30 MHz or greater of separation to be considered nonoverlapping: "Adjacent channel rejection is defined between any two channels with ≥ 30 MHz separation in each channel group defined in 16.4.6.3." Keep in mind that this specification is for 802.11 DSSS. For HR/DSSS (IEEE 802.11-2012, Clause 18), channels must be separated by 25 MHz or greater in order to be considered nonoverlapping.

Figure 6.9 illustrates a 2.4 GHz deployment with no channel planning. Users in the areas where the circles overlap will experience interference. This interference will result in lower overall throughput for the connected users because of the Physical layer (PHY) technologies that wireless LANs use. This interference basically has the same effect as collisions in an Ethernet network, resulting in retransmissions of data.

A correct channel plan will implement channel reuse and ensure that overlapping cells will not use overlapping channels. Channel reuse is using non-overlapping channels—for example 1, 6, and 11 in the 2.4 GHz range—in such a way that the overlapping cells are on different RF channels. Figure 6.10 shows a 2.4 GHz deployment utilizing proper channel reuse. Channel reuse may be accomplished by mapping out the access points on a floor plan and minimizing the chances that the RF cells propagated by the access points do not overlap on the same RF channels. This type of channel plan can de done manually or with site survey software applications. Site survey applications will be discussed in more detail in Chapter 11.

FIGURE 6.9   Users of these access points will experience overlapping channel interference in a multichannel architecture because they are all set to the same channel.

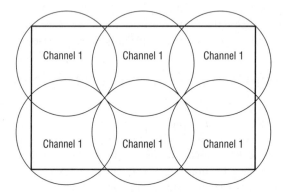

FIGURE 6.10   Co-location of access points with proper channel reuse. Overlapping areas use different channels in a multichannel architecture to prevent interference.

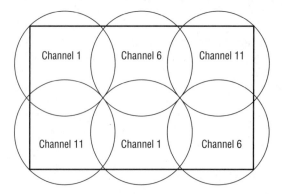

Radio Frequency Range and Speed

How far and fast a radio frequency signal can travel depends on a variety of factors, including line of sight, interference, and the types of materials in the environment. This section discusses these factors.

Line of Sight in Wireless Networking

Radio frequency communication between devices in 802.11 wireless networking uses different types of line of sight. There are two types of line of sight to take into account when planning, designing, and installing wireless networks:

- Visual line of sight
- Direct link radio frequency (RF) line of sight

Visual line of sight is when a transmitter and receiver can "see" each other. In order for wireless networking direct link communication to be successful in an outdoor wireless link, there should be a clear, unobstructed view between the transmitter and receiver. An unobstructed line of sight means few or no obstacles blocking the RF signal between these devices.

In an outdoor wireless LAN installation, direct *RF line of sight* is an unobstructed line between a radio transmitter and receiver. This line will be surrounded by an area of radio frequency transmissions known as the Fresnel zone. The Fresnel zone consists of a number of concentric ellipsoidal volumes that surround the direct RF line of sight between two points, such as an RF transmitter and receiver or two wireless bridges.

In outdoor wireless LAN installations, the RF line of sight, and therefore the radio transmissions between a transmitter and receiver, could be affected if the total area of the Fresnel zone is blocked by more than 40 percent. This blockage can come from a variety of sources, such as trees, buildings, terrain, or other obstacles, including the curvature of the earth over a distance of 7 miles or greater. Figure 6.11 illustrates a Fresnel zone.

FIGURE 6.11   The oval area represents the Fresnel zone RF coverage area between a transmitter and receiver, two wireless bridges.

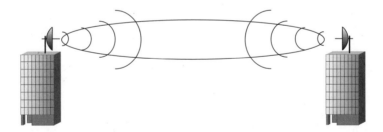

One way to think about line of sight is by the analogy of two people looking at each other. If two people about the same height standing some distance apart are making direct eye contact, they have a good visual line of sight. In addition to being able to see directly in front of them, people have peripheral vision. This peripheral vision gives people the ability to see movement and objects outside of their direct line of sight or direct eye contact. This peripheral vision or side vision is analogous to the Fresnel zone theory.

EXERCISE 6.1

Demonstrating Fresnel Zone and Blockage

Here is one way to demonstrate the Fresnel zone. Focus your eyes at a location on a wall. Make sure there are obstacles or movement off to both left and right sides of your view. Hold your hands down to your sides. Continue to focus your eyes for a minute or so, and then take your right, left, or both hands and slowly raise them from your sides toward the side of your head while blocking your peripheral vision. You'll notice as your hands get closer to the side of your head the view of the objects or movement to the sides will be blocked by your hands. This is an example of a blocked Fresnel zone.

 Sixty percent of the total area of the Fresnel zone must be clear of obstacles in order to have RF line of sight.

Because of the low transmit and receive power and the short distance, a visual line of sight is not required for an indoor wireless LAN deployment. An indoor access point may cover areas that are divided by walls and other obstacles. With this short range and if the radio frequency is able to penetrate the obstacles, wireless communication between a transmitter and a receiver will be successful even when the devices do not have a visual line of sight.

Wi-Fi and Non-Wi-Fi Interference

Interference from a radio frequency point of view occurs when a receiver hears two different signals on the same or close frequency. *Interference* causes received radio frequency signals to be distorted. In wireless LANs, this interference can have a severe impact on the quality of signal received by a wireless device. This distorted or corrupted signal will decrease the amount of data a device can effectively receive, thereby causing less data throughput.

A wireless LAN receiver has similar characteristics to the human ear. Both can hear a range of frequencies. If one person is speaking and a number of people are listening to this speaker, that is analogous to a single transmitter and multiple receivers. If a second person started to speak at the same time, people listening might not be able to understand either speaker. In a sense, they are experiencing interference.

As discussed earlier in this chapter, an IEEE 802.11 wireless network may use the unlicensed 2.4 GHz industrial, scientific, and medical (ISM) band. This band is also used for many other devices, including:

- Cordless phones
- Microwave ovens

- Medical devices
- Industrial devices
- Baby monitors
- Other IEEE 802.11 wireless networks

Because these devices also use radio frequency to operate, and the frequency is in the same unlicensed band as IEEE 802.11 wireless networks, they have the potential to interfere with one another. Although they may coexist in the same RF space, the interference factor needs to be taken into consideration. This can be done as part of the site survey process.

Co-channel and Adjacent Channel Interference

Co-channel or adjacent channel interference occurs when two devices in the same physical area are tuned to close radio frequency channels or the same channel. For example, an access point on channel 1 and another access point on channel 2 in close or hearing range of each other will experience adjacent channel interference. Some of the symptoms of this type of interference are reduced throughput and the equivalent of collisions causing data retransmissions. A new term being used for co-channel interference is "co-channel cooperation," since it is not really interference but rather an increase in the size of the contention domain.

 Co-channel interference is defined as two different radio transmitters using the same frequency. The IEEE 802.11-2012 standard, however, defines interference between channels 1 and 2 as co-channel interference caused by overlapping channels. According to the standard, adjacent channel interference for HR/DSSS and ERP in the 2.4 GHz ISM band is caused by frequencies of greater than or equal to 25 MHz separation, such as channels 1 and 6. The terms *co-channel* and *adjacent* are used loosely in the wireless LAN industry. Please consult specific manufacturers' documentation for their definition. The CWNP program complies with the IEEE standards definition.

Overlapping interference is defined as two devices (such as access points) on the same frequency overlapping one another. For example, two access points in close proximity to each other, one on channel 1 and the other on channel 3, might interfere with each other.

Both adjacent channel interference and co-channel channel interference will cause poor throughput on a wireless network. In a wireless network, co-channel or adjacent channel interference can have the same impact. Figure 6.12 shows that 2.4 GHz ISM band channel 4 and channel 6 overlap.

A properly designed wireless LAN will have overlapping RF cells. Overlapping cells provide continuous coverage for the entire area where the access points are placed. Overlapping cells allow devices to move from one access point to another and maintain a constant connection. A well-designed wireless LAN will also minimize or eliminate overlapping channel interference. This design includes assigning nonoverlapping RF channels to cells that do overlap with each other. In practice, an overlapping cell design will include a 20 to 30 percent overlap to encourage better roaming. Wireless repeaters require a 50 percent overlap to be effective. The frequency in use is determined by how many nonoverlapping channels are available in the band. For example, in the United States, the 2.4 GHz band used for 802.11b/g/n has three nonoverlapping channels—1, 6, and 11. Figure 6.13 shows 2.4 GHz ISM band with three nonoverlapping channels, channels 1, 6, and 11.

FIGURE 6.12   Channel overlap in the 2.4 GHz ISM band

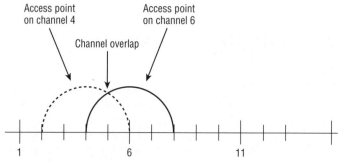

Representation of 2.4 GHz ISM band consisting of 14 channels
Channels 1, 6, and 11 are labeled

FIGURE 6.13   Five channels of separation and 25 MHz of separation between nonoverlapping channels

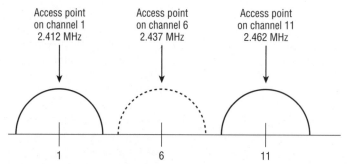

Representation of 2.4 GHz ISM band consisting of 14 channels
Channels 1, 6, 11 are non-overlapping

WLAN/WPAN Interference

The performance of IEEE 802.11 wireless networks can be affected when they are co-located with IEEE 802.15 wireless personal area networks (WPANs). Bluetooth is an example of a wireless personal area network. Like 802.11, Bluetooth devices operate in the

2.4 GHz frequency range and use frequency hopping spread spectrum (FHSS) technology. This functionality in older Bluetooth devices could potentially interfere with IEEE 802.11 wireless networks. Newer versions of Bluetooth that use adaptive frequency hopping (AFH) have less chance of interfering with other wireless networks, including 802.11 wireless networks. Adaptive frequency hopping allows devices such as Bluetooth to adapt to the RF environment by seeking areas of interference and not operating in those specific frequency ranges. This will lessen the chances of 802.15 WPAN devices interfering with 802.11 WLAN devices. This newer technology is proven such that WLAN 802.11 and WPAN 802.15 Bluetooth devices may coexist in the same physical radio chipset.

Environment: RF Behavior

In addition to various types of radio frequency interference, the interaction between RF and the surrounding environment can also affect the performance of IEEE 802.11 wireless networks. RF behavior is the result of environmental conditions, including:

- Reflection
- Refraction
- Diffraction
- Scattering
- Absorption
- Diffusion

Reflection

Reflection occurs when an RF signal bounces off a smooth, nonabsorptive surface such as a table top and changes direction. Reflections can affect indoor wireless LAN installations fairly significantly in certain cases. Depending on the interior of the building—such as the type of walls, floors, or furnishings—there could be a large number of reflected signals. If not properly handled, reflections could cause a decrease in throughput and poor network performance. Figure 6.14 illustrates reflection.

FIGURE 6.14   Radio frequency reflection

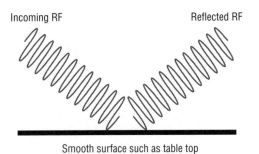

Smooth surface such as table top

Think of a ping-pong game when it comes to reflection. When a ping-pong ball is served or hit, it comes in contact with the table—a smooth, hard surface—and bounces off in a different direction. This is similar to how reflection works with radio frequency.

Refraction

When an RF signal passes between mediums of different densities, it may change speeds and also bend. This behavior of RF is called *refraction*. Glass is an example of material that may cause refraction. When an RF signal comes in contact with an obstacle such as glass, the signal is refracted (bent) as it passes through and some of the signal is lost. The amount of loss depends on the type of glass, its thickness, and other properties. Figure 6.15 shows refraction.

FIGURE 6.15   Radio frequency refraction

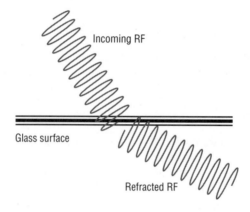

Diffraction

When an RF signal passes an obstacle, the wave changes direction by bending around the obstacle. This RF behavior is called *diffraction*. A building or other tall structure could cause diffraction, as could a column in a large open area or conference hall. Figure 6.16 illustrates diffraction. When the signal bends around a column, building, or other obstacle, the signal weakens, resulting in some level of loss.

FIGURE 6.16 Radio frequency diffraction

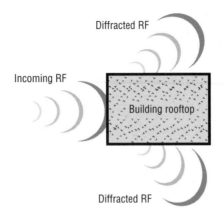

Demonstrating Diffraction: Rock in a Pond

You can demonstrate diffraction by using a pond of still water. Place a large object such as a two-by-four piece of lumber in a pond of still water. After the water settles, try to drop a pebble or small rock off to the side of the piece of lumber. Watch closely and you will see the ripple of the water bend around the lumber, resulting in a diffraction effect.

Scattering

When an RF signal strikes an uneven surface, wavefronts of the signal will reflect off the uneven surface in several directions. This is known as *scattering*. Scattering, illustrated in Figure 6.17, is another form of loss that may severely degrade the RF signal.

FIGURE 6.17 Radio frequency scattering

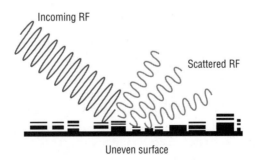

Absorption

When material absorbs an RF signal, no signal penetrates through the material. An example of *absorption* is the human body. The human body has a high water content and will absorb RF signals. This type of absorption can be a problem for wireless network deployments in certain environments. Densely populated areas such as airports and conference halls need to consider absorption when designing a wireless LAN deployment. Figure 6.18 shows absorption.

FIGURE 6.18   Radio frequency absorption

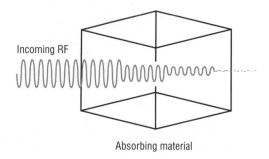

Diffusion

Diffusion occurs when the RF signal naturally widens as it leaves an antenna element. As a result of this widening effect, the transmitted radio frequency signal will decrease in amplitude and be less powerful at any distance from the antenna. This is known as *free space path loss* (FSPL). FSPL is the greatest form of loss factor in a radio frequency link. FSPL is calculated using frequency and distance as variables and entered into a mathematical formula. The receiving antenna is only able to receive a small amount of the transmitted signal because of this widening effect of the diffused signal as it propagates through the air. Any signal that is not received by the intended device is considered loss.

Basic Units of Radio Frequency Measurement

If a person were given a dollar bill, they would be one dollar richer. If this person were given 100 cents, they would still be one dollar richer. From this example, we see 1 dollar = 100 cents and 1 cent = 1/100th of a dollar. One dollar and 100 cents are the same net amount, but a cent and a dollar are different units of currency.

The same is true for radio frequency measures of power. The basic unit of measure for radio frequency is the watt. A wireless access point may be set to an output of 30 mW (milliwatts) of power. A milliwatt is 1/1000 of a watt. Just as in currency cents and dollars are both denominations of money, watts and milliwatts are measurements of RF power. Other units of measurement for RF are dB, dBi, dBd, and dBm.

Absolute Measurements of Radio Frequency Power

The amount of power leaving a wireless access point is one example of an *absolute* measure of power. This is an actual power measurement and not a ratio or a relative value. In other words, this is a measurable amount of power and can be determined with the proper instrument, such as a watt meter. A typical maximum amount of transmit output power from an access point is 100 mW.

The measure of AC power can be calculated using a basic formula. The formula is:

$P = E \times I$

Power (P) equals voltage (E) multiplied by current (I).

A simple example would be to calculate the power from 1 volt and 1 amp. Using the given variables, the formula is:

$P = 1 \text{ volt} \times 1 \text{ amp}$

The answer would be power = 1 watt.

The formula $P = E \times I$ is shown here for reference only to demonstrate the calculation of radio frequency power. You *will not* need to know this formula for the CWTS exam.

Watt (W)

The *watt* (W) is a basic unit of power measurement. It is an absolute value or measurable value. Most wireless networks function in the milliwatt range. Power level in watts is a common measurement in long distance point-to-point and point-to-multipoint connections.

Milliwatt (mW)

One milliwatt (mW) is 1/1000 of a watt. This is a common value used in RF work and IEEE 802.11 wireless LANs. The output power of an access point typically ranges from 1 mW to 100 mW. Most enterprise-grade access points allow you to change the output power. Most SOHO-grade access points have a fixed output power, typically 30 mW. The milliwatt is also an absolute unit of power measurement.

Decibel Relative to a Milliwatt (dBm)

dBm is the power level compared to 1 milliwatt. This is based on a logarithmic function. A good rule to remember is 0 dBm = 1 mW. This value is considered as absolute zero. Using a formula or basic RF calculation rules, you can easily convert any milliwatt value to decibels: 100 mW = 20 dBm, for example.

The dBm is also an absolute unit of power measurement. A dB is an example of a change in power or relative measurement of power where dBm is measured power referenced to 1 milliwatt or an absolute measure of power. The next section discusses relative measurements of power.

Remember, absolute values are measurable values of power such as watt, milliwatt, and decibel milliwatt.

Relative Measurements of Radio Frequency Power

Changes in radio frequency power are known as *relative*. dB and dBi are relative measurements of power. An example would be an RF amplifier. If the input power to an amplifier is 10 mW and the output power is 100 mW, the gain of the amplifier is 10 dB—a change in power.

If the input power to an antenna is 100 mW and the output power is 200 mW, the gain of the antenna is 3 dBi—a change in power. Both of these are examples of changes in power and are known as relative expressions of RF power.

Decibel (dB)

The decibel (*dB*) is a ratio of two different power levels caused by a change in power. Figure 6.19 shows how an amplifier will provide an increase or change in power.

FIGURE 6.19 Output doubled in power from 100 mW to 200 mW from amplifier with a gain or change in power of +3 dB

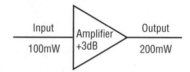

Basic RF Math: The 3s and 10s Rule

This section is beyond the scope of the CWTS exam objectives and is for informational purposes only.

There is a simple way to perform any RF math calculation without having to use logarithms and mathematical formulas. This method is known as the 3s and 10s Rule (or sometimes referred to as the 10s and 3s Rule). If you remember five basic steps, you can perform any RF math calculation. The five basic steps are as follows:

- 0 dBm = 1 mW (starting point)

- Increase by 3 dBm and power in mW doubles or × 2

- Decrease by 3 dBm and power in mW is cut in half or ÷ 2

- Increase by 10 dBm and power in mW is multiplied by 10 or × 10

- Decrease by 10 dBm and power in mW is divided by 10 or ÷ 10

Decibel Isotropic (dBi)

Decibel isotropic (*dBi*) is the unit that represents the gain or increase in signal strength of an antenna. The term *isotropic* in the RF world means energy broadcast equally in all directions in a spherical fashion. An imaginary, perfect antenna is known as an *isotropic radiator*. This is a theoretical concept and is used as a reference and in calculations. dBi will be discussed and used in more detail in Chapter 7. Table 6.6 shows a summary of absolute and relative power measurements.

TABLE 6.6   Absolute and relative measures of power

Absolute power	Relative power
Watt	dB
Milliwatt	dBi
dBm	dBd

Remember, relative values are changes in power from one value to another value. dB, dBi, and dBd measure relative power.

Decibel Dipole (dBd)

The gain of some antennas may be measured in decibel dipole (*dBd*). This unit of measurement refers to the antenna gain with respect to a reference dipole antenna. The gain of most antennas used in wireless LANs is measured in decibel isotropic (dBi); however, some manufacturers may reference the gain of an antenna in dBd. The following simple formula derives the dBi value from the dBd value:

dBi = dBd + 2.14

This formula converts from dBi to dBd:

dBd = dBi – 2.14

 Real World Scenario

dBd vs. dBi

You are a procurement agent working for a manufacturing company. An engineer orders some antennas to be used in a wireless LAN deployment. The part number you received from the engineer on the bill of materials is for antennas that are currently out of stock at your normal supplier. The order has to be placed as soon as possible, but technical support for the vendor is gone for the day and you are not able to get any assistance.

You found what appears to be a reasonable alternative for the requested antennas. However, the gain of the antennas does not exactly match what the engineer documented on the bill of materials. The engineer requested omnidirectional antennas with a gain of 6 dBi. You found what appears to be a comparable alternate with a gain of 6 dBd. It will be necessary for you to determine whether these antennas will work. Not quite understanding the difference, you do some research to determine the difference between dBd and dBi. After searching various websites, you find a formula to convert the two different units:

$$dBi = dBd + 2.14$$

Using your calculator, you enter the value from the specification sheet for the alternate antennas:

$$6 \ dBd + 2.14 = 8.14 \ dBi$$

Unfortunately, the antennas found will not be a good alternate in this example. Back to the drawing board!

Radio Frequency Signal Measurements

It is important to understand the various signal measurements of radio frequency used in wireless LAN technology. Using tools like a wireless adapter client utility or a *spectrum analyzer* will allow you to view different statistics that pertain to a wireless network. Some of these statistics are

- Receive sensitivity
- Radio frequency noise
- Received signal strength indicator (RSSI)
- Signal-to-noise ratio (SNR)

Receive Sensitivity

The basic definition of *receive sensitivity* is the measurable amount of radio frequency signal usable by a receiver. This is also determined by how much radio frequency noise is in the area of the radio receiver. Figure 6.20 shows a wireless adapter client utility that displays statistics, including the strength of signal received.

Radio Frequency Noise

Radio frequency noise is the term for RF signals from sources other than the transmitter and receiver that are in communication. Here is an analogy to help explain. You and a guest are in a crowded open space restaurant for dinner. There are many unrelated conversations occurring at the same time at the various tables throughout the restaurant. If you and your dinner guest momentarily paused in your conversation, you would hear these other conversations, as well as the noise from equipment, telephones, and tables that are being cleared. This would be the restaurant equivalent of radio frequency noise, as shown in Figure 6.21.

FIGURE 6.20   The Orinoco 8494-US IEEE 802.11a/b/g/n USB adapter shows the amount of signal received.

Advanced Status				? X
Network Name (SSID):	Guest	Current Signal Strength:	-65 dBm	Client utility shows a signal strength of −65 dBm
Server Based Authentication:	None	Current Noise Level:	-96 dBm	
Data Encryption:	None	Up Time:	00:11:39	
Authentication Type:	None	802.11b Preamble:		
Message Integrity Check:	None	Current Receive Rate:	108.0 Mbps	
QoS:	WMM	Current Transmit Rate:	108.0 Mbps	
CCKM Authentication:	Off			
Management Frame Protection:	Off	Control Channel:	36	
		Extension Channel:	40	
Associated AP Name:	Unavailable	Control Frequency:	5.180 GHz	
Associated AP IP Address:	Unavailable	Extension Frequency:	5.200 GHz	
Associated AP MAC Address:	00-15-70-C7-C8-80	Channel Set:	United States	
		Channel Width:	20-40	
Power Save Mode:	Normal			
Current Power Level:	13 mW			
Available Power Levels (5 GHz):	50, 40, 25, 20, 13, 10, 9, 8, 7, 6, 5, 4, 3, 2, 1 mW			
Available Power Levels (2.4 GHz):	100, 63, 50, 32, 20, 10, 9, 8, 7, 6, 5, 4, 3, 2, 1 mW		OK	

FIGURE 6.21   Restaurant analogy example of radio frequency noise

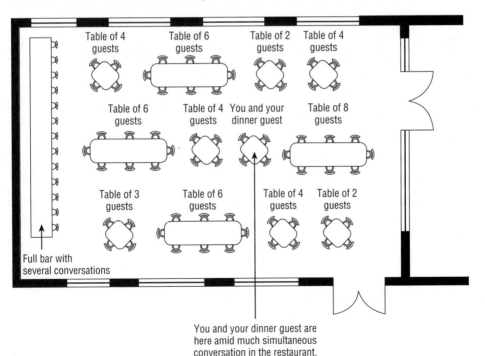

You and your dinner guest are here amid much simultaneous conversation in the restaurant.

In a wireless LAN environment several RF devices may be operating in the same physical space as the wireless transmitter (access point) and receiver (client device). Depending on the level of this radio frequency noise, it may be difficult for the transmitter and receiver to understand each other. In Figure 6.22 a screen capture from a noise analyzer utility shows a wireless basic service set on channel 40 in the 5 GHz UNII-1 band. Also shown is the radio frequency noise floor of about –95 dBm.

FIGURE 6.22 The MetaGeek Chanalyzer Pro software utility shows a noise floor for the tested site of about –95 dBm.

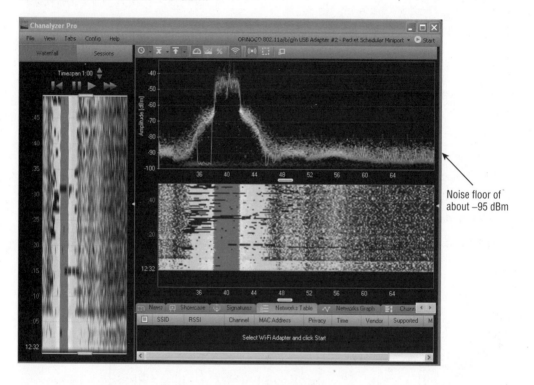

Noise floor of about –95 dBm

Received Signal Strength Indicator (RSSI)

Received signal strength indicator (RSSI) is an arbitrary number assigned by the radio chipset or device manufacturer. There is no standard for this value, and it will not be comparable between devices from different manufacturers. The calculation of the RSSI value is done in a proprietary manner and a wireless device from one manufacturer may indicate different signal strength than that indicated by another, even though they both are receiving the exact same signal and at the same actual amount of radio frequency power. This value is a key determinant of how well the wireless LAN device will perform. How the device is used with the network will determine the required levels of signal for optimal connectivity. Most wireless client device manufacturers allow their chipsets to access the higher data rates as long as they are getting a –70 dB signal or stronger. Wireless VoIP manufacturers recommend deploying so that the client devices can receive a –67 dB or better signal from the access point, a strength that is double the –70 dB required for higher data rate use due to the need for better signaling in QoS communications.

Signal-to-Noise Ratio (SNR)

The *signal-to-noise ratio* (SNR) is the difference between the amount of received signal and the noise floor. Looking back at the restaurant analogy, if you were to continue your conversation and the tables surrounding yours were all speaking at higher volumes, you might not be able to hear your dinner guest very well, because of the amount of noise created in the open area of your table. Looking at this from a wireless LAN perspective, if a client device records a received signal of –85 dBm and the noise floor is –95 dBm, the signal-to-noise ratio will be 10 dB. This value is calculated by subtracting the received signal from the noise. In this case –85 dBm – (–95 dBm) = 10 dB. This would not be an adequate signal-to-noise ratio, because the receiver would have a difficult time determining the difference between the wanted RF signal and the surrounding RF noise. On the other hand, if the received signal is –65 dBm and the noise floor is –95 dBm, then the signal-to-noise ratio will be 30 dB. This value again is calculated by subtracting the received signal from the noise—in this case, –65 dBm – (–95 dBm) = 30 dB. This would be an excellent signal-to-noise ratio because the receiver would easily be able to determine the intended RF signal from the surrounding RF noise. Figure 6.23 illustrates the SNR as seen in a spectrum analyzer tool.

FIGURE 6.23 Graph showing the received signal strength vs. noise floor and the SNR using the Cisco Spectrum Expert spectrum analyzer utility.

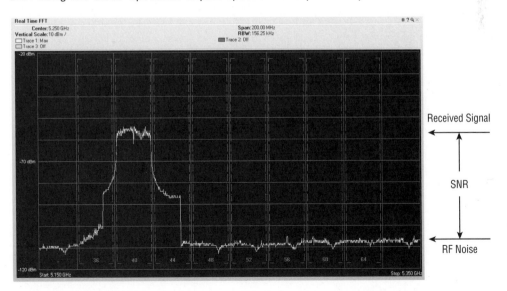

Summary

This chapter explored radio frequency basics and the essential role RF plays in the world of IEEE 802.11 wireless networking. You learned the definition and understanding of RF as it pertains to wireless networking and the basic characteristics or properties of radio frequency such as:

- Wavelength
- Frequency
- Amplitude
- Phase

Then we described devices such as transmitters and receivers and how they communicate. In wireless LAN technology, an example of a transmitter and receiver is an access point and client device. We also discussed the unlicensed RF bands and channels used in the 2.4 GHz ISM and 5 GHz UNII ranges for wireless LAN communications as well as other frequency ranges that may be allowed for use with IEEE 80211 wireless networking depending on the local regulatory agency. Radio frequency coverage and capacity are two important areas that should be considered closely to ensure that a wireless deployment will offer reliable connectivity and perform well for the user base.

We then explained correct channel reuse to minimize interference from the co-location of access points. This chapter explored cause and effect of co-channel interference from sources other than wireless networks operating in the ISM and UNII bands. We also looked at RF behaviors such as reflection, refraction, and absorption, and the impact of building materials and the effect they have on the propagation of radio waves. We discussed RF units of measure both absolute and relative, including the watt, milliwatt, dB, and dBi. Finally we covered various types of radio frequency signal measurements used with IEEE 802.11 wireless networking. These topics included:

- Receive sensitivity
- Radio frequency noise
- Received signal strength indicator (RSSI)
- Signal-to-noise ratio (SNR)

Exam Essentials

Know the basic characteristics or properties of radio frequency.   Understand the characteristics of radio frequency such as wavelength, phase, frequency, and amplitude.

Be familiar with the frequencies used for wireless networks.   Know the unlicensed ISM and UNII bands available for use with wireless networks.

Understand wireless network coverage and capacity.   Know the difference between coverage and capacity and the factors that will have an impact on both.

Know what RF factors will affect the range and speed of wireless networks.   Understand the effects of interference and the devices that cause interference. Be familiar with the environmental conditions that cause reflection, refraction, diffraction, scattering, and absorption. Understand their impact on the propagation of RF signals.

Identify basic RF units of measurement.   Understand the difference between absolute and relative measures of RF power. Define W, mW, dB, dBm, and dBi.

Identify RF signal measurements   Understand receive sensitivity, radio frequency noise, received signal strength indicator (RSSI), and signal-to-noise ratio (SNR).

Review Questions

1. What is the term defining the number of times a cycle of an RF signal will oscillate in one second?

   A. Phase

   B. Frequency

   C. Amplitude

   D. Wavelength

2. How many nonoverlapping channels are available in the unlicensed 2.4 GHz ISM band?

   A. 1

   B. 3

   C. 6

   D. 11

3. The capacity of an access point is dependent on which factors? (Choose two.)

   A. Number of users

   B. Channel reuse

   C. Co-location

   D. Software applications

   E. Frequency

4. When an RF signal passes between media of different densities and may change speeds and bend, the behavior is known as:

   A. Refraction

   B. Reflection

   C. Scattering

   D. Diffraction

5. What two devices use RF to communicate? (Choose two.)

   A. Transmitter

   B. Transistor

   C. Reactor

   D. Reflector

   E. Receiver

6. Which are relative measures of RF power? (Choose two.)

   A. mW

   B. dB

    C. dBm

    D. dBi

    E. Watt

7. In the 2.4 GHz range, what distance between the center frequencies (in megahertz) is required for two channels to be considered nonoverlapping for HR/DSSS?

    A. 5 MHz

    B. 22 MHz

    C. 25 MHz

    D. 30 MHz

8. Two characteristics of RF signals are:

    A. Amplitude

    B. Reflection

    C. Phase

    D. Refraction

    E. Diffraction

9. How many channels are available for wireless LANs to use in the unlicensed UNII-1 band?

    A. 2

    B. 4

    C. 6

    D. 11

10. Which are absolute measures of RF power? (Choose two.)

    A. Watt

    B. dB

    C. mW

    D. dBi

    E. dBd

11. Which two channels are considered nonoverlapping in the 2.4 GHz band?

    A. 1 and 6

    B. 2 and 6

    C. 6 and 10

    D. 11 and 13

12. How many channels are available for wireless LAN use in the unlicensed 2.4 GHz ISM band?

    A. 8

    B. 10

    C. 11

    D. 14

13. The range of a 2.4 GHz signal is mostly dependent on which RF characteristic?

    A. Frequency

    B. Wavelength

    C. Amplitude

    D. Phase

14. Which item has an effect on RF line of sight?

    A. Phase

    B. Obstacles

    C. Interference

    D. Amplitude

15. How many channels are available for wireless LAN use in the unlicensed middle UNII-2e band?

    A. 4

    B. 6

    C. 11

    D. 14

16. As seen in a two-dimensional (X/Y) view, the amplitude of an RF signal is:

    A. Height

    B. Length

    C. Shift

    D. Width

17. An 802.11b channel is how wide in MHz?

    A. 5 MHz

    B. 22 MHz

    C. 25 MHz

    D. 30 MHz

18. When an RF signal bounces off a smooth nonabsorptive surface, the behavior is:

    A. Refraction

    B. Reflection

    C. Scattering

    D. Diffraction

19. What is the gain of an antenna measured in?

   A. dB

   B. dBc

   C. dBi

   D. dBm

20. When RF passes or bends around an obstacle such as a building or column, the behavior is:

   A. Reflection

   B. Refraction

   C. Scattering

   D. Diffraction

Chapter 7

Wireless LAN Antennas and Accessories

THE FOLLOWING CWTS EXAM OBJECTIVES ARE COVERED IN THIS CHAPTER:

✓ **2.3 Identify the purpose, features, and proper implementation of the following types of antennas**

- Omnidirectional/dipole

- Semidirectional

- Highly directional

✓ **2.4 Describe the proper locations and methods for installing RF antennas**

- Internal and external (to the AP) antennas

- Pole/mast mount

- Ceiling mount

- Wall mount

✓ **3.6 Understand and apply basic RF antenna concepts**

- Passive gain

- Beamwidth

- Simple diversity

- Polarization

✓ **3.7 Identify the use of the following WLAN accessories and explain how to select and install them for optimal performance and regulatory domain compliance**

- RF cables

- RF connectors

- Lightning arrestors and grounding rods

Antennas are an essential part of a successful wireless LAN deployment. From the transmitter perspective, an antenna takes the energy from the transmission system, transforms it into radio waves, and propagates it through the free air. From the receiver perspective, an antenna performs the opposite task—it receives the radio waves, transforms them back to AC signals, and finally sends the information to a computer or other wireless device.

Many factors are involved in determining the proper antenna to be used in an application or deployment of a wireless LAN. These factors include:

- Indoor or outdoor installation
- Distance between transmitter and receiver
- Frequency to be used
- Horizontal or vertical orientation/polarization
- Aesthetics
- Cost
- Manufacturer
- Intended use
- Mounting brackets
- Electrical characteristics
- Height
- Location
- Local ordinances

Basic Radio Frequency Antenna Concepts

It is important to understand some of the basic theory, characteristics, and terminology associated with antennas prior to learning how they operate. Becoming familiar with this will help in making decisions when it comes to sales and support of antennas and wireless LAN systems. Some of the terminology for characteristics of antennas is listed here:

Radio Frequency lobes: Shape of the radiation patterns

Beamwidth: Horizontal and vertical angles

Antenna charts: Azimuth and elevation

Gain: Changing the radio frequency coverage pattern (beamwidths)

Polarization: Horizontal or vertical orientation

Radio Frequency Lobes

The term *lobe* has many meanings, depending on the context in which it is used. Typically it is used to define the projecting part of an object. In anatomical terms, an example would be part of the human ear known as the ear lobe. In botanical terms, a lobe is the divided part of a leaf. As a radio frequency technology term, lobe refers to the shape of the RF energy emitted from an antenna element. RF lobes are determined by the physical design of the antenna. The antenna design also determines how the lobes project from an antenna element.

The effect of antenna design, particularly the shape of the RF lobes, is one reason why choosing the correct antenna is a critical part of a wireless LAN design. Antennas may project many lobes of RF signal, some of which are not intended to be usable areas of coverage. The RF lobes that are not part of the main or intended lobe coverage—that is, the rear and side lobes—contain usable RF but are not intended to be used to provide coverage for the wireless LAN cell. They are for the most part unintentional coverage areas and are not part of a good wireless LAN design and planned coverage area. The type of antenna utilized—omnidirectional, semidirectional, or highly directional—will determine the usable lobes. These antennas as well as the RF radiation patterns they project will be discussed in more detail later in this chapter. Figure 7.1 shows an example of RF lobes emitted from an antenna element. The "main signal" is the lobe intended to be used.

FIGURE 7.1 Radio frequency lobes' shape and coverage area are affected by the type and design of an antenna.

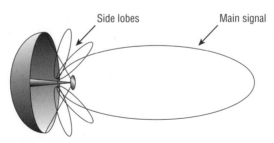

Highly directional parabolic dish antenna

Side lobes Main signal

Antenna Beamwidth

The design of an antenna will determine how radio frequencies propagate and the specific patterns in which the energy propagates from an antenna element. As mentioned earlier, the patterns of energy emitted from an antenna are known as lobes. For antennas, the beamwidth is the angle of measurement of the main RF lobe measured at what is called the half-power point, or −3 dB point. *Beamwidth* is measured both horizontally and vertically, in degrees. It is important to understand that antennas shape the RF coverage or isotropic energy that radiates from the antenna element. Changing types or remaining with the same type of antenna but changing the gain will also change the coverage area provided by the wireless LAN system.

Documents or antenna specifications are available to illustrate the horizontal and vertical beamwidths. Azimuth and elevation charts available from the antenna manufacturer will show the beamwidth angles.

The *azimuth* refers to the horizontal RF coverage pattern, and the *elevation* is the vertical RF coverage pattern. The azimuth is the view from above or the "bird's-eye view" of the RF pattern; in some cases it will be 360°. Think of the elevation as a side view. If you were to look at a mountain from the side view, it would have a certain height or elevation measured in feet or meters. For example, Pikes Peak, a mountain in the front range of the Rocky Mountains, has an elevation of 14,115′ (4,302 meters). Figure 7.2 shows a representation of horizontal and vertical beamwidths. Some predictive modeling site survey software programs will allow the wireless LAN designer to adjust the azimuth and elevation of the antennas used in the predictive modeling design to more closely depict the real world coverage of the wireless LAN system. Wireless LAN site surveys and predictive modeling will be discussed in more detail in Chapter 11, "Performing an RF Wireless LAN Site Survey."

FIGURE 7.2 Horizontal (azimuth) and vertical (elevation) beamwidths measured at the half power, or −3 dB point

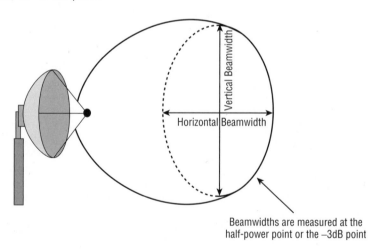

Beamwidths are measured at the
half-power point or the −3dB point

🌐 Real World Scenario

Reading Azimuth and Elevation Charts

Understanding how to read an azimuth and elevation chart is useful from a technical sales, design, or integration perspective. Knowing these patterns will help when making hardware recommendations for customers based on needed coverage and device use. These charts show the angles of radio frequency propagation from both the azimuth (horizontal or looking down, top view) and the elevation (vertical or side view). They give a general idea of the shape of the RF propagation lobe based on antenna design.

Antenna manufacturers test antenna designs in a laboratory. Using the correct instruments, an engineer is able to create the azimuth and elevation charts. These charts show only approximate coverage area based on the readings taken during laboratory testing and do not take into consideration any environmental conditions such as obstacles or interference. The following image shows an example of an azimuth and elevation chart for a semidirectional antenna.

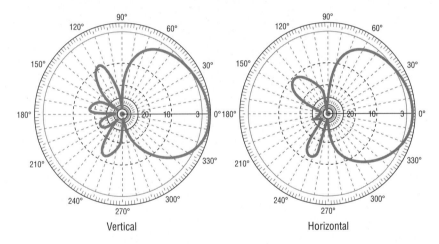

Vertical   Horizontal

Image provided by www.L-com.com

Understanding how to read one of these charts is not complicated. Notice that the chart is a circular pattern with readings from 0° to 360°, and there are many rings within these charts. The outermost ring shows the strongest signal from the testing process of this antenna. The inner rings show measurements and dB ratings less than the strongest measured signal from the outside ring. A good chart will show the most accurate readings from the testing process. A sales or technical support professional can use these charts to get an idea of how the radiation pattern would look based on a specific antenna type and model.

Antenna Gain

The *gain* of an antenna provides a change in coverage that is a result of the antenna focusing the area of radio frequency propagation. This gain is produced from the physical design of the antenna element. In Chapter 6, "Radio Frequency Fundamentals for Wireless LAN Technology," we looked at various characteristics of radio frequency. One of these characteristics is amplitude, which was defined as the height (voltage level) or the amount of power of a sine wave. The amplitude is created by varying voltage over a period of time and is measured at the peaks of the signal from top to bottom. Amplification of an RF signal will result in gain. An antenna is a device that can change the coverage area, thus propagating an RF signal further. Antenna gain is measured in decibels isotropic (dBi), which is a change in power as a result of increasing the isotropic energy. Isotropic energy is defined as energy emitted equally in all directions. The sun is a good example of isotropic energy, emitting energy in a spherical fashion equally in all directions. Figure 7.3 illustrates energy being emitted from an isotropic radiator.

FIGURE 7.3   A perfect isotropic radiator emits energy equally in all directions.

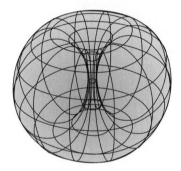

Passive Gain

It's quite intriguing how an antenna can provide *passive gain*, a change in coverage without the use of an external power source. Because of how antennas are designed, they focus isotropic energy into a specific radiation pattern. Focusing this energy increases coverage in a particular direction. A common example used to describe passive gain is a magnifying glass. If a person is standing outside on a beautiful sunny day, the sun's energy is not intense because it is being diffused across the entire earth's hemisphere. Thus, there is not enough concentrated energy to cause any harm or damage in a short period of time. However, if this person were to take a magnifying glass and point one side of it toward the sun and the other side toward a piece of paper, more than likely the paper would start to heat quickly. This is because the convex shape of the magnifying glass focuses or concentrates the sun's energy into one specific area, thus increasing the amount of heat to that area.

Antennas are designed to function in the same way by focusing the energy they receive from a signal source into a specific RF radiation pattern. Depending on the design of the antenna element, as the gain of an antenna increases, both the horizontal and vertical radiation patterns (beamwidths) will decrease or create narrower beamwidths. Conversely, as the gain of an antenna decreases, the beamwidths will increase, making a larger radiation pattern. One exception to this behavior is the omnidirectional antenna. This type of antenna has a horizontal beamwidth of 360°. When the gain is increased or decreased, the beamwidth will remain 360° but the size of this coverage area will increase or decrease depending on the change in the gain. Omnidirectional antennas are discussed in more detail later in this chapter. Figure 7.4 shows a drawing of a wireless LAN system with 100 mW of RF power at the antenna. Because of passive gain, the antenna has the effect of emitting 200 mW of RF power.

FIGURE 7.4 An access point supplying 100 mW of RF power and an antenna with a gain of 3 dBi for an output at the antenna of effectively 200 mW of RF power

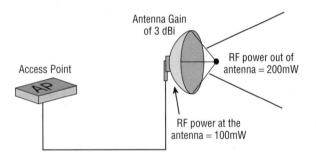

It is important to understand that many local radio frequency regulatory domains or agencies restrict the amount of RF power that can be emitted from an unlicensed RF system. This "system" includes all the components certified by the local regulatory agency and may include the transmitter (access point), the connectors, and the antenna. Changing and increasing the gain of an antenna will increase the amount of effective RF energy leaving the antenna and may violate the regulations set forth by the local regulatory agency and void the certification. The Federal Communications Commission (FCC) has modified what it allows several times, to the point of much confusion for installers trying to remain compliant with the regulations. Additionally, altering the original design in any way may require the entire system to be recertified based on the laws in each RF agency and that agency's interpretation of the term licensed system.

Exercise 7.1 is a simple way to demonstrate passive gain.

EXERCISE 7.1

Demonstrating Passive Gain

You can demonstrate passive gain by using a standard 8.5″ × 11.0″ piece of notebook paper or cardstock.

1. Roll a piece of paper into a cone or funnel shape.

2. Speak at your normal volume and notice the sound of your voice as it propagates through the air.

3. Hold the cone-shaped paper in front of your mouth.

4. Speak at the same volume.

5. Notice that the sound of your voice is louder. This occurs because the sound is now focused into a specific area or radiation pattern, and passive gain occurs.

Active Gain

Active gain will also provide an increase in signal strength. In a wireless LAN system, *active gain* is accomplished by providing an external power source to an installed device. An example of such a device is an amplifier. An amplifier is placed in series in the wireless LAN system and will increase the signal strength based on how much gain it provides.

If an amplifier is used in a wireless LAN system, certain regulatory domains require that the amplifier be certified as part of the system. It is best to carefully consider whether an amplifier is necessary before using such a device in an IEEE 802.11 wireless LAN system. Using an amplifier may nullify the system's certification and potentially exceed the allowed RF limit.

Antenna Polarization

Antenna *polarization* describes how a wave is emitted from an antenna and the orientation of the electrical component or electric field of the waveform. To maximize radio frequency signals, the transmitting and receiving antennas should be polarized in the same direction or as closely as possible. Antennas polarized the same way ensure the best possible RF signal.

If the polarization of the transmitter and receiver are different, the power of the RF signal will decrease depending how different the polarization is. Figure 7.5 shows an example of horizontal and vertical polarized antennas.

With the large number of wireless LAN devices available, it is a challenging task to accomplish the same polarization for all devices on the network. Performing a wireless LAN site survey will show signal strength based on several factors, including polarization of access point antennas. This survey will help determine the received signal strength of the wireless LAN devices. Site surveys and antenna polarization are discussed in more detail in Chapter 11.

FIGURE 7.5 Horizontally and vertically polarized antennas

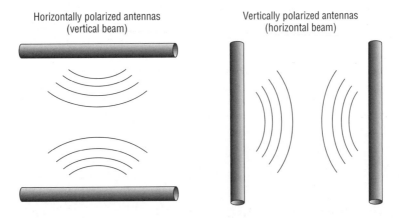

Horizontally polarized antennas (vertical beam)

Vertically polarized antennas (horizontal beam)

Real World Scenario

Antenna Polarization Example

It is fairly simple to demonstrate antenna polarization with a notebook computer or other wireless LAN device and either a wireless network adapter client utility or other third-party software that shows signal strength and/or signal to noise ratio. One such utility is InSSIDer, a free open source Wi-Fi network scanner for Windows XP and above. You can find how to access the InSSIDer program at the download page for this book, www.sybex .com/go/cwts2e. InSSIDer displays the received signal strength from the access points in the receiver area.

You can visualize polarization by performing the following steps. This experiment should be performed using a notebook computer within close proximity to an access point.

1. Verify that you have a supported wireless network adapter.

2. Install and launch the InSSIDer program or other utility that shows signal strength.

3. Monitor the received signal strength indicator (RSSI) value.

4. While monitoring the RSSI value, change the orientation of the notebook computer.

5. Notice the change in the RSSI value (either an increase or decrease) when the orientation of the computer changes with respect to the access point.

This demonstrates how polarity can affect the received signal of a device.

Wireless LAN Antenna Types

The type of antenna that is best for a particular installation or application will depend on the desired radio frequency coverage pattern. Making the correct choice is part of a good wireless LAN design. Using the wrong type of antenna can cause undesirable results, such as interference to neighboring systems, poor signal strength, or incorrect coverage pattern for your design.

Three common types of antennas for use with wireless LANs are:

- Omnidirectional/dipole antennas
- Semidirectional antennas
- Highly directional antennas

This section describes each type of antenna in more detail and provides specifications and installation or configuration information about these antennas.

Omnidirectional Antennas

Omnidirectional antennas are common on most access points of either SOHO or enterprise grade. An *omnidirectional antenna* has a horizontal beamwidth (azimuth) of 360°. This means that when the antenna is vertically polarized (perpendicular to the earth's surface) the horizontal radiation pattern is 360° and will propagate RF energy in every direction horizontally. The vertical beamwidth (elevation) will vary depending on the antenna's gain. As the gain of the antenna increases, the horizontal radiation pattern will increase, providing more horizontal coverage. Keep in mind the beamwidth is still 360°, but it will be a larger 360° area that is covered because of the higher gain of the antenna. However, the vertical radiation pattern will decrease, thus providing less vertical coverage.

The shape of the radiation pattern from an omnidirectional antenna looks like a donut and is known as a torus. Figure 7.6 shows an example of the toroidal radiation pattern of an omnidirectional antenna.

FIGURE 7.6 The omnidirectional radiation pattern has a toroidal shape.

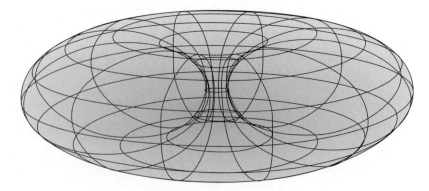

Omnidirectional antennas are one of the most common types of antenna for indoor wireless LAN deployments. Most access points use omnidirectional antennas. Access points come with fixed, removable, or integrated antennas. If the antenna is removable, the installer can replace it with one of different gain. Enterprise-grade access points typically have removable antennas that are sold separately.

Some regulatory domains require the use of proprietary connectors with respect to antennas. These connectors limit access points to the specific antennas tested with the system. Therefore, it is best to consult with the manufacturer of the access point or other wireless LAN transmitting device to determine which antennas may be used with the system.

The most common type of omnidirectional antenna used indoors is known as the "rubber duck antenna." This type of antenna typically has a low gain of 2 dBi to 3 dBi and connects directly to an access point. Rubber duck antennas usually have a pivot point so the polarization can be adjusted vertically or horizontally regardless of how the access point is mounted.

Some antennas will operate in both the 2.4 GHz ISM band and the 5 GHz UNII band and can thus work with a multiband wireless device.

Figure 7.7 shows a rubber duck omnidirectional antenna.

FIGURE 7.7   2.4 GHz rubber duck omnidirectional antenna

Image provided by www.L-com.com.

Omnidirectional Antenna Specifications

In addition to the beamwidth and gain, omnidirectional antennas have various other specifications to be considered, including:

- Frequency range

- Voltage standing wave ratio (VSWR)

- Polarization

- Attached cable length
- Dimensions
- Mounting requirements

Table 7.1 is an example of a specification sheet for a rubber duck omnidirectional antenna.

TABLE 7.1   Omnidirectional antenna specifications

Electrical specifications	
Frequency ranges	2400–2500 MHz
Gain	2.2 dBi
Horizontal beamwidth	360°
Impedance	50 ohm
Maximum power	50W
VSWR	<2:0
Mechanical Specifications	
Weight	0.52 oz. (15 g)
Length	4.7″ (105mm)
Maximum diameter	0.4″ (10mm)
Finish	Matte black
Connector	Reverse polarity SMA plug
Operating temperature	–40°C to 60°C (–40°F to 140°F)
Polarization	Vertical
Flame rating	UL 94HB
RoHS-compliant	Yes

A physical representation of the antenna is also helpful for sales and integration professionals. Figure 7.8 shows the physical specifications diagram for a rubber duck omnidirectional antenna.

Azimuth and elevation charts are usually available to allow visualization of the radio frequency radiation pattern emitted from the antenna. This is useful for a wireless LAN professional to determine the approximate RF propagation pattern. The purpose of these charts, and how to read them, were explained in the Case Study "Reading Azimuth and Elevation Charts" earlier in this chapter. Figure 7.9 shows the charts for a rubber duck omnidirectional antenna.

FIGURE 7.8 Rubber-duck omnidirectional antenna physical specifications

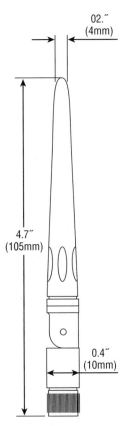

FIGURE 7.9 Vertical (elevation) and horizontal (azimuth) charts for omnidirectional antenna

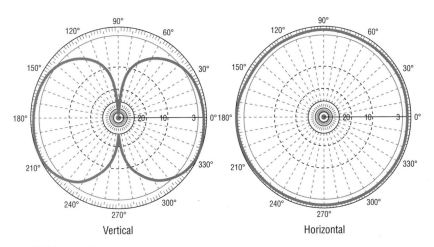

Image provided by www.L-com.com.

Semidirectional Antennas

Semidirectional antennas take radio frequency power from the transmitting system and focus it into a more specific pattern than an omnidirectional antenna offers. *Semidirectional antennas* are available in various types, including patch, panel, sector, and Yagi. These antennas are manufactured for either indoor or outdoor use and are designed to provide more specific coverage by focusing the horizontal radiation pattern to a value of less than 360°. A semidirectional antenna will allow the wireless LAN designer to provide RF coverage to a specific area within a deployment. This coverage area may consist of rooms or areas in which an omnidirectional antenna may not be the perfect solution. For indoor installations, such areas include rectangular rooms or offices, hallways, and long corridors. For outdoor deployments, they include point-to-point and point-to-multipoint bridging installations.

Patch/Panel Antennas

In the wireless LAN world, the terms *patch* and *panel* are commonly used to describe the same type of antenna. The intended use will affect the choice of patch/panel antenna to be used in a specific application. Choosing the correct patch/panel antenna will require knowing the dimensions of the physical area to be covered as well as the amount of gain required. A *patch/panel antenna* can have a horizontal beamwidth of as high as 180°, but usually the horizontal beamwidth is between 35° and 60°. The vertical beamwidth usually ranges between 30° and 80°. Figure 7.10 shows a 2.4 GHz flat patch antenna. Sector antennas are a type of semidirectional antenna that can be configured in an array to provide omnidirectional coverage. Sector antennas are covered in more detail later in this chapter.

FIGURE 7.10   2.4 GHz 8 dBi flat patch antenna

Image provided by www.L-com.com.

🌐 Real World Scenario

Appropriate Use of a Semidirectional Antenna

A small business consultant is tasked with providing wireless LAN access to several offices in a multi-tenant building. The client wants to provide adequate coverage for the offices they lease but would like to minimize the number of access points. The client wishes to use access points and antennas that are aesthetically pleasing, since these offices allow public access. The areas to be covered are rectangular, as shown here:

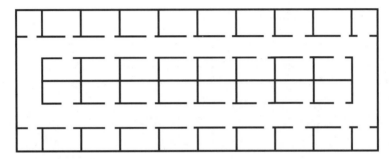

One solution would be to provide several access points using low-gain omnidirectional antennas. The following image illustrates how several access points could be used to provide coverage to this area.

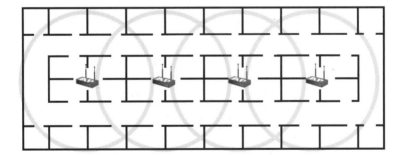

However, the consultant believes that if low-gain rubber duck omnidirectional antennas are used, an access point with significant output power would be required to cover the length of the rooms. In addition, the client wants to minimize the number of access points and make the installation aesthetically pleasing.

An alternate solution is to use a patch antenna on both sides of the office, thereby providing adequate coverage and minimizing the use of access points. The following image shows patch antennas mounted at both ends of the office area as well as the projected coverage area of both antennas.

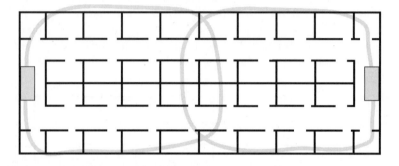

Patch/Panel Antenna Specifications

The specifications for semidirectional antennas such as patch or panel vary based on the design of the antenna. Semidirectional antennas are available in single- or dual-band capability. Semidirectional antennas may be used indoors or outdoors depending on the application. Table 7.2 is an example of a specification sheet for a 2.4 GHz 8 dBi flat patch antenna.

TABLE 7.2   Flat patch antenna specifications

Electrical specifications	
Frequency ranges	2400–2500 MHz
Gain	8 dBi
Horizontal beamwidth	75°
Vertical beamwidth	65°
Impedance	50 ohm
Maximum power	25 W
VSWR	<1.5:1 avg
Mechanical specifications	
Weight	0.4 lb. (.18 Kg)
Dimensions	4.5″ x 4.5″ x 0.9″ (114mm x 114mm x 23mm)
Radome material	UV-inhibited polymer
Connector	12″ N-female

Electrical specifications

Operating temperature	−40°C to 85°C (−40°F to 185°F)
Mounting	Four 1/4″ (6.3mm) holes
Polarization	Horizontal or vertical
Flame rating	UL 94HB
RoHS-compliant	Yes
Wind survival	>150 mph (241 kph)

Wind loading data

Wind speed (mph)	Loading
100	5 lb.
125	7 lb.

A radome cover will protect an antenna from outdoor elements and certain weather conditions. Attenuation from the materials that the radome covers are constructed of will be minimal. They mainly protect the antenna from the collection of elements such as snow and hail.

Azimuth and elevation charts are also available for patch/panel antennas. Figure 7.11 shows the charts for the 2.4 GHz 8 dBi flat patch antenna.

FIGURE 7.11   Vertical (elevation) and horizontal (azimuth) charts for 2.4 GHz 8 dBi patch antenna

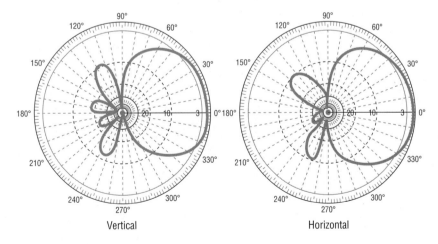

Image provided by www.L-com.com.

Sector Antennas

Sector antennas can be used to create omnidirectional radiation patterns using semidirectional antennas. These antennas are often used for base station connectivity for point-to-multipoint connectivity. *Sector antennas* have an azimuth that varies from 90° to 180°. These are typically configured to offer a total azimuth of 360°. For example, using sector antennas with an azimuth of 120° each would require three antennas in order to get omnidirectional or 360° coverage. This is a common configuration used with cellular phone technology. Figure 7.12 shows a sector panel antenna.

FIGURE 7.12   2.4 GHz 14 dBi 90° sector panel antenna

Image provided by www.L-com.com.

Sector Antenna Specifications

As mentioned earlier, sector antennas are commonly configured in an array to allow semidirectional antennas to provide omnidirectional coverage. This is useful in a campus environment or community arrangement to provide wireless LAN access such as Internet access. Sector antennas will usually have wide horizontal beamwidth (azimuth) and a narrow vertical beamwidth (elevation). Table 7.3 is an example of a specification sheet for a 2.4 GHz 14 dBi 90° sector panel WLAN antenna.

TABLE 7.3 90° sector panel WLAN antenna specifications

Electrical specifications	
Frequency ranges	2400–2500 MHz
Gain	14 dBi
Horizontal beamwidth	90°
Vertical beamwidth	15°
Impedance	50 ohm
Maximum input power	300 W
VSWR	<1.5:1 avg
Front to back ratio	>23 dB
Lightning protection	DC ground
Mechanical specifications	
Weight	4.4 lbs. (2 kg)
Dimensions	20 × 7″ × 3.5″ (500mm × 180mm × 90mm)
Radome material	UV-inhibited plastic
Connector	Integral N-female
Operating temperature	–40°C to 85°C (–40°F to 185°F)
Mounting	2″ (50mm) diameter mast maximum
Polarization	Vertical
Flame rating	UL 94HB
RoHS-compliant	Yes
Wind survival	>130 mph (210 Km/h)
Wind loading data	
Wind speed (mph)	**Loading**
100	32 lb.
125	49 lb.

Figure 7.13 shows the charts for the 2.4 GHz 14 dBi 90° sector antenna.

FIGURE 7.13 Vertical (elevation) and horizontal (azimuth) charts for 2.4 GHz 14 dBi 90° sector panel antenna

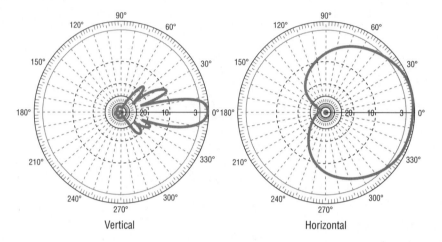

Vertical   Horizontal

Image provided by www.L-com.com.

Yagi Antennas

Yagi antennas are designed to be used indoors in long hallways and corridors, or outdoors for short-range bridging (typically less than two miles). *Yagi antennas* have vertical and horizontal beamwidths ranging from 25° to 65°. The radiation pattern may look like a funnel or a cone. As the signal propagates away from the antenna, the RF coverage naturally widens (diffusion). The aperture of the receiving antenna is much narrower than the signal at that point. This is a result of diffusion, which is the biggest form of loss in an RF link. Figure 7.14 shows a Yagi antenna.

FIGURE 7.14 2.4 GHz 15 dBi Yagi antenna

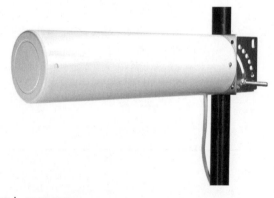

Image provided by www.L-com.com.

Yagi Antenna Specifications

Table 7.4 is an example of a specification sheet for a 2.4 GHz 15 dBi Yagi WLAN antenna.

TABLE 7.4   15 dBi Yagi antenna specifications

Electrical specifications	
Frequency ranges	2400–2500 MHz
Gain	14.5 dBi
–3 dB beamwidth	30°
Impedance	50 ohm
Maximum power	50 W
VSWR	<1.5:1 avg
Lightning protection	DC short
Mechanical specifications	
Weight	1.8 lbs. (.81 kg)
Dimensions – Length × diameter	18.2″ × 3″ (462mm × 76mm)
Radome material	UV-inhibited polymer
Connector	12″ N-female
Operating temperature	–40°C to 85°C (–40°F to 185°F)
Mounting	1-1/4″ (32mm) to 2″ (51mm) diameter masts
Polarization	Vertical and horizontal
Flame rating	UL 94HB
RoHS-compliant	Yes
Wind survival	>150 mph (241 kph)
Wind speed (mph)	**Loading**
100	12 lb.
125	19 lb.

Figure 7.15 shows the charts for the 2.4 GHz 14 dBi Yagi antenna.

FIGURE 7.15   Vertical (elevation) and horizontal (azimuth) charts for 2.4 GHz 14 dBi Yagi antenna

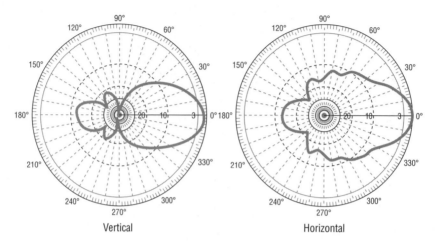

Vertical   Horizontal

Image provided by www.L-com.com.

Outdoor Installation of Yagi Antennas

A Yagi antenna may be in a weatherproof enclosure. This is not required but may be useful in outdoor installations. The weatherproof enclosure will prevent collection of certain elements such as snow and ice. Radome covers are available for parabolic dish antennas for the same purpose.

Highly Directional Antennas

Highly directional antennas are typically *parabolic dish antennas* used for long-range point-to-point bridge connections. These antennas are available with a solid reflector or a grid. Some manufacturers of parabolic dish antennas advertise ranges of 25 miles or more depending on the gain and the environmental conditions. Parabolic dish antennas have very narrow horizontal and vertical beamwidths. This beamwidth can range from 3° to 15° and has a radiation pattern similar to that of a Yagi, with the appearance of a funnel. The beamwidth starts very narrow at the antenna element and naturally widens because of diffusion. Because these antennas are designed for outdoor use, they will need to be manufactured to withstand certain environmental conditions, including a wind rating and appropriate mounting. Grid antennas can provide similar coverage and are less susceptible to wind loading. Figure 7.16 shows a parabolic dish antenna.

FIGURE 7.16   5 GHz 28.5 dBi parabolic dish antenna

Image provided by www.L-com.com.

Highly Directional Antenna Specifications

Table 7.5 is an example of a specification sheet for a 2.4 GHz 30 dBi grid parabolic dish antenna. Notice that the vertical and horizontal beamwidths of this antenna are 5.3°, very narrow compared to other antenna types.

TABLE 7.5   2.4 GHz 30 dBi grid parabolic dish antenna specifications

Electrical specifications	
Frequency ranges	2400–2500 MHz
Gain	30 dBi
Horizontal beamwidth	5.3°
Vertical beamwidth	5.3°
Impedance	50 ohm
Maximum power	100 W
VSWR	<1.5:1 avg

TABLE 7.5   2.4 GHz 30 dBi grid parabolic dish antenna specifications *(continued)*

Mechanical specifications

Weight	35 lbs. (16 kg)
Dimensions	59″ diameter (1.5 m)
Grid material	Galvanized steel
Operating temperature	–40° C to 85° C (–40° F to 185° F)
Mounting	1-1/4″ (32mm) to 2″ (51mm) diameter masts
Polarization	Vertical
Flame rating	UL 94HB
Wind survival	>134 mph

Shipping Specifications

Shipping carton size	(L x W x H) 62″ × 17″ × 32″ (1.6m × 0.43m × 0.81m)
Shipping weight	50 lbs. (22.7 kg)

Wind speed (mph)	Loading
100	61.8 lb.
125	97 lb.

Figure 7.17 shows the charts for the 15 2.4 GHz 30 dBi grid parabolic dish antenna.

FIGURE 7.17   Vertical (elevation) and horizontal (azimuth) charts for 2.4 GHz 30 dBi grid antenna

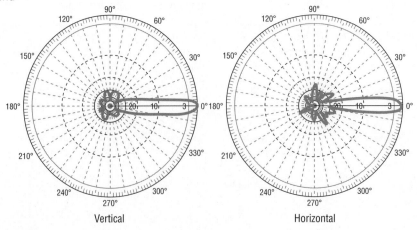

Vertical   Horizontal

Image provided by www.L-com.com.

Shipping a Parabolic Dish Antenna

One thing to consider regarding the sale and procurement of a highly directional parabolic dish antenna is the size and shipping weight. Since these antennas are much larger and heavier than other antennas used in wireless LANs, shipping cost may be a factor. Some specification sheets will detail shipping information for this reason.

Radio Frequency Cables and Connectors

Radio frequency cables play a role in various wireless LAN deployment situations. For example, cables may be used to connect access points and client devices to antennas or to connect other devices that may used in wireless networking. Several factors need to be taken into consideration when using cables in a wireless LAN system, including these:

- Type of cable
- Length of cable
- Cost of cable
- Impedance rating

Choosing the correct cable for use in wireless LAN systems is an important part of a successful wireless LAN deployment. The right cable for the right job will help ensure that *signal loss*—a decrease in signal strength—is minimized and performance is maximized.

Radio Frequency Cable Types

The type of cable used will depend on the application. Many systems use cables to extend from the wireless device such as an access point to an antenna located outside of a building. It is important to choose the correct type of cable in order to optimize the performance of the wireless LAN system. Cables vary in diameter, and the application will determine the type of cable to use. For example, connecting a wireless LAN adapter on a notebook computer to an external antenna requires a specific type of cable that should be short and flexible. Thick, rigid cables are best used for longer runs. The radio frequency range in which the cable will be used also is important to consider. Where the cable is used will determine the radio frequency rating of the cable. For example, wireless LANs use 50 ohm cable, whereas television (such as satellite and cable) will use 75 ohm cable. Using cable with the correct rating will minimize voltage standing wave ratio (VSWR), a phenomenon discussed in the section "Impedance and VSWR." Figure 7.18 shows a spool of high-quality 50 ohm cable.

FIGURE 7.18   L-com spool of low-loss 400-series coaxial bulk cable

Image provided by www.L-com.com.

Radio Frequency Cable Length

The length of a cable used in a wireless LAN system is another factor to consider. A cable of even a very short length will have some level of attenuation or loss. As a reminder, loss is a decrease in signal strength. This decrease in signal strength means less overall performance and throughput for users of the wireless LAN. Professionally manufactured cables typically are available in many standard common lengths. Best practices recommend using the correct length and minimizing connections. For example, if a run from an access point to an external antenna is 27', it would be best to use a single cable as close to that length as possible. Connecting two or more pieces of cable together will increase the loss to the system. One might be tempted to use a longer piece, such as 50', but this is not recommended since the extra length will add loss to the system.

Figure 7.19 shows a short length of cable known as a pigtail used to connect a standard cable to a proprietary cable. If an RF cable is used or extended, the attenuation that is introduced can be offset with the use of an amplifier or with a higher-gain antenna. An amplifier will provide active gain and an antenna will provide passive gain. Keep in mind that using an incorrect amplifier may void the system certification and that using a higher-gain antenna may exceed the rules set by the local RF regulatory agency.

Radio Frequency Cable Cost

Cable cost may also play a role in the type of cable to be used. The old saying "you get what you pay for" is true with cables as well. I recommend using high-quality name-brand

RF cables to optimize the performance of your system. Premium cables may come at a higher price, but the benefit of better quality signal is the main advantage.

FIGURE 7.19   Short pigtail adapter cable

Image provided by www.L-com.com.

Impedance and VSWR

Impedance is the measurement of alternating current (AC) resistance. It is normal to have some level of impedance mismatch in a wireless LAN system, but the impedances of all components should be matched as closely as possible in order to optimize performance of the system. Impedance mismatches can result in what is called *voltage standing wave ratio (VSWR)*. A large impedance mismatch can cause high level of VSWR and will have an impact on the wireless LAN system and transmitted or received signal.

Electrical resistance is measured in ohms. IEEE 802.11 wireless LAN devices have an impedance of 50 ohms.

Radio Frequency Connectors

In a wireless LAN system, radio frequency connectors are used to join devices together, allowing the RF signal to transfer between the devices. These devices may connect access point to antenna, antenna to cable, cable to cable, or various other components to each other. RF connectors also cause an impedance mismatch to some degree and increase the level of VSWR. To minimize the effects of VSWR, best practices suggest keeping the use of connectors to a minimum. Using connectors can also result in *insertion loss*. Insertion loss is usually minor by itself, but it can contribute to overall loss in a system, thereby resulting in less RF signal and less throughput.

Using Proprietary Connectors for Regulatory Domain Compliance

Some regulatory domains require the use of *proprietary connectors* on antennas and antenna connections in wireless LAN systems. These proprietary connectors prevent an installer or integrator from unintentionally using an antenna that might exceed the maximum amount of power allowed for the transmission system. Although these connectors are considered proprietary, many manufacturers share proprietary connectors:

- MC connectors are used by Dell, Buffalo, IBM, Toshiba, and Proxim-ORiNOCO.

- MMCX connectors are used by 3Com, Cisco, Proxim, Samsung, Symbol, and Motorola.

- MCX connectors are used by Apple and SMC devices.

- RP-MMCX connectors are used by SMC devices.

Standard RF connectors may be used in wireless LAN systems to connect devices that are not part of the point connecting to the antenna. For example, an access point connecting to a length of cable that is then connected to an amplifier could use a standard RF connector. The cable connecting the amplifier to the antenna would require a proprietary connector. Figure 7.20 shows examples of common RF connectors.

FIGURE 7.20 Several common RF connectors used with wireless LANs

Image provided by www.L-com.com.

Factors in Antenna Installation

Several factors are important to consider when you are planning to install a wireless network. These include earth curvature, multipath, and radio frequency line of sight. This section includes information about how to take these factors into account when planning a wireless installation.

Addressing the Effects of Earth Curvature

Beyond seven miles, the curvature of the earth will have an impact on point-to-point or point-to-multipoint wireless LAN connections. Therefore, it is important to add height to the antenna in order to compensate for the *earth curvature*, sometimes referred to as earth bulge. A formula is used to calculate the additional height of antennas when a link exceeds seven miles. However, this is beyond the scope of the CWTS exam objectives and is not discussed in this book.

Antenna Placement

The installation location and placement of antennas depend on the type of antenna and application in which it will be used. When installing antennas, consider the placement based on the design of the wireless LAN and the intended use of the antenna. When antennas are used outdoors, lightning arrestors, grounding, and adherence to local codes, laws, and government regulations must be followed as well as good RF design. Increasingly, local ordinances dictate how or if outdoor antennas can be mounted for looks as well as safety. Lightning arrestors and grounding methods are discussed later in this section.

Omnidirectional Antenna Placement

Placement of an omnidirectional antenna will depend on the intended use. Some omnidirectional antennas can be connected directly to an access point or may be integrated within the access point. In this configuration, the installation is fairly straightforward; it involves simply attaching the antenna to the access point or using the integrated antenna. Omnidirectional antennas are usually placed in the center of the intended coverage area. High-gain omnidirectional antennas are typically used in outdoor installations for point-to-multipoint configurations. This configuration is more complex because more than likely it requires mast or tower mounting. The exact placement depends on the intended coverage area as well as the gain of the antenna.

Semidirectional Antenna Placement

Semidirectional antennas may be used for either outdoor or indoor installations. When mounted indoors, a patch/panel antenna typically will be mounted flat on a wall with the connector upward for connections to a cable or directly to an access point. A template with the hole placement may be included for ease of installation. These antennas usually will use four mounting holes (one in each corner) to securely fasten the antenna to the wall. Yagi antennas can also be mounted either indoors or outdoors. The most common installation is outdoors for short-range point-to-point or point-to-multipoint bridging solutions. This will require a mounting bracket such as a tilt and swivel for wall mounting or U-bolts and plate for mast or pole mounting.

Highly Directional Antenna Placement

Highly directional antennas such as a parabolic dish are almost always used exclusively in outdoor installations. This type of antenna is used mostly for long-range point-to-point bridging links and will require installation on building rooftops or antenna towers. Alignment for long-range links is critical for reliable communications. Software and hardware tools are available for the installer to use for accurate alignment. As with other outdoor installations, secure mounting is essential in order to maintain safety and link reliability.

Minimizing the Effects of Multipath Using Antenna Diversity

In Chapter 6, we discussed some of the behaviors of radio frequency, including reflection, refraction, scattering, and diffraction. To review, reflection is caused by an RF signal bouncing off a smooth, nonabsorptive surface and changing direction. Indoor environments are areas that are prone to reflections. Reflections are caused by the RF signal bouncing off walls, ceilings, floors, and furniture; thus some installations will suffer from reflection more than others. The effect of reflection will be a decrease in signal strength due to a phenomenon called *multipath*. Multipath is the result of several wavefronts of the same transmission signal received out of phase at slightly different times. This can cause the receiver to be confused about the received signals. The result is corrupted signal and less overall throughput. Figure 7.21 illustrates multipath.

FIGURE 7.21   Effects of multipath

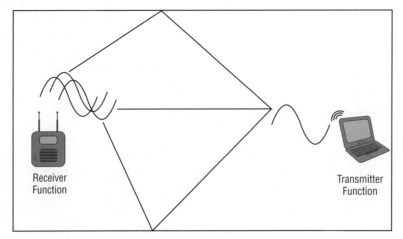

Receiver
Function

Transmitter
Function

Think of multipath as an echo. If you were to stand near a canyon and speak to somebody at a high volume some distance away, the other person would notice an echo. This echo is due to the fact that the sound of your voice is reflecting off the canyon walls. Therefore, the other person is hearing variations of your voice at slightly different times—as with RF multipath, several wavefronts of the same signal are arriving out of phase.

Antenna diversity is one way to help reduce the effects of multipath. *Antenna diversity* is a technology used in wireless LANs where a station (access point or client device) will utilize two antennas combined with one radio to decrease the effects of multipath. Using multiple antennas and some additional electronic intelligence, the receiver will be able to determine which antenna will receive and send the best signal. In diversity systems, two antennas are spaced at least one wavelength apart. This allows the receiver to use the antenna with the best signal to transmit and receive. With respect to radio frequency diversity, the antennas are required to be of the same design, frequency, gain, and so on.

Diversity Antenna Orientation

When you are using a diversity system such as an access point, it is important to have both antennas oriented the same way. They cannot be used to cover different areas. Using diversity antennas in an attempt to provide coverage for different areas will defeat the purpose of the diversity design.

Combating Effects of Wind and Lightning in WLAN Installations

Weather conditions such as rain, snow, and sleet typically do not affect wireless LAN communications unless the conditions are extreme or snow and sleet collect on antenna elements. However, some weather conditions that can affect wireless communication are wind and lightning.

Most outdoor antennas that can be affected by wind will have wind-loading data in the specification sheet. *Wind loading* is the result of wind blowing at high speeds and causing the antenna to move.

Lightning can destroy components connected to a network if the antenna takes either a direct or an indirect lightning strike. A properly grounded lightning arrestor will help protect wireless LAN and other networking equipment from indirect lightning strikes.

Lightning Arrestors

Transient or induced electrical currents are the result of an indirect lightning strike in the area of a wireless LAN antenna system. *Lightning arrestors* are an in-series device installed after the antenna and prior to the transmitter/receiver. Although this device will not provide protection from a direct lightning strike, it will help protect against an indirect lightning strike, which can damage electronics at distances away from the source of the strike. When the induced electrical currents from a lightning strike travel to the antenna, a lightning arrestor will shunt this excess current to ground, protecting the system from damage. Figure 7.22 shows a lightning arrestor.

FIGURE 7.22   L-com AL6 series 0-6 GHz coaxial lightning and surge protector

Image provided by www.L-com.com.

Grounding Rods

A *grounding rod* is a metal shaft used for grounding a device such as an antenna used in wireless networking. The rod should be driven into the ground at least 8' deep. Grounding rods are available in various types of steel, including stainless, galvanized, and copper clad. They are also available in a variety of diameters and lengths. Depending on the local electrical code, the grounding system should measure resistance between 5 and 25 ohms. Local code should also be consulted regarding material, diameter, and length of grounding rods. You should not share grounding rods with other equipment because interference or damage may occur.

It is imperative to install a grounding rod properly to ensure correct operation. If installing a grounding rod and other lightning protection equipment is beyond the knowledge level of the wireless engineer or installer, it is best to have a professional contractor perform the job.

Installation Safety

Professional contractors should be considered in the event you are not comfortable with performing the installation of a wireless LAN antenna yourself. Installing antennas may require bonded or certified technicians. Be sure to check local building codes prior to performing any installation of a wireless LAN antenna. Never underestimate safety when installing or mounting antennas. All safety precautions must be adhered to while performing an installation. The following are some general guidelines and precautions to be considered for a wireless LAN antenna installation:

- Read the installation manual from the manufacturer.
- Always avoid power lines. Contact with power lines can result in death.
- Always use the correct safety equipment when working at heights.
- Correctly install and use grounding rods when appropriate.
- Comply with regulations for use in the area and for use of towers as well.

Antenna Mounting

In addition to choosing the correct antenna to be used with a wireless LAN system, you must take into account the antenna mounting. The required antenna mounting fixture will depend on the antenna type, whether it will be used indoors or outdoors, and whether it will be used for device/client access or bridging solutions such as point-to-point or point-to-multipoint. It is best to consult with the antenna or device manufacturer to determine which mounting fixture is appropriate for use based on the intended deployment scenario. The following are several mounting types that may be used for a wireless LAN antenna solution:

- Internal and external (to the AP) antennas
- Pole/mast mount
- Ceiling mount
- Wall mount

Internal and External (to the Access Point) Antennas

Some wireless access points allow the use of either integrated or external antennas. Most modern controller-based and cooperative access points provide integrated antennas, and some have connectors to allow for the use of external antennas. Integrated antennas may be a better solution, mostly to match the aesthetics requirements of the organization where the access point will be used. Integrated antennas make an access point less noticeable if it is hanging from a standard 8'–10' high ceiling. Integrating them will also prevent individuals from tampering with antennas that if external might be within a person's reach. Tampering could be an issue in areas that are accessible to the general public, such as installations in educational, library, and medical environments.

It is important to take the mounting orientation into consideration when using access points with integrated antennas. The access point may be designed to be mounted on a ceiling. If you were to mount this type of access point on a wall, the radiation patterns would change, and this might create a coverage problem, especially with omnidirectional antennas.

One disadvantage of access points with integrated antennas is that the antennas cannot be changed to any other type. Basically you would be committed to using the antennas that are part of the access point and would be unable to add an antenna with higher gain or a different radiation pattern. Access points that have external antenna connectors allow the user to add different antennas that may be better suited to the environment or installation location. The external antennas will allow for a higher gain and possibly a different radiation pattern. Using an external antenna usually requires a software configuration that will disable the integrated antenna when external antennas are installed. You should not be able to use both the integrated and external antennas simultaneously. Many indoor access point models that use internal antennas offer the same coverage as their external antenna model counterparts This, however, will vary based on the manufacturer.

WARNING   When using wireless access points with integrated antennas, it is important to take the mounting into consideration. Some access points of this style are intended to be mounted on a ceiling or a wall, but not both. Mounting an antenna in a way it is not designed for will produce undesirable results, including radio frequency coverage problems.

Pole/Mast Mount

Pole/mast mounts typically consist of a mounting bracket and U-bolt mounting hardware. The mounting bracket is commonly L-shaped. One side of the bracket has a hole to mount an omnidirectional or similar antenna. The other side of the bracket has predrilled holes for fastening the bracket to a pole using U-bolts. Figure 7.23 shows an example of a heavy-duty mast mount.

FIGURE 7.23   Heavy-duty mast mount with U-bolts

Image provided by www.L-com.com.

Exercise 7.2 describes the basic steps for installing an omnidirectional antenna using a mast mount adapter.

EXERCISE 7.2

Installing a Pole/Mast Mount

1. Attach the mounting bracket to the mast using the supplied hardware.

2. Remove the antenna mounting bolt and washer from the base of the antenna.

3. Insert the antenna into the hole in the top of the mounting bracket. Without overtightening, securely fasten the antenna to the mounting bracket using the washer and antenna mounting bolt.

4. For outdoor installations, remember to use the proper sealant for weatherproofing when connecting the cable to the antenna.

Ceiling Mount

It may be necessary to mount certain antennas or access points with attached or integrated antennas from a ceiling. Many antennas can be mounted directly to a hard ceiling made from concrete, drywall, or similar material. Another possibility is a drop ceiling with acoustic tiles. Regardless of the type of ceiling in question, follow the manufacturer's instructions on the appropriate fixture to be used for mounting and detailed instructions for ceiling mounts. Figure 7.24 shows an example of a ceiling mount antenna.

FIGURE 7.24 L-com 2.3 GHz to 6 GHz 3 dBi omnidirectional ceiling mount antenna

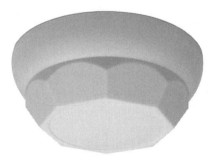

Image provided by www.L-com.com.

Wall Mount

Antennas or access points with attached antennas may need to be mounted to a wall based on the use or site survey results. Just as with a ceiling mount, follow the manufacturer's instructions on the appropriate fixture for wall mounting. When mounting an antenna to the wall, consider the polarization of the antenna. Keep in mind that some antennas are designed to be mounted on the ceiling; these types should not be mounted on a wall. This is especially true for access points with integrated antennas. It is best to try to match the polarization of the access points and the wireless client devices. In other words, if the access point's antennas are vertically polarized, the wireless client devices should be polarized in the same manner to promote better connectivity. However, with the wide variety of newer wireless client devices available this is getting harder to achieve. Choosing the correct antenna and mounting position is typically part of a wireless LAN site survey. Site surveys will be discussed in more detail in Chapter 11.

Maintaining Clear Communications

Several factors affect whether two wireless devices can communicate with each other. These factors include line of sight (both visual and RF) and Fresnel zone. Indoor wireless LAN installations use a low amount of radio frequency transmit power, usually around 30 mW to 50 mW, and will be able to communicate effectively even if the client device does not have a line of sight with an access point. This is because the RF will be able to penetrate obstacles such as walls, windows, and doors. Outdoor installations usually use a much higher output transmit power and will require an RF line of sight for effective communication.

Visual Line of Sight

Visual *line of sight* (LoS) is defined as the capability of two points to have an unobstructed view of one another. A visual LoS is usually not necessary for communications using IEEE 802.11 wireless LAN systems; it is implied with RF LoS. If a wireless LAN engineer was planning to connect two buildings together using wireless LAN technology, one of the first things the engineer would do is to verify that there is a clear, unobstructed view between the planned locations in order to provide an RF LoS.

Radio Frequency LoS

For two devices to successfully communicate at a distance via radio frequency, including a point-to-point or point-to-multipoint connection, a clear path for the RF energy to travel between the two points is necessary. This clear path is called RF LoS. This RF LoS is the premise of the Fresnel zone.

Fresnel Zone

The *Fresnel zone* for an RF signal is the area of radio frequency coverage surrounding the visual LoS. The width or area of the Fresnel zone will depend on the specific radio frequency used as well as the length or distance of the signal path. There is a formula used to calculate the width of the Fresnel zone at the widest point. However, that is beyond the scope of the CWTS exam objectives and is not shown in this book.

In an outdoor point-to-point or point-to-multipoint installation, it is important for the Fresnel zone to be clear of obstructions for successful communications to take place between a radio frequency transmitter and receiver. Best practices recommend maintaining an obstruction-free clearance of the least 60 percent for the Fresnel zone in order to have acceptable RF LoS. Maintaining a clear RF LoS becomes more difficult as the distance between two points increases. Obstructions can cause the Fresnel zone to be blocked enough for communications to suffer between a transmitter and receiver. Such obstructions include:

- Trees
- Buildings or other structures
- Earth curvature
- Natural elements such as hills and mountains

Figure 7.25 illustrates the Fresnel zone between two highly directional antennas.

FIGURE 7.25   Visualization of Fresnel zone

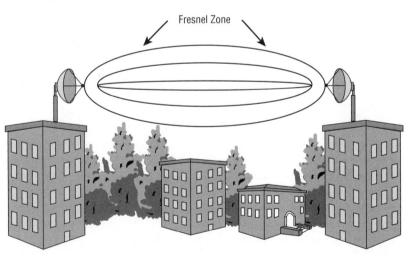

In order to stay clear of obstructions, carefully plan your antenna placement and antenna height. Keep in mind that a wireless LAN link may cross public areas in which an integrator or installer will have no control over the environment. There is a possibility, depending on the environmental conditions, that an IEEE 802.11 wireless LAN link may not be a feasible solution due to the inability to maintain an RF LoS. You should perform an outdoor site survey prior to the procurement and installation of wireless LAN hardware to ensure the installation and operation of the wireless LAN will be successful.

Summary

Antennas are a critical component in a successful operation of a wireless LAN. In this chapter, you learned about radio frequency signal characteristics and basic RF antenna concepts, including these:

- Radio frequency lobes
- Beamwidth (horizontal and vertical measurements)
- Passive and active gain
- Horizontal and vertical polarization of antennas

By understanding these characteristics and concepts, a sales engineer, integrator, or other wireless LAN professional can help choose the best antenna to be used for a specific use.

Understanding the radio frequency propagation patterns of various antenna types as well as the recommended use of an antenna will assist in deciding which antenna is best suited for the desired application. As discussed in this chapter, antennas are available in various types:

- Omnidirectional
- Semidirectional
  - Patch/panel
  - Sector
  - Yagi
- Highly directional
  - Parabolic dish

Omnidirectional antennas are one of the most common types of antenna used for indoor applications of wireless networking. Omnidirectional antennas provide a horizontal radiation pattern of 360°. Other antennas such as patch/panel, Yagi, or parabolic dish can be used if justified by the intended use. You learned about the radiation patterns of each of these types of antennas as well as how each may be used.

A proper mounting fixture is required to ensure safety and correct operation of the antenna and wireless network. In this chapter we looked at various methods for mounting antennas, including integrated and external (to the access point), pole/mast mount, ceiling mount, and wall mount.

Finally, you learned about other factors to be considered when choosing and installing an antenna for use with wireless LANs. The other areas of concerns are:

- Visual line of sight
- Radio frequency line of sight
- Fresnel zone

Understanding these concepts will help you achieve more successful deployment, operation, and use of antennas in wireless LANs.

Exam Essentials

Understand RF signal characteristics and basic RF concepts used with antennas.   Know the difference between passive and active gain. Understand that antennas use passive gain to change or focus the radio frequency radiation pattern. Understand the difference between beamwidth and polarization.

Know the different types of antennas used in wireless networking.   Be familiar with different types of antennas used with wireless networking, including omnidirectional antennas, semidirectional antennas, and highly directional antennas. Understand the various radiation patterns each of these antennas is capable of.

Identify various RF cables, connectors, and accessories used in wireless LANs. **Understand that, depending on the local regulatory body, proprietary connectors may be required for use with antennas. Know that cables will induce some level of loss in a wireless LAN system. Be familiar with the types of connectors available.**

Identify the mounting options of antennas used in wireless networking.   Antennas may be integrated or external to the wireless access point. Identify different types of antenna mounts, including internal and external (to the access point), pole/mast, ceiling, and walls.

Understand additional concepts regarding RF propagation.   Understand and know some of the additional concepts when choosing and installing antennas used with wireless LANs. These concepts include visual line of sight, radio frequency line of sight, and Fresnel zone.

Review Questions

1. Omnidirectional antennas have a horizontal beamwidth of _____ degrees.
    A. 90
    B. 180
    C. 270
    D. 360

2. Antennas provide an increase in RF coverage by using _____ gain.
    A. Active
    B. Passive
    C. Positive
    D. Maximum

3. Horizontal beamwidth is _____ to the earth's surface.
    A. Parallel
    B. Perpendicular
    C. Positive
    D. Negative

4. An access point requires _____ antennas for diversity functionality.
    A. One
    B. Two
    C. Three
    D. Six

5. What device is used to shunt transient current to ground in the event of an indirect lightning strike?
    A. Lightning striker
    B. Lightning arrestor
    C. Lightning prevention
    D. Lightning breaker

6. Amplifiers provide an increase in signal strength by using _____ gain.
    A. Active
    B. Passive
    C. Positive
    D. Maximum

7. Highly directional antennas are typically used for _____ connectivity.

  A. Short-range

  B. Omnidirectional

  C. Long-range

  D. Dipole

8. You are a network engineer. While moving a handheld wireless LAN device, you notice that the signal strength increases when the device is moved from a horizontal to a vertical position. This is because the _____ is changing.

  A. Polarization

  B. Wavelength

  C. Frequency

  D. Diffusion

9. RF line of sight is required for what type of IEEE 802.11 WLAN installation? (Choose two.)

  A. Point-to-point

  B. Scattered

  C. Point-to-multipoint

  D. Reflected

  E. Refracted

10. Which can cause a loss of signal strength? (Choose two.)

  A. Antenna

  B. Amplifier

  C. Cable

  D. Connector

  E. Transmitter

11. An IEEE 802.11g access point requires a minimum of how many antennas to move data?

  A. One

  B. Two

  C. Four

  D. Six

12. 802.11a access points support which antenna technology to help reduce the effects of multipath?

  A. Adjustable gain

  B. Antenna diversity

  C. Adjustable polarization

  D. Antenna multiplexing

13. The following graphic shows what type of antenna?

Image provided by www.L-com.com.

   A. Omnidirectional

   B. Yagi

   C. Patch/panel

   D. Parabolic dish

14. Which weather element would commonly have an effect on a wireless LAN system?

   A. Rain

   B. Snow

   C. Wind

   D. Hail

15. Wireless network cables and devices have impedance (AC resistance) of _____ ohms.

   A. 10

   B. 25

   C. 50

   D. 75

16. The curvature of the earth will have an impact on the wireless LAN signal after how many miles?

   A. 2

   B. 7

   C. 10

   D. 25

17. A patch antenna is an example of what type of antenna?

    A. Semidirectional

    B. Omnidirectional

    C. Highly directional

    D. Dipole-directional

18. An azimuth chart shows which RF radiation pattern?

    A. Vertical

    B. Horizontal

    C. Positive

    D. Negative

19. A point-to-point wireless link requires what percent of the Fresnel zone to be clear in order to be considered to have an acceptable RF line of sight?

    A. 0

    B. 20

    C. 40

    D. 60

20. The image below shows what type of antenna?

Image provided by www.L-com.com.

    A. Highly directional

    B. Dipole-directional

    C. Omnidirectional

    D. Semidirectional

Chapter 8

Wireless LAN Terminology and Technology

THE FOLLOWING CWTS EXAM OBJECTIVES ARE COVERED IN THIS CHAPTER:

✓ **1.2 Define basic characteristics of and concepts relating to Wi-Fi technology**

- Network discovery via active and passive scanning
- Power saving operation
- Data rates and throughput
- Dynamic rate switching
- 802.11 authentication and association
- The distribution system and roaming
- Infrastructure and ad hoc modes
- BSSID, SSID, BSS, ESS, BSA, IBSS
- Protection mechanisms

This chapter will look at some of the terminology used in IEEE 802.11 wireless networking. 802.11 wireless LANs may be configured in one of two modes: ad hoc or infrastructure mode. We will discuss both of these modes, as well as how the technology is applied and its advantages and disadvantages. In addition, we will examine some of the technical aspects, such as naming the wireless LAN and identifying the devices through Layer 2 MAC addressing or logical names. You will also learn about the methodologies a wireless LAN device or client station uses to locate and connect to the wireless network (these include passive and active scanning as well as the authentication and association processes.

It is important to know how IEEE 802.11 wireless LAN infrastructure devices such as access points are connected using a common wired or wireless distribution system. This distribution system allows access points to communicate with each other and gives the associated and connected wireless LAN devices the capability to roam or move between access points and maintain consistent connectivity across the wireless LAN.

Other wireless LAN technology factors are important to understand when studying IEEE 802.11 wireless networking. This chapter will discuss the differences between data rates and throughput. A sales or technical support specialist should be able to understand and explain why, for example, an IEEE 802.11n access point advertises a maximum data rate of up to 600 Mbps but in many cases the data transfers are half or less than half of this advertised data transfer rate.

Finally, we will look at IEEE 802.11 protection mechanisms in depth and explain why they are needed for backward compatibility and the effect they may have on the data transfer rate.

Some of the topics we will see in this chapter have been briefly touched on in earlier chapters. One of the objectives of this chapter is to tie the terminology and topics together. In wireless LAN technology education, it can be somewhat challenging to cover certain parts of the technology without touching lightly on some other topics. This chapter will tie some of the loose ends together and help you to better understand how IEEE 802.11 wireless networks operate.

Wireless LAN Modes of Operation

Wireless LANs can be configured to operate in different modes for device and user access. Two common modes for access are ad hoc mode and infrastructure mode. These two modes can be broken down into three different configurations:

- Independent basic service set (IBSS)
- Basic service set (BSS)
- Extended service set (ESS)

Each of these configurations will be discussed in more detail in this chapter. The application/deployment scenario for a wireless LAN is the determining factor for the best mode to use. The IBSS configuration does not require the use of an access point and unless specifically justified is not commonly used in enterprise wireless LAN deployments. In addition, if not properly implemented the IBSS can introduce security vulnerabilities, such as potentially bridging the wired network infrastructure to an unsecured wireless network. The most common configuration for an IEEE 802.11 wireless LAN is infrastructure mode, which uses at least one access point. Infrastructure mode requires a minimum of one access point but can consist of up to thousands of access points. The access points are connected by a common medium known as the distribution system. We will look at each of these modes and the details of how they are configured.

The Independent Basic Service Set

It is important to understand what the *independent basic service set* (IBSS) is, how it works, and potential uses, advantages, and disadvantages. This wireless LAN operation mode uses no access points and consists of only wireless devices or client computers. Communication occurs only among devices that are part of the same IBSS. Unlike an access point, this mode has no centralized control or manageable security or accounting features. Figure 8.1 shows devices in an IBSS.

FIGURE 8.1   Example of an independent basic service set (IBSS)

Wireless Client Device   Wireless Client Device

Wireless Client Device   Wireless Client Device

Certain parameters must be set on the devices that wish to participate in an IBSS. These parameters must be the same on all the devices in order for them to effectively communicate with one another. Three common parameters set on devices that belong to the same IBSS are:

- Service set identifier (SSID)
- Radio frequency channel
- Security configuration

The Service Set Identifier

The *service set identifier* (SSID) is a common parameter used in all wireless LAN operation configurations. Although it is discussed here, it also pertains to the other configurations discussed later in this chapter, such as the basic service set (BSS) and extended service set (ESS). The SSID is the logical name of the service set used to identify the wireless network. The SSID is used by devices to select a wireless network to join. This is accomplished through processes that are known collectively as the discovery phase and include passive and active scanning, both of which will be discussed later in this chapter.

In some cases, naming a wireless network can be a tough decision. Organizations that deploy a wireless network may already have a naming convention in place for such scenarios. If not, a decision will need to be made regarding the wireless network names (SSIDs) used for access points and other devices to identify the wireless LAN.

Every device that wishes to be part of the same wireless LAN IBSS, BSS, or ESS will use a common network name, the SSID. (See Figure 8.2 for an IBSS example.) For infrastructure devices such as access points, the SSID parameter is manually set on the access point. From the client access side, the SSID is a user-configurable parameter that can be set manually in the wireless client software utility or received automatically from networks that broadcast this information element.

FIGURE 8.2   IBSS, ad hoc, or peer-to-peer network using common configuration parameters

SSID = ABCD
Channel 1
WPA Personal

SSID = ABCD
Channel 1
WPA Personal

SSID = ABCD
Channel 1
WPA Personal

SSID = ABCD
Channel 1
WPA Personal

The SSID name should be unique and should not divulge who you are or the location of the wireless LAN devices, unless you are trying to create a wireless hotspot or a public accessible IEEE 802.11 wireless network. For example, if a fictitious bank by the name of ABC Bank used an SSID that included ABC_Bank, it would tell an intruder where the wireless network is and could be a potential security threat because a financial institution is a target. It is important to understand if the proper wireless LAN security is enabled, the SSID name should not be an issue, but there is no point in broadcasting certain types of information. Rather than using the bank name in the SSID, consider a unique name that does not describe the business or location.

The SSID is case sensitive and has a maximum limit of 32 characters or, as specified in the IEEE 802.11 standard, 32 octets.

SSID Hiding

Most manufacturers of small office/home office (SOHO) and enterprise-grade access points allow the SSID to be hidden from view for devices attempting to locate a wireless network. In this case a client device would need to know and specify the SSID in the client utility profile in order to connect to the network. Even though this is not an effective way to secure a wireless network and should not be used to do so, it is a practice some choose to use for various reasons. Some disadvantages to not broadcasting the SSID are that it may cause an increase in roaming times in an enterprise deployment and in a SOHO deployment cause neighbors to deploy on the same channel that you are using because they are unable to see your network. SSID hiding (also known as a closed network) will be discussed in more detail in Chapter 9, "Wireless LAN Security Basics."

Figure 8.3 shows an example of entering the SSID in the Microsoft Windows 7 AutoConfig wireless configuration client utility for an ad hoc network. First you select "Set up a wireless ad hoc (computer-to-computer) network" in the Set Up A Connection Or Network dialog box; then you enter the SSID on the "Give your network a name and choose security options" Properties page.

The Radio Frequency Channel

The IBSS wireless network configuration requires a user to set the specific radio frequency channel that will be used by all devices that are part of the same IBSS network. This is accomplished in the client utility software for the network adapter. Some client software utilities set this automatically, in which case the IBSS will use the channel automatically specified. You may also be able to specify the RF channel in the advanced properties of the wireless network adapter device driver properties.

It is important to understand that all wireless devices in any common IBSS must be communicating on the same radio frequency channel. If the client utility does allow a channel to be set, the channel chosen is up to the user but based on the local regulatory domain in which the network is used. Additional devices wishing to join the IBSS must do so by scanning, either passively or by use of active scanning. Figure 8.4 shows an example of setting the RF channel on a notebook computer.

FIGURE 8.3   Entering the SSID and other parameters in the Microsoft Windows 7 wireless configuration client utility

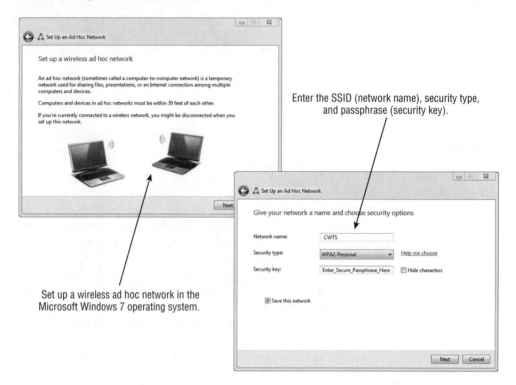

IBSS Security

With IBSS networks, there is no centralized control and no security management features. Security is left up to the individual user or wireless device. If a user inadvertently shares a resource, it could expose sensitive information and pose security threats. This can be a concern for many enterprise installations, and therefore the use of an IBSS is against corporate security policy in many organizations.

IBSS Terminology

The wireless LAN industry uses several different terms to identify an IBSS. The term used is up to the manufacturer or a specific implementation. An IBSS is usually identified by one of three terms:

▪   Independent basic service set (IBSS)

- Ad hoc

- Peer-to-peer

FIGURE 8.4   Setting the RF channel for an IBSS, ad hoc wireless network in the Intel 5100 IEEE 802.11a/g/n wireless network adapter driver Advanced settings page

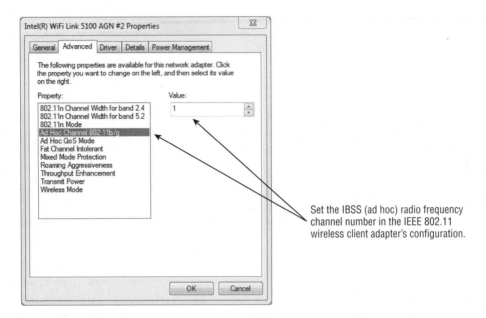

Regardless of the terminology used—*IBSS*, *ad hoc*, or *peer-to-peer*—it comes down to wireless LAN devices connecting to each other without the use of an access point or other wireless infrastructure device. All devices in an IBSS network work independently of one another, and there is no centralized management or administration capability. This type of connection may be useful in homes or small offices for ease of installation but is rarely if at all used with enterprise or corporate wireless networks.

Advantages and Disadvantages of an IBSS

The advantages and disadvantages of an IBSS network will vary depending on the application.

Some of the advantages of IBSS are as follows:

Easy to Configure   To create an IBSS, the user only needs to specify an SSID, set the radio frequency channel, and enable the security settings.

No Investment in Access Point Hardware   An IBSS can be created with the IEEE 802.11 wireless LAN adapter that is built into the wireless computer or other device. No infrastructure device such as an access point is required to connect the wireless LAN devices together.

Some disadvantages of IBSS are as follows:

Limited Radio Frequency Range   Because radio communications is two-way, all devices need to be in a mutual communication range of one another in order to operate effectively.

No Centralized Administration Capability   In many large or enterprise deployments, IBSS connectivity is against corporate security policy because it is impossible to manage such networks centrally.

Not Scalable   There is no set maximum number of devices that can be part of an IBSS network, but the capacity of such networks is low compared to other types of networks.

Difficult to Secure   Some computer operating systems have made the setup of an IBSS wireless network very easy for any type of user. These users may inadvertently share or allow access to sensitive or proprietary information. This security threat is worse if an IBSS user is also physically connected to a wired network and provides a bridge from an unsecured or unmanaged wireless network to a company's wired network infrastructure.

A wireless LAN device such as a notebook computer configured as an IBSS device can be a potential security threat if it is also connected to a wired network infrastructure. It could provide a bridge for unsecured wireless access to the company's wired network. In this configuration, potential intruders would have access to information from a corporate network by connecting to the unsecured ad hoc network. For this reason, this type of configuration is against corporate security policies of many companies. Many organizations use wireless intrusion prevention systems to detect and shut down wireless ad hoc networks. It is important to inform visitors and contractors who may be physically connected to the company's infrastructure when ad hoc networks are against the corporate security policy to prevent potential security issues.

Setting up an IBSS network is similar to setting up a workgroup for an operating system such as Microsoft Windows. All devices with the same workgroup name will be able to communicate with each other sharing resources such as files, printers, and so on.

The Basic Service Set

The *basic service set* (BSS) is the foundation of the wireless network. This mode consists of an access point connected to a network infrastructure and its associated wireless devices. This is considered the foundation because it may be one of many access points that form a wireless network. With a BSS setup, each access point is connected to a network infrastructure, also known as the distribution system (DS), which allows connected wireless LAN devices to access network resources based on the appropriate permissions the wireless device or user has access to. The radio frequency area of coverage depends on several factors, such as the antenna gain and RF output power settings; this area of coverage is known as the *basic service area* (BSA). Any IEEE 802.11 wireless device in radio range and part of the BSA with the correct configuration parameters, including the SSID and security settings, will be able to successfully connect to the access point. Figure 8.5 shows an example of a BSS.

FIGURE 8.5   Basic service set consisting of a single access point connected to a distribution system and associated devices

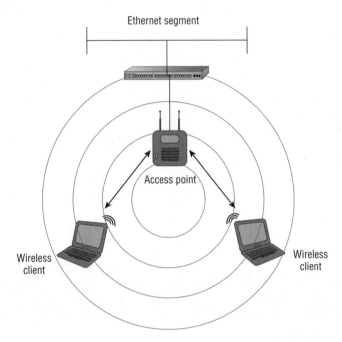

As mentioned earlier, infrastructure mode consists of a wireless access point connected to a distribution system. The BSS consisting of one access point is a common implementation in many homes, SOHO, or small to medium businesses (SMBs). The decision to use a single access point depends on several factors, among them the size of the location, how the wireless network is used, and how many wireless devices will be connected.

Just as in an IBSS configuration, several parameters need to be configured for a BSS. These include the SSID or name of the network, the radio frequency channel to be used, and any security parameters that are set on the BSS. The access point will broadcast these and other parameters about the wireless network to devices that want to connect to the BSS, thus requiring minimal configuration on the wireless client side. Unlike the independent basic service set, in a BSS the radio frequency channel is set on the access point and not on the wireless client device.

Advantages and Disadvantages of a BSS

A BSS has many benefits, advantages, and disadvantages. Some of the advantages are as follows:

- Uses intelligent devices with a large feature set to provide users with consistent, reliable, and secure communications to a wireless network.

- Useful in a variety of situations: homes, SOHO, and small to large businesses.

- Very scalable; you can increase the coverage and capacity of a BSS by adding more access points.

- Centralized administration and control.

- Security parameters and specific access can be set centrally.

Some of the disadvantages of a BSS are as follows:

- Incurs additional hardware costs compared to IBSS.

- Usually will require a site survey to determine radio frequency coverage and capacity requirements.

- Must be connected to a network infrastructure known as the distribution system, either wired or wireless.

- Additional knowledge required for configuration and deployment.

Figure 8.6 shows configuring the SSID on an access point.

FIGURE 8.6   Graphical user interface for a Cisco Linksys access point configuring the SSID

The Extended Service Set

As stated in the IEEE 802.11-2012 standard, an *extended service set* (ESS) is defined as a "set of one or more interconnected basic service sets (BSSs) that appears as a single BSS to the logical link control (LLC) layer at any station (STA) associated with one of those BSSs." In basic terms, this can be one or more access points connected to a common wired or wireless distribution system. An ESS is a common configuration in most wireless LAN deployments for small to medium businesses as well as large enterprise organizations.

In most cases, an ESS would be used to provide consistent and complete coverage across an entire organization. An ESS can be thought of as several basic service sets (BSSs) that must have matching parameters, such as SSID and security settings. If the SSIDs of two access points do not match, then they are considered separate basic service sets, even though they are connected by a common network infrastructure. It is the distribution system connecting these together and a common network name (SSID) that makes up the ESS. In most cases, the basic service area for each BSS will overlap to allow roaming (transition) from one BSS to another. Figure 8.7 shows an example of an extended service set (ESS).

FIGURE 8.7 Two basic service sets connected by a common distribution system, making an extended service set

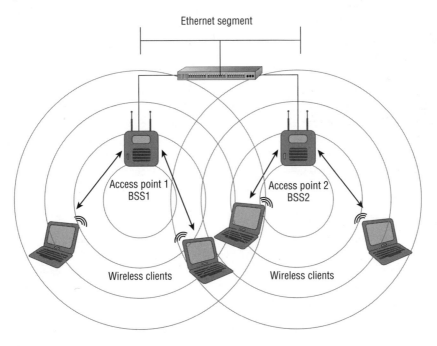

Roaming between access points is a critical component of wireless LAN technology in most modern wireless network deployments. This is because the wireless LAN is now a major part of every corporate network. Many envision a complete wireless network for all communications, including data, voice, and video. Roaming is so important that the IEEE added the 802.11r amendment to provide a standardized methodology for client station roaming and fast secure transition within the wireless LAN.

The Basic Service Area

The basic service area (BSA) is the area of radio frequency coverage or the RF cell that encompasses a wireless access point and its associated stations. A wireless client device will be contained in the basic service area as long as it has enough required receive signal strength to maintain an association state with the wireless access point.

Know Your Abbreviations: SSID vs. ESSID vs. BSSID

It is easy to confuse the abbreviations (acronyms) for several of the wireless LAN terms we have learned. This sidebar will summarize the differences.

SSID (Service Set Identifier)

SSID (service set identifier) is the network name and provides some segmentation of the wireless network.

ESSID (Extended Service Set Identifier)

Although not defined by the IEEE 802.11 standard or amendments, *extended service set identifier* (ESSID) is a term that some manufacturers use in place of SSID. For the most part, ESSID and SSID are synonymous terms for the name or segmentation of a wireless network. The term used will vary among manufacturers. The term ESSID was adopted by some manufacturers because it implies more than one access point is using the same SSID and security settings connected to a common distribution system.

BSSID (Basic Service Set Identifier)

It is sometimes easy to confuse the *basic service set identifier* (BSSID) with the SSID or name of the network. The BSSID is defined as the unique identifier, Media Access Control (MAC) address of the basic service set. It is important to note that some manufacturers may allow for several BSSIDs to be connected to a single access point radio or for a single common BSSID to be shared among many access points.

To review, the MAC address is the unique identifier of a network adapter or what is known as the hardware address. The radio in an access point is also a network adapter. The difference between a wired and a wireless network adapter is simply that no Ethernet jack is available on a wireless adapter. Instead, a radio is used for Layer 1 communications.

The MAC address is a 48-bit IEEE 802 format address that uniquely identifies the network interface adapter—or, in this case, radio. The format of the BSSID is *XX:XX:XX:YY:YY:YY* where *X* is the number assigned to a manufacturer and *Y* is the unique hardware address of the device.

Although the BSSID uniquely identifies the access point's radio using a MAC address, the SSID is broadcast as the name of the network in order to allow devices to connect. Some devices allow for multiple SSIDs, which use multiple BSSIDs for a single radio. This lets a single access point connected to a wired infrastructure provide multiple WLANs.

In an ad hoc or IBSS network there is no access point for centralized communication. Instead, wireless LAN devices communicate directly with each other. Because there is no access point in this configuration, the BSSID is a randomly generated number that has the same format as the 802 MAC address and is generated by the first ad hoc wireless device at startup.

Connecting to an IEEE 802.11 Wireless Network

In order for a device to successfully connect to a wireless network, several different frame exchanges must take place. Various frame types allow for specific functions to occur. They include the authentication and association process, reserving the medium, exchanging data, and power save functions. The following section introduces some of the frame types and the roles they play in wireless networking.

IEEE 802.11 Frame Types

As discussed in Chapter 6, "Radio Frequency Fundamentals for Wireless LAN Technology," devices communicate by sending radio frequency waves to each other through the air. These RF waves carry the digital data from one device to another. At this stage, the information traveling through the air is organized into what are known as frames. These frame types play various roles depending on the information being sent. Wireless LANs use three different frame types.

Management Frames

Management frames are used to manage the network. Management frames assist wireless LAN devices in finding and connecting to a wireless network. This includes advertising the capabilities of the WLAN and allowing connections by the authentication and association process. Management frames are exchanged only between immediate wireless devices such as an access point and client device and never cross the Data Link layer (Layer 2) of the OSI model. It is important to understand that management frames are always transmitted at the lowest mandatory data rate of the service set so that all stations on the same radio frequency channel in the basic service area can understand them. The following are examples of management frames:

- Beacon
- Probe request
- Probe response
- Authentication
- Association request
- Association response

Control Frames

Control frames are used to control access to the wireless medium by allowing devices to reserve the medium and acknowledge data. In addition, some control frames are used to request data from the access point after returning from a power save state and with IEEE 802.11 protection mechanisms to allow wireless device coexistence. Some examples of control frames are as follows:

- RTS
- CTS
- CTS to Self
- PS-Poll
- ACK

Data Frames

As their name implies, data frames are used to carry data payload or Layer 3 information between wireless devices.

A special type of data frame is the null data or null function frame, which helps implement power save features and is not used to carry any data payload. There is also a variant of the null frame called the QoS null frame, which is used with quality of service functions. Examples of data frames include:

- Data
- QoS data
- Null data

The details of the specific functions of each of these frame types are beyond the scope of this book and the CWTS exam objectives, but some of these frames needed to be briefly introduced in order to explain upcoming topics. These include a wireless device "listening" for a network to join, supplying the appropriate credentials, and finally connecting to send data to the network infrastructure.

Wireless Network Discovery

Wireless network discovery is the process of a client device looking for wireless networks and identifying the parameters of the network, including the SSID, supported data rates, and security settings. The discovery phase consists of the passive scanning and active scanning processes. Wireless network discovery prepares a wireless client device to perform an IEEE 802.11 authenticat ion and association, which will allow a device access to the wireless network.

Passive Scanning

The first part of the discovery phase in IEEE 802.11 wireless networking is known as *passive scanning*. This process allows wireless LAN devices to "listen" for information about wireless networks in the radio receiving area of the wireless network or the basic service area (BSA). During the passive scanning process, wireless LAN devices will listen for specific information to make them aware of networks in the area. An analogy to this process would be using an FM radio tuner to scan through the entire band listening for a station to tune in to. The radio will scan through the band listening for different stations. Once a desired station is heard, the person listening can stop on that specific radio station.

As mentioned earlier in this chapter, management frames assist wireless LAN devices in finding and connecting to a wireless network. An example of a management frame that works in the discovery phase or passive scanning is a beacon frame. This frame for the most part is an advertisement of the wireless network. It carries specific information about the access point or basic service set such as the SSID, the radio frequency channel that it is operating on, the available data rates it is configured for, the security parameters, and much more. During the passive scanning phase, wireless devices listen for beacons advertising the details about the wireless networks in the area or radio range of the client device. Wireless LAN devices are constantly listening for beacon frames. Figure 8.8 shows a wireless LAN client passively scanning and listening for an access point to connect with.

By default, beacons broadcast at about 10 times a second. This value is actually 1024 microseconds and is identified as the target beacon transmission time (TBTT). Although this interval can be changed, it is recommended to do so only if necessary or recommended by the manufacturer. In some cases, manufacturers may suggest specific timing intervals for such frames as beacons.

FIGURE 8.8   An example of passive scanning with a wireless LAN client listening for access points in the basic service area

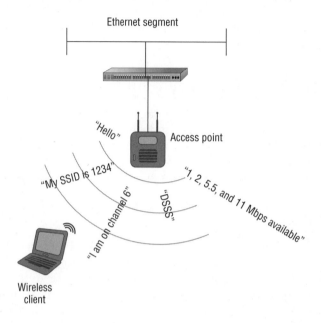

Figure 8.9 shows a packet analyzer capturing beacon frames generated from an access point.

FIGURE 8.9   Packet analyzer capture of beacon frames

00:14:A8:53:5F:C0	Ethernet Broadcast	00:14:A8:53:5F:C0	47%	802.11 Beacon
00:14:A8:53:5F:C0	Ethernet Broadcast	00:14:A8:53:5F:C0	45%	802.11 Beacon
00:14:A8:53:5F:C0	Ethernet Broadcast	00:14:A8:53:5F:C0	44%	802.11 Beacon
00:14:A8:53:5F:C0	Ethernet Broadcast	00:14:A8:53:5F:C0	44%	802.11 Beacon
00:14:A8:53:5F:C0	Ethernet Broadcast	00:14:A8:53:5F:C0	44%	802.11 Beacon
00:14:A8:53:5F:C0	Ethernet Broadcast	00:14:A8:53:5F:C0	44%	802.11 Beacon
00:14:A8:53:5F:C0	Ethernet Broadcast	00:14:A8:53:5F:C0	45%	802.11 Beacon
00:14:A8:53:5F:C0	Ethernet Broadcast	00:14:A8:53:5F:C0	47%	802.11 Beacon

Active Scanning

Active scanning is the second part of the wireless LAN discovery phase. In *active scanning*, wireless LAN devices wishing to connect to a network send out a management frame known as a probe request. The function of this management frame is to find a specific wireless access point to connect with. Depending on the wireless client utility software used, if an SSID is specified in the client utility software active profile, the device will join only a network with the matching SSID that is specified. An exception to this is a probe request that contains a "wildcard SSID" or a "null SSID." The IEEE 802.11 standard requires all access points to respond to a "null" or broadcast probe request. This type of probe request frame will not specify an SSID value and will rely on the access points to provide the SSID in the probe response frame. The probe request and probe response frames are discussed in more detail later in this chapter.

Access points constantly listen for probe request frames. Any access point within hearing range of the wireless device and having a matching SSID sends out a probe response frame to the wireless device. If more than one access point responds, the device selects the "best" access point to connect with based on certain factors such as signal strength and signal quality. Figure 8.10 illustrates the active scanning process.

FIGURE 8.10   Wireless client device sending a probe request frame to access points in radio range

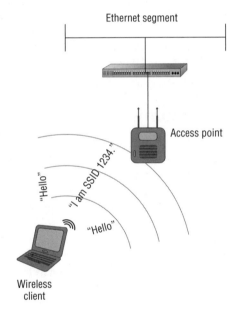

Frames Used for Active Scanning

During the active scanning process, two frames are exchanged between the device and the access point.

1. The wireless LAN device sends a broadcast probe request frame to all devices, including access points within radio range.

2. The access point(s) send a probe response frame to the device so it can identify the parameters of the network before joining.

Figure 8.11 shows a packet analyzer capturing frames of the active scanning process.

FIGURE 8.11   Packet analyzer capture of probe request and probe response frames

00:19:7E:43:4E:E8	Ethernet Broadcast	Ethernet Broadcast	74%	802.11 Probe Req
00:14:A8:53:5F:C0	00:19:7E:43:4E:E8	00:14:A8:53:5F:C0	48%	802.11 Probe Rsp
00:19:7E:43:4E:E8	00:14:A8:53:5F:C0		75%	802.11 Ack

> The IEEE 802.11 standard requires access points to respond to devices that are sending a null or blank SSID. The standard refers to this as a wildcard SSID. It is important not to confuse this with disabling the SSID broadcast on an access point. Most wireless equipment manufacturers provide the capability to set the access point not to respond to a probe request with a null or wildcard SSID. If the AP is set not to respond to such probe requests, the wireless device is required to have the SSID specified in the client utility in order to connect to the BSS.

IEEE 802.11 Authentication

Authentication in general is defined as verifying or confirming an identity. We use a variety of authentication mechanisms in our daily lives, such as logging onto a computer or network at home or at the office, accessing secure sites on the Internet, using an ATM machine, or showing an identification badge to get access to a building.

IEEE 802.11 devices must use an authentication process in order to access network resources. This IEEE 802.11 authentication process differs from conventional authentication methods such as providing credentials, a username and password to gain access to a network. The *authentication* discussed here is wireless device or IEEE 802.11 authentication, required in order for the device to become part of the wireless network and participate in exchanging data frames. (Providing credentials such as a username and password or a preshared key is a different type of authentication, to be discussed in Chapter 9.) The IEEE 802.11 standard addresses two types of IEEE authentication methods: open system and shared key.

IEEE 802.11 Open System Authentication

This 802.11 authentication method is defined by the IEEE 802.11 standard as a null authentication algorithm and is a two-step authentication process. Two management frames are exchanged between the device and the access point during open systems authentication. For the most part, open system authentication cannot fail unless other security measures such as MAC filtering are put in place that will prevent the device from accessing the network. Keep in mind that IEEE 802.11 open system authentication always exists, even with the most secure wireless LANs. It is used to allow the wireless station to connect to the access point and then after association use additional credentials such as a passphrase or username and password pair for authentication. If the wireless station did not perform an open system authentication and association first, there would be no way to use additional security mechanisms. IEEE 802.11 open system authentication is the only valid authentication process allowed with newer wireless LAN security amendments and interoperability certifications for the network to be considered a robust security network (RSN).

Open system authentication is a very simple process. A wireless LAN device will ask an access point, "Can I be a part of this network?" and the access point will respond, "Sure, come join the party." So there really is no validation of identity. *Open system authentication* is considered a two-way frame exchange because two authentication frames are sent during this process. It is not a request and response situation; it is authentication and success.

Figure 8.12 illustrates open system authentication.

FIGURE 8.12   A wireless client authenticating to an access point using open system authentication

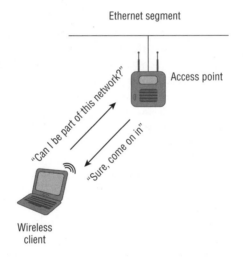

Ethernet segment

Access point

"Can I be part of this network?"

"Sure, come on in"

Wireless client

Open system authentication does not provide any type of data encryption. With open system authentication, Wired Equivalent Privacy (WEP) is optional and can be used for data encryption if desired. WEP will be discussed in more detail in Chapter 9.

These are the two steps used for open system authentication. One management frame is sent in each step.

1. The wireless LAN device wanting to authenticate sends an authentication frame to the access point. This frame is acknowledged by the access point.

2. The access point accepting the authentication sends a successful authentication frame back to the device. This frame is acknowledged by the authenticating device.

Figure 8.13 shows a packet capture of the two-way open system authentication frame exchange.

FIGURE 8.13 Packet capture of open system authentication

00:19:7E:43:4E:E8	00:14:A8:53:5F:C0	00:14:A8:53:5F:C0	75%	802.11 Auth
00:14:A8:53:5F:C0	00:19:7E:43:4E:E8		47%	802.11 Ack
00:14:A8:53:5F:C0	00:19:7E:43:4E:E8	00:14:A8:53:5F:C0	50%	802.11 Auth
00:19:7E:43:4E:E8	00:14:A8:53:5F:C0		75%	802.11 Ack

IEEE 802.11 Shared-Key Authentication

Shared-key is another authentication method defined by the IEEE 802.11 standard. It is a little more complex than open system authentication. This IEEE 802.11 authentication method is a four-way frame exchange. During *shared-key authentication*, four management frames are sent between the wireless device wanting to join the wireless network and the access point. Shared-key authentication differs from open system authentication in that shared-key authentication is used for both IEEE 802.11 authentication and data encryption.

Shared-key authentication is considered flawed because the authentication key and therefore the encryption (WEP key) used could be captured by an intruder. If an intruder were to capture the four wireless frames used during the shared-key authentication process, they would be able to use this information with the appropriate software and extract the security (WEP) key. Shared-key authentication requires the use of Wired Equivalent Privacy (WEP) for both wireless device authentication and data encryption. Because WEP is mandatory with shared-key authentication, an intruder could potentially identify the WEP key used for the network by capturing the authentication process using a wireless packet analyzer. Shared-key authentication therefore should be avoided whenever possible and is not allowed when using newer IEEE 802.11i, WPA, or WPA2 security methods.

Some manufacturers have removed the option to set shared-key authentication, both in infrastructure devices such as access points and bridges and in client software utilities. Some legacy devices may still use shared-key authentication as the only authentication option. If this is the case, steps need to be taken to protect the integrity of the network and also to identify an appropriate upgrade path for the devices using IEEE 802.11 shared-key authentication.

Figure 8.14 illustrates the four frames exchanged during the shared-key authentication process.

As mentioned earlier, because WEP is mandatory with shared-key authentication, it makes a system vulnerable to intrusion. Therefore, open system authentication is considered more secure than shared-key authentication when WEP is used with open system authentication. This is because WEP is used to encrypt the data only and not used for the IEEE 802.11 authentication process. WEP was designed as a way to protect wireless networking users from casual eavesdropping.

FIGURE 8.14   Shared-key authentication uses a four-way frame exchange.

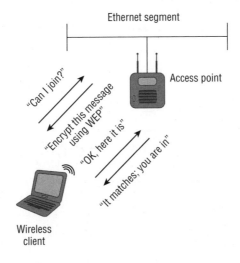

Frames Used for Shared-Key Authentication

An 802.11 wireless device must perform an IEEE 802.11 authentication to the wireless network prior to associating according to the 802.11 standard. The following steps show the four-way frame exchange used for shared-key authentication. This method should not be used but is shown here to illustrate the process.

1. The wireless LAN device wanting to authenticate sends an authentication frame to the access point. This frame is acknowledged by the access point.

2. The access point sends a frame back to the WLAN device that contains a challenge text. This frame is acknowledged by the WLAN device.

3. The WLAN device sends a frame back to the access point containing an encrypted response to the challenge text. The response is encrypted using the device's WEP key. This frame is acknowledged by the access point.

4. After verifying the encrypted response the access point accepts the authentication and sends a "successful authentication" frame back to the device. This final frame is acknowledged by the device.

Figure 8.15 shows the four authentication frames used in shared-key authentication.

FIGURE 8.15 Packet capture of four frame exchange 802.11 shared-key authentication

00:19:7E:43:4E:E8	00:14:A8:53:5F:C0	00:14:A8:53:5F:C0	88%	802.11 Auth
00:14:A8:53:5F:C0	00:19:7E:43:4E:E8		44%	802.11 Ack
00:14:A8:53:5F:C0	00:19:7E:43:4E:E8	00:14:A8:53:5F:C0	45%	802.11 Auth
00:19:7E:43:4E:E8	00:14:A8:53:5F:C0		84%	802.11 Ack
00:19:7E:43:4E:E8	00:14:A8:53:5F:C0	00:14:A8:53:5F:C0	88%	802.11 Auth
00:14:A8:53:5F:C0	00:19:7E:43:4E:E8		42%	802.11 Ack
00:14:A8:53:5F:C0	00:19:7E:43:4E:E8	00:14:A8:53:5F:C0	44%	802.11 Auth
00:19:7E:43:4E:E8	00:14:A8:53:5F:C0		87%	802.11 Ack

IEEE 802.11 ASSOCIATION

IEEE 802.11 *association* takes place after a wireless device has been successfully 802.11 authenticated either by open system authentication or by shared-key authentication. In the association state, the authenticated device can pass traffic across the access point to the network infrastructure or other associated wireless devices, allowing access to resources that the device or user has permissions to access. After a device is authenticated and associated, it is considered to be part of the basic service set. A device must be 802.11 authenticated before it can be associated. Figure 8.16 illustrates the association process, and Figure 8.17 shows frames used during the association process.

FIGURE 8.16 Authentication and association

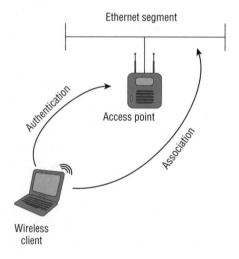

FIGURE 8.17 Packet capture of the association request and association response process

00:19:7E:43:4E:E8	00:14:A8:53:5F:C0	00:14:A8:53:5F:C0	78%	802.11 Assoc Req
00:14:A8:53:5F:C0	00:19:7E:43:4E:E8		44%	802.11 Ack
00:14:A8:53:5F:C0	00:19:7E:43:4E:E8	00:14:A8:53:5F:C0	50%	802.11 Assoc Rsp
00:19:7E:43:4E:E8	00:14:A8:53:5F:C0		71%	802.11 Ack

After successful association, the IEEE 802.11 authentication and association process is complete. Keep in mind that this is very basic access to the network using either open system authentication or WEP for authentication and encryption. After this process is complete, more sophisticated authentication mechanisms such as IEEE 802.1X/EAP (which provides user-based authentication) or preshared key (passphrase) can be used to secure the wireless network. These and other security components will be discussed in more detail in Chapter 9.

Frames Used for IEEE 802.11 Association

After a successful 802.11 authentication, the association process will begin. Association allows a wireless device to send information across the access point to the network infrastructure.

1. Wireless LAN device sends an association request frame to the access point. This frame is acknowledged by the access point.

2. The access point sends an association response frame to the device. This frame is acknowledged by the associating device.

IEEE 802.11 Deauthentication and Disassociation

It is worthwhile to understand that the opposite of authentication and association can occur in a wireless LAN. These events are known as *deauthentication* and *disassociation*. Deauthentication occurs when an existing authentication is no longer valid. This can be caused by a wireless LAN device logging off from the current connection or roaming to a different BSS. A disassociation occurs when an association to an access point is terminated. This may occur when the associated wireless LAN device roams from one BSS to another. Both deauthentication and disassociation are notifications and not requests. Since neither can be refused by either side, they are both considered automatically successful from the sender's perspective. Unless IEEE 802.11w is implemented, deauthentication can also be a security issue. These frames can be used for denial of service attacks or to hijack a wireless device. Both deauthentication and disassociation frames are management frames. Figure 8.18 shows how disassociation and deauthentication frames would look on a packet analyzer.

FIGURE 8.18 Packet capture of disassociation and deauthentication frames

00:19:7E:43:4E:E8	00:14:A8:53:5F:C0	00:14:A8:53:5F:C0	77%	802.11 Disassoc
00:14:A8:53:5F:C0	00:19:7E:43:4E:E8		50%	802.11 Ack
00:14:A8:53:5F:C0	00:19:7E:43:4E:E8	00:14:A8:53:5F:C0	48%	802.11 Deauth
00:19:7E:43:4E:E8	00:14:A8:53:5F:C0		74%	802.11 Ack

Intrusion tools are available that will continuously send deauthentication frames to a device. Use of this type of tool is considered a denial-of-service (DoS) attack. An intruder may also use a deauthentication frame to force a device to reauthenticate to an access point causing the device to be hijacked. This as well as other possible intrusion techniques will be discussed in Chapter 9. The 802.11w amendment provides enhancements to the IEEE 802.11 standard that enables data integrity, data origin authenticity, replay protection, and data confidentiality for selected IEEE 802.11 management frames including authentication.

The Distribution System

In wireless LAN technology, the *distribution system* (DS) is the common network infrastructure to which wireless access points are connected; it can be wired or wireless. In most cases this would be an Ethernet segment. In this capacity, the access point acts like a Layer 2 translational bridge. A *translational bridge* is defined as a device used to connect two or more dissimilar types of LANs together, such as wireless (IEEE 802.11) and Ethernet (IEEE 802.3). From a receiver's perspective, this allows an access point to take information from the air (the communication medium in wireless networking) and make a decision either to send it back out to the same wireless radio or to forward it across to the distribution system. An access point can do this because it has enough intelligence to determine if a data frame is destined to be sent to the distribution system or if it should stay on the originating wireless side of the network. This is possible because the access point knows whether a device is part of the wireless LAN side through the authentication and association methods mentioned earlier. Figure 8.19 shows an example of a distribution system.

FIGURE 8.19   Two access points connected to a common distribution system, in this case IEEE 802.3, Ethernet

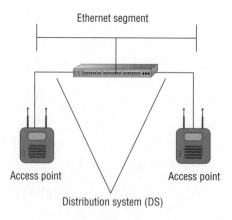

The distribution system is a network segment that consists of one or more connected basic service sets. As mentioned earlier, according to the original IEEE 802.11 standard, one or more interconnected basic service sets make up an extended service set. The distribution system allows wireless LAN devices to communicate with resources on a wired network infrastructure or to communicate with each other through the wireless medium. Either way, all wireless frame transmissions will traverse through an access point.

In some cases it may be feasible and justified to use a *wireless distribution system* (WDS). Unlike the wired distribution system mentioned earlier, a wireless distribution system will connect basic service sets together using wireless LAN technology. Typically the best way to use a WDS is to use two different radio technologies in the same access points. For example, using the 2.4 GHz band for wireless device access and the 5 GHz band for the distribution system will limit contention and provide associated devices a better experience because one radio is used for device access and the other creates the WDS. Figure 8.20 shows an example of a wireless distribution system.

FIGURE 8.20   Two dual-band access points used to create a wireless distribution system

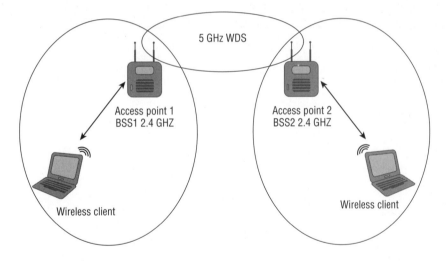

Data Rates

The speed at which wireless devices are designed to exchange information is known as the *data rate*. As mentioned in Chapter 5, "Physical Layer Access Methods and Spread-Spectrum Technology," these rates will differ depending on the wireless standard, amendment, spread spectrum type, or Physical Layer technology in use. Table 8.1 shows data rates for various WLAN technologies. Data rates do not accurately represent the amount of information that is actually being transferred between devices and a wireless network. Figure 8.21 shows an 802.11a/g/n wireless LAN adapter in a notebook computer reading a data rate of 300 Mbps. To learn more about the actual amount of information transferred, see the next section, "Throughput."

TABLE 8.1 Data rates based on spread spectrum type

Standard/amendment	Technology	Data rates
802.11	FHSS	1 and 2 Mbps
802.11	DSSS	1 and 2 Mbps
802.11b	HR/DSSS	5.5 and 11 Mbps; 1 and 2 Mbps from DSSS
802.11a	OFDM	6, 9, 12, 18, 24, 36 and 48 Mbps
802.11g	ERP-OFDM	6, 9, 12, 18, 24, 36 and 48 Mbps
802.11n	HT-OFDM	Up to 300 Mbps

FIGURE 8.21 Windows 7 wireless configuration utility showing a data rate of 300 Mbps for an IEEE 802.11a/g/n wireless LAN adapter

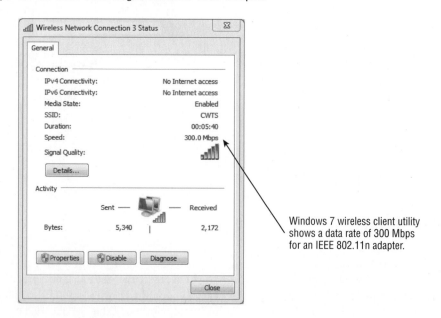

Windows 7 wireless client utility shows a data rate of 300 Mbps for an IEEE 802.11n adapter.

Throughput

Unlike data rate (the maximum amount of information theoretically capable of being sent), *throughput* is the amount of information actually being correctly received or transmitted. Many variables affect the throughput of information being sent. Some of these include:

- Spread spectrum or Physical Layer technology type in use
- Radio frequency interference
- Number of wireless devices connected to an access point

For example, an 802.11g wireless access point has a maximum data rate of 54 Mbps. With one user connected to this access point, chances are the best throughput that could be expected is less than 50 percent of the maximum, or about 20 Mbps. If more users connect to the same access point, the throughput for each user would be even less, because of the contention between users sharing the same wireless medium. Figure 8.22 shows an example of actual throughput for an 802.11a/g/n wireless LAN adapter.

FIGURE 8.22   Actual throughput of an IEEE 802.11a/g/n 300 Mbps wireless LAN adapter

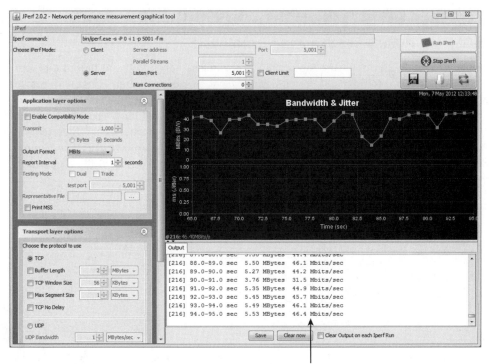

JPerf performance test utility showing an average throughput of about 44 Mbps using an IEEE 802.11a/g/n wireless adapter

---

Packing and Shipping Data: A Throughput Analogy

Packing and shipping an item in a cardboard box is a way of looking at data rate versus throughput. You have a cardboard box that is rated to have a maximum capacity of two cubic feet. You want to send a fragile item such as a vase to somebody else. The vase if measured would really only take about one cubic foot of space. However, this is a very fragile item, and you want to make sure it gets to the destination without any damage. So rather than just put the vase by itself in a box with a capacity of one cubic foot, you want to protect it with some packing material such as bubble wrap. Wrapping the vase in bubble wrap will take an additional one cubic foot of space.

The data rate is analogous to the box capable of holding two cubic feet of material. The one-cubic-foot vase is analogous to the actual data being sent. The packing material is analogous to the contention management and other overhead that causes the throughput to be less than the theoretical capacity of the WLAN device.

In Exercise 8.1 you will measure the throughput of your own wireless network.

EXERCISE 8.1

Measuring Throughput of a Wireless Network

In this activity, you will measure throughput of a wireless network. If you have the proper equipment, it is not too difficult. If you already have an existing wireless network set up with a computer connected to the wired side or distribution system, you have a good part of the setup done. This exercise uses the JPerf software program for Microsoft Windows. JPerf is a graphical front-end program for IPerf from SourceForge. JPerf does require that Java be installed on the computer. The following step-by-step instructions assume a wireless access point already configured with TCP/IP settings as well as SSID. To perform this exercise, you will need the following equipment:

- Two computers

- Java installed on both computers

- One wireless access point

- One Ethernet cable

- One wireless network adapter

- JPerf software (jperf-2.0.2.zip)

The JPerf software is available from code.google.com/p/xjperf. Click the Downloads tab to complete the download.

Complete the following steps to measure throughput:

1. Connect the required equipment as shown in the graphic.

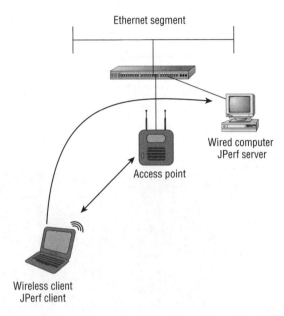

Ethernet segment

Wired computer
JPerf server

Access point

Wireless client
JPerf client

2. Create a folder named Jperf on the C:\ drive on both computers and extract the contents of the jperf-2.0.2.zip file you downloaded to the Jperf folder you created. This folder needs to be created at the root or C:\ in order for the remaining steps to work as written.

3. On the computer connected to the wired distribution system, open a command prompt. This will vary based on the operating system in use. For example, if you are using Windows XP or above, select Start ➢ All Programs ➢ Accessories ➢ Command Prompt.

4. In the command prompt window, type the command **ipconfig** at the C:\ prompt and note the IP address of this computer.

```
C:\WINDOWS\system32\cmd.exe

C:\>ipconfig

Windows IP Configuration

Ethernet adapter Wireless Network Connection:

        Connection-specific DNS Suffix  . :
        IP Address. . . . . . . . . . . . : 192.168.100.35
        Subnet Mask . . . . . . . . . . . : 255.255.255.0
        Default Gateway . . . . . . . . . :

C:\>
```

5. This computer will act as the JPerf server. In the open command window, type **cd\Jperf** at the C:\ prompt and press the Enter key. This will put you in the proper location of the JPerf program you copied to this computer in step 2.

6. Enter the following command to start the JPerf server: **jperf.bat**. After a few seconds, the JPerf 2.0.2 - Network Performance Measurement Graphical Tool window will appear.

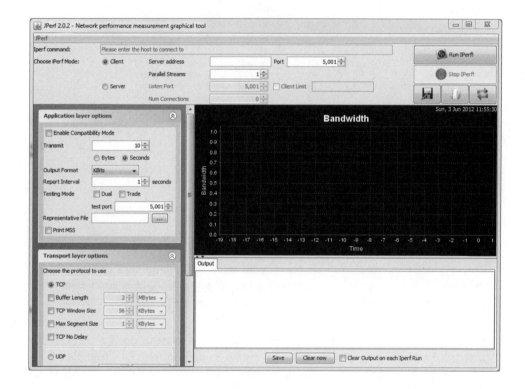

7. In the Application Layer Options section, click the Output Format drop-down box and select the MBits option. This will show the results in megabits per second.

8. Click the Server radio button.

9. Click the Run IPerf! button in the upper-right corner of the window.

1. Select MBits.

2. Select Server.

3. Click the Run IPerf! button.

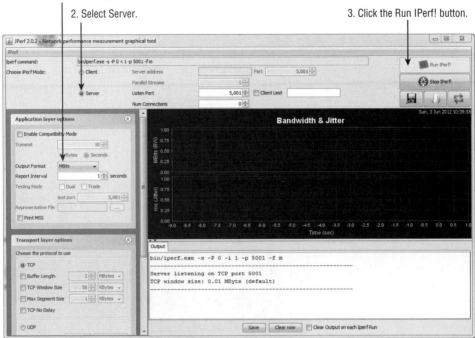

10. The JPerf server is now ready for throughput testing.

11. On the computer with a wireless network adapter, connect to your access point using the wireless network adapter. This computer will act as the JPerf client for throughput testing.

12. On this same computer, open a command prompt.

13. In the command prompt window, type the command **ipconfig** at the C:\ prompt and verify the IP address of this computer.

14. Verify connectivity to the JPerf server by typing the following command: **ping** {*IP address*}.

    You will need to replace {*IP address*} with the server address you recorded in step 4. You should see several replies if you are correctly connected to the server through the access point.

15. This computer will act as the JPerf client. In the open command window, type the command **cd\jperf** at the C:\ prompt and press Enter.

This will put you in the proper location of the JPerf program you copied to this computer in step 2.

16. In the command prompt window, type the following command to launch the JPerf graphical program: **jperf.bat**.

After a few seconds the JPerf 2.0.2 - Network Performance Measurement Graphical Tool window will appear.

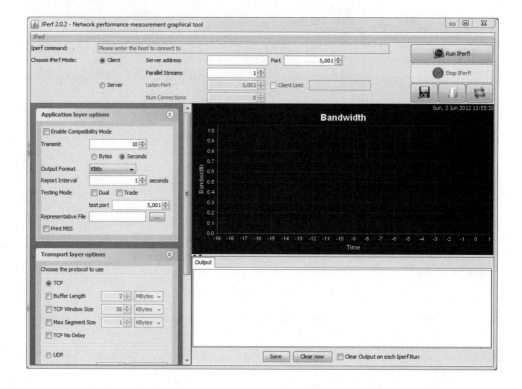

17. In the Application Layer Options section, click the Output Format drop-down box and select the MBits option. This will show the results in megabits per second.

18. Click the Client radio button, and in the Server Address field enter the IP address of the server that you recorded in step 4.

19. Click the Run IPerf! button in the upper-right corner.

20. After 10 seconds the test will be complete and in the program window you will see the actual throughput recorded using the JPerf program.

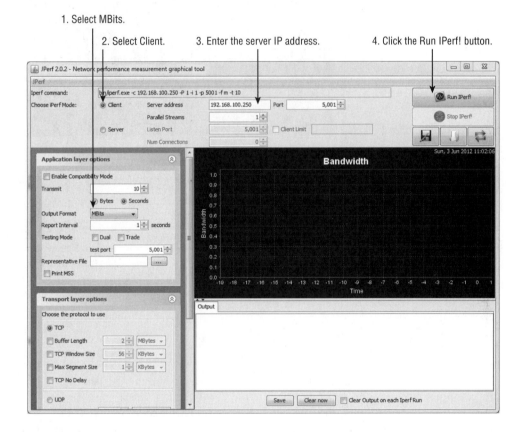

21. Close the JPerf program window on both computers.

When you are finished, you can delete the JPerf program and folder you created in step 2.

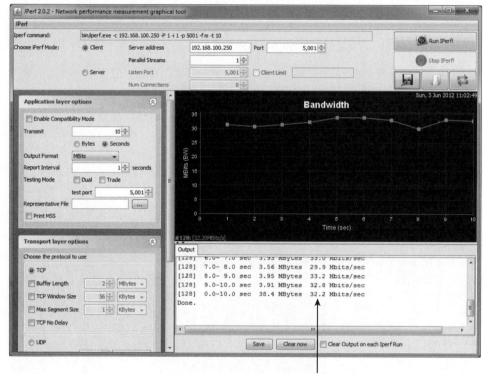

Test shows 32 Mbps of data throughput.

Dynamic Rate Switching

When a wireless device moves through the basic service area (BSA) or as the distance from the access point increases, the data rate will decrease. Conversely, as the wireless device moves closer to the access point, the data rate can increase. This is called *dynamic rate switching* (DRS), also known as dynamic rate shifting and even dynamic rate selection. This process allows an associated wireless device to adapt to the radio frequency in a particular location of the BSA. DRS is typically accomplished through proprietary mechanisms set by the manufacturer of the wireless device. The main goal of dynamic rate switching is to improve performance for the wireless device connected to an access point. As a wireless device moves away from an access point, the amount of received signal will decrease because of the free space path loss. When this occurs, the modulation type will change because the radio frequency signal quality is less and thus a lower data rate will be realized.

Remember from Chapter 5 that different data rates use different modulation technologies. Using a less complex modulation type at a lower data rate will provide better overall performance as the station moves away from the access point. Figure 8.23 illustrates how dynamic rate switching works. As the wireless device moves away from the access point, the data rate will decrease. Keep in mind the opposite is true as well. As a wireless device moves closer to an access point, the data rate will increase.

FIGURE 8.23 A graphical representation of dynamic rate switching

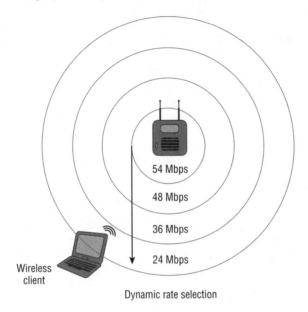

54 Mbps

48 Mbps

36 Mbps

24 Mbps

Wireless
client

Dynamic rate selection

Wireless LAN Roaming or Transition

In wireless LAN technology, *roaming* is the term for what happens when a wireless device moves from one basic service set or access point to another. Roaming was not addressed in the original IEEE 802.11 standard. This process is typically accomplished in a proprietary manner based on how the manufacturer chooses to implement it. Manufacturers use different criteria to initiate roaming from one access point to another. There was an amendment to the IEEE 802.11 standard (IEEE 802.11F, Inter-Access Point Protocol) that was ratified in June 2003 as a recommended practice intended to address multivendor access point interoperability. However, this recommended practice was implemented by few if any manufacturers, and it was withdrawn by the IEEE 802 Executive Committee in February 2006. The next attempt to standardize roaming between access points is IEEE 802.11r. This driving force behind this amendment to the standard was to allow for fast secure transition with wireless voice devices.

When a wireless LAN device moves through a BSA and receives a signal from another access point, it needs to make a decision whether to stay associated with the current access point or to reassociate with the new access point. This decision when to roam is proprietary and based on specific manufacturer criteria. Some of these criteria manufacturers use are:

- Signal strength
- Signal-to-noise ratio
- Error rate
- Number of currently associated devices

When a wireless LAN device chooses to reassociate to a new access point, the original access point will hand off the association to the new access point as requested from the new access point. Keep in mind it is the wireless client device that initiates the move to a new access point. This move is done over the wired network or distribution system based on how the manufacturer implemented the roaming criteria. Figure 8.24 illustrates a notebook computer roaming from one access point to a new access point.

FIGURE 8.24   The roaming process for a wireless LAN

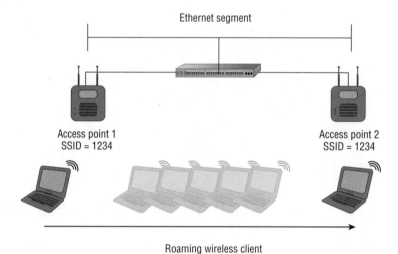

Roaming wireless client

Frames Used for Reassociation (Roaming)

When a device moves or "roams" to a new access point, it needs to associate to the new access point. Because the device is already associated, in order to connect to the new access point it must complete a reassociation process.

1. A wireless LAN device sends a reassociation request frame to the new access point. This frame is acknowledged by the new access point.

2. The new access point sends a reassociation response frame to the wireless device after handoff across the distribution system from the original access point has occurred. This frame is acknowledged by the reassociating wireless device.

Figure 8.25 shows reassociation request and response frames in a packet analyzer.

FIGURE 8.25   Packet capture of the reassociation process

00:19:7E:43:4E:E8	00:14:A8:53:5F:C0	00:14:A8:53:5F:C0	77%	802.11 Reassoc Req
00:14:A8:53:5F:C0	00:19:7E:43:4E:E8		50%	802.11 Ack
00:14:A8:53:5F:C0	00:19:7E:43:4E:E8	00:14:A8:53:5F:C0	45%	802.11 Reassoc Rsp
00:19:7E:43:4E:E8	00:14:A8:53:5F:C0		74%	802.11 Ack

The 802.11r amendment to the standard was ratified in 2008 and is now part of the IEEE 802.11-2012 Standard. This amendment is for fast BSS transition (FT) and allows for fast secure roaming for devices between basic service sets. The main objective of this amendment is to support voice over IP (VoIP) technology.

IEEE 802.11 Power Save Operations

Many wireless LAN devices are portable and use DC battery power to some degree. A wireless network adapter uses DC power to operate, and in some cases this could be a significant drain on the battery in the device. This is especially true with newer IEEE 802.11n wireless adapters that support MIMO technology. The original IEEE 802.11 standard addresses power saving operation. This power save operation is designed to allow a wireless LAN device to enter a dozing state in order to conserve DC power and extend battery life. If the wireless LAN device is plugged into a consistent power source such as an AC outlet, there is no reason to implement power save features. However, portable devices that are mobile and may not have access to an AC power source should consider using power save operations. The original IEEE 802.11 standard addressed two different power save modes: active mode (AM) and power save (PS) mode. In some cases, power save (PS) mode is considered legacy because the IEEE 802.11e amendment for quality of service addresses new, more efficient power save mechanisms. Although the original PS mode may be considered legacy, it is still widely used in many devices. As mentioned earlier in this chapter in the section "IEEE 802.11 Frame Types," a data frame known as a *null function frame* is used with power management and does not carry any data but is used to inform the access point of a change in power state.

Active Mode

In *active mode* (AM) a wireless LAN device or station (STA) may receive frames at any time and is always in an "awake" state. In this case, the wireless LAN device is not relying on battery power; thus, there is no reason for the device to assume a low power state, and it will never doze. Some manufacturers refer to active mode as continuous aware mode (CAM).

Power Save Mode

In *power save* (PS) mode, the wireless LAN device or station (STA) will doze or enter a low power state for very short periods of times. At specific time intervals, the device will "listen" for selected beacons and determine if any data is waiting for it (buffered) at the access point. The beacon frame contains information for associated devices regarding power save. When a wireless LAN device associates to an access point, the device receives what is known as an *association ID* (AID). The association ID is a value that will represent that device in various functions, including power save mode. The beacon frame contains an indicator for each AID associated device to let wireless devices know whether they have data waiting for them or buffered at the access point. If it is determined that the access point does have data buffered for a specific device, the device will send a control frame message (PS-Poll frame) to the access point to request the buffered data. Figure 8.26 shows where power save mode can be set in the advanced settings of the wireless adapter device driver.

FIGURE 8.26   The driver settings for an Intel 5100 IEEE 802.11a/g/n wireless adapter and power save mode setting

Power save mode may cause some amount of overhead for the wireless LAN device, and there is a trade-off in performance. With power save mode enabled, the battery life will be extended; however, performance will suffer to some degree because the device will not be available to receive data continuously. The device will only be able to receive buffered data during the "awake" state. Power save mode is common in applications where battery conservation is important, such as barcode scanners, voice over Wi-Fi phones, and other handheld devices.

> ### 🌐 Real World Scenario
>
> #### Use of Power Save Mode in Barcode Scanners
>
> Organizations such as retail, manufacturing, and warehousing have been using 802.11 wireless LAN technologies for many years. Many of these businesses use wireless LAN devices such as barcode scanners in addition to notebook computers and other portable devices. Barcode scanners are used heavily for inventory and asset tracking purposes. These devices must run for many hours at a time, typically in 8- or 10-hour shifts for individuals who may be using them. Applications such as this greatly benefit from using IEEE 802.11 power save features and extending battery life of wireless LAN devices. This minimizes downtime because batteries in these devices will not have to be changed or recharged as often during a work shift.

Automatic Power Save Delivery

The IEEE 802.11e Quality of Service amendment to the standard fueled the need for more efficient power save mechanisms in wireless networking. Depending on the implementation and requirements, legacy power save modes may not be efficient enough to work with applications that use QoS, such as voice and video. *Automatic power save delivery* (APSD) differs from the original power save mode in that a trigger frame will wake a device in order to receive data. APSD is a more efficient way of performing power save functions. It works well with time-bound applications that are subject to latency, such as voice and video.

IEEE 802.11 Protection Mechanisms

In order to allow newer, faster wireless LAN technology such as 802.11g and 802.11n devices to communicate with older, slower wireless devices, technology called protection mechanisms was designed to allow for backward compatibility. The mechanisms available depend on which amendment to the standard is used. Protection mechanisms will provide the backward compatibility needed to allow different technologies to coexist in the same radio frequency space.

There are two broad categories of protection mechanism:

- Extended rate physical (ERP) protection mechanism for IEEE 802.11g networks
- High throughput (HT) protection mechanism for IEEE 802.11n networks

Each category includes several modes for specific situations.

IEEE 802.11g Extended Rate Physical Protection Mechanisms

In order for IEEE 802.11g and IEEE 802.11b devices to coexist in the same basic service area, the wireless access point must use *extended rate physical (ERP) protection*. Most manufacturers of IEEE 802.11 wireless LAN equipment will provide options when it comes to coexistence. These options usually include the capability to set an access point to one of three modes:

- IEEE 802.11b only mode: DSSS and HR/DSSS
- IEEE 802.11g only mode: ERP-OFDM
- IEEE 802.11b/g mixed mode: DSSS, HR/DSSS, and ERP-OFDM

IEEE 802.11b-Only Mode

This mode requires setting an access point to operate in 802.11b-only mode. This involves disabling all the IEEE 802.11g ERP-OFDM data rates of 6, 9, 12, 18, 24, 36, 48, and 54 Mbps and allowing only DSSS data rates of 1 and 2 Mbps and HR/DSSS rates of 5.5 and 11 Mbps. Enabling this mode limits the maximum data rate to 11 Mbps. Setting an access point to this mode has limited applications such as using legacy IEEE 802.11b-only capable devices, for example.

IEEE 802.11g-Only Mode

This mode is the opposite of 802.11b-only mode. It disables all of the IEEE 802.11b DSSS and HR/DSSS data rates of 1, 2, 5.5, and 11 Mbps, and it allows the IEEE 802.11g ERP-OFDM data rates of 6, 9, 12, 18, 24, 36, 48, and 54 Mbps. This operation mode is useful in an environment where backward compatibility to 802.11b is not required, such as an environment where all devices connecting have IEEE 802.11g capability, and the through-put needs to be maximized; thus there are no IEEE 802.11b devices in use.

IEEE 802.11b/g Mixed Mode

Most deployments in the 2.4 GHz ISM band use this mode for communications. This allows devices that support the IEEE 802.11g amendment and IEEE 802.11b devices to operate together in the same BSA and associated to the same access point. As mentioned in Chapter 2, "Introduction to Wireless Local Area Networking," throughput will decrease when IEEE 802.11b devices and IEEE 802.11g devices are both associated to the same access point.

Extended Rate Physical (ERP) mixed mode uses control frames to reserve the wireless medium. Two options are available:

Request to Send/Clear to Send (RTS/CTS)   One option of control frames that are used as a protection mechanism to reserve the RF medium.

Clear to Send (CTS) to Self   A single frame used as a protection mechanism. This is a common implementation used by wireless LAN equipment manufacturers. A benefit of using this frame is less overhead than the RTS/CTS process.

Both RTS/CTS and CTS-to-Self control frames allow wireless devices using different Physical Layer technologies to share the wireless medium and help to avoid collisions. These control frames specify how much time is needed for a frame exchange between the transmitter and a receiver to complete. This time value is processed by all devices in the basic service area that are not part of the frame exchange. Once this time has expired, the wireless medium is considered clear.

IEEE 802.11n High-Throughput Protection Mechanisms

IEEE 802.11n devices operate in either the 2.4 GHz or the 5 GHz band. Backward compatibility for IEEE 802.11a/b/g devices needs to be taken into consideration. The IEEE 802.11n amendment identifies several different modes for *high-throughput (HT) protection* mechanisms. These mechanisms are known as HT protection modes and are a set of rules that devices and access points will use for backward compatibility:

- Mode 0–Greenfield mode
- Mode 1–HT nonmember protection mode
- Mode 2–HT 20 MHz protection mode
- Mode 3–HT mixed mode

These modes are constantly changing based on the radio frequency environment and associated wireless devices. The goal with IEEE 802.11n wireless networks is to get to Mode 0–Greenfield mode. With today's wireless networks and WLAN technology, we are more than likely at Mode 3–HT mixed mode or possibly even one of the other two modes in most cases.

Mode 0–Greenfield Mode

Mode 0 or *Greenfield mode* allows high-throughput (HT) devices only. These HT devices must also share operational functionality and they must match; for example, they must all support 20 MHz or 20/40 MHz channels only. If an IEEE 802.11n (HT) access point is set to 20/40 MHz channel width and a client capable of only 20 MHz wide channels associates, the connection is not considered Greenfield mode. Mode 0 does not allow IEEE 802.11a/b/g devices using the same RF channel. IEEE 802.11a/b/g devices will not be able to communicate with an access point in Greenfield mode. Transmissions from these devices will cause collisions at the access point, causing some degradation in throughput because it is seen by the HT system as radio frequency interference. Greenfield mode is what we as wireless network designers and administrators are working toward achieving, but it may be some time before we are there because of backward compatibility and legacy wireless devices.

Mode 1–HT Nonmember Protection Mode

All devices in Mode 1 or *HT nonmember protection mode* must be HT-capable. When a non-HT device—that is, an IEEE 802.11a/b/g access point or wireless client device—is within the hearing range of the HT access point and on the same 20 MHz channel or one of the 20/40 MHz wide channels, this protection mode will be activated.

Mode 2–HT 20 MHz Protection Mode

All devices in Mode 2 or *HT 20 MHz protection mode* must be HT-capable as well. The operation of this protection mode is based on the fact that 802.11n devices can use 20 MHz or 20/40 MHz wide channels. Mode 2 means that at least one 20 MHz HT station is associated with the HT 20/40 MHz access point and that the access point provides compatibility for 20 MHz devices.

Mode 3–HT Mixed Mode

Mode *3* or *HT mixed mode* is used if one or more non-HT stations are associated in the BSS. This mode allows backward compatibility with non-802.11n or IEEE 802.11a/b/g wireless devices. This is the likely the most common mode for IEEE 802.11n HT networks today because of the need for backward compatibility and the legacy IEEE 802.11 wireless devices that are still in use on most wireless networks.

Additional HT Protection Modes

Two other HT protection modes are also available:

- Dual CTS is a Layer 2 protection mechanism that is used for backward compatibility between IEEE 802.11n HT and IEEE 802.11a/b/g devices.
- Phased coexistence operation (PCO) is an optional BSS mode with alternating 20 MHz and 20/40 MHz phases controlled by a PCO-capable access point.

Summary

Wireless LANs can operate in two modes: either ad hoc mode, which means no access points are used, or infrastructure mode, where an access point provides a central point of communication for the wireless LAN devices. In this chapter, we looked at these modes of operation as well as the service sets IEEE 802.11 networks use. We looked at the three configurations for wireless LANs:

- Independent basic service set (IBSS)
- Basic service set (BSS)
- Extended service set (ESS)

In this chapter we discussed the configuration of each, along with some of the advantages and disadvantages of each configuration—from an IBSS, which uses no access points, to a BSS or ESS, which uses one or many access points. Some of the configuration parameters, such as SSID and radio frequency channel, and how they are used were also explained. Some of these acronyms are very close in spelling and sound similar when spoken. It is important to understand the differences among the following abbreviations:

- Service set identifier (SSID)
- Extended service set identifier (ESSID)
- Basic service set identifier (BSSID)

- Independent basic service set (IBSS)
- Basic service set (BSS)
- Extended service set (ESS)
- Basic service area (BSA)

For example, SSID is the name of the wireless network, and the BSSID is the unique identifier MAC address of the AP radio.

In addition to explaining the different configurations and terminology used, we looked at the processes wireless devices use to connect to and become part of a wireless LAN, including:

- Wireless discovery
- Passive scanning
- Active scanning
- IEEE 802.11 authentication
- IEEE 802.11 association

The discovery processes of passive scanning (listening for beacons) and active scanning (joining a wireless LAN) are important parts of starting the connection process. This continues with 802.11 authentication—in most cases open system—and the 802.11 association process. Once these processes are complete, the device finally becomes part of the wireless network, enabling it to pass traffic across to the access point to the network infrastructure.

We also saw the components and technology that play a role with IEEE 802.11 wireless networks, such as:

- Distribution system (DS)
- Wireless distribution system (WDS)
- Data rate (what is advertised)
- Throughput (what is actual)

Both a wired distribution system, in most cases Ethernet, and a wireless distribution system using radios and access points provide connectivity for wireless infrastructure. We looked at the differences between data rate and throughput. It is important to understand that an access point may have a data rate of 54 Mbps or even up to 600 Mbps, but throughput (the actual data transmission rate) is typically less than half of the data rate. Because wireless LANs are contention based, data throughput will be even less when more devices connect to the network.

Dynamic rate switching—a client transferring more or less data depending on the proximity from an access point as well as roaming or moving through the basic service areas and being able to maintain connectivity—was also discussed in this chapter. Finally, the chapter covered the important topics of power save mode and protection mechanisms. With power save mode, a wireless LAN device is able to extend battery life by entering into a low-power state or "doze" for very short periods of time. This permits the device to consume less battery power, therefore allowing connectivity for longer periods of time without changing or recharging the battery. The modes discussed were:

- Active mode

- Power save mode (PS)

- Automatic power save delivery (APSD)

It is beneficial to understand the differences in power save capabilities among these modes.

Lastly, we discussed IEEE 802.11 protection mechanisms and the importance of these methods in order to provide backward compatibility and coexistence to older technology devices:

- Extended rate physical (ERP) protection for IEEE 802.11g

- High throughput (HT) protection for IEEE 802.11n

We looked at some highlights of both protection mechanism technologies for IEEE 802.11g and 802.11n networks.

Exam Essentials

Understand the different operation modes for IEEE 802.11 wireless networks.   Know the difference between infrastructure and ad hoc mode as well as the use of both.

Be familiar with the different service sets used with wireless networking.   Understand the differences among IBSS, BSS, BSA and ESS.

Identify the terminology used with IEEE 802.11 wireless networking.   Understand the differences among SSID, ESSID, and BSSID. Know which one identifies the name of a network and which one identifies the physical address of an access point.

Know the process that devices use to join a wireless LAN.   Understand the process and operation of discovery, passive scanning, active scanning, IEEE 802.11 authentication, and IEEE 802.11 association.

Understand the differences between distribution systems as well as data transfer.   Identify the differences as well as the function of a distribution system and wireless distribution system and roaming between each. Know the differences between data rate and throughput as well as dynamic rate switching.

Identify the power-save capabilities of IEEE 802.11 wireless networks.   Know the various power-save modes of both legacy and Wi-Fi Multimedia (WMM), including active mode, power save mode, and APSD.

Know the various protection mechanisms available for both IEEE 802.11g and 802.11n wireless networks.   Be familiar with the two protection mechanisms: ERP protection mechanisms and HT protection mechanisms. Understand that these mechanisms provide coexistence for newer and legacy wireless LAN devices.

Review Questions

1. When a wireless LAN device listens for beacon frames, it is participating in which phase?

   A. Power save

   B. Passive scanning

   C. Active scanning

   D. Authentication

2. You are a sales engineer connected to an IEEE 802.11a access point with a mobile computer. As you move away from the access point, the connection speed slows to the next lowest supported data rate. The change in data rate is described by which term?

   A. Dynamic frequency selection

   B. Transmit power control

   C. Dynamic rate switching

   D. Transmit save mode

3. An independent basic service set (IBSS) consists of how many access points?

   A. 0

   B. 1

   C. 2

   D. 4

4. Wireless LAN devices in an 802.11a peer-to-peer network will connect to which device(s)?

   A. An access point

   B. 802.11g client devices

   C. 802.11a client devices

   D. A wireless switch

5. As a device moves away from an access point, which of the following is true regarding dynamic rate switching?

   A. Data rate decreases

   B. Output power decreases

   C. Data rate increases

   D. Output power increases

6. A service set identifier (SSID) has a maximum limit of how many characters or octets?

   A. 8

   B. 16

   C. 32

   D. 128

7. You are a technical support engineer and receive a call from a customer regarding a problem with their wireless network connection. The building has an ESS network with five 802.11g access points. The customer claims that when they move from their office to a conference room using the 802.11g network they lose their connection and cannot connect to the access point in the conference room. Which is the most likely cause for this user to lose their connection when they roam on the wireless network?

   A. Different RF channel

   B. Mismatched SSID

   C. Different BSSID

   D. Mismatched association

8. A beacon frame advertises information about the wireless network. A beacon frame is what type of frame?

   A. Data

   B. Control

   C. Management

   D. Detail

9. In order for a wireless client to become completely part of the basic service set, it must first _____ and then _____

   A. Associate, authenticate

   B. Authenticate, associate

   C. Deauthenticate, authenticate

   D. Disassociate, authenticate

10. The process in which a wireless LAN client connection moves from one access point to another is called _____.

   A. Reauthentication

   B. Roaming

   C. Rebuilding

   D. Roving

11. In order to set up an ad hoc network, a user must know which two parameters? (Choose two.)

   A. SSID

   B. BSSID

   C. Channel

   D. MAC address

   E. Protection mode

12. The open system authentication process uses how many frames?

   A. One

   B. Two

C. Three

D. Four

13. You are a help desk support technician at a retail department store and you receive a call from a manager in the administrative offices. He complains that the performance of his 802.11g notebook computer decreases several times throughout the day. Upon visiting the customer, you realize several people are performing inventory using 802.11b barcode scanners in the adjacent room. What is most likely the cause of the poor performance for the manager's notebook computer?

    A. Association

    B. Authentication

    C. ERP protection

    D. HT protection

14. Which items describe a service set identifier (SSID)? (Choose two.)

    A. 32 characters maximum

    B. 64 characters maximum

    C. Is case sensitive

    D. Is not case sensitive

15. A basic service set identifier (BSSID) is the unique identifying MAC address of the _____.

    A. AP radio

    B. AP Ethernet port

    C. Router

    D. Client

16. When an IEEE 802.11g wireless LAN consists only of wireless client stations, the network is operating as what type of basic service set?

    A. Active

    B. Independent

    C. Passive

    D. Infrastructure

17. You are a technical support engineer and provide help desk support for the network in a manufacturing company. You receive a call from the sales manager, who wants to know how power save operations should be set up on her notebook computer to optimize the system performance. The notebook computer is plugged into an AC power source and rarely used on battery. Which mode would you recommend her to set on the wireless adapter?

    A. Power save mode

    B. Association mode

    C. Active mode

    D. Passive mode

18. According to the IEEE 802.11 standard, an extended service set (ESS) consists of how many interconnected basic service sets?

   A. One or more

   B. Two or more

   C. Three or more

   D. Four or more

19. The IEEE 802.11 association process happens after which phase?

   A. Authentication

   B. Distribution

   C. Deauthentication

   D. Reauthentication

20. A basic service set (BSS) consists of how many access points?

   A. Zero

   B. At least one

   C. At least two

   D. At least four

Chapter 9

Wireless LAN Security Basics

THE FOLLOWING CWTS EXAM OBJECTIVES ARE COVERED IN THIS CHAPTER:

✓ **6.1 Identify and describe the following legacy WLAN security technologies**

  ▪ SSID Hiding

  ▪ WEP

  ▪ MAC Filtering

✓ **6.2 Understand the basic operation of and implementation best practices for the following WLAN security technologies**

  ▪ WPA and WPA2-Personal

  ▪ WPA and WPA2-Enterprise

  ▪ 802.1X/EAP

  ▪ AAA and RADIUS

  ▪ Encryption – TKIP/CCMP

✓ **6.3 Understand the basic functions and implementation best practices for the following WLAN security technologies**

  ▪ Role based access control (RBAC)

  ▪ Virtual private networking (VPN)

  ▪ Wireless intrusion prevention systems (WIPS)

  ▪ Captive portals

  ▪ Network management and monitoring systems

Security in many ways means defining your level of acceptable risk and protecting yourself to at least that level. This can vary greatly based on industry, budget, and the types and ages of devices supported. Security is a very important part of wireless networking, just as it is in any other type of computer networking or information technology. When the IEEE 802.11 standard was first ratified back in 1997, it addressed a basic security concept called Wired Equivalent Privacy (WEP). However, this security solution was considered weak and was easily compromised early on. In this chapter, we will look at some of the legacy wireless LAN security technologies used with standards-based wireless networking, including:

Service set identifier (SSID) hiding

Media access control (MAC) filtering

Wired Equivalent Privacy (WEP)

We will also take a look at some of the vulnerabilities of these legacy technologies and see why they should not be used for securing a wireless LAN. You will learn about some of the newer security methods available based on the IEEE 802.11i amendment and now included in the IEEE 802.11-2012 standard. These security methods are also part of the Wi-Fi Alliance certifications, WPA and WPA 2.0. We will explore small office/home office (SOHO) security solutions and enterprise-level security solutions. These include:

Preshared key

Passphrase

User-based authentication

IEEE 802.1X/EAP

Remote Access Dial-In User Service (RADIUS)

Authentication, authorization, and accounting (AAA)

In Chapter 2, "Introduction to Wireless Local Area Networking," we discussed some of the certifications available from the Wi-Fi Alliance that pertain to wireless LAN security. This chapter will explore further some of the concepts of passphrase, preshared key, and 802.1X/EAP. We will also discuss encryption methods such as TKIP and CCMP, which are ways to scramble computer data and are used with wireless LANs.

One thing that is often overlooked is security from a remote location, such as a wireless hotspot. In this chapter, you will learn about virtual private networking (VPN) solutions and how they can be used to secure wireless connections for users connecting to the corporate network from a remote wireless network. Wireless intrusion prevention systems (WIPS) are also becoming popular in today's wireless LAN world. If WIPS is implemented correctly, these solutions can provide a wealth of information as well as protection for your network infrastructure and wireless devices. Finally, we will look at basic functions and implementation best practices for role-based access control (RBAC), captive portals, and network management and monitoring systems.

Introducing IEEE 802.11 Wireless LAN Security

The importance of computer network security is often underestimated, and wireless LAN security is no different. "I don't understand why I need to secure my access point." "I don't have anything on my computer that would be of interest to anybody other than me." "I tried to enable security on my wireless, but I couldn't get it to work so I just turned it off." These are some of the common excuses many technical support engineers or consultants used to hear from people when it came to wireless security. In the early days of IEEE 802.11 wireless networking, security was weak. This led to much vulnerability, which in turn made wireless networking not a very attractive solution for many enterprise deployments, especially those concerned about security.

With the improvements in standards-based wireless LAN security, partly thanks to the Wi-Fi Alliance certifications as well as the IEEE 802.11i amendment to the standard, wireless LANs have become a major part of many enterprise networks in all industries and businesses. Because wireless networks are inherently unbounded, it is possible to have more security protecting wireless communication than what is used to secure most wired LANs. This is the case in many wireless LAN implementations.

Wireless LAN Threats and Intrusion

Computer networks have always been the target of various types of intrusion techniques. Wireless networks are no different—in fact, wireless networks are more vulnerable to intrusion because the communication is not bounded by any physical media such as an Ethernet cable. This key vulnerability in wireless networking is the use of the air, a shared unbounded medium. The level of security applied to a wireless network will depend on a couple of factors:

- What are you trying to protect?
- What are you trying to prevent?

There are many security concerns related to wireless networking. Some of these concerns arise because wireless LANs use radio frequency for communication and the open air as the medium. Others are a threat to either wired or wireless networks. The following list identifies some of these concerns and threats:

- Eavesdropping
- Radio frequency denial of service (DoS)
- Media access control (MAC) address spoofing
- Hijacking
- Man-in-the-middle attacks
- Peer-to-peer attacks
- Encryption cracking

Although many of these threats or methods of intrusion are common, advanced security solutions such as wireless intrusion prevention systems (WIPS) are available to help discover and mitigate some of them. Figure 9.1 illustrates some of the vulnerabilities with wireless networking.

FIGURE 9.1 Wireless LANs are subject to many potential security threats.

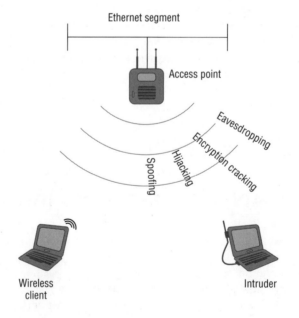

🌐 **Real World Scenario**

Locking the Door of Your Automobile

Let's take a quick look at an analogy that may make network security easier to understand. You need to run some errands on a Saturday afternoon and decide to go to the market to pick up some supplies. When you arrive at your destination, you leave your automobile but do not lock the door. Who could potentially enter your vehicle? The answer is anybody who attempts to open the door. Locking the door of your vehicle will prevent the casual intruder from being able to enter through the door. Therefore the lock on your door is one layer of security that could be used to prevent a potential intruder from entering your vehicle.

So, with the door locked, now who could potentially get into your vehicle? The answer is two different individuals: first, you (because you have the key to the door); second, a potential intruder who could compromise the lock on the door. As you can see, locking the door provides a layer of security and will prevent the casual intruder from entering your vehicle, but it will not prevent a determined intruder.

Now let's add a second layer of security. In addition to locking the door you set an alarm on your vehicle. You now have two layers of security: the door lock and the alarm. For an intruder to gain access to your vehicle, they would now need to have the knowledge and the ability to overcome two layers of security. First, they would need the ability to compromise the lock on the door, and then they would need the knowledge to disable the alarm, both without being noticed. The number of potential intruders has decreased significantly, from those who can just open the unlocked door, to those who have the knowledge to not only compromise the door lock but also disable the alarm.

IEEE 802.11 Standard Security

Even though wireless LAN security has greatly increased over the years, it is important to understand the original IEEE 802.11 standard as it relates to wireless LAN security. It is important to be aware of some of the basics or building blocks prior to getting into more sophisticated areas of security. From a security viewpoint, the original standard addressed two areas of security: authentication and data privacy. Both of these are common components of computer network security. In computer networking, *authentication* is defined as a way of confirming an identity; basically, it determines that you are who you say you are. Data privacy is ensuring that information or data is understandable only by the individuals or groups it is intended for, the sender and the intended receiver.

One way many people may think of authentication is to supply a username and password in order to log onto a computer. Another would be to supply the appropriate logon before performing an activity like Internet banking. To review from Chapter 8, "Wireless LAN Terminology and Technology," the original IEEE 802.11 standard addresses two types of authentication: open system authentication and shared-key authentication. These authentication types are different from the examples described earlier, which most people are familiar with. IEEE 802.11 authentication is performed by the wireless LAN protocol and, except for shared-key authentication, does not require user intervention.

IEEE 802.11 Open System Authentication

To review from Chapter 8, this type of authentication is a two-step process, a two-frame exchange, and is one of the simplest ways to provide an authentication process. IEEE 802.11 open system authentication cannot fail except for circumstances such as a network adapter having a bad device driver. This authentication is what is known as a *null authentication*, which for the most part means it doesn't really authenticate anything at all. For example, if a wireless client device such as a notebook computer wants to join the wireless network, it will "ask" the access point if it can authenticate, and the access point will always accept.

IEEE 802.11 Shared-Key Authentication

Also discussed in Chapter 8, IEEE 802.11 shared-key authentication is a four-step process, not to be confused with WPA or WPA2 personal mode, which uses a preshared key for authentication. The main difference between open system and shared-key authentication is that with shared-key authentication, Wired Equivalent Privacy (WEP) is required in order for it to function correctly. This is because shared-key authentication uses WEP for both 802.11 authentication and for data payload encryption. But WEP is not secure, so it makes shared-key authentication weak and vulnerable to intrusion. WEP was intended only to protect wireless network users against casual eavesdropping and for authentication with shared key. Figure 9.2 shows how to set either open system or shared-key authentication on an enterprise-grade access point.

FIGURE 9.2   Cisco 1250 series IEEE 802.11n wireless access points SSID security settings

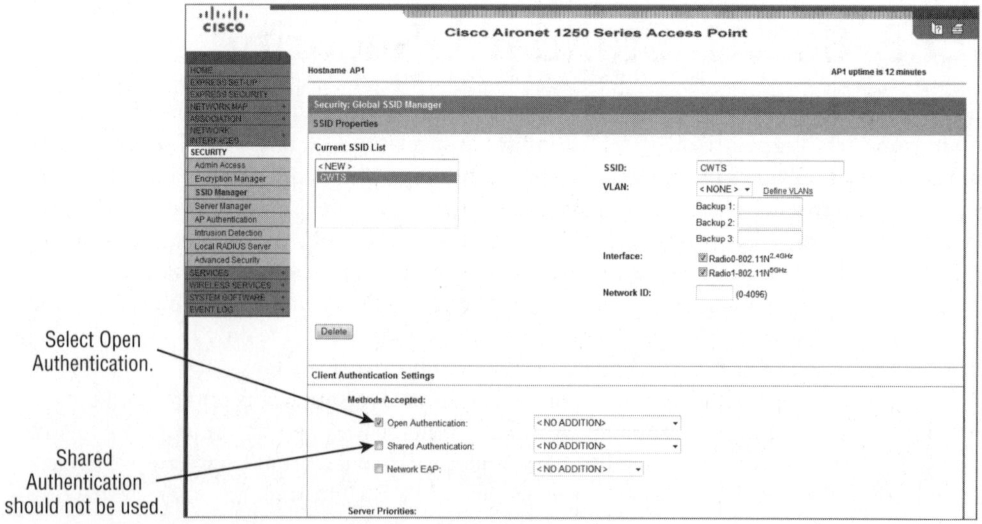

Early Wireless LAN Security Technologies

Because of the way security was defined in the original IEEE 802.11 standard, manufacturers of wireless LAN equipment were able to design different ways a user could secure a wireless LAN. But even though these methods looked good on paper, they did not do much to provide a good security solution. Some of these common wireless LAN security methods and legacy security solutions discussed here are:

- Service set identifier (SSID) hiding (closed network)

- Media access control (MAC) filtering

- Wired Equivalent Privacy (WEP)

If some of these are considered legacy wireless LAN security methods, why is it important to discuss them? You need to understand these solutions because there are still some wireless network implementations that may use some or all of them as part of a wireless security solution. Because standards-based wireless LAN technology has been around for over a decade, many early adopters had no choice but to use these security techniques. Over the years, wireless LAN security has improved tremendously; however, it is a fact that some of these early adopters still have legacy wireless devices that will not support the latest and greatest security technology such as WPA or WPA2. Therefore these solutions may still currently play a role in the wireless network infrastructure.

The Service Set Identifier

As you'll recall from Chapter 8, the service set identifier (SSID) is a logical name for the wireless network and was designed to be used for wireless device segmentation. The SSID will allow wireless devices such as notebook computers to identify and connect to a wireless LAN using the discovery phase, which includes the passive and active scanning processes. There are a couple of ways this connection can be accomplished. Passive scanning occurs when the wireless client device listens for beacons frames. The SSID is specified in a beacon frame in the SSID information element. As discussed in Chapter 8, the beacon frame is an advertisement of the wireless network. The beacon frame by default is set to broadcast at about 10 times a second. The beacon frame will advertise the SSID of the wireless network during this interval.

You can specify that the SSID of the wireless LAN be joined in the wireless client software utility of the connecting wireless device. In this case, a wireless client will send a probe request frame with the intent of joining that particular network. The IEEE 802.11 standard requires access points to respond to all probe requests that have a matching SSID or what is known as a wildcard SSID (an SSID with a value of 0), also referred to as a null SSID. A wildcard SSID is used when a client device does not specify the SSID in the wireless client software utility. If a wireless client device is scanning or looking for a wireless network to join, they will see the wireless network because the beacon frame is broadcasting the SSID. Most manufacturers of SOHO and enterprise access points provide the option not to broadcast the SSID in beacon frames. This is commonly known as disabling the SSID broadcast, SSID hiding, or a closed network and is discussed in the next section.

SSID Hiding

Most manufacturers of IEEE 802.11 wireless LAN equipment provide the capability to disable SSID broadcasting, as shown in Figure 9.3. Another term for this process is *SSID hiding*. SSID hiding allows a user to remove the SSID that would normally appear in broadcast beacon frames. If the SSID is not being broadcast, the wireless network may not be seen by the wireless client devices that do not have that wireless network's SSID specified in their client software utility. If somebody knows the SSID, they would be able to enter it into their wireless client device software and then be able to connect to the wireless network.

FIGURE 9.3   The Motorola RFS6000 wireless LAN controller allows you to disable SSID broadcast.

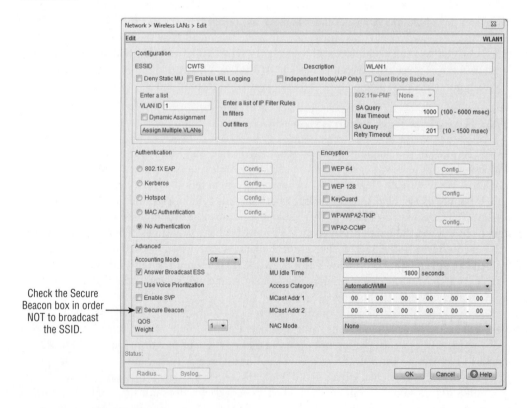

Check the Secure Beacon box in order NOT to broadcast the SSID.

In the early days of wireless networking, people would hide the SSID, believing that would secure the network because it was not visible to devices passively scanning for a network to join. This was a misconception, because even though the SSID is not being broadcast in these beacon frames, it can still be identified in other wireless frames, such as the probe response frame. This means that anyone with a wireless scanning utility such as a packet analyzer would be able to determine the SSID of a wireless network by monitoring the frames that are sent through the air. Therefore, hiding the SSID should *not* be used as a way to secure a wireless network.

Hiding the SSID is sometimes used to prevent the wireless network from being seen by those who should not be connecting to it. Many organizations will hide the SSIDs of all the wireless networks except for the open guest network. This is sometimes done to help reduce unnecessary technical support calls from someone who may try to connect to a wireless LAN that they do not have access to. However, this method is not intended to secure the wireless network.

The Media Access Control Address

To review, the media access control (MAC) address is a unique hardware identifier of a computer network device. This 6-byte address is the Layer 2 address that allows frames to be sent to and received from a device. Figure 9.4 shows the MAC address of a wireless network adapter viewed with `ipconfig.exe`. An important point here is that the MAC address is unique, and no two network devices should ever have the same Layer 2 MAC address. In a wireless network, MAC addresses are easily visible to anyone using a wireless packet analyzer or wireless network scanning software utility. These addresses are required for a network device to send and receive information; therefore, they cannot be encrypted and are visible to anyone with the knowledge to view them.

FIGURE 9.4   The Windows command-line utility `ipconfig.exe` will display MAC addresses.

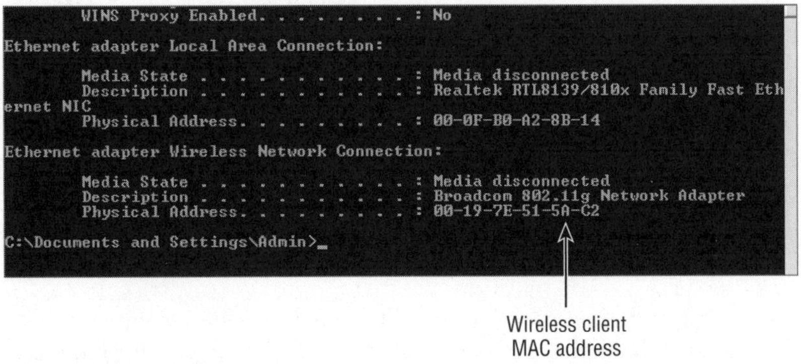

```
        WINS Proxy Enabled. . . . . . . . : No
Ethernet adapter Local Area Connection:

        Media State . . . . . . . . . . : Media disconnected
        Description . . . . . . . . . . : Realtek RTL8139/810x Family Fast Eth
ernet NIC
        Physical Address. . . . . . . . : 00-0F-B0-A2-8B-14

Ethernet adapter Wireless Network Connection:

        Media State . . . . . . . . . . : Media disconnected
        Description . . . . . . . . . . : Broadcom 802.11g Network Adapter
        Physical Address. . . . . . . . : 00-19-7E-51-5A-C2

C:\Documents and Settings\Admin>_
```

Wireless client
MAC address

MAC Address Filtering

Since IEEE 802.11 wireless LAN device technology operates at the lowest two layers of the OSI model, the Physical layer and the Data Link layer, the MAC address plays a big role in wireless networking. Manufacturers of wireless LAN equipment provide a feature known as *MAC address filtering*. Its purpose is to either allow or disallow access to the wireless network by restricting which MAC addresses can IEEE 802.11 authenticate and associate to a wireless network. Figure 9.5 is an example of how to apply a MAC address filter on an access point.

FIGURE 9.5   Linksys WRT54G MAC filter setup

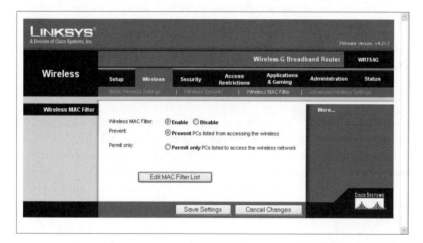

This looks great on paper but is a weak security feature, because it can be easily compromised. Remember, wireless networks use the air as their access medium to communicate, and radio frequency is what exchanges the information between devices. So if an intruder were to monitor the air with a tool such as a wireless packet analyzer or wireless scanning utility software program, they would be able to see all the wireless traffic within hearing range of their wireless device. Because wireless LAN devices communicate with each other using MAC addressing, all of these addresses would be visible to whoever wants to see them.

MAC Address Spoofing

Because MAC addresses are visible to anyone who wants to take the time to see them by using the correct software utility, they create a potential problem for those who implemented MAC address filtering. An intruder can easily perform a task called *MAC address spoofing*. This involves tricking the wireless device into thinking its unique MAC address is something other than what is encoded in the actual network card.

There are several ways for an intruder to accomplish MAC address spoofing. It can be done with software programs such as SMAC or within the computer operating system—for example, in the Microsoft Windows Registry. All options and configuration settings in the Windows operating system are stored in this hierarchical database known as the Windows Registry. If someone wanted to spoof the MAC address of a wireless network adapter using this database, they might (depending on the adapter) be able to enter a new MAC address value in the device driver's configuration, which would then be stored in the Windows Registry. Another option is to change the Windows Registry value directly using the Registry Editor tool built into Windows. This would be considered a modifiable MAC address. MAC addresses may also be stored in a configuration file, and in nonvolatile memory. Keep in mind that changing the MAC address in the Registry or in a configuration file changes only the software reference that the operating system sees and uses. It does not change what is known as the burned-in address (BIA) or the hard-coded address, which is unmodifiable.

IEEE 802.11 Authentication and Data Encryption

As discussed earlier in this chapter, authentication is defined as validating an identity. Authentication also gives the capability to control access to a system. In the original IEEE 802.11 standard, this is accomplished by using either IEEE 802.11 open system or shared-key authentication. Since open system authentication is a null authentication method and except for special circumstances it cannot fail, the wireless device will always authenticate. IEEE 802.11 shared-key authentication, on the other hand, uses *Wired Equivalent Privacy* (WEP) for wireless device authentication as well as for data payload encryption. Encryption is the process of modifying information from its original form to make it unreadable except by those who know the technique or the method in which the data was modified. In the original IEEE 802.11 standard, data encryption was accomplished by using WEP. In order for a device to pass information across an access point, it must first IEEE 802.11 authenticate, and then associate.

About Wired Equivalent Privacy

From a security perspective, one major drawback to any wireless network is the fact that all information, including data payload, travels through the air from one device to another. This makes wireless LANs vulnerable to eavesdropping and inherently less secure than bounded networking using other networking technology such as Ethernet. With IEEE 802.11 open system authentication, all information is broadcast through the air in plain text. What this means is that anyone with knowledge of how to use a wireless packet analyzer or other wireless scanning software program can easily see all the information that is passing between devices through the air.

WEP was designed as a way to protect wireless networking from casual eavesdropping. The original IEEE 802.11 standard states that the use of WEP is optional. The manufacturer supplies the capability, but it is up to the user of the wireless device to implement it.

In wireless LANs, WEP can be used in one of two ways: with IEEE 802.11 open system authentication to encrypt the data only or with shared-key authentication, which is used for wireless device authentication and for data encryption. The original standard specified only 64-bit WEP, which consists of a 40-bit key plus 24-bit WEP initialization vector (IV).

How to Use WEP

WEP is fairly simple to implement. It requires all wireless devices to have the same WEP key. The WEP key can be either 64-bit or 128-bit; however, the standard required only 64-bit WEP. One disadvantage to WEP is that it uses static keys, which means all wireless devices—access points, bridges, and client stations—must have the same key and the key must be manually entered into them. Any time the key is changed, it must be changed on all of the wireless device that are on the same SSID. No matter which you use, 64-bit WEP or 128-bit WEP, you are still only using a 24-bit IV. 64-bit WEP uses a 40-bit secret key and a 24-bit IV. 128-bit WEP uses a 104-bit secret key but still only the 24-bit IV, making both vulnerable to the same attacks. Gathering a number of these IVs allows an attacker to crack your key in minutes.

Some governing bodies no longer allow the use of WEP. Payment Card Industry (PCI), for example, no longer allows the use of WEP for securing wireless networks. If you are still using WEP, it should be a high priority to move away from this legacy security technology as quickly as possible.

Figure 9.6 shows configuring an enterprise-grade access point for WEP. Table 9.1 describes the characteristics of the two types of WEP keys.

FIGURE 9.6   Cisco 1250 series IEEE 802.11n wireless access point WEP key settings

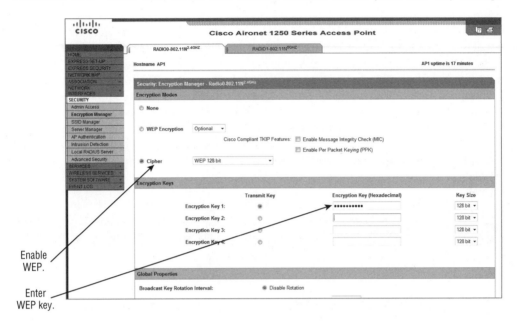

TABLE 9.1   Characteristics of the two types of WEP keys

Key length	# of ASCII characters	# of hex characters
64 bit	5	13
128 bit	10	26

One major disadvantage of using WEP is that it was compromised early on and is therefore not secure. It is easy to capture data using a wireless packet analyzer; with a little knowledge and correct software utilities, cracking a WEP key is a simple feat. This made WEP a weak security solution, but it was pretty much the only solution available at the time of early IEEE 802.11 wireless networking.

With today's newer and more sophisticated software tools and technology, WEP can be cracked easily and quickly. WEP will be discussed in more detail in the section "IEEE 802.11 Encryption Methods" later in this chapter.

IEEE 802.11 SOHO and Enterprise Security Technologies

The IEEE 802.11i amendment to the standard provided much improvement in the ways wireless LANs can be secured. Enterprise-based wireless LANs are now capable of the most up-to-date security solutions available in the industry. This amendment to the standard introduced what is known as the Robust Secure Network (RSN). In order for wireless LAN equipment to create an RSN, it must be RSN capable or 802.11i compliant, which means it will optionally support Temporal Key Integrity Protocol (TKIP) and it must also support Counter Mode with Cipher-Block Chaining Message Authentication Code Protocol (CCMP). The Wi-Fi Alliance has released several certifications that pertain to wireless networking: WPA and WPA 2.0 for SOHO and enterprise deployments, and WPS for the home user.

The following section discusses Wi-Fi Protected Setup (WPS). This topic is not included in the exam objectives but is explained here for your reference.

Wi-Fi Protected Setup PIN-Based or Push-Button Configuration Wireless Security

Many manufacturers of SOHO-grade wireless LAN equipment have adopted either PIN-based or push-button wireless security. Both of these solutions simplify the process of securing a wireless network either for the SOHO environment or for home-based users. As discussed in Chapter 2, the Wi-Fi Alliance has branded a certification for push-button and PIN-based security called Wi-Fi Protected Setup. The Wi-Fi Protected Setup certification (WPS) addresses both of these solutions.

In December 2011 a security flaw was reported with WPS. This allegedly allowed an intruder to recover the personal identification number (PIN) used to create the 256-bit preshared key. Disabling certain features or a firmware update may be available to provide adequate protection. Keep in mind that this solution to the issue may only be possible with newer-model wireless routers. You should check with the manufacturer to determine if a solution (either a software setting or firmware upgrade) is available for a specific device. See Chapter 2 for more details about this security hole.

PIN-Based Security

Personal identification number (PIN) functionality is required in order for a wireless device to be Wi-Fi Protected Setup (WPS) certified. PIN-based security requires a unique PIN to be entered on all devices that will be part of the same secure wireless network. A PIN will come as either a fixed label or sticker on a device, or it can be dynamically generated in the setup utility and shown on the computer screen. It is important to understand the difference between a PIN and a passphrase, password, shared key, or preshared key. A PIN is a number; the acronym spelled out means "personal identification number." Therefore a PIN will only consist of numbers. Passphrases and the others may contain combinations of numbers, letters, and special characters. The registrar device in the case of a wireless LAN is the access point. The access point will detect when a new wireless device that supports WPS is in radio range. When this device tries to join the network, the registrar will prompt the user to enter the unique PIN. Once the PIN is entered, the process authenticates the device and encrypts the network data sent to and from the device. Figure 9.7 shows an example of PIN-based wireless security.

FIGURE 9.7   D-Link wireless access point with PIN-based security

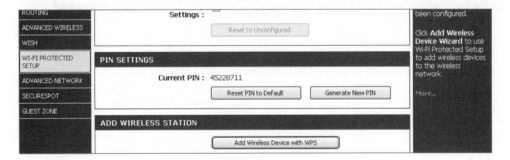

Push-Button Configuration Security

Push-button security or push-button configuration (PBC) allows users to configure wireless LAN security with "the push of a button," making setting up wireless security a one-step process. When a user pushes a hardware button on the wireless residential gateway (wireless router) and clicks a software button in the software utility for the network adapter installed in the client device wanting to associate, push-button security creates a connection between the devices, configures the network's SSID, and turns on security. This allows a secure connection among all devices that are part of the wireless network. Figure 9.8 shows an example of push-button security. The Linksys version of push-button security is called SecureEasySetup (SES).

FIGURE 9.8   Linksys WRT54G wireless residential gateway/router with push-button security (SES)

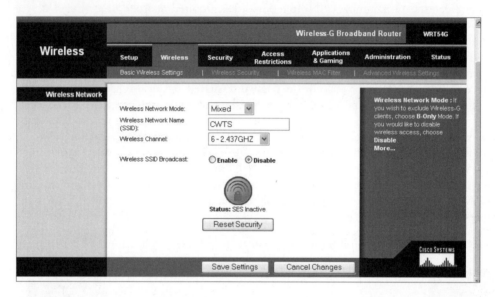

In order to use SES, all devices, including the wireless residential gateway/router and the wireless client adapters, must support the feature. First a button is pushed on the wireless residential gateway/router; then a button (a software setting in the wireless client utility) is clicked on the wireless device(s). Usually in less than a minute the process is complete and all devices have a secure connection. Only those devices within radio frequency hearing range that are participating in the process will become part of the secure network.

Support for both PIN and PBC configurations is required for access points; client devices at a minimum must support PIN. A third, optional method, near field communication (NFC) tokens, is also supported. A USB flash drive (memory card or solid-state storage drive with a USB interface) may be used to store and transfer credentials. Many SOHO equipment manufacturers have Wi-Fi Protected Setup–certified devices on the market today. Some include:

- Belkin
- Broadcom
- D-Link
- Linksys
- Netgear
- TRENDnet
- ZyXEL

For these and other manufacturers that support Wi-Fi Protected Setup (WPS), visit the Wi-Fi Alliance website at www.wi-fi.org.

Wi-Fi Protected Access and WPA2 Personal Security

Passphrase-based security was designed with the SOHO or home-based user in mind. This type of security allows a user to create a very secure wireless LAN solution without the experience or knowledge necessary to configure enterprise-level components such as an 802.1X/EAP and a RADIUS server. Passphrase-based security requires all wireless devices that are part of the same wireless network to have the same 256-bit preshared key (PSK) in order to securely communicate. The capability to derive a secure key of this length would be a daunting task; to ease the burden of having to create a long secure key, the passphrase was introduced. This works by requiring the user to enter a strong passphrase on all wireless devices that are part of the same wireless LAN to be secured. The benefit of a passphrase is it can be a sequence of words or other text that is memorable only to the user who created it. After the passphrase is entered into the device, with the help of an electronic algorithm from the IEEE 802.11i amendment, it will create a 256-bit preshared key.

Passphrase Characteristics

The characteristics of the passphrase are as follows:

- It consists of 8 to 63 ASCII (case sensitive) or 64 hexadecimal characters.
- It creates a 256-bit preshared key.
- The longer and more random the passphrase, the more secure it will be.
- Weak passphrases can be compromised.

Several software programs and websites have random password generators to aid in the generation of strong passphrases. One such website is Gibson Research Corporation. GRC's Ultra High Security Password Generator can be found at www.grc.com/passwords.htm.

Figure 9.9 shows how to configure a passphrase on a SOHO access point.

FIGURE 9.9   D-Link wireless access point preshared key passphrase settings

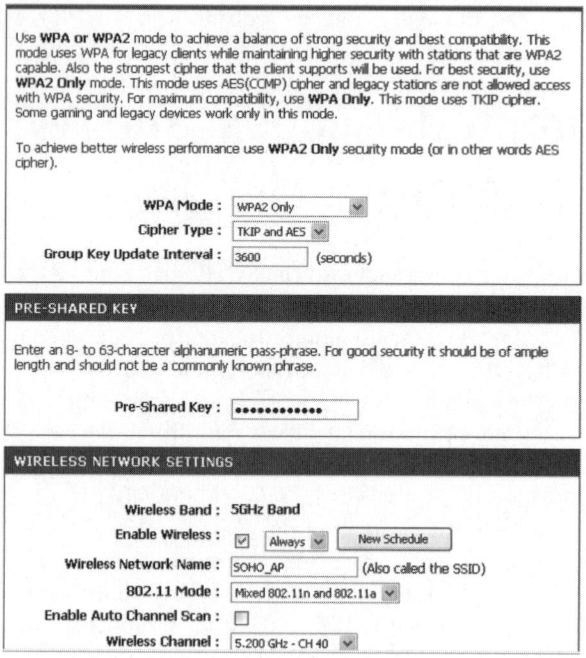

Use **WPA or WPA2** mode to achieve a balance of strong security and best compatibility. This mode uses WPA for legacy clients while maintaining higher security with stations that are WPA2 capable. Also the strongest cipher that the client supports will be used. For best security, use **WPA2 Only** mode. This mode uses AES(CCMP) cipher and legacy stations are not allowed access with WPA security. For maximum compatibility, use **WPA Only**. This mode uses TKIP cipher. Some gaming and legacy devices work only in this mode.

To achieve better wireless performance use **WPA2 Only** security mode (or in other words AES cipher).

WPA Mode :	WPA2 Only ▾
Cipher Type :	TKIP and AES ▾
Group Key Update Interval :	3600 (seconds)

PRE-SHARED KEY

Enter an 8- to 63-character alphanumeric pass-phrase. For good security it should be of ample length and should not be a commonly known phrase.

Pre-Shared Key : ●●●●●●●●●●●●

WIRELESS NETWORK SETTINGS

Wireless Band :	5GHz Band
Enable Wireless :	☑ Always ▾ New Schedule
Wireless Network Name :	SOHO_AP (Also called the SSID)
802.11 Mode :	Mixed 802.11n and 802.11a ▾
Enable Auto Channel Scan :	☐
Wireless Channel :	5.200 GHz - CH 40 ▾

WPA and WPA2 Enterprise Security

Concerned about problems connected with MAC address filtering and WEP, the industry drove the development of additional, improved wireless security solutions. One of these solutions also operates at Layer 2 and is an IEEE standard. This advanced enterprise-level solution is known as IEEE 802.1X, also called user-based security. User-based security allows an administrator to restrict access to a wireless network and its resources by creating users in a centralized database. Anyone trying to join the network will be required to authenticate as one of the users by supplying a valid username and password. After successful authentication, the user will be able to gain access to resources for which they have permissions. This type of mutual authentication is more secure than the previously mentioned passphrase security method.

IEEE 802.1X/EAP

IEEE 802.1X/EAP consists of two different components used together to form an enterprise computer network security solution. IEEE 802.1X/EAP is defined in the IEEE 802.11-2012 Standard but was originally part of the IEEE 802.11i amendment. We'll first discuss the IEEE 802.1X standard and then Extensible Authentication Protocol (EAP). Then we'll combine the technology and terms to form IEEE 802.1X/EAP.

IEEE 802.1X

IEEE 802.1X is a port-based access control method and was designed to work with IEEE 802.3 Ethernet wired networks. However, this standard was adapted into the wireless world as an alternative, more powerful solution to legacy 802.11 wireless LAN security technologies. Wireless devices that use 802.1X technology are identified using different terminology than that used in IEEE 802.11 standards-based wireless networking:

- Supplicant (wireless client device)
- Authenticator (wireless access point)
- Authentication server RADIUS or AAA authentication server)

Figure 9.10 illustrates the 802.1X/EAP process for a wireless LAN.

FIGURE 9.10   Wireless LAN client authenticating to a RADIUS server using IEEE 802.1X/EAP

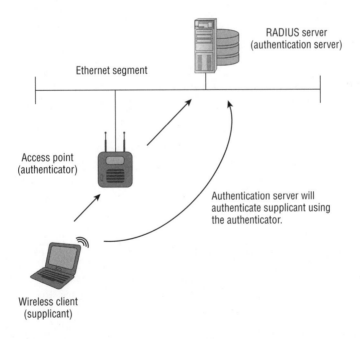

Supplicant   The supplicant is another name for the wireless client device attempting to connect to the wireless network. This typically is the software security component of the wireless client device and the IEEE 802.1X terminology.

Authenticator   The authenticator is the IEEE 802.1X term for the wireless access point or wireless LAN controller. The authenticator acts as a middleman between the wireless supplicant and the authentication server. When the supplicant requests to join the wireless network, the authenticator passes the authentication information between the two devices.

Authentication Server   The term "authentication server" is used by the IEEE 802.1X standard to identify the server that will authenticate the wireless supplicant. The authentication server receives all information from the authenticator. The authentication server may be an AAA or a RADIUS server; both are explained later in this chapter.

Extensible Authentication Protocol

IEEE 802.1X is a framework that allows for an authentication process. The authentication process used with IEEE 802.1X is *Extensible Authentication Protocol* (EAP). The IEEE 802.1X standard will employ some EAP type to complete this process. Many types of EAP are available in the industry that can be used with IEEE 802.11 wireless networking. These vary from proprietary solutions to very secure standard solutions. Examples of some popular EAP types include:

- EAP-TLS
- TTLS (EAP-MSCHAPv2)
- PEAP (EAP-MSCHAPv2)
- EAP-FAST

These and other EAP types allow a user to authenticate to a wireless network in several ways, including credentials such as username/password or certificate-based authentication.

The details of EAP and how it works are beyond the scope of the CWTS certification and exam objectives. For more information, refer to other CWNP materials.

IEEE 802.1X and EAP Together: IEEE 802.1X/EAP

Now it is time to put these two parts together to form the IEEE 802.1X/EAP authentication process. This authentication process is typically used for enterprise-level security but can be and is sometimes used in smaller wireless installations. As mentioned earlier, a variety of EAP types are available in the industry that work very well with IEEE 802.11 wireless LAN deployments. The EAP type chosen will depend on the environment in which the wireless LAN is used. EAP types vary in specifications, costs, and complexity. Figure 9.11 shows IEEE 802.1X/EAP configuration on a cloud-based wireless network management system.

FIGURE 9.11 Aerohive HiveManager Online cloud-based IEEE 802.1X/EAP configuration screen

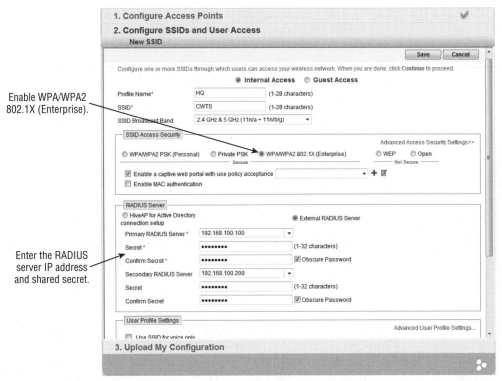

Remote Authentication Dial-In User Service

Remote Authentication Dial-In User Service (RADIUS) is a networking service that provides centralized authentication and administration of users. RADIUS started as a way to authenticate and authorize dial-up networking users. A remote user would dial up to a network using the public switched telephone network (PSTN) and a modem. A modem from a modem pool on the receiver side would answer the call. The user would then be prompted by a remote access server to enter a username and password in order to authenticate. Once the credentials were validated, the user would then have access to any resources for which they had permissions. Figure 9.12 illustrates the remote access service authentication mechanism.

In this example, the remote access client would be the computer dialing into the network, and the remote access server would be the one performing the authentication for the dial-up user. As computer networks grew in size and complexity and remote access technology improved, there was a need to optimize the process on the remote access server side. This is where RADIUS provides a solution. RADIUS took decentralized remote access services databases and combined them into one central location, allowing for centralized user administration and centralized management. It eased the burden of having to manage several databases and optimized administration of remote access services.

FIGURE 9.12 Remote user authenticating to a remote access server (RAS)

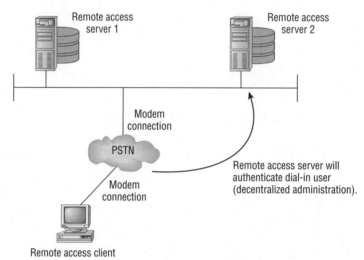

A company does not need a large number of RADIUS servers. For a small to medium-sized company, one RADIUS server should be sufficient (with a backup if possible). Larger enterprise organizations may need several RADIUS servers across the entire wide area network. In wireless networking, the wireless access point can act as a RADIUS client, which means it will have the capability to accept requests from wireless client devices and forward them to the RADIUS server for authentication. Figure 9.13 shows this configuration.

As Figure 9.13 shows, the remote access client is now the wireless access point. The wireless client device is authorized as a user in the database of the RADIUS server. The RADIUS server is the authenticating server or database. A RADIUS server may also be known as an authentication, authorization, and accounting (AAA) server. In this configuration, it will authenticate users and provide access to the resources for which they have permissions. In addition, it will keep track of all transactions by accounting.

Authentication, Authorization, and Accounting

The *Authentication, Authorization, and Accounting* (AAA) protocol provides a framework to allow secure access and authorization as well as keep track of the user's activities on a computer network including wireless networks. AAA is commonly part of a RADIUS server's functionality. The three components that work together in the AAA protocol are:

- Authentication
- Authorization
- Accounting

FIGURE 9.13   Wireless access point configured as a RADIUS client device

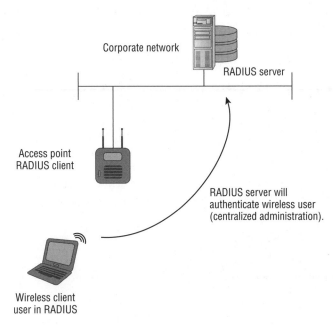

The First Part of AAA—Authentication

As you learned earlier in this chapter, authentication is defined as a way of confirming or validating an identity; for the most part it validates that you are who you say you are. Enterprise IEEE 802.11 wireless networks commonly use IEEE 802.1X/EAP or user-based authentication technology. In addition to username and passwords, wireless networks may also use other authentication methods, including digital certificates and smart cards, to name a few.

The Second Part of AAA—Authorization

For wireless networking, authorization provides access to network resources that a wireless device or user has the appropriate permissions or rights to use. These permissions could be tied to an individual user object but can also be tied to a group object. After a user authenticates, the AAA protocol will then allow for the authorization process. Authorization can be on a per-user or per-group basis. In IEEE wireless networking technology, authorization is commonly used for wireless LAN functionality, including bandwidth controls, time restrictions/controls, and quality of service (QoS) policies.

The Third Part of AAA—Accounting

Accounting is the last part or third "A" in the Authentication, Authorization, and Accounting (AAA) protocol. Accounting will keep track of every place on the network a user visits or everything done on the network. Basically, it monitors all network activity.

This can be used for something as simple as tracking resource usage for software or hardware upgrade purposes or for technology budgeting purposes. Accounting can be used to determine what technology different areas of the organization are using and how they will be able to contribute to the cost of this technology.

IEEE 802.11 Encryption Methods

In the most basic sense, encryption consists of taking information and scrambling it so only the sender and intended recipient that know the encryption method are able to decipher the encrypted information. In addition to authenticating and verifying an identity, encryption also needs to be considered for wireless networking. In the IEEE 802.11 standard, three different encryption mechanisms can be used on a wireless network to protect data traffic:

- Wired Equivalent Privacy (WEP)
- Temporal Key Integrity Protocol (TKIP)
- Counter Mode with Cipher Block Chaining Message Authentication Code Protocol (CCMP)

Wired Equivalent Privacy

As discussed earlier in this chapter, Wired Equivalent Privacy (WEP) was an optional encryption method specified in the original IEEE 802.11 standard. WEP was only intended to protect wireless network users against casual eavesdropping and for IEEE 802.11 shared-key authentication. As discussed, this encryption method is considered legacy and was compromised early on, making it a weak solution to use with modern wireless networks. With early deployments of standards-based wireless networking, WEP was the only solution available, which made it very popular. At that time, the capability to crack WEP was available but that did not mean anyone could do it. Initially, cracking WEP required a large amount of data, some knowledge of the process, and usually a software program to extract the WEP key. Newer technology has made cracking WEP a very simple process. WEP can be cracked in minutes rather than hours, days, or weeks and almost anyone can do it. The fact that WEP is available in two key lengths—64-bit or 128-bit—makes no difference to the experienced intruder. WEP uses the RC4 stream cipher for bit-level encryption. The problem with WEP does not lie in RC4 but in how it was used in the encryption process. One reason WEP is vulnerable to intrusion is because of something called an initialization vector (IV). The 24-bit IV is broadcast in the clear or unencrypted. This being the case, it exposes a weakness in the way WEP was designed, thereby allowing it to be compromised.

Is WEP Still Used?

WEP is weak and because of vulnerabilities can be cracked. Therefore, using WEP is not a recommended solution to secure wireless computer data. Many countries have not fallen under PCI's scrutiny yet and still use WEP to protect wireless networks. Older voice over Wi-Fi phones and barcode scanners may still use WEP.

As a general rule, it is best not to use WEP as a security measure for protection of a wireless network and its users. However, there are still some deployments that use devices with wireless networking that have limited capabilities when it comes to security. WEP may be the only security option they have. If upgrading the devices to something that supports higher-level security is not an option, the organization may have no choice but to use WEP. If this is the case, it is important for the network administrator to use appropriate device segmentation for the WEP-enabled devices in order to not compromise the entire network infrastructure. One way to do this is to consider the use of a virtual local area network (VLAN). This gives the administrator the ability to separate wireless devices that may be potentially compromised because of WEP from other devices that are capable of more advanced security solutions.

There are many software programs available to allow someone with limited knowledge to be able to crack WEP. As mentioned earlier, newer, more sophisticated tools allow WEP to be cracked in minutes. If a wireless network has the capability of more advanced security such as 802.11i, WPA, or WPA 2.0, one of those should be used instead of WEP. An appropriate device upgrade path should be evaluated in order to eliminate the use of WEP in any capacity on the wireless network.

Preventing WEP from Being Cracked with a Patented Technology Called *WEP Cloaking*

You are a network consultant and have been assigned the task to evaluate a wireless network in a retail establishment that currently uses wireless barcode scanners for a variety of applications. You determine that these devices currently have no security solution enabled. After evaluating the system, you come to the conclusion that the only possible wireless security solution that can be applied to these devices is WEP.

You know from experience that WEP is not secure and can be compromised. Therefore you make a recommendation to the IT manager to upgrade all of the wireless barcode scanners to support a higher level security such as WPA 2.0 to adequately secure the data. You are told by the IT manager that unfortunately the budget for the current year will not allow hardware upgrade of the devices. This being the case, you have an alternate solution. This organization currently is considering a WIPS solution.

The capability to crack WEP has been available for many years through a variety of freeware WEP cracking tools. There are 23 known attacks against the original 802.11 encryption standard for either 64-bit or 128-bit WEP. Through the use of sophisticated utilities, WEP can be cracked in minutes regardless of the key strength. One solution known as WEP Cloaking allows organizations to operate WEP-encrypted networks securely and preserve their existing investment in mobile devices such as barcode scanners. This patented WEP Cloaking technology will make these popular freeware cracking tools useless. This solution would allow the company to maintain the current barcode scanner technology and still provide a secure wireless solution for the organization. Keep in mind that WEP Cloaking is one manufacturer's method to protect legacy devices forced to use WEP until they can be replaced with newer, more secure devices.

Temporal Key Integrity Protocol

Temporal Key Integrity Protocol (TKIP) was designed as a firmware upgrade to WEP. TKIP added several enhancements to the WEP algorithm and was the foundation for the Wi-Fi Protected Access (WPA) certification from the Wi-Fi Alliance. These enhancements include:

- Per-packet key mixing of the IV to separate IVs from weak keys
- A dynamic rekeying mechanism to change encryption and integrity keys
- 48-bit IV and IV sequence counter to prevent replay attacks
- Message Integrity Check (MIC) to prevent forgery attacks
- Use of the RC4 stream cipher, thereby allowing backward compatibility with WEP

Configuring a wireless network to use TKIP is a fairly straightforward process. It can be accomplished either by using the web interface available on most SOHO access points or by using the web interface or command-line interface for enterprise-level access points. For the wireless client devices, TKIP will be configured through the client software utility. Some older wireless hardware devices may not support TKIP. If this is the case, replacement of the hardware will be necessary in order to take advantage of newer security solutions. Figure 9.14 shows how to configure TKIP using WPA on a wireless LAN controller.

TKIP/RC4 uses a 48-bit IV and can be compromised in the same way as WEP if a weak key is used. Using a stronger technique such as CCMP/AES is a better solution.

Counter Mode with Cipher Block Chaining Message Authentication Code Protocol

Counter Mode with Cipher Block Chaining Message Authentication Code Protocol (CCMP) is a mandatory part of the IEEE 801.11i amendment, now in the IEEE 802.11-2012 standard and part of Wi-Fi Protected Access 2.0 (WPA2) certification from the Wi-Fi Alliance. CCMP uses the *Advanced Encryption Standard* (AES) algorithm block cipher. CCMP is mandatory for robust security network (RSN) compliance. If an RSN is required to comply with an industry or governmental regulation, CCMP must be used. CCMP is also intended as a replacement to TKIP. Because of the strong encryption CCMP provides, it may require replacement of legacy hardware. In some cases, it may use a separate chip to perform computation-intensive AES ciphering.

Configuration of CCMP is similar to that of TKIP, discussed earlier. The main difference with CCMP is that older hardware may not support it and it is a stronger encryption solution. Figure 9.15 shows configuring the CCMP method using WPA2.

FIGURE 9.14   Motorola RFS6000 wireless LAN controller security configuration screen

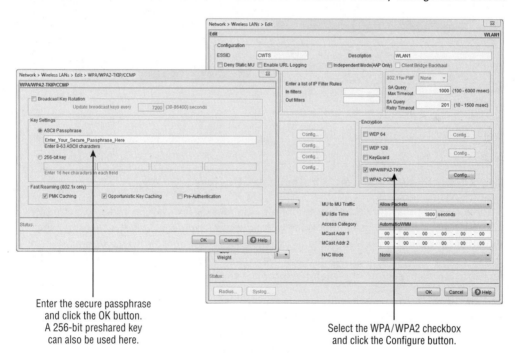

Enter the secure passphrase
and click the OK button.
A 256-bit preshared key
can also be used here.

Select the WPA/WPA2 checkbox
and click the Configure button.

FIGURE 9.15   Cisco 1250 series IEEE 802.11n wireless access point security configuration selection

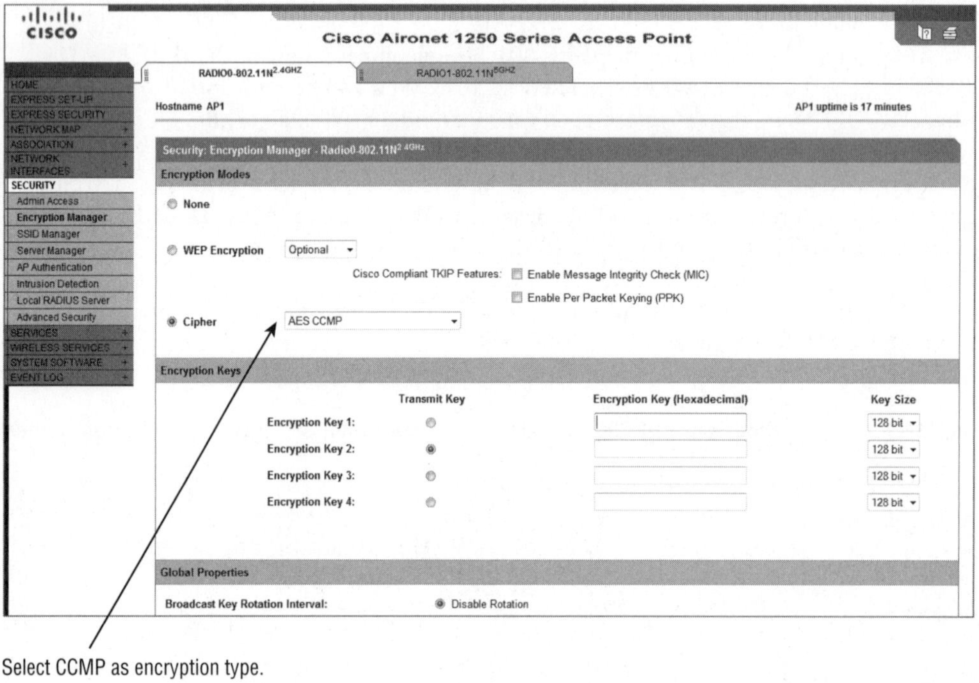

Select CCMP as encryption type.

Upgrading the Firmware on Wireless LAN Devices

In some cases, it may be necessary to upgrade the device firmware in order to get either TKIP or CCMP capability. It is important to follow the manufacturer's instructions when upgrading firmware to prevent damage to the device. Improper firmware upgrades or a loss of power during the upgrade process may render the device unusable or require the device to be sent back to the manufacturer for repair.

Some of the security technologies we just discussed are part of the Wi-Fi Alliance interoperability testing for standards-based wireless LAN equipment. As mentioned in Chapter 2, equipment certified for both WPA and WPA2 can function in either personal or enterprise modes. Table 9.2 shows the details of both WPA and WPA 2 certifications.

TABLE 9.2   Details of the Wi-Fi Alliance WPA and WPA 2 certifications

Wi-Fi Alliance security method	Authentication method	Encryption/cipher method
WPA – Personal	Passphrase	TKIP/RC4
WPA – Enterprise	IEEE 802.1X/EAP	TKIP/RC4
WPA 2 – Personal	Passphrase	CCMP/AES or TKIP/RC4 (optional)
WPA 2 – Enterprise	IEEE 802.1X/EAP	CCMP/AES or TKIP/RC4 (optional)

Role-Based Access Control

Role-based access control (RBAC) is a way of restricting access to only authorized users. This access is from authentication based on specific roles rather than user identities. It was designed to ease the task of security administration on large networks. RBAC has characteristics similar to those of a common network administration practice—the creation of users and groups. RBAC may also fit well under the authorization part of AAA because it has very similar characteristics.

To give a user on a computer network access to a network resource, best practices recommend creating a group object, assigning the group permissions to the resource, and then adding the user object to the group. This method allows any user who is a member of the group to be granted access to the resource. Role-based access control can be used for various activities users may perform while connected to a wireless LAN, including limiting the amount of throughput, enforcing time restrictions, or controlling access to specific resources such as the Internet.

Let's look at an example. Your organization consists of several departments that use resources available on the wireless network. The departments are sales, engineering, and accounting. Each department has specific requirements for what and when they need to access from the wireless LAN. This is where RBAC would be a great fit. If the network administrator wanted to restrict access to the wireless LAN for the sales department from 8:00 a.m. to 5:00 p.m., she could create a role using this feature. If the engineering department was using too much bandwidth, a role could be created to restrict throughput for that department. These are a couple of examples where RBAC can work with a wireless LAN.

Virtual Private Networking

Virtual private networking (VPN) is the capability to create private communications over a public network infrastructure such as the Internet. The security solutions discussed earlier in this chapter are Layer 2 security solutions; that is, all such solutions work at Layer 2 of the OSI model. By contrast, VPNs are Internet Protocol–based—they typically operate at Layer 3 of the OSI model but some will work at Layer 2. Figure 9.16 illustrates VPN technology in relationship to the OSI model.

FIGURE 9.16   OSI model representation of a Layer 3 VPN security solution

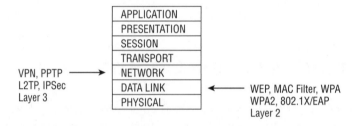

Prior to the ratification of the IEEE 802.11i amendment to the standard, VPN technology was prevalent in enterprise deployments as well as in remote access security. Since Layer 2 security solutions have become stronger (mostly thanks to the 802.11i amendment and the Wi-Fi Alliance WPA and WPA2 certifications), VPN technology is not as widely used within enterprise LANs. However, VPN still remains a powerful security solution for remote access in both wired and wireless networking.

VPNs consist of two parts—tunneling and encryption. Figure 9.17 illustrates a VPN tunnel using the Internet. A standalone VPN tunnel does not provide data encryption, and VPN tunnels are created across Internet Protocol (IP) networks. In a very basic sense, VPNs use encapsulation methods where one IP frame is encapsulated within a second IP frame. The encryption of VPNs is performed as a separate function.

FIGURE 9.17   Representation of a VPN tunnel

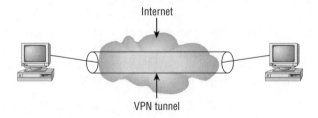

Real World Scenario

Shipping a Crate Using VPN Technology

An analogy for the VPN process is shipping a locked crate from one location to another. You are a technical support engineer for the headquarters office of a company that has five offices in different locations around the world. You get a telephone call from a co-worker at one of the remote offices. She needs to replace an access point with a newer model at the remote office. You need to ship the pre-configured replacement access point to her using a common carrier. You want to ensure that the access point arrives at the destination location without coming into physical contact with anybody other than the intended recipient.

The access point is analogous to the *IP frame*. You put the access point into a crate that has a combination lock to secure it. This crate containing the access point is analogous to the *second IP frame*, or the one that *encapsulates* the original IP frame.

You ship the crate to the destination using a common carrier, which would be analogous to the *public infrastructure* over which the encrypted data is sent. Many other packages are shipped by this common carrier, but no one will be able to see the contents of the crate because they do not know the combination to the lock (the encryption method).

When the access point arrives at the destination, the recipient (the technical support engineer for the remote office) must know the combination of the lock on the crate in order to open it to retrieve the access point. So you tell her the combination over the telephone. This is analogous to the *encryption method*. Over a secure telephone line, only you (the sender) and she (the recipient) know the combination to the lock. The tech support engineer will be able to unlock the crate using the combination you supplied her, and she will be able to retrieve the access point.

Two common types of VPN protocols are:

- Point-to-Point Tunneling Protocol (PPTP)
- Layer 2 Tunneling Protocol (L2TP)

Point-to-Point Tunneling Protocol

Developed by a vendor consortium that included Microsoft, *Point-to-Point Tunneling Protocol* (PPTP) was very popular because of its ease of configuration and was included in all Microsoft Windows operating systems starting with Windows 95. PPTP uses Microsoft Point-to-Point Encryption (MPPE-128) Protocol for encryption. This process provides both tunneling and encryption capabilities for the user's data.

> **WARNING** If the PPTP configuration uses MS-CHAP version 2 for user authentication on a wireless network, it can be a security issue. This authentication process can be captured using a wireless protocol analyzer or other scanning software program and potentially allow someone to perform a dictionary attack, allowing them to acquire a user's credentials and eventually giving them the capability to log on to the network. A dictionary attack is performed by software that challenges the encrypted password against common words or phrases in a text file (dictionary). Therefore, using PPTP on a wireless network should be avoided. Keep in mind that the security vulnerability is not PPTP itself; it is that the authentication frames on a wireless LAN can be captured by an intruder, who can then acquire user credentials (username and password) and be able to gain access to the VPN.

Layer 2 Tunneling Protocol

Layer 2 Tunneling Protocol (L2TP) is the combination of two different tunneling protocols: Cisco's Layer 2 Forwarding (L2F) and Microsoft's Point-to-Point Tunneling Protocol (PPTP). L2TP defines the tunneling process, which requires some level of encryption in order to function. With L2TP, a popular choice of encryption is Internet Protocol Security (IPSec), which provides authentication and encryption for each IP packet in a data stream. Since L2TP was published in 1999 as a proposed standard and because it is more secure than PPTP, L2TP has gained much popularity and for the most part is a replacement for PPTP. L2TP/IPSec is a very common VPN solution in use today. PPTP should not be used when L2TP is available.

Components of a VPN Solution

A VPN solution consists of three components:

- Client side (endpoint)
- Network infrastructure (public or private)
- Server side (endpoint)

In many cases, both client side and server side are known as VPN endpoints. The infrastructure in many cases is a public access network such as the Internet. The client-side endpoint typically consists of software, allowing it to be configured for the VPN. This software is available at a nominal cost from a variety of manufacturers. Newer Microsoft Windows operating systems include VPN client software for both PPTP and L2TP. Figure 9.18 shows a VPN client configuration screen.

Wireless LAN client devices have the capability to be a VPN client endpoint. The VPN can terminate either at an access point or across the Internet to the corporate network. Figure 9.19 shows a common example of a wireless client device connecting to a wireless hotspot to access the corporate network.

FIGURE 9.18 Microsoft Windows 7 Professional built-in VPN client utility configuration

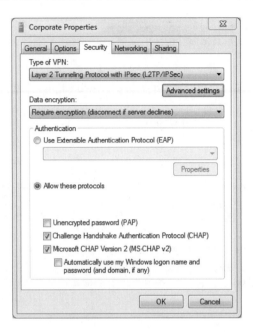

FIGURE 9.19 Wireless LAN client using a wireless hotspot to connect to a corporate office using VPN technology

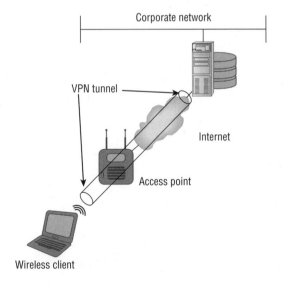

In Exercise 9.1, you will explore the built-in VPN client software utility in Windows 7 Professional.

EXERCISE 9.1

Setting Up a VPN

In this exercise, you will set up a VPN connection using the built-in VPN client utility in Microsoft Windows 7 Professional.

1. Click Start ➢ Control Panel. The Control Panel window appears.

2. Click the View Network Status And Tasks link under the Network And Internet heading in the Control Panel window. The Network and Sharing Center window appears.

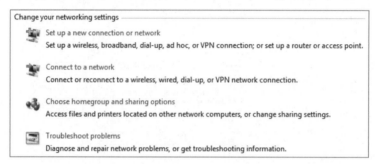

3. In the Change Your Network Settings menu, click the Set Up A New Connection Or Network link. The Set Up A Connection Or Network – Choose A Connection screen appears.

4. Select Connect To A Workplace – Set Up A Dial-Up Or VPN Connection To Your Workplace, and click Next. The Connect To A Workplace – How Do You Want To Connect? screen appears.

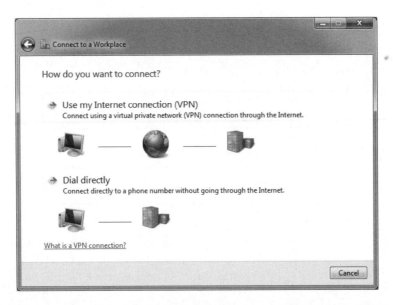

5. Click Use My Internet Connection (VPN). The Connect To A Workplace – Do You Want To Set Up An Internet Connection Before Continuing? screen appears. Click I'll Set Up An Internet Connection Later. The Connect To A Workplace – Type The Internet Address To Connect To screen appears.

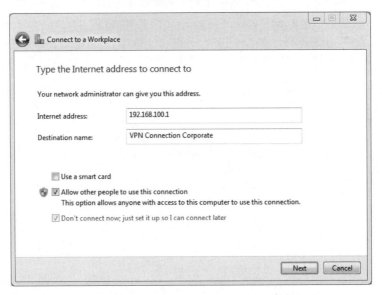

6. In the Internet Address text box, type the IP address or hostname of the remote VPN server you wish to connect to. In the Destination Name text box, type your selected name for the VPN connection and click Next. The Connect To A Workplace – Type Your User Name And Password screen appears.

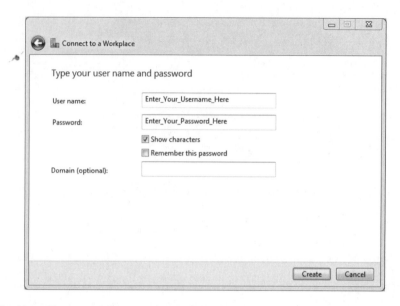

7. In the User Name and Password text boxes, enter a valid username and password and click Create.

8. The Connect To A Workplace – The Connection Is Ready To Use screen appears; click Close. The Network and Sharing Center appears.

9. To use your VPN connection, click the Connect To A Network link. The Currently Connected To screen will appear. Click the name of the VPN connection you created in step 6. The Connect VPN Connection dialog box appears, prompting for a username and password.

10. Enter a valid username and password and also domain if required and click Connect to connect to your VPN server. Once your credentials have been validated by the VPN server, you will have access to the network through the VPN you created.

The Wireless Intrusion Prevention System

In wireless networking, a *wireless intrusion prevention system* (WIPS) is a software/hardware solution that monitors the radio waves and, using a wireless hardware sensor, can report captured information to software to be recorded in a server database (this differs from other network monitoring and management systems discussed later in this chapter). The WIPS solution will then be able to take the appropriate countermeasures to prevent wireless network intrusions. These countermeasures are based on identifying the intrusion by comparing the captured information to an intrusion signature database within the WIPS server. Figure 9.20 shows a WIPS dashboard that displays a Layer 1 radio frequency jamming denial of service (DoS) attack that was recorded.

There are many advantages to using a WIPS. Some of them include:

- Captures information by 24/7 monitoring

- Detects threats to the wireless infrastructure such as DoS attacks and rogue access points

- Notifies you about threats through a variety of mechanisms

- Supports integrated spectrum analysis

- Includes elaborate reporting systems

- Ensures compliance with corporate security policy and legislative compliance

- Retains data for forensic investigation

- Uses hardware sensors for monitoring

24/7/365 Monitoring   With a WIPS, monitoring of the wireless network can be accomplished 24 hours a day, seven days a week, to help identify potential attacks, including DoS, either from Layer 1 RF or from Layer 2 software such as a deauthentication storm. A WIPS also finds rogue (unauthorized) access points and misconfigured wireless devices.

Detection and Mitigation   Unlike many wireless intrusion detection systems (WIDS), WIPS has the capability to detect and react. WIPS solutions will automatically respond to threats against a wireless LAN by stopping the device or process that contains the threat before it has a chance to cause any damage to the wireless network.

FIGURE 9.20   AirMagnet Enterprise dashboard

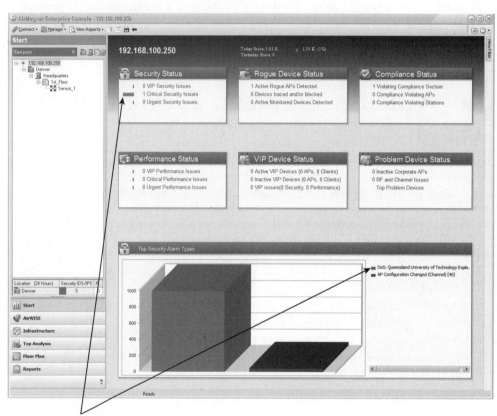

AirMagnet Enterprise detects
an RF denial-of-service (DoS)
attack that was reported.

Notification of Threats   WIPS solutions have the capability to provide notifications to network administrators based on alerts and alarms of potential threats that the WIPS encounters during monitoring. These notifications can be provided in a variety of ways, such as email or pager.

Integrated Spectrum Analysis   This feature allows an administrator to view the state of a remote radio environment at a branch office or remote location. This allows the accurate diagnosis of radio spectrum problems, including Layer 1 DoS attacks.

Elaborate Reporting Systems   In addition to standard reports, most WIPS solutions allow network administrators to create their own customized reports in a short period of time. These reports will enable an organization to meet the specific requirements of audit groups, either internal or external to the organization.

Regulatory Policy Compliance   A WIPS will have the capability to help ensure that an organization maintains the necessary legislative compliance. Compliance requirements include Health Insurance Portability and Accountability Act (HIPAA) and Payment Card Industry (PCI).

Retains Data for Forensics   Many WIPS solutions can retain data that may be used in forensics investigations. The WIPS will provide the documented proof an organization may require to take the appropriate action based on events recorded. WIPS solutions will require fine-tuning to some degree to eliminate misrepresentation of the threat signatures the system will detect. This starts with a baseline of the environment, allowing the administrator to gauge the levels of detection and reaction.

Uses Hardware Sensors for Monitoring   WIPS solutions will use either dedicated hardware sensors or share the sensor functionality with access points. These sensors will collect data by monitoring the air 24/7 and allowing information to be reported to a server database.

WIPS Configuration and Maintenance

Although a WIPS solution is a valuable tool to use for wireless LAN monitoring and detection/mitigation of wireless intrusions, it needs to be set up, configured, and maintained correctly. Installing a WIPS system without setting the appropriate thresholds and baselines may result in unreliable or unusable collections of information. For example, if an organization is concerned about deauthentication attacks, such as forcing a "deauthentication storm" (sending many consecutive deauthentication frames), this setting will need to be enabled on the WIPS system with the appropriate threshold setting in order to be detected. Remember from Chapter 8 that deauthentication occurs when an existing authentication is no longer valid, and it can be caused by a wireless LAN device logging off from the current connection or roaming to a different BSS. If an intruder sends just a couple of deauthentication frames to a wireless device in an attempt to force them to reauthenticate, and thus perform a hijack attack, the activity may fall under the threshold set for the deauthentication frames that are monitored and could be missed. The bottom line is that proper setup, configuration, and maintenance of a WIPS system all need to be carefully considered. Figure 9.21 shows the policy setup screen for a WIPS.

Overlay and Integrated WIPS Technology

A WIPS requires hardware sensors for monitoring and sending the data to the WIPS server. These sensors can be dedicated devices (only used for monitoring) or can share functionality with the wireless access points. The terminology used for these WIPS sensors is:

- Overlay WIPS sensors
- Integrated WIPS sensors

FIGURE 9.21 AirMagnet Enterprise WIPS policy configuration

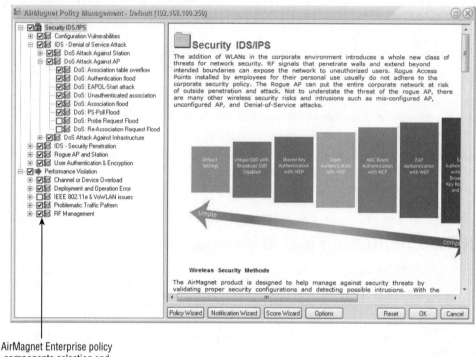

AirMagnet Enterprise policy
components selection and
threshold settings

Overlay WIPS Sensors

Overlay WIPS sensors are dedicated wireless devices that have physical characteristics similar to those of wireless access points but are only used for scanning the air and sending data to a WIPS server. These devices are passive and will not interfere with other wireless LAN devices such as access points. This type of sensor does not need to be implemented on a 1:1 deployment. In other words you do not need one WIPS sensor with every one access point. WIPS sensors are commonly installed in a 1:3 or 1:4 ratio. Figure 9.22 shows how a WIPS overlay solution uses dedicated sensors.

It is best to check with the WIPS manufacturer to determine the recommended number of dedicated sensors. Some wireless site survey software tools will specify the number and locations of the sensors required, based on the wireless network design. One disadvantage to the overlay solution is extra cost for the dedicated sensors. Some manufacturers allow a wireless access point to run as a dedicated sensor; for these, the cost would be the same as the wireless access point.

FIGURE 9.22   The WIPS overlay installation uses separate devices.

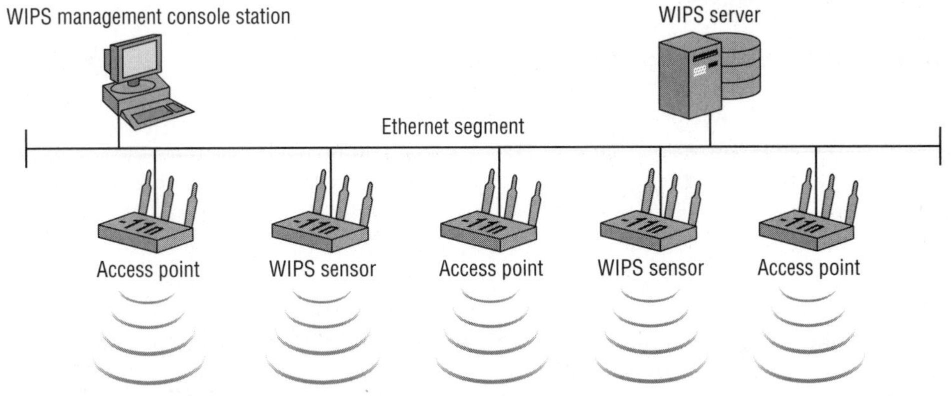

WIPS management console station   WIPS server

Ethernet segment

Access point   WIPS sensor   Access point   WIPS sensor   Access point

Integrated WIPS Sensors

Integrated WIPS sensors are part of a wireless access point's functionality. An integrated sensor may have a dedicated radio for full-time WIPS monitoring, or it may share a radio with the access point for part-time WIPS monitoring. A dedicated WIPS radio that is built into the wireless access point will be able to monitor the air and send data directly to the WIPS server full time. This would be the radio's only function. One benefit to this type of sensor is that the cost will be less than that of the overlay system, because it does not requires separate dedicated WIPS sensors. However, the cost may be a little higher than if it were only an access point because of the additional radio for the WIPS capability. The other type of integrated WIPS sensor is the one that shares a radio with the access point. The downside to this is that the WIPS monitoring will only be part-time and will not be able to capture everything that is going on. Figure 9.23 shows a WIPS integrated solution, consisting of a WIPS sensor and access point in the same device (wireless access point).

FIGURE 9.23   WIPS integrated solution sensor radio built into a wireless access point

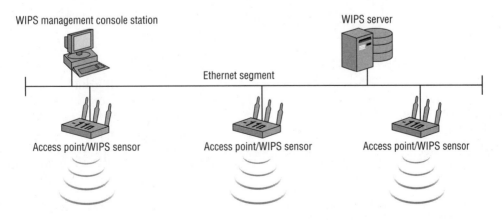

WIPS management console station   WIPS server

Ethernet segment

Access point/WIPS sensor   Access point/WIPS sensor   Access point/WIPS sensor

 **Real World Scenario**

Integrated WIPS Sensor Analogy

Think about this analogy. An after-hours security officer is sitting at a desk watching the security monitors for any unauthorized access or other activities that could be a security violation. The officer hears a noise down the hall and leaves his post to investigate. Because he has stepped away from the desk, he cannot be watching the security monitors at the same time. Therefore an unauthorized person may be able to enter the area without being noticed by the security officer. This is similar to the way an access point that is a part-time integrated WIPS sensor and that is servicing wireless client devices may not be able to see and detect potential WIPS violations. For example, if the wireless access point is providing voice over wireless access, because of QoS features the access point will prioritize the wireless voice frames and may forgo the WIPS monitoring. This will result in the WIPS server not being able to capture potential wireless intrusions or other wireless security violations.

Making the decision to use an overlay or integrated WIPS may be a tough one. It may come down to what you are trying to prevent and what you are trying to protect. It may also come down to cost. The bottom line is this: If you are planning to install a WIPS, evaluate the advantages and disadvantages of each type carefully. One of the main goals of a WIPS is to enforce functional (technical) corporate security policy 24/7/365.

The Captive Portal

A *captive portal* is a process that redirects a user to an authentication source of some type before they will be allowed wireless network access. This authentication source in the form of a web page will require a user to "authenticate" in some way and may include the following:

- Enter user credentials (username and password).
- Input payment information.
- Agree to terms and conditions.

When one or more of these methods is complete, a wireless device will then be able to access the network and use whatever resources they have permission to access. Most if not all public access wireless networks should have some type of captive portal enabled. This will help to protect both the provider (host) and the user of the wireless network. At a minimum, requiring the user to agree to terms and conditions via a captive portal should be implemented.

Most enterprise-grade wireless access points, including cooperative access points and wireless LAN controllers, have "built-in" captive portal capabilities that are fairly straightforward to implement.

Wireless Network Management and Monitoring Systems

Wireless network management and monitoring systems are software- or hardware-based solutions that allow a wireless network engineer to both control and administer wireless infrastructure devices and collect information that may be used to troubleshoot and resolve wireless LAN issues. The information collected may consist of either Physical Layer information (radio frequency) or Data Link Layer information (wireless LAN frames).

In the early days of standards-based IEEE 802.11 wireless networking, only autonomous access points for the most part were available; there was no centralized management or control. (Autonomous access points are discussed in Chapter 2.) To manage these infrastructure devices, you would need to configure each device separately. This could be done by connecting either through the command-line interface or a web-based interface, and individual configuration worked well if only a few infrastructure devices were installed.

However, as the need for wireless LAN technology grew, so did the number of devices or access points. Managing a large number of infrastructure devices manually was not feasible. This is where the *wireless network management system* (WNMS) evolved. The WNMS is a centralized solution that was originally available in either software form to run on a server or hardware form to run as a standalone network appliance. (We'll look at a third option, cloud-based WNMS solutions, next.) A WNMS would allow a network engineer to manage and control the entire wireless LAN centrally. These centralized management systems are available from many manufacturers for use with their own infrastructure devices and are available as vendor-neutral solutions to work with many different manufacturers' equipment. A WNMS may also incorporate WIPS technology for a complete wireless network management, monitoring, and security solution. Figure 9.24 shows a WNMS dashboard.

WNMS: Software, Hardware, or Cloud?

As you just learned, a WNMS is available in different forms—software that will run on a server, hardware that will run on a dedicated appliance, and now cloud-based WNMS solutions. This newest option is growing in popularity. With the evolution of standards-based wireless LAN technology, the wireless LAN controller worked as a substitute for WNMS, offering control and management of the complete wireless LAN infrastructure. However, as the wireless networks continued to grow, so did the need for a WNMS. Figure 9.25 shows a cloud-based wireless network management system.

FIGURE 9.24 Aruba Networks Airwave Wireless Network Management Software Platform

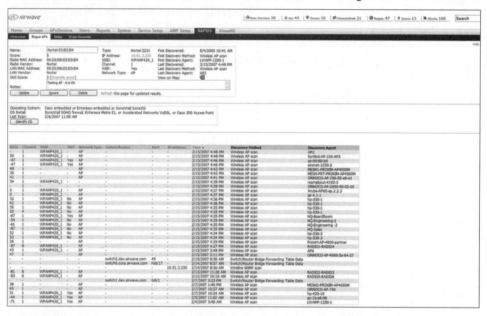

FIGURE 9.25 Aerohive HiveManager NMS cloud-based WNMS

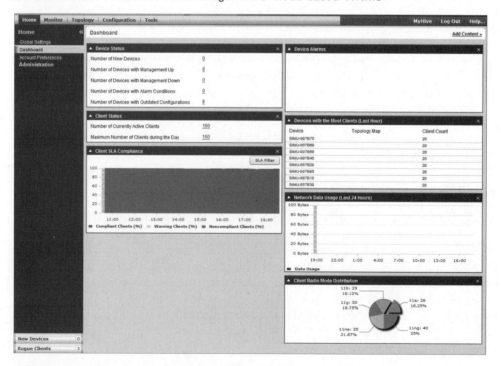

Listed here are some of the WNMS solutions available from various manufacturers:

Manufacturer	Solution	Description
Aerohive	HiveManager NMS	Cloud-based, public or private cloud using a virtual machine
Aruba Networks	AirWave	Also vendor-neutral or multi-vendor
Cisco Systems	Cisco Wireless Control System (WCS)	
Hewlett Packard	HP Intelligent Management Center (IMC)	
Meraki		Cloud-based
Motorola	AirDefense Services Platform (ADSP)	Hardware appliance or virtual machine
Xirrus	Xirrus Management System (XMS)	Software-, appliance-, or cloud-based

Keep in mind that some manufacturers allow management of both wireless and wired infrastructures from one platform, creating a "unified" management of the entire network.

Wireless Network Monitoring

In addition to wireless network management solutions, you need to understand wireless network monitoring solutions. These monitoring solutions are in addition to the WIPS you learned about earlier in this chapter. They allow a wireless network engineer to monitor the performance of a wireless network at the Physical layer and the Data Link layer for both troubleshooting and security information gathering purposes.

Physical Layer Monitoring

Physical Layer monitoring allows the wireless network engineer to see what is happening in the air as it relates to radio frequency. This is usually accomplished with the use of a spectrum analyzer, which allows an engineer to "see" the radio frequency and thus detect potential interference issues and also security issues. Interference from both wireless LAN devices and other wireless devices such as two-way radios or microwave ovens will be visible with the help of a spectrum analyzer. The spectrum analyzer will also detect Layer 1 security issues such as a narrow-band or wide-band radio frequency denial-of-service (DoS) attack. Figure 9.26 shows how a spectrum analyzer can see the Physical layer information and detect potential security threats.

FIGURE 9.26   The MetaGeek Chanalyzer spectrum analyzer shows an RF DoS attack using a narrow-band jamming device.

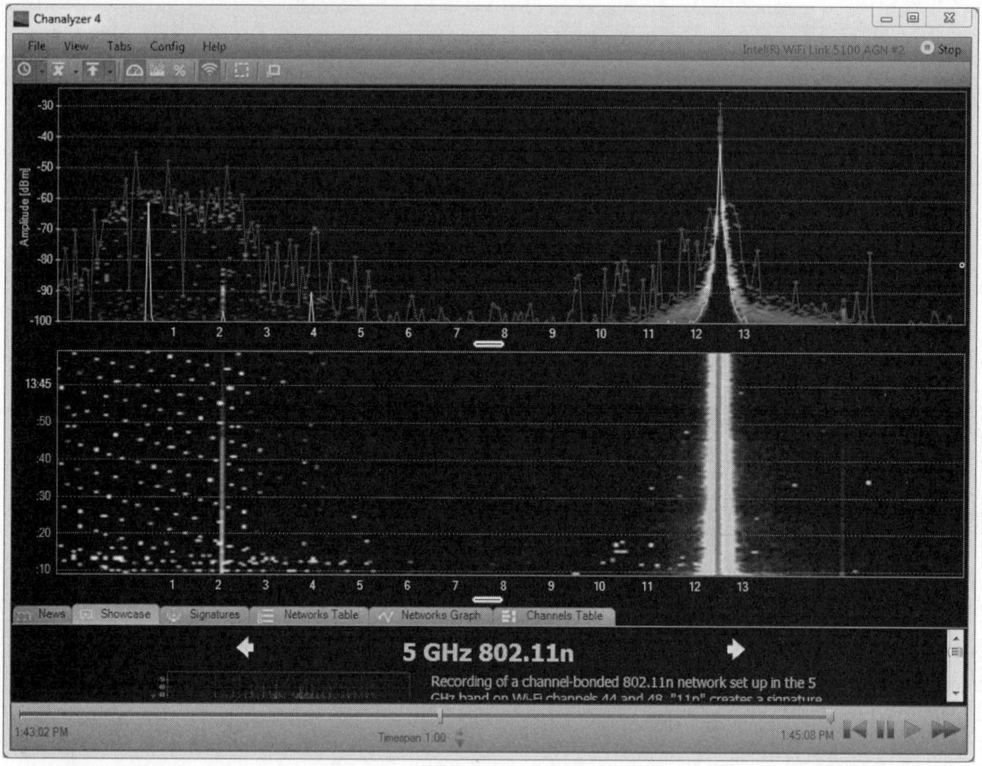

Some manufacturers of wireless LAN spectrum analyzers are:

Manufacturer	Solution	Comments
AirMagnet/Fluke Networks	Spectrum XT	
Cisco Systems	Cisco Spectrum Expert	Formerly Cognio
Fluke Networks	AirCheck Wi-Fi Tester	Handheld device
MetaGeek	Chanalyzer	

Data Link Layer Monitoring

Data Link layer monitoring means looking at the Layer 2 information; it allows a network engineer to view the wireless LAN frames that traverse the air and provides the opportunity to view both potential performance and security issues. Protocol analysis tools allow the engineer to view both frame exchanges and frame decoding by expanding on the captured wireless frames. From a security point of view, these tools can provide valuable wireless network information for both the wireless network engineer as well as a potential intruder. The wireless network engineer will be able to find potential security configuration issues that could open the door to intruders. If an intruder were to capture wireless frames, such as the preshared key 4-way handshake, they might (depending on how strong the passphrase is) be able to use a dictionary attack software program and determine the pass-phrase; this would allow them to gain access to the wireless network and potentially see a user's encrypted data.

Some wireless LAN analyzers are able to capture and reconstruct TCP/IP frames and reconstruct a session and allow web pages to be seen or email messages to be read directly from the captured wireless frames. Keep in mind that this is possible on an open wireless network or one on which the intruder has been able to capture the frames that allow them to access the wireless LAN and to decode the data frames. Some common wireless LAN protocol analyzers are:

Manufacturer	Solution	Comments
AirMagnet/Fluke Networks	WiFi Analyzer	
MetaGeek	Eye P.A.	
Tamosoft	Commview for WiFi	
Wildpackets	OmniPeek Network Analyzer	
Wireshark		Formerly Ethereal

Some of these packet analyzers (among others) will perform wireless LAN analysis and work with wired LANs.

Many manufacturers of wireless LAN packet analyzers offer trial versions of their software to allow you to "try before you buy." Visit the manufacturers' websites for more information on how to obtain a trial version of their software.

The topic of regulatory compliance, discussed next, is not included in the exam objectives but is explained here for your own reference.

Industry Regulatory Compliance

It is very important for companies, organizations, and businesses that collect private or personal information from individuals to secure that information appropriately. In recent years, there have been several legislative regulations that various businesses are required to conform to. This legislation regulates how data is handled for businesses such as health care, retail, financial, and others. Plans for complying with them are known as legislative compliances. When using wireless networks, companies must verify any additional requirements from a security perspective that may be needed when dealing with regulatory compliance. This section briefly describes some of these legislative compliance requirements.

PCI Compliance

PCI stands for Payment Card Industry and is a regulation requiring companies to adhere to security standards created to protect card information pertaining to financial transactions. According to the PCI Standards Council, in order to be PCI-compliant a company must meet the following six requirements:

- Build and maintain a secure network.

- Protect cardholder data.

- Maintain a vulnerability management program.

- Implement strong access control measures.

- Regularly monitor and test networks.

- Maintain an information security policy.

 For more information on PCI, visit the PCI Security Standards Council website at www.pcisecuritystandards.org.

HIPAA Compliance

HIPAA is the abbreviation for the United States Health Insurance Portability and Accountability Act of 1996. The goal of HIPAA is to provide standardized mechanisms for electronic data exchange, security, and confidentiality of all healthcare-related computer information and data. HIPAA consists of two parts:

- HIPAA, Title I

- HIPAA, Title II

If someone loses or changes their job, Title I of HIPAA protects their health insurance coverage.

In the information technology industries, Title II is what most people mean when they refer to HIPAA; it establishes mandatory regulations that require extensive changes to the way that healthcare providers conduct business by securing computer information and data.

 For more information on HIPAA, visit the U.S. Department of Health and Human Services website at www.hhs.gov/ocr/hipaa.

Summary

In this chapter, we briefly discussed network intrusion and the impact it can have on a wireless LAN. We also took a look at IEEE 802.11 security methods and a quick review from Chapter 8 of the authentication types defined in the IEEE 802.11 standard, open system and shared key. We explored some of the IEEE 802.11 WLAN security technologies, including:

- SSID hiding
- MAC address filtering
- Wired Equivalent Privacy (WEP)

We discussed the vulnerabilities in each of these solutions. We showed an example of how the SSID could be hidden from view and also discussed why this is not a good security method—because other wireless frames contain the SSID, and it can be found even though it is removed from a beacon frame. You saw how MAC address filtering can be spoofed using freeware utilities downloadable from the Internet or through the computer operating system. We also looked at the last of three security solutions, WEP, and illustrated how it could be compromised; as you learned, it is a weak wireless security solution.

In addition to the legacy security solutions, we explored some of the more modern solutions:

SOHO and home-based solutions

- Passphrase/preshared key
- Push-button or PIN-based configuration

Enterprise-based solutions

- 802.1X/EAP
- RADIUS and AAA

You learned that encryption consists of taking information and scrambling it so that only the sender and the intended recipient, who know the algorithm, will be able to decipher the data. We looked at three types of encryption used in IEEE 802.11 wireless networking:

- WEP
- TKIP
- CCMP

Role-based access control (RBAC) is a component for administration of wireless networks that allows access and authorization based on individual groups and users and other parameters.

We also discussed virtual private networking (VPN), commonly a Layer 3 solution that provides a secure connection over a public infrastructure such as the Internet. You saw how VPN technology can be a solution for wireless network users from a remote location to access corporate or other networks from a hotspot or other unsecured wireless LAN. We also compared PPTP and L2TP and discussed the differences between them. PPTP using MS-CHAP version 2 is not a good security solution for wireless LANs, because the authentication can be captured and potentially compromised through a dictionary attack.

You saw how a captive portal can be used to redirect a user to a web authentication page requiring authentication or an agreement of terms and conditions prior to getting network access.

Products are available for enterprise wireless LANs that will monitor the airwaves 24/7 and record all activity detected by the wireless sensors. We discussed these solutions, known as a wireless intrusion prevention system (WIPS), which have the capability to detect and react to a potential intrusion on the wireless network. You learned that WIPS sensors are available in an overlay or integrated technology. Wireless network management systems (WNMS) are available in software-, hardware-, or cloud-based solutions. A WNMS will allow for centralized management and control of the wireless and possibly wired infrastructure. A WNMS may have some WIPS capability.

We also addressed the functionality and features of these solutions. Finally, we discussed regulatory compliances such as the Health Insurance Portability and Accountability Act (HIPAA) and Payment Card Industry (PCI), and the importance of securing computer data for industries such as healthcare, retail, and financial.

Exam Essentials

Be familiar with 802.11 legacy security technologies.   Know the characteristics and features of security methods, including service set identifier (SSID), media access control (MAC) filtering, and Wired Equivalent Privacy (WEP), and the weaknesses or vulnerabilities of each.

Understand passphrase-based security.   Identify the components of passphrase-based security that are commonly used for SOHO and home wireless networks. Understand that a passphrase will create a 256-bit preshared key for wireless security.

Identify IEEE 802.1X/EAP user-based security components.   Know the features and use of IEEE 802.1X port-based access control, Extensible Authentication Protocol (EAP), and Remote Authentication Dial-In User Service (RADIUS). Understand the components that make up an Authentication, Authorization, and Accounting (AAA) server.

Understand Layer 3 wireless virtual private network (VPN) security solutions.   Know how a VPN operates as well as the components of the VPN solution. Understand the differences between Point-to-Point Tunneling Protocol (PPTP) and Layer 2 Tunneling Protocol (L2TP).

Be familiar with the wireless intrusion prevention system (WIPS).   Know what a WIPS solution is and the benefits it can provide an organization to help manage wireless LAN security. Understand the differences between overlay and integrated WIPS sensors, including their advantages and disadvantages.

Know the differences between wireless network management and monitoring systems.   Identify some of the features and benefits of a wireless network management system (WNMS) and the different platforms that are available. Understand that wireless network monitoring systems include wireless packet analyzers and allow a network engineer to view statistics regarding the network health and security.

Review Questions

1. Which security methods do IEEE 802.11n access points support? (Choose three.)

   A. WPA Enterprise

   B. WEP

   C. PPTP

   D. RBAC

   E. MAC filters

   F. IPSec

2. Both _____ and _____ are wireless LAN security methods that support shared key security. (Choose two.)

   A. WPA2 Personal

   B. WPA2 Enterprise

   C. 802.1X/EAP

   D. WEP

   E. WPA Enterprise

3. Which security feature provides the strongest security for a home-based wireless network?

   A. SSID hiding

   B. Passphrase

   C. MAC filters

   D. 128-bit WEP

4. You need to attend a business meeting out of town that requires air travel. You are at the airport and have some extra time. While waiting to board your plane you decide to check your office email using an IEEE 802.11g wireless hotspot access point at the airport. In order to provide a secure connection, you would enable your notebook computer to use _____.

   A. Passphrase security

   B. WEP

   C. A VPN to the corporate network

   D. IEEE 802.1X/EAP to the corporate network

5. A _____ filter is used to allow or deny wireless barcode scanners access to an 802.11b/g network.

   A. WEP

   B. IPSec

   C. SSID

    D. RF

    E. MAC

6. The security amendment to the IEEE 802.11 standard requires _____.

    A. WEP

    B. CCMP

    C. TKIP

    D. PPTP

    E. VPN

7. Which process is a VPN solution intended to provide for users connecting to a network?

    A. Secure Layer 3 transmissions over a public network infrastructure

    B. Secure Layer 2 transmissions over a public network infrastructure

    C. Secure Layer 3 transmissions over a corporate network infrastructure

    D. Secure Layer 2 transmissions over a corporate network infrastructure

8. Which function does RBAC provide?

    A. Restricts access to authorized users or groups

    B. Provides access to only network administrators

    C. Streamlines hardware installation

    D. Allows users to install software

9. Hiding the service set identifier of a wireless LAN will require a user to _____ in order to gain access to the wireless network.

    A. Enter a username and password when prompted

    B. Call the help desk and ask for a new password

    C. Enable the SSID broadcast on the client device

    D. Know the SSID and enter it manually

10. Remote Authentication Dial-In User Service (RADIUS) requires users on a wireless network to perform what function?

    A. Access the corporate network using only the PSTN and a modem.

    B. Call in to the help desk service and request a username and password.

    C. Enter a username and password that will be centrally administered.

    D. Request remote assistance to help solve a software problem on a computer.

11. The IEEE 802.1X standard identifies the authenticator as another term for the _____ in wireless networking.

    A. Client device

    B. Access point

    C. RADIUS server

    D. EAP server

12. Which data encryption/authentication method is identified in the original IEEE 802.11 standard?

    A. TKIP

    B. AES

    C. CCMP

    D. WEP

    E. EAP

13. You are a wireless network administrator monitoring the reports for a recently installed wireless intrusion prevention system. You receive an alert notifying you of high levels of RF activity detected from an access point operating as a sensor and currently set to channel 6. Which problem could be causing the alert? (Choose two.)

    A. Interference from a neighboring access point

    B. RF deauthentication storm

    C. RF denial-of-service (DoS) attack

    D. Misconfigured client workstation

    E. RF encryption attack

14. The length of a WEP key is typically_____ or _____.

    A. 5-bit, 10-bit

    B. 13-bit, 26-bit

    C. 64-bit, 128-bit

    D. 128-bit, 256-bit

    E. 192-bit, 256-bit

15. Which security solution is mandatory for client devices in order to be considered Wi-Fi Protected Setup certified?

    A. WEP

    B. PIN

    C. WPA

    D. PBC

    E. TKIP

16. A newly configured wireless intrusion prevention system will _____.

    A. Require a network administrator to monitor for intrusions

    B. Automatically monitor the network for potential attacks

    C. Require an administrator to manually shut down a rogue access point

    D. Automatically notify a network administrator regarding a firmware upgrade

17. You are a network administrator and are asked for a security recommendation regarding older wireless 802.11-compliant VoIP handsets. The company does not have the budget to upgrade the equipment at this time. Which would be the best recommendation you could provide?

    A. Don't worry about securing the handsets because voice transmissions cannot be deciphered.

    B. Carefully plan a strategy using WEP and VLANs.

    C. Use a VPN solution with L2TP/IPSec.

    D. Use a CCMP/AES Layer 2 solution.

18. A weakness with MAC address filtering is that it allows an intruder to _____.

    A. Crack the encryption.

    B. Spoof an address.

    C. Cause an RF DoS attack.

    D. Steal user authentication.

19. What type of wireless network device is PIN-based security most commonly used with?

    A. SOHO brands that support WPA 2.0

    B. Enterprise brands that support WPA 2.0

    C. SOHO brands that support WPS

    D. Enterprise brands that support WPS

20. Layer 2 Tunneling Protocol commonly uses which encryption method?

    A. IPSec

    B. PPTP

    C. AES

    D. WEP

    E. MPPE

Chapter

10

Wireless LAN Site Survey Basics

THE FOLLOWING CWTS EXAM OBJECTIVES ARE COVERED IN THIS CHAPTER:

✓ **4.1 Understand and describe the requirements to gather information prior to the site survey and do reporting after the site survey**

- Gathering business requirements
- Interviewing stakeholders
- Gathering site-specific documentation including existing network characteristics
- Identifying infrastructure connectivity and power requirements
- Understanding RF coverage requirements
- Understanding application requirements

This is the first of two chapters discussing wireless LAN site surveys. This chapter covers site survey planning and the business aspects related to a wireless LAN site survey, including gathering business requirements, interviewing the appropriate people, and gathering additional information regarding the location in which the network will be installed. Chapter 11, "Performing an RF Wireless LAN Site Survey," will discuss the technical aspects of performing a site survey.

Early deployments for wireless LANs in many cases required only a onetime site survey. This is because wireless LAN technology was fairly static and the radio frequency dynamics of the locations in which these networks were installed did not change much. However, thanks to the rapid pace at which wireless LAN technology and deployments are growing and the increasing use of other devices that use unlicensed radio frequency, site surveys can be an ongoing process for the areas where these wireless networks are installed. Although there are no set rules about when or how wireless site surveys should be performed, there are guidelines that many manufacturers suggest based on deployment scenarios for wireless networks that use their equipment.

In this chapter you will learn about site survey requirements such as understanding the business requirements for the intended use of the wireless LAN and asking plenty of questions by interviewing department managers and users to help determine the applications and security requirements for the proposed network. Gathering information is a major part of a site survey to ensure a successful deployment. You will also learn about the importance of documenting every step, from the design to the installation, and the validation of the wireless network.

Wireless LAN Site Surveys

The main objectives of a wireless LAN *site survey* are to find areas of *RF coverage* and RF interference sources as well as installation locations for hardware infrastructure devices such as access points, bridges, antennas, and any other devices that will be used with the wireless LAN. This will help ensure that applications to be used—both hardware and software—will be supported by the wireless network. Site surveys vary in complexity, depending on the organization or location in which a wireless network will be used.

As mentioned earlier, there is not a specific set of rules that must be followed. However, many manufacturers of wireless LAN equipment have guidelines and suggestions when it comes to a wireless site survey and where this survey fits into the process of design and implementation of the wireless network.

Knowing and understanding the expectations of the client or business in regard to the wireless LAN is a critical part of a successful deployment. To understand these client expectations, you have to gather much information. This includes interviews and meetings with all those who will be affected by the installation of the wireless LAN, which encompasses nearly all departments of the company in most installations.

The scope of the wireless LAN site survey is dependent on many factors, some of which include:

- Size of physical location
- Intended use of the network
- Number of users and devices
- Wireless client device capabilities
- The wireless LAN environment
- Performance expectations
- Bring-your-own-device (BYOD) acceptance

Size of Physical Location

Depending on the size of the physical location where the wireless network will be installed, a complete wireless LAN site survey may not be necessary. For example, a small sandwich shop wishes to offer free wireless Internet access as a convenience for its patrons who choose to have a meal there. This sandwich shop is approximately 1,200 square feet, has seating for about 15 people, and is located in a small street retail mall. In this case, a single access point would more than likely be sufficient for the number of users who access the wireless network at any one time and the type of data being sent across the access point.

Although a full-blown site survey determining areas of RF interference coverage and interference would more than likely not be required, it would still be beneficial to visit the location and determine the best place for the access point. In a situation like this, what I like to call a "site survey lite" may be all that is necessary. This would include testing the area to determine the best RF channel to use as well as access point mounting, consideration of aesthetics, and connecting to the wired network for access to the Internet.

A larger installation will require a more extensive site survey and may include either a manual physical RF site survey or a predictive modeling site survey using elaborate software. Manual and predictive modeling site survey software will be discussed in more detail in Chapter 11.

Intended Use of the Network

Looking at the sandwich shop scenario again, chances are the intended use of this wireless network will consist of patrons staying online for short periods of time and browsing the Internet or checking email. It is unlikely that many users would be performing any high-end or bandwidth-intensive applications on this type of connection. Therefore, the single–access point model would be sufficient for this deployment. With larger installations, the use of the network may include bandwidth-intensive applications such as electronic imaging, computer-aided design, or database programs and would have an impact on the number of access points that would be required in order to provide adequate performance.

Number of Users and Devices

The number of users or devices that will be accessing a wireless network is also a factor in determining the number of access points required, which in turn will determine the scope of a site survey. It has already been established that in our sandwich shop example a single access point would be sufficient based on the size of the location and the intended use of the network. However, as the number of actual wireless-enabled devices grows and because of the added capacity requirements, the need for additional access points will also increase. In a case where more than one access point is required, a more extensive wireless site survey is also required.

Wireless Client Device Capabilities

In addition to the number of users and wireless client devices, it is important to understand the types of devices that will be connected to the wireless LAN and what their capabilities are. For example, notebook computers or handheld devices such as tablets and smart phones all have specific functionality and will need to meet certain requirements. This type of device could be performing tasks as simple as basic web browsing or checking email. Other possible device types include Wi-Fi–enabled voice handsets that may need their own SSIDs for quality of service functionality and operate in the 5 GHz UNII band or barcode scanners that will be keeping track of inventory.

Part of the wireless site survey planning process is to question the appropriate people regarding the types of devices and understanding what their capabilities are to ensure that expectations of the users will be met. Some of the capabilities that need to be considered are:

- IEEE 802.11b/g only
- IEEE 802.11a or dual band capable
- IEEE 802.11n capable and number of transmit and receive radio chains
- MIMO capabilities, such as the number of spatial streams or transmit beamforming
- Notebook computers, desktop computers, or tablets
- Radio Frequency Identification (RFID) tags for location services
- Wi-Fi–enabled voice handsets and the operating frequency
- Wi-Fi–enabled smart phones

Future devices that will be used with the wireless LAN must be evaluated. This includes the expansion of the wireless LAN, new technology that may be introduced based on the business model, and bring-your-own-device (BYOD) acceptance. See Chapter 4, "Wireless LAN Client Devices," for more information regarding the various wireless client devices that are used with IEEE 802.11 wireless networking.

The Wireless LAN Environment

Understanding the environment in which the wireless LAN will be deployed and the wireless client devices that will be used in the environment is another important factor that sometimes is overlooked. Different environments will have different concerns. For example, an area that may have excess radio frequency noise, an area with harsh environmental conditions such as temperature fluctuations, or industrial areas have their own set of challenges. Different environments that may have their distinct type of challenges include:

- General office spaces: Walls and attenuation values
- Office cube farms: Density
- Medical: Hospitals or medical centers
- Industrial: Machine shops or factories
- Educational: High quantity of mobile devices

These are a few examples or different environments that may use IEEE 802.11 wireless LANs and will need to be considered as part of the wireless LAN site survey. In Chapter 2, "Introduction to Wireless Local Area Networking," you learned about some of the various deployment scenarios for common wireless LAN network types.

Performance Expectations

Keeping in mind that wireless networks are half-duplex and contention based, and many factors will affect the performance of a wireless LAN, including the number of wireless devices, types of software and hardware applications used, location, and the number of infrastructure devices providing access. These infrastructure devices include access points and bridges. Part of a wireless LAN site survey involves defining what the customer expects for performance of the network. A mutual understanding of the factors that affect performance as well as how they will be dealt with is imperative from the beginning of the wireless LAN site survey process.

Bring-Your-Own-Device Acceptance

With the number of IEEE 802.11–enabled devices continually growing, the need for increased wireless LAN capacity is also becoming a major concern. *Bring your own device* (BYOD) describes the recent increase in company employees bringing their own personal IEEE 802.11–enabled mobile devices to their place of work and using these devices to access company resources including the Internet, printers, software applications, and file servers. Take a moment and think about the number of IEEE 802.11–enabled devices you may have in your possession, office or home. These devices include:

- Notebook computers
- Smart phones
- Tablet devices
- Wireless printers

- Wireless video cameras
- Wireless household appliances
- DVD or Blu-ray players
- Wireless-capable televisions

This list represents just some of the devices that are used daily and are now IEEE 802.11 wireless capable. The average family of four may have as many as 20 wireless LAN devices in the home, and this number will increase as wireless LAN technology advances. When companies or organizations allow employees to bring their personal wireless devices to the office or place of work, that opens up an entire set of potential issues. These issues include security, technical support, and wireless infrastructure capacity concerns.

BYOD, Wireless LAN Capacity, and RF Site Surveys

If employees are allowed to bring their own devices to their place of business, you must take this into consideration when designing a wireless network and performing an RF site survey. Because IEEE 802.11 wireless LANs are contention based and use a shared medium, the added number of devices will impact the performance if the network is not properly designed. BYOD may require smaller RF cells and additional wireless access points in order to offer adequate performance for the number of devices. In addition to the load factor, the types of technology used—IEEE 802.11a/b/g/n—will have an impact on the need for backward compatibility. Figure 10.1 shows how a number of personal devices can have an impact on the capacity of a wireless LAN.

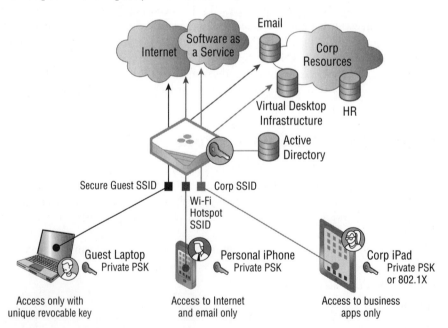

FIGURE 10.1 Aerohive shows the various personal devices that may be connected to a wireless LAN.

Gathering Business Requirements

Gathering information is typically the first step of a wireless LAN design and implementation. As mentioned, the business model or type of business where the wireless LAN will be deployed is a major part of deciding the level of a wireless LAN site survey. The type of business will determine the needs and use of a wireless network. Knowing the applications used—both hardware and software—is a critical part of a wireless LAN deployment as this will affect recommendations such as the number and locations of access points. Expectations can make or break a wireless LAN deployment. The expectations of the wireless network must be discussed, evaluated, and documented up front. To completely understand what the customer expects, you will need to gather information from various areas of the business. A high-quality site survey is going to require many questions to be asked and answered, including the following:

Bandwidth Needs   How much bandwidth will be required for users of the wireless network? The types of applications in use will have an impact on this. Most manufacturers have wireless LAN design guides that you can reference for various deployment scenarios.

Coverage Area   In what rooms or areas of the buildings is wireless LAN coverage expected? This is becoming the entire location in most cases.

Applications Used   What type of applications—either hardware or software—are used at the facility? This may include computer-aided design, digital imaging, databases, and voice over wireless LAN.

Wireless Devices Used   What type of wireless devices will be used? These include notebook computers, handheld scanners, wireless phones tablets, and other devices, whether company owned or BYOD.

Desired IEEE 802.11 Technologies   What type of IEEE 802.11 infrastructure (IEEE 802.11a/b/g/n) would be best suited to the specific environment and deployment?

IEEE 802.11 wireless networks were once considered extensions of wired networks, providing access to a few users in areas exceeding the physical distance of Ethernet or other wired medium in place. IEEE 802.11 wireless LAN technology continues to grow and is now a major part of every area in a business, corporation, or company's computer network infrastructure. It is difficult to find any business or organization that does not provide some type of IEEE 802.11 wireless network access. Fully understanding the *business requirements* is part of a successful wireless LAN site survey and deployment. This section looks at case studies of designing for the wireless networking requirements of different types of businesses or other organizations.

General Office/Enterprise

Office buildings and other enterprise installation locations may consist of walled offices or open spaces with many cubicles. This type of installation usually will require infrastructure devices to aesthetically fit the environment and may require antennas to be mounted to drop ceilings with the access points located out of sight. Figure 10.2 shows an example of a floor plan for an office deployment.

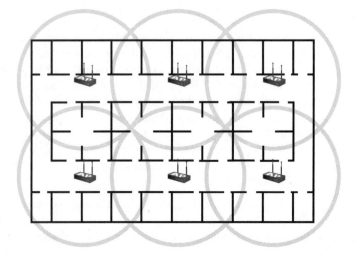

FIGURE 10.2 A small office wireless LAN installation using omnidirectional antennas

These installations may have a high density of users and therefore require more access points to handle the number of wireless devices connected to the network. The software and hardware applications used in these environments will need to be closely evaluated to ensure optimal performance for the user base. Chances are that interference sources in this type of deployment would be limited mostly to computer networking, and radio frequency challenges may be limited.

Case Study—Enterprise

A case study by Aruba Networks discusses a wireless LAN deployment for Ariba, a provider of enterprise commerce software systems.

Customer

- Ariba
- Commerce software
- Sunnyvale, CA

Objective

- Integrate a seamless IEEE 802.11 wireless solution without disrupting wired network
- Provide VPN support for a diverse OS environment, including Mac, Linux, and Windows clients
- Add centralized wireless management and RF spectrum management

- Scale to support hundreds of simultaneous users
- Ensure multilayered wireless security that addresses authentication, encryption, rogue AP detection, and policy management

Solution

- One Aruba MMC-5000 Mobility Controller
- 44 Aruba 52 dual-purpose 802.11a+b/g access points
- Three Aruba 800 Mobility Controllers
- ArubaOS Mobility Software

Result

- Enhanced user experience
- Centralized security and control for entire wireless LAN
- Remote RF visibility and monitoring
- Seamless integration with existing wired network

 Read the complete case study at the Aruba Networks website, www.arubanetworks.com.

Manufacturing

Deploying a wireless network in a manufacturing environment will not be as straightforward as general office/enterprise or some other deployment types. Manufacturing environments have a completely different set of challenges, including equipment other than IEEE 802.11 devices that operate in the 2.4 GHz ISM band, which means RF interference can be a major issue.

In addition to interference, physical aspects of the structure itself such as high ceilings and large manufacturing facilities create mounting, accessibility, and RF signal concerns. Equipment installed in manufacturing facilities may have to withstand harsh environmental conditions such as extreme temperature, grease, and dirt.

Case Study—Manufacturing

FN Manufacturing, LLC is a precision machining manufacturer specializing in the production of small arms and is located in Columbia, SC. FN Manufacturing selected Xirrus equipment to deploy IEEE 802.11n wireless LAN coverage for four paper manufacturing and warehousing units. A case study describes the details of this solution.

Customer

- FN Manufacturing, LLC

- Located in Columbia, SC
- Precision machining manufacturer

Objective

- Wireless coverage for four paper manufacturing and warehousing units
- Enough bandwidth to accommodate multiple business applications
- Secure network for client and company information

Solution

- 80 percent fewer devices, cable pulls, and switch ports to cover multiple buildings with one wireless array located in each
- Coverage with high-gain directional antennas
- Distributed intelligence in each array
- Easy installation and network integration with onboard switch, firewall, and management

Result

To comply with Department of Defense regulations, FN Manufacturing upgraded to Xirrus 802.11n wireless arrays to ensure reliable wireless connectivity for their crucial business applications. Xirrus provided a resilient wireless network to run mission-critical inventory and order management across all of their facilities, using the fewest devices possible. With the Xirrus network, using wireless handheld scanners for RFID tracking of items became effortless—greatly increasing the efficiency, productivity, and flexibility of FN Manufacturing's operations.

 Read the complete case study at the Xirrus website, www.xirrus.com.

Warehousing

Warehousing presents unique challenges for wireless networking. Like manufacturing environments, warehouses are typically large facilities with high ceilings, making for a potentially difficult site survey and installation. In addition, one of the biggest concerns with warehousing deployments is the storage of products and materials. Certain types of product in large quantities, such as paint and other liquids, can cause excessive RF behaviors such as refraction, absorption, and reflection, thereby affecting performance of the wireless network. Liquids, especially stored in large quantities, will have an absorbing effect on RF. Other products, such as those made of paper or cardboard, will also have an impact. These issues should be evaluated closely as part of the site survey process for a warehouse implementation. As the inventories for these products change, so will the effect of the RF behaviors.

Case Study—Warehousing

Cellynne Corporation/Stefco Industries selected Xirrus to deploy 802.11abg+n Wi-Fi arrays across their Florida headquarters and manufacturing facility. A case study describes the details of this solution.

Customer

- Cellynne Corporation/Stefco Industries
- Fully integrated paper manufacturer capable of processing pulp into a wide variety of premium paper and towel products
- Corporate headquarters—Haines City, FL

Objective

- Wireless network to deliver pervasive connectivity for wireless scanners on forklifts, handheld scanners, and notebook computers
- Reliable Wi-Fi coverage throughout the offices, manufacturing, and distribution ware-housing.
- Easy-to-deploy and easy-to-manage network
- Upgradeable infrastructure as business and technology needs change

Solution

- Xirrus 802.11abg+n Wi-Fi arrays across the Florida headquarters and manufacturing facility.
- The Xirrus Wi-Fi array integrates up to 24 802.11abg+n radios coupled with a high-gain directional antenna system into a single device along with an onboard multigigabit switch, Wi-Fi controller, firewall, dedicated Wi-Fi threat sensor, and an embedded spectrum analyzer.
- Provides more than enough bandwidth, security, and control to replace switched Ethernet to the desktop as the primary network connection and results in 75 percent fewer devices, power, cabling, switch ports, and installation time than a traditional "thin" AP architecture.

Result

Using an array architecture with directional antennas eliminated the need for an additional 18 access points, cable runs, and switch ports. It also saved Cellynne Corporation/Stefco Industries over 8,600 kWh of energy each year.

- Reliable Wi-Fi platform for critical business applications
- Flexible Wi-Fi infrastructure as performance needs increase
- Secure Wi-Fi connection to protect against internal/external threat

Read the complete case study at the Xirrus website, www.xirrus.com.

Retail/Point of Sale

Retail and point-of-sale (PoS) deployments may have some characteristics similar to those of the warehousing environment. In addition to a large quantity of products such as paper and liquids, there may be RF interference sources in businesses that sell appliances and electronics. The use or demonstration of items such as microwave ovens, two-way radios, consumer-grade IEEE 802.11 access points, and computers may cause interference issues that need to be evaluated.

Security is another major concern for this type of business in order to protect information such as credit card numbers and personal identification numbers (PINs). Some major retailers are now using the wireless network to broadcast or announce in-store specials to patrons visiting the store; they can do this using a variety of mechanisms, including text messages or email. The personal devices that many people have in their possession may also have an effect on interference.

Healthcare/Medical

Healthcare deployments such as hospitals can be a challenging installation for many reasons. These environments will have both wireless LAN and wired LAN devices that operate in the 2.4 GHz ISM band; therefore interference may be a critical factor for both the WLAN deployment and the other medical devices that use the same frequencies. Some areas in hospitals—such as the intensive care unit, emergency room, or operating rooms—may have limitations on the type of wireless that may be installed, whereas others may require coverage throughout the entire hospital.

IEEE 802.11 wireless LAN technology has greatly improved the way hospitals function by allowing doctors, nurses, and lab technicians to use notebook computers as well as other portable devices including IEEE 802.11–capable tablets while working with patients and staff members. In addition to aiding the hospital infrastructure, wireless LANs are used by patients and visitors quite extensively. This gives patients recovering at a hospital and their visitors the capability to use the Internet to access information. Once again the number of personal wireless-enabled devices may have an impact on the wireless LAN installed.

Case Study—Healthcare

A case study by Cisco Systems for Hennepin County Medical Center describes a wireless LAN deployment for the healthcare industry.

Customer

- Hennepin County Medical Center

- Healthcare
- Minneapolis, MN

Objective

- Improve hospital-wide communication, productivity, and patient care
- Increase bandwidth and RF coverage to support next-generation mobile applications and communication systems that improve clinical workflow
- Implement a unified wireless network supporting the needs of an integrated biomedical and IT department

Solution

- A unified wireless network simplifies management and facilitates 802.11n upgrade.
- 802.11n access points support a wide range of bandwidth-intensive mobile devices and services over one secure unified wireless infrastructure.
- A wireless control system enables easy location of RF equipment throughout the hospital.

Results

- Improved staff communication, as well as accuracy, efficiency, and safety of patient care through increased bandwidth and coverage from 802.11n deployment
- Increased responsiveness of mobile clinicians and helps ensure business continuity by enhancing network reliability
- Improved management efficiency of the wireless network, maximizing biomedical and IT resources

---

 Read the complete case study at the Cisco website, www.cisco.com.

Government/Military

Government agencies and military installations need to be taken into consideration for IEEE 802.11 wireless networking. One of the biggest concerns for wireless LAN deployments in these environments is security. Some government or military agencies do not allow any wireless LAN access and have what is known as a "No Wi-Fi" policy. In a situation like this, a site survey is still required because the wireless LAN deployment, instead of allowing access to network resources, will be used to monitor the air and to keep all unauthorized wireless access out.

For government and military agencies that do allow wireless access to resources and the Internet, security is of the utmost concern. Government and military installations may span large campuses similar to those in educational deployments such as universities and may require outdoor point-to-point or point-to-multipoint connections. In this case, an outdoor site survey will be required.

Case Study—Government

A case study for the city of Gilroy, CA, discusses an outdoor wireless deployment by Cisco Systems for public safety.

Customer

- City of Gilroy
- Municipal government
- Gilroy, CA

Objective

- Support real-time traffic monitoring system to improve traffic flow
- Find more efficient way for mobile public safety vehicles to share information in the field
- Enhance public image of the city's downtown
- Provide broadband service capability for citizens in downtown

Solution

- Deployed secure, flexible outdoor wireless network to support a variety of governmental and public-facing applications

Result

- Improved traffic flow through busy intersections and overall driving experience in the city
- Improved the ability of public safety officers to take full advantage of mobile computing capabilities
- Helped enhance the city's reputation as a forward-thinking technological community
- Provided Wi-Fi public access for citizens

Read the complete case study at the Cisco website, www.cisco.com.

Education

Education deployments will vary in size and complexity. Some of the factors that play a role in educational IEEE 802.11 wireless deployments include density and coverage. For example, a large university campus may have tens of thousands of students and thousands of access points covering many acres of land and many buildings. As mentioned in Chapter 2, some educational institutions are implementing a "one-to-one" initiative—in other words, the goal is to have one Internet-accessible device for every one student. This type of initiative will introduce density and capacity concerns, because of the potentially high number of students in a single classroom. Educational institutions, whether an elementary school, a high school, or a college campus, should always consider starting with an RF wireless site survey and follow best practices from the equipment manufacturer to ensure a successful deployment.

Case Study—Education

A case study from Aerohive shows how Allegany County Public Schools, located in Cumberland, MD, was facing growing pains that come with embracing high-tech trends. They required a wireless network that could accommodate an influx of Apple iPads and other popular Wi-Fi–enabled mobile devices.

Customer

- Allegany County Public Schools
- Consisting of 24 schools
- Approximately 9,000 students
- Approximately 700 staff members

Requirements

- Accommodate influx of iPads and other IEEE 802.11wireless mobile devices
- Enable students to use same device in the classroom and home
- Enable multiple devices to connect to wireless network simultaneously
- Increase security to accommodate new wireless traffic

Solution

- Provide ubiquitous wireless LAN coverage across the entire school system
- Replace its existing controller-based 802.11a/b/g wireless network
- Install Aerohive's controller-less, 802.11n-compliant wireless platform

Result

- Running 4,000 computers on its network and 2,000 laptops on rolling carts
- Using HiveManager to monitor wireless network and all client activity
- Students and teachers using iPads for everything from data collection to video
- Employs a three-tier security for allowing devices on wireless network

 Read the complete case study at the Aerohive Networks website, www.aerohive.com.

Public Access, Hotspots, Hospitality

Public access, hotspots, and hospitality IEEE 802.11 wireless LAN installations may need to accept connections from a wide variety of client devices, including IEEE 802.11a/b/g/n devices. In many cases, consumer-brand notebook computers will be limited to IEEE 802.11b/g or now 802.11b/g/n technology. Backward compatibility with these technologies is essential because the infrastructure will have no control over the type of client device that may connect. If backward compatibility is not taken into consideration, some devices may not be able to connect and use the wireless network resources.

Although many wireless LAN deployments should take these factors into consideration, it is especially important in environments in which the infrastructure has little or no control over the client device population that may be connecting to the wireless LAN. This type of network includes public access installations such as hotels or resorts, restaurants, airports, arenas, and other small to large service businesses.

Case Study—Hospitality

A case study for the American Airlines Center in Dallas, TX, by Aruba Networks discusses an example of a wireless LAN deployment for the hospitality industry.

Customer

- American Airlines Center
- Sports and entertainment venue
- Dallas, TX

Requirements

- Secure in-seat wireless concession application
- Provide on-demand 802.11 a/b/g service to media and visitors
- Use a single wireless network to provide different access and security rights to different users
- Provide centralized policy management for wired and wireless users
- Provide high-speed VPN termination of IPSec and PPTP tunnels
- Allow plug-and-play installation and automated configuration
- Support existing third-party access points already in use

Solution

- Aruba MMC-5000 Mobility Controller
- More than 50 Aruba AP-60/61 dual-purpose 802.11a/b/g access points
- ArubaOS Mobility Software, VPN Server, Adaptive Radio Management, and Wireless IDS

Benefits

- Reduced operational management and capital expense
- Plug-and-play deployment

- Per-user roles and policies automatically enforced upon authentication
- Remote troubleshooting
- Secures third-party "thick" access points

 Read the complete case study at the Aruba Networks website,
www.arubanetworks.com.

Interviewing Stakeholders

Understanding the intended use of an IEEE 802.11 wireless LAN is a critical part of a successful deployment. Who better to explain what the wireless network will be used for than those who will be using it? Those performing a site survey may not necessarily understand the functional aspects of a certain type of business, so it is critical to get input from all who will be using the wireless network. Department managers, business unit managers, and team leaders usually know the function of their specific areas of the organization the best. Therefore they will also know the needs and requirements of users of the wireless network and how a successful deployment will help increase job productivity.

I recommend you create some type of checklist or formal site survey questionnaire to use during the interview process. This will ensure specific details about the business and proposed wireless deployment are not missed. The use of such forms helps ensure uniform, repeatable interviews. These forms can also become part of the documentation and final deliverable that will be presented to the customer. Although there are some general questions that can be asked, there will be more specific questions based on the business model of the organization or the wireless LAN to be installed. Figure 10.3 shows an example of notes that can be taken during the information gathering stage and the wireless site survey specifics.

```
Objective
Survey dates
Testing procedure
General network description
Proposed WLAN components
Existing wireless system
RF spectrum analysis
Area-by-area analysis
Contact list


1.      Project Objective
        Site Description
2.      Wireless LAN Evaluation Process
3.      Existing Wireless LAN Configuration
4.      Ethernet Network
5.      Wireless LAN Assessment
6.      RF Coverage Test Results
7.      Recommended Network Changes
8.      Contacts
9.      Warranty
```

FIGURE 10.3 Sample checklist showing some information collected for a wireless LAN site survey

Some generic interview questions that will pertain to most installations are as follows:

Has a site survey ever been performed in the past?   It is good to know whether a site survey has previously been performed at a location. Although the previous site survey is only as good as the person who performed it, it may be beneficial and a timesaver to have some information available. Depending on when it was performed, a previous site survey report may not be accurate—physical changes to the location may have taken place—for example, additions of rooms or walls or changes to the interior design.

Are any blueprints, floor plans, or any other site-specific documentation available?   Blueprints, floor plans, or other documentation about the location are critical in performing an RF wireless site survey. If this information is not available it may have to be created, which in turn would create an additional expense for the company or customer. The accuracy of these documents needs to be considered in order to provide ideal site survey results.

How many devices and users anticipate using the wireless network?   The number of expected devices on the wireless network is valuable information to have. Knowing the number of devices and users will help determine the amount of infrastructure equipment, such as access points and bridges, that will be required for the deployment. Discussing with department managers the number of devices and users on the network as well as the number of working shifts will help provide adequate planning. Also knowing whether users are allowed to bring their own devices will be beneficial.

Will public access be required?   If public access to the wireless network is required, that will potentially affect the number of infrastructure devices such as access points required for the deployment. In addition to the equipment, security, captive portal and backward compatibility should be taken into account in this situation.

Is there any preference for a specific manufacturer's equipment?   It is a recommended practice for a site survey to be performed with the same manufacturer's equipment that will be used in the deployment. So any customer preference for equipment manufacturer must be determined at the initial phases of the site survey. This will ensure good results based on the design of the wireless network.

What is the coverage area?   The intended coverage area of the facility also needs to be addressed. This helps provide a surveyor with information to accurately estimate how long a physical site survey may take and roughly estimate the amount of hardware required. Knowing the coverage area will also help determine any unexpected obstacles that may occur as part of the site survey process.

Is an existing IEEE 802.11 wireless network in place?   If an existing IEEE 802.11 wireless network is in place, it needs to be addressed as part of the site survey process. Questions need to be asked, such as:

- What technology is currently in use, IEEE 802.11a, IEEE 802.11b/g, or IEEE 802.11n?
- How many wireless devices and users does the network currently support?
- Where are the access points located?
- What is the wireless network used for?

Knowing the answers to these and other questions will help determine the role, if any, that the existing IEEE 802.11 wireless network will play in the new deployment. Keep in mind that some organizations may have quite an extensive existing wireless network and may be in the process of upgrading to newer or different technology. If this is the case, it will need to be determined whether any of the existing network components can or will be used with the new deployment. Photographs of existing equipment used in a deployment are always useful. Figure 10.4 shows a photograph of an existing IEEE 802.11a/b/g access point with diversity antennas.

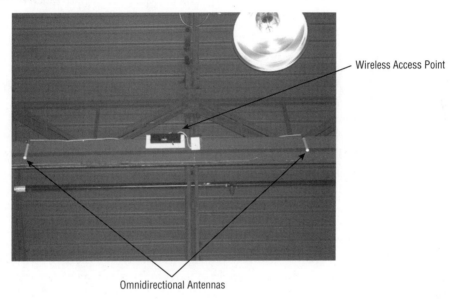

FIGURE 10.4   An IEEE 802.11a/b/g dual-band access point on a ceiling 35 feet high

Are there any known areas of RF interference?   Information regarding known areas of RF interference is very useful in a site survey. It will save time if previous knowledge of RF interference is made available as part of the site survey process.

Are there any known areas that may lack RF coverage?   Just as previous knowledge of areas affected by RF interference is valuable, the lack of RF coverage in specific areas is also very good to know. This will help a surveyor determine any special situations that may be addressed during the site survey process. This may require testing of various types of antennas to help provide RF coverage in areas that are currently lacking.

What type of applications will be used?   It is important to know the types of applications that will be used. Applications—either software or hardware—will affect the load and number of access points or other infrastructure devices required. These applications include bandwidth-intensive software, voice over wireless, and so on. The surveyor should also become familiar with any special circumstances that may be required to support these applications—for example, the frequency or IEEE 802.11 technology that may be required for the wireless devices to operate.

Will voice or other applications that require quality of service be used?   If applications (such as voice handsets) are planned for the location, this will have an impact on the site survey and design of the wireless network. Because these types of applications have greater requirements for signal quality and signal strength as well as fast transition, this will need to be taken into consideration during the site survey. Additional density and more access points may be required.

Video over wireless LAN is another application that may require quality of service. Like voice, video is subject to latency and may involve special design requirements. Video over wireless LAN is used in applications ranging from sports venues to security surveillance and monitoring.

Is roaming required?   In most cases, the answer to this question is yes. This is especially true with networks that will be using voice handsets. Voice handsets are one of the most commonly used wireless LAN devices that require seamless roaming and secure transition capabilities. Although notebook computers and tablets may require roaming, voice and video applications are time bounded and subject to latency issues. Fast, secure transitions may also be required for roaming. If so, the amount of overlap between RF cells would need to be closely looked at to ensure reliable sessions for the devices connected to the network.

Is Power over Ethernet (PoE) required?   In most medium to large installations, the answer to this question is yes. Understanding the PoE requirements is another essential part of the wireless LAN site survey. The capabilities as well as the number of devices expected to use PoE—including wireless access point, hardwired Ethernet IP phones, and security cameras—will play a role in the design and types of equipment used in the wireless network.

What are the wireless security requirements?   Although security is not necessarily part of an RF site survey, as much information as possible on the security requirements is very helpful with the design of the wireless network. Some security solutions may require additional hardware or software that would have to be taken into account for the network design.

Will an escort be required?   In many cases, people are not allowed to roam freely throughout a business. An escort might be and usually is needed to walk through a location with an outside contract site surveyor. In addition, the escort and surveyor will need access to areas that may be locked or secure, such as wiring closets and computer rooms. Escorts may be from various parts of the company, hospital, or organization, including facilities, information technology, medical staff, and security.

Are there any legislative compliance requirements?   Depending on the type of business in which the wireless network will be installed, there may be legislative or other compliance requirements. For example, medical institutions may have to meet HIPAA requirements, and retail establishments may require PCI compliance. These need to be taken into consideration as part of a wireless LAN site survey and deployment.

Are you following corporate policies?   You should use any written corporate policy as a guideline or offer suggestions for changes in the policy to accommodate other wireless LAN requirements. The wireless LAN site survey questioning process should bring any policy-related issues to light for discussion and/or change if needed.

Manufacturer Guidelines and Deployment Guides

The information just presented includes some types of questions that need to be addressed during the site survey process. Keep in mind that the actual questions and details depend on the business model and the implementation of the wireless network. For site survey and deployment guides, check with the manufacturer of the equipment that you will use. These guides will provide additional information that is helpful in generating a list of questions and concerns that will need to be addressed.

A sample sensor placement site survey form can be found on the download page for this book, www.sybex.com/go/cwts2e.

Defining Physical and Data Security Requirements

Understanding the security requirements of both the physical environment and the user data is another design aspect of a wireless network. Because wireless LANs use radio frequency to send and receive information such as computer data, wireless LANs are vulnerable to something known as *RF jamming*, which is caused by RF interference and can be either intentional or unintentional. As the name implies, RF jamming disrupts RF communications. If an intruder wants to wreak havoc in a wireless network, they can use an RF signal jammer to cause interference on the same RF bands used by the wireless network. The only way to protect against this kind of activity is through physical security. *Physical security* includes blocking RF signals from either entering or leaving a location. This could be done in a variety of ways—shielding materials can include metal, paint, or even wallpaper. If physical security is a concern where the wireless network will be installed, this needs to be taken into consideration during a site survey and design stages.

For reasons beyond their control, some organizations may still require the use of legacy IEEE 802.11 security solutions for *data security*—ensuring that information such as computer data is received by the intended recipients without tampering during transit. This may include legacy hardware or software devices that have limited security capabilities. If legacy security solutions are used, special considerations may need to be taken into account from an infrastructure design perspective. This could mean using more access points or potentially using virtual local area network (VLAN) technology, which involves defining broadcast domains in a Layer 2 network. Other, more advanced security solutions may require additional hardware or software for both the infrastructure and devices accessing the network. It is important to understand that wireless LAN deployments should never violate or circumvent a corporate security policy. Security solutions were discussed in Chapter 9, "Wireless LAN Security Basics."

Gathering Site-Specific Documentation

Documentation for the location where a wireless network will be installed will make a surveyor's job much easier and result in a smoother overall deployment. Drawings and other documentation pertaining to the following list can provide valuable information:

- Floor plans
- Blueprints
- Proposed location of furnishings
- Electrical specifications

Floor Plans and Blueprints

Gathering any site-specific documentation that exists, such as floor plans or blueprints, is helpful for a site survey. This documentation is useful to a variety of individuals who will be participating in a wireless LAN design and deployment. The documentation can be used during a physical or predictive RF site survey and spectrum analysis to note areas of importance. Having floor plans and blueprints available allows a surveyor to document specific parts of a site survey such as location of access points and other wireless devices. If a predictive modeling site survey is used, an electronic version of a floor plan can be imported into the software program to help streamline the surveyor's job. The standard formats for floor plan (map) files vary from product to product for most modeling software, but they typically include DWG, PDF, JPG, PNG, GIF, and TIF. Figure 10.5 shows a site survey software program that allows for various file formats to be imported.

Blueprints or floor plans will also help those who install cable and mount hardware and if necessary can be provided to electricians for AC power installation.

Furnishings

The proposed types and location of furnishings or other items that may affect RF signal propagation or penetration are also good to know if the information is available. This will help during the design and site survey phase to determine access point locations and pinpoint other things that may affect RF signals, such as reflection, refraction, diffraction, and absorption. Unfortunately, most floor plan documents do not specify this kind of information, because in many cases furnishings are not permanent fixtures and can change. Some organizations will have this information stored in asset documentation using spreadsheets or databases. Many times it will be up to the surveyor to determine where the furnishings or equipment are located and the effect it may have on the radio frequency.

Be sure to gather information about the following:

- In an office or enterprise environment, furnishings may consist of desks, cabinets, chairs, and other items.

- In warehousing and retail environments, furnishings will include storage racks and shelving as well as product inventories.

- In manufacturing environments, information should be gathered about the location of industrial equipment used in the manufacturing process and about equipment used to move product throughout the factory.

- In medical environments, furnishings or equipment will include devices that may cause interference and operate in the same frequency range as the proposed wireless network. Storage of items used within the hospital or medical environment for patients and employees may also affect RF coverage.

- In educational environments, the location of lockers and internal windows are important, as are the types of materials used in the walls, such as concrete blocks with and/or without sound dampening material inside. All of these factors will have an effect on the RF propagation.

These are just some examples of the types of furnishings and other items that may affect a wireless LAN deployment and are factors to consider.

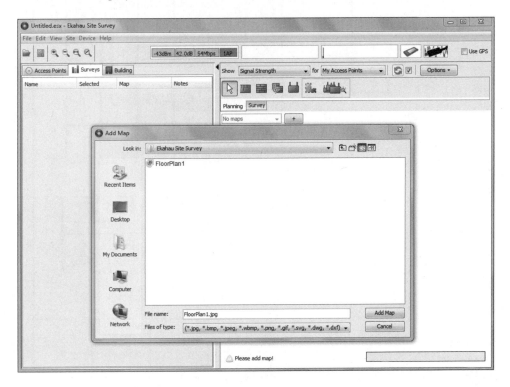

FIGURE 10.5 Importing a floor plan map using the Ekahau Site Survey program

Electrical Specifications

Documentation of the electrical specifications of the environment is helpful in determining whether the current electrical implementation will be sufficient to handle the proposed wireless network deployment. This will allow the site survey process to determine whether any upgrades need to be made in order to support devices that may be using Power over Ethernet or if the existing infrastructure is sufficient. It is best to gather information regarding electrical power sources, electrical panel information, existing wiring, and location of electrical outlets.

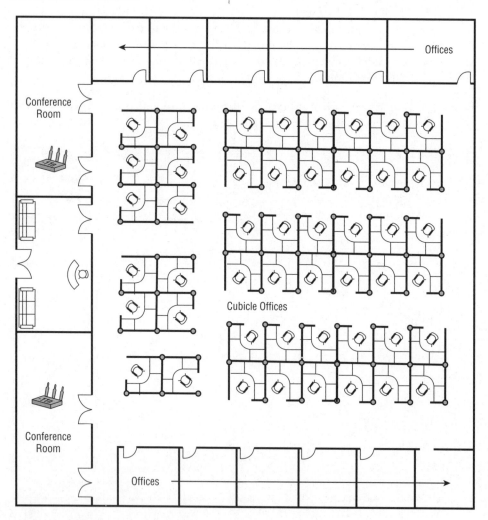

FIGURE 10.6 Floor plan with an existing wireless LAN deployment

Documenting Existing Network Characteristics

Documentation is a major part of any business, and computer networks are no exception. In order to have a successful deployment of a wireless network, it is critical to know the details of the *existing network infrastructure* as well as future implementations, upgrades, and modifications. These existing infrastructures may include a wired or wireless network already in place and functioning that may be upgraded or in a new deployment. Figure 10.6 shows a floor plan with an existing wireless deployment of only two access points providing wireless access for the conference rooms. This information can be used as part of the new wireless site survey and design.

Documentation of networks is usually the responsibility of the IT department. Some organizations may lack good documentation of the existing network infrastructure. If this is the case, additional work may be required prior to starting a wireless site survey.

Existing IEEE 802.11 Wireless Networks   One of the questions that must be asked during the interview process is to determine the scope of any existing IEEE 802.11 wireless networks. If this type of wireless network does exist (as it often does), it will need to be dealt with during the site survey and design procedure. The questions that are asked regarding the existing wireless network will help determine the role it is going to play. If the existing network is going to remain in place, understanding its technical details and how to work it into the design of the new or upgraded deployment will help you create a successful and productive wireless LAN deployment.

Existing IEEE 802.3 or Other Wired Networks   In addition to knowing of any existing wireless networks, you should know about the wired network infrastructure. Any existing documentation on the wired network infrastructure will help streamline the process for connecting the IEEE 802.11 wireless components of the network. The wired infrastructure is discussed in more detail in the next section of this chapter.

Identifying Infrastructure Connectivity and Power Requirements

Why are there so many wires in wireless networking? Wireless networks require some type of wired infrastructure for many reasons, including connecting access points together, allowing wireless device and user access to network resources, providing access to a wide area network, allowing Internet connectivity, and supplying electrical power.

Network infrastructure connectivity plays a big role in wireless networking. A wireless LAN site survey will require additional information about the network infrastructure and power requirements. In a sense, a wireless site survey also requires a wired or infrastructure survey. Information regarding the wired network includes:

- Location of wiring closets
- Wired infrastructure network devices in use

- Connection speed between sites
- Electrical power requirements

Location of Wiring Closets   A *wiring closet* is a room (usually secured) containing electrical power and cabling for voice and data that is terminated and connected to infrastructure devices such as switches and routers. In most cases these locations are noted on the floor plan or blueprint documents, but that may not always be the case and you will need to find them if they are not noted. When deploying a wireless network, you should know not only the physical locations of wiring closets but also the capacity of existing infrastructure devices. This is important because wired connections such as IEEE 802.3 Ethernet have specific limits for cable lengths, and infrastructure devices such as access points and bridges will have to be placed within these physical limits of infrastructure connectivity. For example, the IEEE 802.3 Ethernet standard has a physical maximum cable length of 328 feet (or 100 meters) for unshielded twisted pair wiring.

In addition to cable length, the feasibility of running the Ethernet cable from the wiring closet to the desired location must be considered. For example, the intended location for an access point may be on a ceiling without any access from above. In this case, lack of accessibility could pose a problem for installation of the Ethernet cabling from the wiring closet and/or AC power to the devices.

Wired Infrastructure Network Devices in Use   The wired infrastructure devices in use may have an impact on a successful deployment of a wireless LAN. An evaluation of the infrastructure devices by a WLAN site surveyor or a network infrastructure professional may be required to determine if any additional hardware or changes must be made prior to deploying a WLAN. If the infrastructure devices, such as Layer 2 switches and routers, are not adequate to support a new wireless deployment, additional hardware may need to be purchased.

Connection Speed between Sites   The connection speeds and type of connections between sites should be evaluated to determine any bottlenecks that could affect the overall network performance. Placement of authentication servers and other network resources may be affected by the speed of these links.

Electrical Power   Since all wireless LAN infrastructure devices, including access points, bridges, and wireless switches, require an AC power source, and these devices may be supplying Power over Ethernet (PoE) to the infrastructure devices, verification of an adequate AC power supply must be performed. The AC power sources are sometimes taken for granted or not taken into consideration, which could pose a problem during the installation phase. It is also important to determine what local ordinances may apply and what they allow you to do for a wireless LAN installation.

Because PoE is used not only in infrastructure devices but also with IP telephones, security cameras, and other users' devices, it may be necessary to perform calculations and verify that the power supply to the wiring closet will be adequate to support the powered infrastructure (including the PoE devices). Electrical components of a wiring closet may need to be upgraded to support a new wireless LAN deployment. Newer wireless LAN technologies such as IEEE 802.11n MIMO systems may require more DC power than is currently available with IEEE 802.3af PoE, based on this amendment to the Ethernet standard.

If these technologies will be used, the power requirements will need to be carefully considered to verify that enough DC power will be available to the end powered devices. Some manufacturers provide IEEE 802.3at (with new PoE capabilities) endpoint or midspan devices to provide the necessary amount of DC voltage for certain PoE-capable devices. All manufacturers of IEEE 802.11 wireless equipment claim the capability to power newer dual-band IEEE 802.11n access points with standard 802.3af power. I recommend that you read the specification data sheet for the access point or other wireless device to determine the type of PoE required and if IEEE 802.3af or IEEE 802.3at will be required for the device.

Understanding Application Requirements

Understanding the application requirements for software applications is another important part of a successful wireless LAN deployment. The types and number of applications used will affect the performance and the capacity of an IEEE 802.11 WLAN. Some software applications are very bandwidth intensive and will require more resources to perform effectively as designed. Examples of these applications include computer-aided design (CAD) and database programs. By contrast, other applications, such as checking email or casual Internet browsing, are not bandwidth intensive.

Application Effects on Wireless LAN Capacity

As mentioned earlier, some types of software that an organization may use, such as CAD and database applications, will have a tremendous effect on the performance of a wireless LAN. These applications require special attention when designing a wireless LAN because the acceptable capacity of the access points will be less than other applications that do not require as many resources, such as email programs or working with word processors. The infrastructure resources that will be impacted include the processing power and memory capacity of the wireless access points and the speed of the wired infrastructure itself, such as 100 Mbps or 1000 Mbps (Gigabit).

This in turn will affect the RF site survey. The wireless LAN site survey will be impacted because the location where the WLAN is installed may require more infrastructure devices or access points. Other applications, such as voice over wireless LAN, may introduce another entire set of issues. This type of deployment may use only the 5 GHz band for wireless voice technology, and therefore the wireless site survey must be performed accordingly.

Understanding RF Coverage and Capacity Requirements

A major aspect of a wireless LAN site survey is to understand and verify the RF coverage and capacity requirements based on the network design. In Chapter 6, "Radio Frequency Fundamentals for Wireless LAN Technology," you learned about coverage versus capacity and the differences between them. A WLAN site surveyor will need to verify these requirements as part of the site survey. This can be accomplished either manually or automatically through a predictive process, both to be discussed in more detail in Chapter 11.

To review, the wireless coverage and capacity requirements are going to depend on several factors such as:

- Physical size of the area to be covered
- Number of users or devices accessing the wireless network, including bring your own device (BYOD)
- Software or hardware applications in use
- Obstacles and propagation factors based on the environment
- Radio frequency range of the network to be installed
- Wireless LAN hardware to be used
- Output RF power of the transmitters
- Receive sensitivity of the receivers

In addition to an RF coverage analysis, an *RF spectrum analysis* will be beneficial. An RF spectrum analysis allows a site surveyor to view areas of RF coverage as well as interference sources and non-IEEE 802.11 wireless devices. This topic will be discussed further in Chapter 11. Although a spectrum analysis is not required, it does allow a site surveyor to view sources of RF in the locations where a wireless LAN will be deployed.

The following sections, "Client Connectivity Requirements" and "Antenna Use Considerations," cover topics not included in the CWTS exam objectives but are valuable information. This information is included here for your own reference.

Client Connectivity Requirements

Client devices that will be connecting to the wireless LAN also need to be considered as part of a site survey. This includes knowing the radio type, antenna type, gain, orientation, portability, and mobility of the device. Keep in mind that a wireless client device is both a radio frequency transmitter and a receiver. The client must be able to hear the access point and the access point must be able to hear the client device. The RF cell size will vary from device to device. It is beneficial to survey with the type of devices that will be used with the wireless LAN whenever possible. Understanding the type and function of client devices will have an impact on the design of the wireless network. Common wireless client devices include:

- Notebook computers
- Tablets
- Pocket computers
- Smart phones
- Barcode scanners
- Point-of-sale devices
- Voice handsets

Other wireless devices used in various wireless LAN applications include but are not limited to:

- Desktop computers
- Printers and print servers
- Manufacturing equipment
- Video cameras

Many environments have both desktop and notebook computers as wireless client devices. These devices may or may not require roaming capability. Office and enterprise deployments commonly use handsets for voice communications. Although it is fairly difficult to take all potential wireless client devices into consideration, it is best to understand the type of devices that will be used. This information can be obtained through the interview process and the gathering information stage of the site survey. Figure 10.7 shows various wireless client devices.

Images courtesy of Cisco Systems, Inc. Unauthorized use not permitted.

FIGURE 10.7   Client devices that are used with IEEE 802.11 wireless networking include external wireless client adapters, internal wireless client adapters, and voice over wireless LAN handsets

Antenna Use Considerations

In Chapter 7, "Wireless LAN Antennas and Accessories," you saw various types of antennas and accessories. The antenna used in any deployment will depend on the specific scenario. As part of the site survey, various antenna types may need to be used for testing purposes to determine the best antenna for a specific application. In some cases, the customer may want a specific type of antenna, such as omnidirectional mounted directly to the access points. Others may be using access points without external antenna capabilities.

Some businesses are concerned about aesthetics and are particular about the appearance of an antenna and the mounting location. The proper antenna selection will ensure correct coverage as intended by the design and site survey of the wireless LAN. The antenna type used will determine the propagation pattern of the radio frequency and is a significant part of a successful wireless LAN deployment. The antenna used in various deployments will depend on the business model in which the network is installed. Listed are some examples of the business models discussed earlier in this chapter and the type of antennas that may be used in these implementations:

General Office/Enterprise   General office/enterprise solutions usually require complete coverage throughout the entire location. In many cases, this type of installation will require access points mounted out of sight and aesthetically pleasing antennas. This could be an omnidirectional antenna mounted to a ceiling tile or integrated within an access point.

Manufacturing   Manufacturing environments are usually industrial facilities with high ceilings and various types of manufacturing and industrial equipment. These environments may use a combination of omnidirectional and semidirectional antennas due to the physical architecture of the buildings. The antennas also may need to withstand harsh environmental conditions such as extreme temperature fluctuations and dirt.

Warehousing   Warehousing implementations have some characteristics in common with manufacturing. The buildings that house this type of business are in many cases large open areas with high ceilings allowing the storage of large volumes of product and equipment. Antenna mounting needs to be looked at very closely to ensure that equipment such as forklifts used to move product do not come in contact and damage antennas. Warehousing also may use a combination of omnidirectional and semidirectional antennas for proper coverage. Figure 10.8 shows a sample floor plan for a combination small office/warehouse deployment using a combination of omnidirectional and semidirectional antennas.

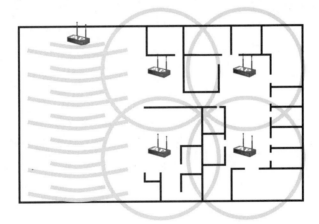

FIGURE 10.8   Small office/warehouse floor plan showing RF coverage using different antenna types

Retail/Point of Sale (PoS)   Retail/point-of-sale installations may have to accommodate publicly accessible areas as well as warehousing and storage in the back of the buildings. In this type of installation, antennas will be a combination of omnidirectional and semidirectional. The devices may consist of computers as well as other handhelds such as wireless barcode scanners or portable wireless devices. Appropriate antenna selection and gain need to be considered to ensure the devices have good signal connectivity to the infrastructure. In many cases, the public areas will require aesthetics to be taken into account in antenna selection. In the storage part of the building, antennas are similar to those described in warehousing.

Healthcare and Medical   Many healthcare and medical deployments are publicly accessible, so aesthetics and security are both important. Antenna types that fit the environment and are not accessible to the public are commonly used. Some healthcare facilities, such as hospitals, may require the use of only omnidirectional antennas mounted to the autonomous access point or integrated into an access point. Others may allow semidirectional antennas such as Yagis to cover long hallways and corridors.

Government and Military   Government and military wireless environments are usually not publicly accessible and in many cases are campus based and require outdoor solutions as well as indoor. In these installations, antennas mounted directly to an access point or semidirectional antennas may well fit the environment. For outdoor point-to-point or point-to-multipoint, highly directional antennas such as parabolic dish may be required.

Education   Education deployments are typically campus based and may require the use of outdoor antennas to connect buildings together. However, for indoor solutions, ensuring the antennas will fit the environment and not be tampered with needs to be evaluated. These deployments may use a combination of omnidirectional and semidirectional antenna types. Some locations may require the use of enclosures for the infrastructure devices to ensure security of the physical devices. In these cases, special connectors and antenna adapters may be required.

Public Access, Hotspot, and Hospitality   Public access, hotspot, and hospitality sites are publicly accessible locations that will require aesthetics and security when it comes to antenna selection, as with some of the previous examples. These deployments can use a combination of omnidirectional, semidirectional, and highly directional antennas.

 Real World Scenario

Typical Steps Used in a Wireless LAN Site Survey

Listed here are some basic steps to provide an overview of the wireless LAN site survey process. Keep in mind these steps may vary slightly based on the location and the type of wireless LAN deployment.

1. Gathering Information and Discussing Business Requirements   Determine the need and intended use of the wireless LAN and interview appropriate individuals. Explain the site survey process and provide an overview of wireless networking. Doing so will help minimize unnecessary delays caused by people who are not included in the process but should have been and are unaware of the wireless LAN and site survey.

2. Project Timeline and Planning   Understand and document the extent and estimated timeline of the survey process and deployment. This will include all stages of the wireless site survey from start to finish, such as design, deployment, and verification. Because the wireless site survey may include people from many different areas such as facilities, IT, engineering, and so on, everyone must be on the same track.

3. Site Visit and Predesign Audit It is a good idea to make a visit to the location in order to get an idea of any issues that may not be visible on a blueprint or floor plan. This will also allow for checking the RF propagation with a test access point if feasible. Performing a wireless LAN site survey without a site visit—especially a predictive modeling survey—can be done, but that will come with some risks. Knowing what you are dealing with will minimize mistakes caused by not knowing the environment and therefore possibly making inaccurate assumptions.

4. Wireless LAN Design Determine areas of RF coverage and interference as well as potential placement of access points and other infrastructure devices. This will be done with an onsite manual site survey, a predictive modeling site survey, or a combination of both. An RF spectrum analyzer can be used to view the air to determine the areas of RF interference.

5. RF Spectrum Analysis and RF Testing Perform testing of the proposed design and verify RF sources of interference. Also verify coverage and lack of coverage. Although an RF spectrum analysis is not a required part of the wireless LAN site survey process, it is highly recommended. Knowing the potential RF interference may impact the wireless LAN design as a whole. It will be much easier to deal with potential RF issues up front rather than after the wireless LAN is deployed. Testing specific areas or audit points with an access point will allow the surveyor to determine the coverage and how the RF propagates from the access point.

6. Deployment of Infrastructure Devices Install the infrastructure devices as described by the design. This may or may not be done by the same person who performed the wireless site survey and in many cases it is not. This means that clear, concise documentation and instructions must be provided to the installer. This will reduce the risk of having to make unnecessary visits back to the location for corrections or adjustments because of mistakes that could have been avoided.

7. Verification of RF Coverage Perform verification testing and spot checks of RF coverage per the design. Make necessary adjustments based on the results of RF testing. Verification testing may consist of spot checks in key areas (audit points) or could include the entire facility. It is important to be certain the wireless LAN will operate as designed. Sometimes cost or budget may not allow for a verification of the entire location, but I recommend it whenever possible. If the entire area cannot be checked, determining the audit points should be done carefully and should be completed in the early stages of the site survey. If needed, make adjustments to allow the wireless LAN to operate as designed.

8. Support Provide technical support for wireless LAN deployment. This involves maintaining the wireless LAN infrastructure and includes RF spectrum monitoring and making the necessary adjustments to adapt to the dynamics of environment. This can be done manually or automatically, depending on the capabilities of the IEEE 802.11 technology that is deployed.

Summary

In this chapter, we explored the business aspects of wireless LAN site surveys. We looked at the objective of a site survey, which is to find areas of RF coverage, interference, and hardware installation locations. We considered the factors determining the complexity of a site survey. These factors include:

- Size of physical location
- Intended use of network
- Number of users and devices
- Performance expectations
- Bring-your-own-device (BYOD) acceptance

In this chapter you saw the importance of gathering information as well as the types of information required to successfully perform a wireless LAN site survey and the design of a wireless network. We looked at several examples of deployment scenarios and case studies from different manufacturers of wireless LAN equipment as to the benefits and solutions of a wireless LAN deployment, which is the result of a successful site survey.

Anyone designing a wireless LAN needs to understand completely the expectations of how the network will perform in the environment before deploying the network. These expectations will be met by asking the right questions of the right people—managers and users of the wireless network—since they are the ones who will be using it. We explored the types of questions that may be asked to provide information that will allow for a successful wireless LAN site survey and deployment.

We also discussed taking into consideration the physical and data security requirements of the wireless network. This is part of a site survey because it will have an impact on the final design, including the number of access points and the physical and data security solutions. Having the appropriate documentation is a key element to a successful deployment. If documents such as floor plans and blueprints are not available, they may need to be created as part of the site survey and design process and may require additional cost for the customer. Accurate documentation will also help streamline some of the site survey process and deployment of a wireless LAN hardware. Accurate documentation will help with the installation of cabling and access points and minimize questions about the installation.

It is essential to know the location and type of existing networks, both wired and wireless. If existing wireless networks are in place, you must determine what role, if any, they will play in the new deployment or upgrade. Identifying the location of wiring closets and evaluating power requirements are two other important tasks in a site survey.

In this chapter you learned about RF coverage requirements and the factors to be taken into consideration to ensure proper coverage throughout the location where the wireless network is installed. Finally, client connectivity requirements and other considerations were discussed. The types of wireless client devices that will be used, such as notebook computer, tablet, or barcode scanner, must be evaluated. Antenna orientation to ensure correct polarization will need to be considered during the site survey process. We also looked at the type of antennas commonly used in a particular deployment scenario.

Exam Essentials

Understand the business requirements of a wireless LAN.   Be familiar with the necessary business information required for successful wireless LAN site survey. These business requirements include bandwidth needs, expected coverage area, and hardware and software applications used in devices and technologies.

Know various types of business models.   Understand that the site survey process will vary based on the business model in which a wireless LAN is deployed. These will include enterprise, manufacturing, healthcare, and public access, to name a few.

Understand the interview process.   Know who you should interview and the type of questions to ask during the site survey and design process. This will help ensure a more successful wireless LAN deployment.   Identify the importance of site-specific documentation.

Identify the importance of site-specific documentation.   Know the various types of documentation required based on the business model for the wireless LAN site survey. This includes blueprints and floor plans as well as other important documentation.

Know the importance of identifying existing networks.   Understand the details of existing wired and wireless networks and be able to define the characteristics of both, such as wiring closet location and power requirements.

Understand the application requirements for the wireless LAN.   Know that different applications, both software and hardware applications, will have an effect on the wireless LAN design and the site survey must take this factor into consideration.

Be familiar with RF coverage requirements.   Know the factors involved with providing adequate RF coverage within a wireless LAN deployment.

Review Questions

1. The main objectives of a wireless LAN site survey are to determine _____ and _____. (Choose two.)
    A. RF coverage
    B. Cost of equipment
    C. RF interference
    D. Manufacturer's equipment
    E. Which client devices to purchase

2. What factor usually determines whether a wireless LAN site survey is required?
    A. Number of access points
    B. Geographic location of business
    C. Number of wiring closets
    D. Number of servers on site

3. The first step of a wireless LAN site survey is typically _____.
    A. Determining the RF coverage
    B. Installing access points
    C. Gathering business requirements
    D. Documenting existing networks
    E. Interviewing managers and users

4. Enterprise office area wireless LAN deployments commonly use _____ antennas for most installations.
    A. Omnidirectional
    B. Semidirectional
    C. Yagi
    D. Parabolic dish

5. You are a wireless network engineer contracted to perform a site survey for a company that manufactures widgets. The wireless site survey will require a physical walk-through of the area. One concern in this implementation is interference from existing _____.
    A. Wireless 3G internet devices
    B. Cellular telephones
    C. 900 MHz two-way radios
    D. 2.4 GHz ISM band devices
    E. CB radios

6. Implementations that may have existing non-wireless LAN devices that will potentially interfere with a 2.4 GHz wireless LAN deployment most likely fall under what business model?

   A. Office

   B. Government

   C. Healthcare

   D. Education

7. You are hired to perform a wireless LAN site survey for a large enterprise company with over a thousand employees. You need to come up with a list of questions to ask users of the wireless network. Which question would be the most relevant for the user community?

   A. Where are the wiring closets?

   B. Do you have any floor plans available?

   C. What applications do you use?

   D. Do you have an equipment manufacturer preference?

   E. What is the RF coverage area?

8. A wireless LAN site survey and design includes defining _____ and _____ security requirements to help protect against RF jamming and protect the integrity of information. (Choose two.)

   A. Physical

   B. Access point

   C. Data

   D. Device

   E. Infrastructure

9. Which device is the best candidate to use the roaming features of an IEEE 802.11n wireless computer network?

   A. Notebook computer

   B. Tablet

   C. Voice handset

   D. Wireless camera

10. Which of the following is a main factor in determining the number of access points required for an IEEE 802.11n wireless LAN deployment?

   A. Type of client devices in use

   B. Number of client devices

   C. Manufacturer of client devices

   D. Antennas in client devices

11. Interviewing managers and users will help determine which part of the site survey process?

    A. Performance expectations

    B. Locations of UNII band interference

    C. Creating floor plans

    D. Locations of access points

12. Which of the following can be imported into a commercial site survey program to assist in predicting the RF coverage of access points?

    A. Electrical specifications

    B. Access point models

    C. Bandwidth requirements

    D. Floor plans

    E. Cost estimates

13. Warehouse inventory such as paint and other liquids in large quantities can cause which RF behavior?

    A. Reflection

    B. Refraction

    C. Diffraction

    D. Absorption

    E. Scattering

14. You are a wireless LAN consultant contracted to assist in a site survey for a retail outlet that will deploy an 802.11n WLAN. You've been asked to participate in an initial meeting with top management to determine the details of a site survey. What topics would most likely be discussed at this meeting? (Choose two.)

    A. Business requirements

    B. Available antenna types

    C. Recommended manufacturer hardware

    D. Bill of materials

    E. Applications in use

    F. Purpose of the wireless LAN

15. A wireless LAN will be deployed in a hospital. Which criterion would be addressed when discussing a potential RF jamming attack?

    A. Data security

    B. Access point security

    C. Physical security

    D. Infrastructure security

    E. Wiring closet security

16. You are a wireless LAN consultant hired to perform a site survey for a hotel. You need to interview the management and staff regarding the proposed installation of the wireless network. Which of the following is an appropriate question to ask the hotel manager?

    A. Is PoE used in the hotel?

    B. What are the aesthetic requirements?

    C. Which areas lack RF coverage?

    D. Which areas have RF interference?

17. Which of the following will be the most likely reason in determining the number of access points required for a wireless LAN deployment?

    A. Applications used

    B. Security requirements

    C. Equipment manufacturer

    D. Ceiling height

18. RF coverage of access points depends on which factor?

    A. Wiring closet location

    B. Access point output power

    C. Electrical power requirements

    D. Floor plans and blueprints

19. Which of the following is *not* a requirement for the initial gathering of technical information for a wireless LAN site survey in a new deployment scenario?

    A. Number of users

    B. Applications in use

    C. Other wireless networks

    D. Cost of equipment

20. Which wireless LAN deployment scenario uses mostly omnidirectional antennas mounted directly to an access point?

    A. Manufacturing

    B. Warehousing

    C. Office building

    D. Sports arena

Chapter

11

Performing an RF Wireless LAN Site Survey

THE FOLLOWING CWTS EXAM OBJECTIVES ARE COVERED IN THIS CHAPTER:

✓ **4.2 Define and differentiate between the following WLAN system architectures and understand site survey concepts related to each architecture. Identify and explain best practices for access point placement and density.**

  ▪ Multiple channel architecture (MCA)

  ▪ Single channel architecture (SCA)

✓ **4.3 Describe the primary purpose and methodology of manual and predictive site surveys**

✓ **4.4 Define the need for and the use of a manual site survey tool and differentiate between the following manual site survey types**

  ▪ Active surveys

  ▪ Passive surveys

✓ **4.5 Differentiate between manual and predictive site surveys**

  ▪ Advantages and disadvantages of each site survey methodology

✓ **4.6 Define the need for and use of site survey software or a protocol analyzer in a manual site survey as it relates to identifying, locating, and assessing nearby WLANs**

✓ **4.7 Differentiate between site survey methods for indoor and outdoor wireless service**

✓ **4.8 Define the need for and use of a spectrum analyzer in a site survey**

  ▪ Identification and location of interference sources

  ▪ Differentiation of Wi-Fi and non-Wi-Fi interference sources

✓ **4.9 Understand industry best practices for optimal use of directional and omni-directional antennas in site surveys**

This is the second of two chapters on the subject of wireless LAN site surveys.

In Chapter 10, "Wireless LAN Site Survey Basics," you learned about the business aspects of a site survey, which included gathering of information such as the business requirements for the wireless network, interviewing managers and users, and gathering site-specific documentation. It is important to have all the necessary groundwork prior to starting a physical wireless RF site survey. Having all the correct information in hand will allow for a complete and thorough survey, which in turn will result in a successful wireless LAN deployment.

In this chapter, you will see some of the components of performing an RF wireless LAN site survey, including determining areas of RF interference by using a spectrum analyzer. Taking into consideration both Wi-Fi and non-Wi-Fi interference sources and understanding how this interference will affect the deployment are also important parts of performing a site survey. We will also look at different types of site surveys, both manual and predictive modeling. We will discuss the two types of manual site surveys, passive and active, and show the advantages and disadvantages of both. Understanding the steps involved and the details of each site survey type will help a wireless LAN engineer determine the best methodology to use. You will learn about some of the tools that may be used in a site survey, including wireless protocol analyzers and wireless scanners. Finally, we will look at the two different types of channel architecture and best practices for hardware placement, including access points and antennas, as well as some of the limitations you may encounter during the physical site survey process.

The Physical Radio Frequency Site Survey Process

After all the up-front work is completed, such as gathering of information, including the business requirements and site-specific documentation, defining physical and data security requirements, and interviewing managers and users, it is time to start the physical RF site survey process and the wireless LAN design. This is one of the most important parts of a successful wireless LAN deployment. This process includes locating areas and sources of RF interference as well as RF coverage (or lack thereof), and determining the locations of access points, bridges, sensors, and other infrastructure devices that will be used with the wireless network. The following sections detail the entire physical wireless site survey process and guidelines. The RF physical site survey is a very subjective topic and people have different opinions on how the entire process works. In many cases, this process can be tailored based on the individual needs or requirements of the location where the wireless LAN will be installed. The following steps should be viewed as recommendations or guidelines:

1. Arrange a walkthrough of the entire location, which may often require being escorted by an authorized person.

2. Take thorough notes.

3. Perform an RF spectrum analysis.

4. Determine preliminary placement of infrastructure devices.

5. Perform on-site testing to verify the design.

6. Determine actual placement of infrastructure devices.

7. Install infrastructure hardware as specified.

8. Perform on-site verification testing and make adjustments to verify the design meets the specifications.

9. Deliver the final site survey report.

In today's wireless LAN world, an RF site survey can be considered an ongoing process. Just a few years ago, not nearly as many wireless networks existed as do today, so the interference factor was not as significant. With the RF dynamics constantly changing and more devices using RF for communications, it is up to the network engineer to take into consideration that site requirements may also be constantly changing. Therefore, the RF site survey may need to be updated periodically.

Radio Frequency Spectrum Analysis

The wireless LAN site survey includes finding areas of RF coverage and RF interference as well as locations for hardware, such as access points, bridges, and other infrastructure devices. Although radio frequency is not visible to the human eye, some tools are available to "see" a visual representation of the RF. A common tool is the RF *spectrum analyzer*. Figure 11.1 shows a spectrum analyzer view of the 2.4 GHz ISM band with the access point set to channel 1. Spectrum analyzers will vary in cost and complexity depending on the frequency ranges they are designed to work with.

Some spectrum analyzers are available that are designed specifically for the wireless LAN market. These usually work only in the license-free radio bands and are typically less expensive because of spectrum limitations. Spectrum analyzers allow you to view the physical layer of communication between devices used in wireless networking. Wireless LAN spectrum analyzers are available in PC card models, devices that attach to a USB port on the computer, and instrumentation-style devices that can be used for applications other than wireless networking. Figure 11.2 shows an example of a WLAN spectrum analyzer that connects to a USB port on a computer.

FIGURE 11.1 Chanalyzer Pro shows RF capture of an IEEE 802.11b/g access point on channel 1.

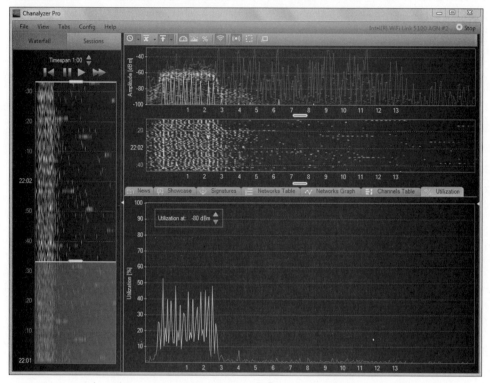

FIGURE 11.2 MetaGeek DBx spectrum analyzer for IEEE 802.11a/b/g/n networks operating in the 2.4 GHz and 5 GHz frequency ranges

Some manufacturers of wireless LAN equipment integrate spectrum analyzer tools into devices such as wireless LAN access points or wireless LAN controllers for constant monitoring of the radio frequency. Others offer standalone products that can be used to monitor more specific areas. Listed here are some manufacturers of wireless LAN spectrum analyzers:

Product	Website
AirMagnet Spectrum XT	www.flukenetworks.com
BumbleBee Handheld	www.bvsystems.com
Motorola AirDefense	www.airdefense.net
Wi-Spy by MetaGeek	www.metageek.net

The ability to analyze the RF allows a site surveyor to find areas that lack coverage, also known as *dead spots*, as well as interference caused by other devices and other IEEE 802.11 wireless networks that operate in the same radio frequency range. Although a spectrum analysis is not a requirement for a wireless LAN site survey, it is beneficial in most medium- to large-scale deployments of wireless networks. Because of the vast number of devices that use unlicensed radio bands, spectrum analysis can be considered an ongoing process. Performing regular spectrum analysis gives wireless LAN engineers the capability to monitor the area in which wireless LAN devices are located for RF interference and other issues. Figure 11.3 shows an example of a USB-based spectrum analyzer designed for IEEE 802.11 wireless networks.

FIGURE 11.3 AirMagnet SpectrumXT USB Spectrum Analyzer

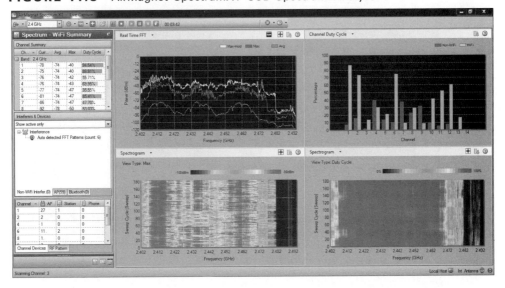

Wi-Fi and Non-Wi-Fi Interference Sources

The performance of a wireless network can be significantly affected by various types of interference sources. Interference may be either intentional or unintentional and caused both by IEEE 802.11 wireless networks and by other devices that also operate in the 2.4 GHz ISM or 5 GHz UNII band. The use of portable and mobile devices that employ radio frequency for communication continues to rise, so interference from these devices is also more prevalent. As mentioned in previous chapters of this book, these interfering devices typically operate in the unlicensed radio spectrum 2.4 GHz ISM band. Other sources of interference from the industrial, medical, and scientific communities will also affect the amount of interference. *Non-Wi-Fi interference* in the ISM band can be caused by devices such as these:

- Microwave ovens
- Cordless telephones
- IEEE 802.15 Bluetooth devices
- Medical equipment
- Manufacturing or industrial equipment
- Wireless video cameras
- Radar systems (5 GHz bands)

FIGURE 11.4 Microwave oven operating at maximum power for 30 seconds and IEEE 802.11b/g access point on channel 1

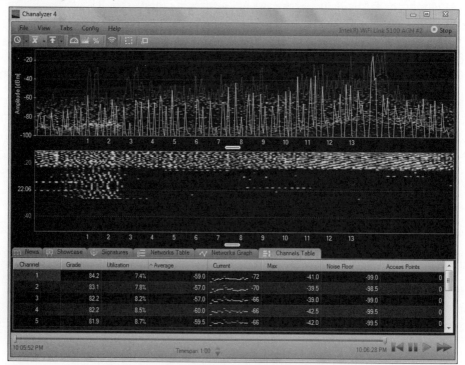

This is by no means a complete list, but it does contain some of the devices used daily that may cause some level of interference in the world of wireless networking. Figure 11.4 shows an example of interference caused by a microwave oven. This figure shows a spectrum analyzer capture that ran for approximately 30 seconds. Microwave ovens operate in the 2.4 GHz frequency range and, depending on the unit, may cause interference with IEEE 802.11 wireless networks.

In Exercise 11.1, you will use the Chanalyzer spectrum analysis software from MetaGeek to look at some sample radio frequency captures.

EXERCISE 11.1

Using Spectrum Analysis

In this exercise, you will install the Chanalyzer software program by MetaGeek. This software will allow you to view some predefined RF captures that are available as part of the program. To perform actual captures, you will need to purchase one of the Wi-Spy analyzers available at www.metageek.net. Chanalyzer 4 can be downloaded from www .metageek.net or at the download page for this book, www.sybex.com/go/cwts2e at no charge.

1. Download the Chanalyzer 4 software package; as of this writing, the program is named Chanalyzer-4-Installer.msi. Execute the program. Depending on the version of the Microsoft OS you are using, you may see an Open File – Security Warning dialog box. Click the Run button to continue. The setup wizard will appear.

2. Click Next to start the installation process. The license agreement will appear.

3. Read the license agreement; then select the I Agree button and click Next. The Select Installation Folder screen will appear.

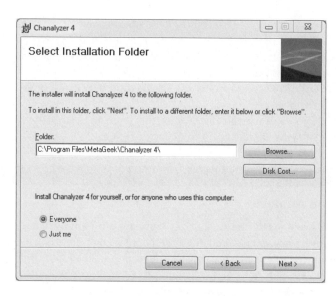

4. Click Next to accept the default installation folder.

5. Click Next on the Confirm Installation screen to start the installation process. Depending on the version of the Microsoft OS you are using, you may see a User Account Control dialog box. Click Yes to continue the installation. The Chanalyzer 4 program will now be installed on your computer. The Installation Complete screen will appear.

6. Click Close to complete the installation process and exit the installer program. The Chanalyzer 4 program is now installed on your computer.

7. Start the Chanalyzer 4 program by choosing Windows Start ➢ All Programs ➢ MetaGeek ➢ Chanalyzer 4. The Chanalyzer 4 for Wi-Spy display will appear on your screen.

8. The Showcase tab should be selected. If not, select it now. Click the 802.11g box to view the sample recording for an 802.11g network 2.4 GHz on Channel 6 capture.

9. Click the large white arrow to start viewing the recording. While observing the screen, let the sample recording run for approximately 1 minute and notice the capture change as the program displays the recorded session. This sample recording runs for 1 minute and 2 seconds. If desired, you can pause the capture or rewind by using the controls on the bottom-right corner of the Wi-Spy window.

10. Select a new capture by clicking the Showcase tab near the bottom of the screen. The additional sample captures screen will appear in the Showcase window.

11. Use the scroll bar to move down and view the sample recordings. Click the 5 GHz Phone box. Scroll back up and click on the large white arrow to view the sample recording for a 5 GHz cordless phone capture.

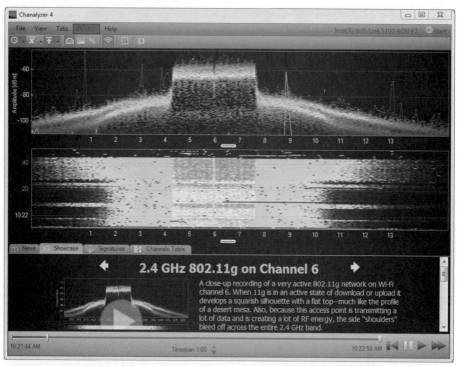

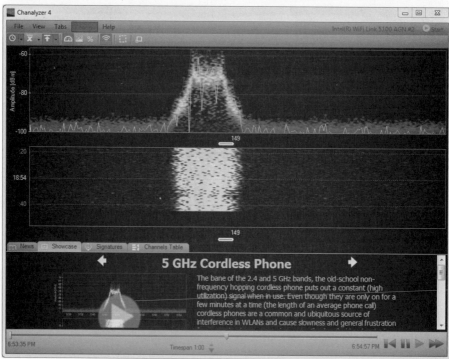

12. While observing the screen, let the sample recording run for approximately 1 minute and notice the capture change as the program displays the recorded session. This sample recording runs for 1 minute and 22 seconds. As with all the sample captures, you can pause, restart, or rewind the capture by using the controls on the bottom-right corner of the Chanalyzer 4 window.

13. Use the scroll bar to move down and view the other sample recordings.

14. Continue to view the other sample recordings by clicking on the 5 GHz 802.11n, 802.11b/g, Microwave, and Video Camera and other sample recordings and repeating steps 9–10.

After you have completed this exercise, you can remove the Chanalyzer 4 program from your computer.

The Wi-Spy spectrum analyzer device is available in several models. This device will plug into an available USB port on your computer. The Chanalyzer 4 program used in this exercise is the same you would use to perform actual captures with the Wi-Spy device from MetaGeek.

Wi-Fi Interference

Wi-Fi interference is caused by IEEE 802.11 wireless LAN devices that operate in the 2.4 GHz ISM or 5 GHz UNII band. In some cases, this is the largest source of interference for wireless LANs. There are two types of Wi-Fi interference: co-channel interference (other devices on the same channel) and adjacent channel interference (other devices on overlapping channels). See the sidebar "Standards vs. Industry Definitions" for more about how these terms are distinguished in the industry generally and by the CWNP exam.

The following network types will cause Wi-Fi interference:

- FHSS networks: 2.4 GHz (Legacy)
- DSSS networks: 2.4 GHz
- ERP-OFDM networks: 2.4 GHz
- OFDM: 5 GHz
- HT-OFDM: 2.4 GHz and 5 GHz (802.11n)

Wi-Fi devices that cause interference can be operating in either infrastructure mode or ad hoc mode. The number of devices that are part of the wireless network will also determine the extent of the interference. In Chapter 5, "Physical Layer Access Methods and Spread-Spectrum Technology," we discussed different types of spread-spectrum technologies that wireless networks use to communicate. FHSS, DSSS, ERP-OFDM, OFDM, and HT-OFDM are technologies used for IEEE 802.11 wireless networking in the 2.4 GHz and 5 GHz bands. However, some of these technologies are used in non–wireless LAN devices as well. For example, Bluetooth devices operating in the 2.4 GHz ISM band also use FHSS technology for communication. Zigbee devices operate in the 2.4 GHz band and use DSSS technology for communication. Depending on the manufacturer, 2.4 GHz cordless phones may use either

FHSS or DSSS. Performing an RF spectrum analysis is one way you can determine the source of this type of interference. If an instrumentation spectrum analyzer (a calibrated device that has the capability to view entire radio spectrums) is used, it will be necessary to understand how to interpret the data collected as well as how to operate the device.

It is important to note that IEEE 802.11 FHSS wireless LANs are legacy and rarely found with today's installations. I mention them here because although it is unlikely, you could possibly encounter them. Also, FHSS is used with other wireless technologies.

Standards vs. Industry Definitions

The following information is from the "Exam Terms" document available from www .cwnp.com and was added here for clarification. Be sure to read the entire document prior to attempting any CWNP certification exam.

The 802.11 standard loosely defines an adjacent channel as any channel with non-overlapping frequencies for the DSSS and HR/DSSS PHYs. With ERP and OFDM, the standard loosely defines an adjacent channel as the first channel with a nonoverlapping frequency space.

This contradicts how the term "adjacent channel interference" is typically used in the marketplace. Most Wi-Fi vendors use this term to loosely mean both interference resulting from overlapping cells and interference resulting from the use of overlapping frequency space. For example, vendors typically use this terminology in a case where AP-1 (channel 1) is located near AP-2 (channel 2).

The CWNP Program has decided to define two separate terms for clarity: Adjacent Overlapping Channel (for example, channels 1 and 2 that are overlapping, and are directly next to each other in the band) and Adjacent Non-overlapping Channel (for example, channels 1 and 6, which are the first immediately side-by-side channels that do not overlap). Channels 1 and 7, 1 and 8, and so on are simply considered nonoverlapping channels and are not adjacent.

Adjacent channel interference is a performance condition that occurs when two or more access point radios are providing RF coverage to the same physical area using overlapping frequencies. Simultaneous RF transmissions by two or more of these access point radios in the same physical area can result in corrupted 802.11 frames because of the frequency overlap. Corrupted 802.11 frames cause retransmissions, which results in both throughput degradation and latency.

Co-channel interference is a performance condition that occurs when two or more independently coordinated access point radios are providing RF coverage to the same physical area using the same 802.11 channel. Additional RF medium contention overhead occurs for all radios using this channel in this physical area, resulting in throughput degradation and latency.

Performing a Manual Radio Frequency Wireless LAN Site Survey

Although some in the industry consider the manual wireless LAN RF site survey process "old school," it provides some of the most accurate results. A manual site survey requires a physical walkthrough of the area, recording information to determine the performance of clients and devices that will be connected to the wireless network. This type of site survey can be very accurate because the surveyor is recording actual statistics, such as:

- Signal strength
- Signal-to-noise ratio (SNR)
- Data rate of connected devices
- Radio Frequency interference

These measurements are recorded while physically moving through the facility or location. Recommended received signal strength and signal-to-noise ratio (SNR) values are discussed later in this chapter. Small-scale manual site surveys can be performed inexpensively by using either a wireless client adapter with site survey functionality, one of several freeware/shareware utilities, or commercial software designed specifically for this type of application. Figure 11.5 shows an example of a free site survey software program.

FIGURE 11.5   Ekahau HeatMapper – Wi-Fi Coverage Mapping Site Survey Software Utility is a free download from Ekahau.

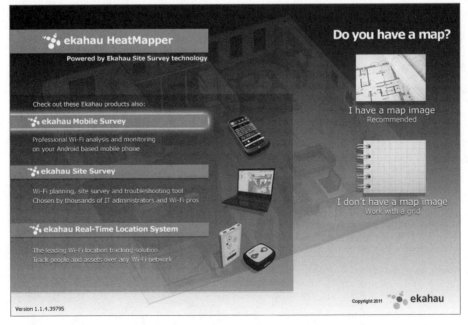

The manual site survey process can be used for recording measurements to determine the actual placement of hardware infrastructure devices and for spot checking, locating other IEEE 802.11 wireless networks, or verification after a predictive site survey has determined the placement of these devices. Not too long ago this manual process was the only way to perform a wireless LAN site survey. The main advantage of the manual process is accuracy. One disadvantage is that it can be very time-consuming depending on the extent of the installation. Some of the basic steps include:

1. Obtaining a floor plan or blueprint of the location to be surveyed

2. Performing a radio frequency spectrum analysis

3. Testing access point placement

4. Taking photographs of access point placement with a digital camera for documentation

5. Analyzing the site survey results

Obtaining a Floor Plan or Blueprint

The first step in a manual site survey is to review a floor plan or blueprint of the location. Many in the industry refer to a floor plan as a "map." This could be a simple sketch and is required to note access point placement as well as readings. The readings to note on the floor plan include signal strength and signal-to-noise ratio values from client devices. Figure 11.6 shows a basic floor plan of a small office building. The floor plan should be marked with approximate access point locations. In some cases, a floor plan or CAD drawing of the location may not be available. Depending on the size of the location, a fire evacuation plan could be photographed or scanned in and used as a starting point to create a drawing and may be adequate for the site survey.

FIGURE 11.6   Approximate access point locations

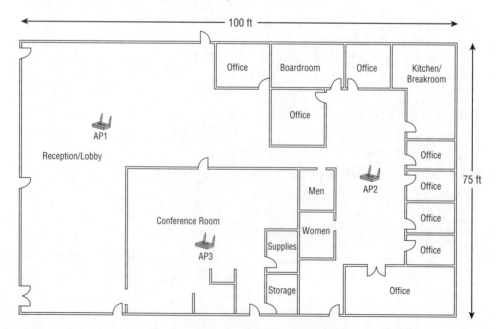

The floor plan and approximate access point locations used in these examples are for illustration purposes only.

Identifying Existing Wireless Networks

As part of a manual site survey, you should identify existing wireless LANs in the area, noting locations that include possible sources of radio frequency interference and may have an impact on the wireless LAN that will be installed. Using a device or software program designed specifically for wireless networks would be ideal. However, freeware or shareware programs may be satisfactory. Figure 11.7 shows an example of a software program that can be used to find existing IEEE 802.11 wireless networks.

FIGURE 11.7 The AirMagnet Wi-Fi Analyzer can be used to view existing IEEE 802.11 wireless networks.

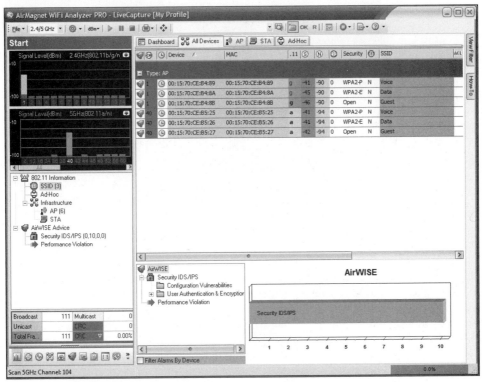

Testing Access Point Placement

Once you have identified potential locations for access points, you can start testing the proposed access point placement. This can be done by temporarily mounting an access point at the desired location to get the most accurate results. In some cases, a tool or fixture made specifically for wireless LAN site surveys or even a tall ladder could be used as a temporary mounting solution. Refer to the documentation that was created prior to going on-site for mounting locations.

It is always best to use test access points from the same manufacturer and, if possible, the same model that will be used in the actual deployment during the pre and post deployment manual site survey process. This practice will yield a better outcome than using generic access points during testing. Figure 11.8 shows an example of a temporary mounting solution.

FIGURE 11.8   Access point temporarily mounted using an expandable light pole

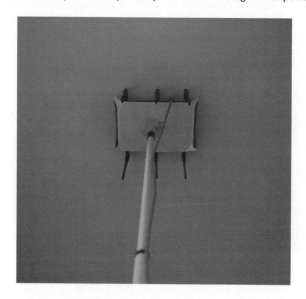

Using one or possibly two temporarily mounted access points, document the results of the testing while moving around the facility. One testing method is to IEEE 802.11 authenticate and associate to the test access points using the site survey computer. A passive process (listening to all access points in the area) may also be used for this type of site survey. The area to be tested should include a reasonable proximity around the temporarily mounted access point. The extents should be the desired minimum received signal threshold, −67 dBm for example. The information recorded and documented will depend on the surveyor but commonly includes signal strength and signal-to-noise ratio. It may be necessary to make adjustments of access point mounting during the testing process, based on the results of the onsite testing process. It would be beneficial to test an actual wireless client device and software application that will be used with the network in order to see if the performance meets expectations. Software-assisted programs as described later in this chapter are commonly used for a site survey of any size in today's wireless LAN deployments.

Analyzing the Results

Once all the testing is complete, it is necessary to perform an offline analysis to determine the final placement of access points or other infrastructure devices that may be used in the wireless LAN deployment. This may include making adjustments from the original plan prior to testing or possibly adding and removing access points. The use of various antennas may also need to be analyzed and documented.

Advantages and Disadvantages of Manual Site Surveys

Listed here are some of the advantages and disadvantages of the manual site survey process:

- Advantages
  - Very accurate because it is based on actual readings
  - Physical characteristics of building are physically tested (attenuation values)
  - Allows verification of actual RF signal coverage
  - Allows marking exact installation locations of hardware while on-site
- Disadvantages
  - Can be very-time consuming
  - Usually only one access point is used for testing, so readings will need to be merged
  - Requires a physical walkthrough of entire location
  - Many areas require an escort and special clearances for access

> WLAN equipment used in a manual site survey should be from the same manufacturer as the hardware that will be installed in the actual deployment. This will minimize any potential issues from variations between manufacturers' devices.

Software-Assisted Manual Site Survey

The manual site survey technique discussed earlier in this section may be adequate for smaller deployments or for organizations that have limited resources and budget. Manual site surveys can also be accomplished with the aid of commercial software programs designed specifically for this process. These programs vary in cost, complexity, and features and contain many advanced features, including:

- Capability to perform both passive and active surveys
- Capability to import floor plans with support for many graphic formats, including JPG, BMP, and CAD formats

- Capability to record critical data such as signal and signal-to-noise ratio
- Visual representation of RF signal propagation of surveyed areas
- Postsurvey offline analysis of collected data

The Passive Wireless LAN Site Survey

A *passive site survey* consists of monitoring the air and recording the radio frequency information from all wireless access points and wireless client stations or devices in the "hearing range" of the surveying station and includes radio frequency information from your own and neighboring devices. This type of site survey does not require an IEEE 802.11 authentication and association to an access point, and no traffic is passed between the survey station and the access point. A passive survey will provide an overall snapshot of the RF in use in or around the location, including RF noise and other IEEE 802.11 wireless networks in the area. It is used to get an overall picture of the wireless LAN access points that are transmitting within the area being surveyed. Figure 11.9 shows an example of a commercial site survey application in passive mode.

FIGURE 11.9   Ekahau Site Survey (ESS) showing passive survey

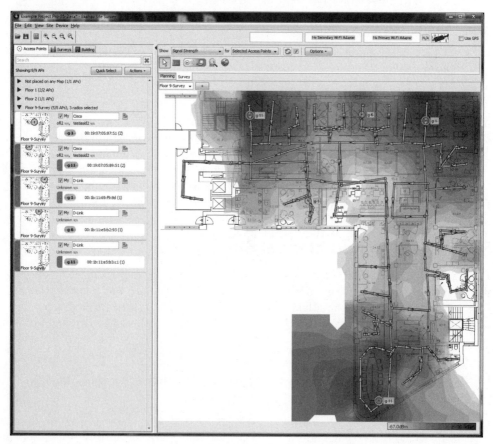

Since passive site surveys do not require an association to an access point, all radio frequencies will be detected, displayed, and recorded. Most commercial software applications with this functionality will have the capability to filter on specific access points from the information that was recorded.

The Active Site Wireless LAN Survey

An *active site survey* consists of a survey device such as a notebook computer associating to an access point prior to taking readings and collecting the data. Some claim this type of manual survey will provide more accurate results because of this direct IEEE 802.11 authentication and association to an access point. The association of the survey device to an access point will actively send and receive some basic RF information to and from the access point, allowing the information about signal strength and noise levels to be recorded. Figure 11.10 shows a commercial site survey performing an active site survey.

FIGURE 11.10   AirMagnet Survey showing an active site survey

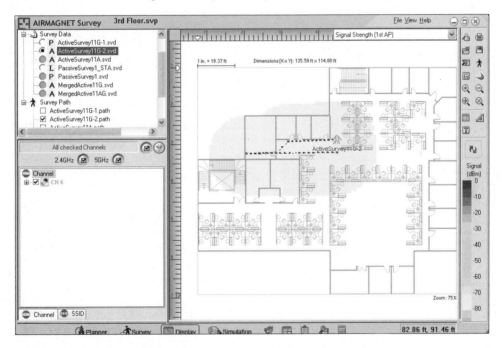

Performing either a passive or active site survey using software involves many of the same steps discussed in "Performing a Manual Radio Frequency Wireless LAN Site Survey" earlier in this chapter. The main difference is the features and capabilities that are available in these commercial software packages. These elaborate features will eliminate the need to manually document and record all the information obtained while walking the area because the program handles this task for the surveyor.

In Exercise 11.2 you will explore the Ekahau HeatMapper site survey program. If you have a floor plan of your area, you can perform an actual manual wireless site survey.

EXERCISE 11.2

Installing Ekahau HeatMapper

In this exercise, you will begin by installing the Ekahau HeatMapper, a free Wi-Fi site survey tool.

Ekahau HeatMapper specifications:

- Wi-Fi coverage mapping tool

- Free of charge

- No official support provided

Ekahau HeatMapper requirements:

- Laptop computer running Windows XP, Windows Vista, or Windows 7 (64-bit or 32-bit)

- 512 MB of RAM

- 1 GB hard disk space

- 500 MHz or faster processor

- Wireless network adapter (internal or external)

The Ekahau HeatMapper program is available free of charge from Ekahau and is available at www.Ekahau.com. The Ekahau HeatMapper allows you to see your wireless network: It shows the wireless coverage of any access point on the map. It also locates all the audible access points, and shows their configurations and signal strength—in real time and on the map (floor plan).

1. Download the Ekahau HeatMapper program, which has the filename Heatmapper-Setup.exe, from the Ekahau website and execute the program. Depending on the version of the Microsoft OS you are using, you may see a User Account Control dialog box. Click the Yes button to continue. The Ekahau HeatMapper Setup wizard will appear.

2. Click Next to start the installation process. The license agreement will appear.

3. Read the license agreement, and then select the I Agree button and click Next. The Choose Install Location screen will appear.

4. Click Next to install the default installation folder. Depending on the version of the Microsoft OS you are using, you may see a Windows Security dialog box appear.

5. Click the Install button to continue if you choose to continue with the installation. The Ekahau HeatMapper program will now be installed on your computer. The Installation Complete screen will appear.

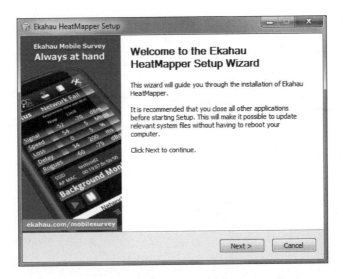

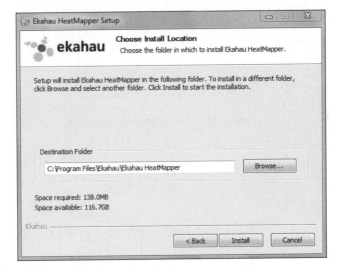

6. Click Finish to complete the installation process and exit the installer program. The Ekahau HeatMapper program is now installed on your computer, and the program will start. The Ekahau HeatMapper home screen (shown in Figure 11.5 earlier) will appear.

7. Click on the "I have a map image" box to start using the program.

8. Browse to the location containing the floor plan image that you plan to use for the survey.

9. Select the image and click the Choose Image button. The Ekahau HeatMapper home screen will return, displaying the floor plan image you imported. If the Quick Help screen appears, you can click the small arrow button in the right center of the screen to minimize the help window.

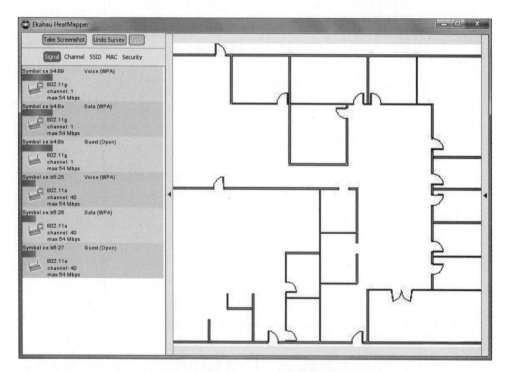

10. Click on the area of the floor plan where you are currently located. You will notice access points on the left side of the screen that the HeatMapper program detects.

11. Take your laptop and start walking around the facility slowly.

12. Left-click your current location on the map as you walk.

13. Right-click when you stop walking. After right-clicking, you will see the combined coverage heatmaps of all access points.

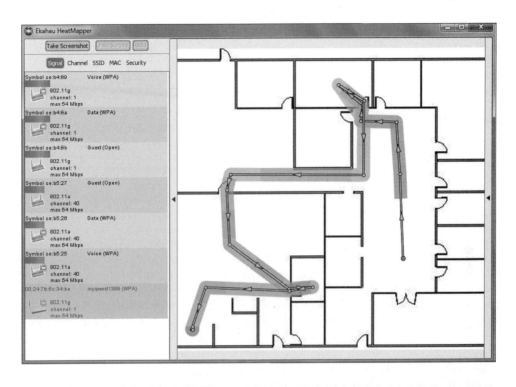

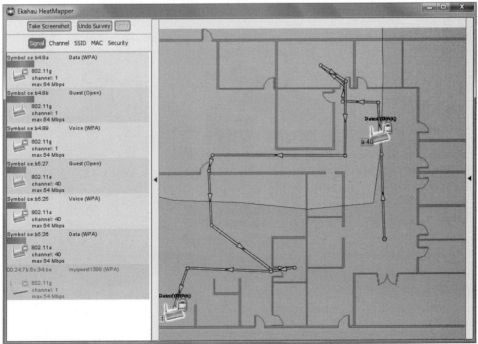

14. Move the mouse over an AP to see the coverage of a single access point.

15. Hide and show the AP list by clicking the small arrow button on the left side center of the screen.

16. Experiment with the HeatMapper program by clicking on the various access point options: Signal, Channel, SSID, MAC, and Security.

17. Click the Take Screenshot button to save an image of the current survey.

18. Close and exit the Ekahau HeatMapper program.

Manual Site Survey Toolkit

To perform a manual site survey, you need a toolkit containing essential components. A floor plan or blueprint is required to record data collected during a manual site survey. If an assisted software program is used, both an electronic version of the floor plan and a paper printout are necessary. Site survey toolkits will vary in complexity and cost. Planning the equipment and tools you will need for a manual site survey is very important. I recommend you take everything you will need and not take items you will not need. Taking items you do not need creates an unnecessary burden. Many times you may be the only person performing the physical survey, and you need to realize the limits. You can create your own site survey kit based on what you will need, or you can purchase a kit from a manufacturer that is built specifically for this purpose. Figure 11.11 shows a wireless LAN IEEE 802.11n MIMO site survey kit from TerraWave Solutions.

FIGURE 11.11   802.11n MIMO site survey kit from TerraWave Solutions contained in a durable and airline-approved transportable carrying case

Image provided by: www.terrawave.com.

The following lists some items that may be included in a Wireless LAN site survey kit. Keep in mind this covers some of the most common items and the kit will vary based on the site survey and the person performing the site survey.

Spectrum Analyzer (Optional but Recommended)   A spectrum analyzer is an optional but recommended item that may be used in an RF wireless LAN site survey. This device will sweep the area to look for devices that may cause interference with the deployment and locate all the radio frequency information in the area. Spectrum analyzers vary in cost and features, as discussed earlier in this chapter. Although "optional," this tool is highly recommended.

Wireless Access Points   One or two access points are needed to take signal measurements during the manual site survey process. It is important to use access points from the same manufacturer and if possible the same model that will be installed, to simulate what will be used in the actual installation. If this cannot be achieved, try to get an access point that is as close as possible to those that will be used in the deployment.

I recommend that you set the test access points' output power level at about 50 percent or less during the site survey. This usually requires lowering the default power, which in many cases is set at maximum. This will allow for adjustments after installation to help compensate for potential differences from when the space was originally surveyed. The output power settings used will be determined by the individual performing the site survey. It is also important to keep in mind that if you are performing a site survey for both the 2.4 GHz and 5 GHz bands, the amount of RF transmit power as well as the gain of the antennas must be taken into consideration because of the difference in wavelength, which will in turn affect the range.

Wireless Client Device Such as a Notebook Computer   A device to take measurements from the client side is an important component of the site survey kit. This can be a notebook computer or tablet with appropriate software to take signal measurements. Size and weight should be considered as well. A Wi-Fi, VoIP handset may also be used for locations that are considering WLAN voice over Internet Protocol capabilities. It is best to try to match the survey client devices with those that will actually be used by the users of the wireless network. However, this is not required.

Portable Battery Packs or Extension Cords   Portable battery packs to temporarily power the wireless access points are highly recommended. However, if these are not available, extension cords are a good substitute. The disadvantage of extension cords is that they require accessible AC power outlets, which might not be available at all sites. Also, they may be difficult to use and can be cumbersome. An extra battery pack for the survey device is also recommended. Battery packs specifically designed for wireless LAN site surveys are available from a variety of manufacturers. Most battery packs will last longer than the surveyor.

Various Antennas (If Required)   If antennas other than those mounted directly to an access point will be used in the deployment, a variety of these antennas should be on hand for testing during the site survey process. If 802.11n technology will be tested during the site survey, appropriate 802.11n antennas will be required as part of the site survey kit. If you do not plan to use different antennas, there is no value in taking them along during the survey.

Temporary Mounting Hardware   Mounting hardware for temporarily mounting access points and antennas should also be considered, including expandable poles, brackets, tape, and nylon tie straps. You may have to be creative when it comes to temporary mounting. It is critical to make safety a number-one priority when performing this task.

Measuring Device, Either Tape or Wheel   A measuring tape or wheel is recommended for measuring distance to wiring closets and distance between access points and any other areas where distance is of importance. Laser measuring tools are also available, but many are only capable of short distances. If possible it would be beneficial to have both a tape or wheel and a laser measuring device.

Digital Camera   As they say, a picture is worth a thousand words. Using a digital camera to take photographs of situations that may be difficult to explain in writing is a great help. This also adds quality to wireless site survey reports. Digital camera technology is now very inexpensive and most smart phones and tablets have this capability built in. I recommend taking many digital photographs when possible, especially in those areas that may be difficult to describe in writing. It is better to have the photographs if the need arises than to wish you had them. Photographs of potential access point locations are valuable should physical limitations of the facility come into question. Also, photographs of existing devices are useful to determine if they are damaged or poorly deployed and need to be revisited as part of the new device deployment.

Pens, Pencils, Markers, and Paper   Documentation is a critical part of wireless site surveys as well as all other areas of the network. Keeping thorough and accurate notes will allow the surveyor to document areas of importance. Even with the advanced portable technology you have in your possession, it is always a good idea to have paper and writing utensils. Markers can also be used to identify the locations where access points will be installed.

Ladders and Lifts   Ladders or lifts are required for mounting temporary access points and antennas. The height of the ladder or lift will depend on the mounting locations for the access points. Keep in mind that the surveyor may not be allowed to use a ladder or lift at certain locations or in some areas. You may have to work with the facility manager to get someone who will be able to perform this task.

Movable Cart   A movable cart or dolly to move all equipment used for the site survey will ease the burden of getting the equipment moved safely around the facility. Depending on the amount of site survey equipment and the number of access points, batteries, poles, ladders, and so on, it can be a cumbersome task to move all this around. This is especially true in larger facilities, and carts make this task much easier.

Performing a Predictive Modeling Site Survey

A predictive modeling site survey can be an accurate way to design a wireless LAN without having to spend time on-site performing a physical walkthrough and testing of the entire location. A *predictive modeling site survey* is a software-based site survey in which a floor plan (map) or drawing of the area to be surveyed is imported into the program. The program then simulates the radio frequency propagation from access points by using the attenuation properties of various structural components. The surveyor can trace over walls, windows, doors, and other elements of the physical location in order to estimate the RF attenuation and show how the RF propagates based on the environment. This type of site survey can be performed in several different ways depending on the equipment used. You can use a standalone commercial software program designed specifically for this purpose or, in some cases, manufacturers build this site survey functionality directly into a wireless LAN controller. Some manufacturers now have web-based wireless site survey programs, and the design is performed online.

This type of site survey requires the wireless engineer or surveyor to input a floor plan drawing of the facility, such as a CAD, JPEG, BMP, or other format file, directly into the software program or the controller. Then details such as the attenuation values of the facility are added. This information includes:

- Type of walls: for example, drywall, brick, or poured concrete
- Thickness of walls
- Types of windows, including glass, thickness, and coating
- Type of doors, such as hollow core, solid core, fire doors, wood, steel
- Location of certain types of furnishings, such as cubicle offices
- Height of the ceiling

One thing to keep in mind about a predictive modeling site survey is that the accuracy and final results are only as good as the information that was input into the program. Basically it equates to "garbage in, garbage out." It is essential for the surveyor to use accurate information about the location, including the attenuation value of all the building materials. Figure 11.12 shows a predictive modeling wireless LAN site survey tool.

Here are some the advantages and disadvantages of using the predictive modeling site survey process:

- Advantages
    - Limited time on-site
    - Does not require a complete physical walkthrough for testing, but a site visit is recommended.
    - Allows for easy adjustment of access point locations and settings
    - Can model different scenarios

- Disadvantages
  - Surveyor may be unfamiliar with the location's physical characteristics
  - Accuracy limited to data input within program
  - Requires extensive knowledge of physical properties of the installation area including attenuation values

FIGURE 11.12 Motorola LANPlanner showing a predictive modeling site survey

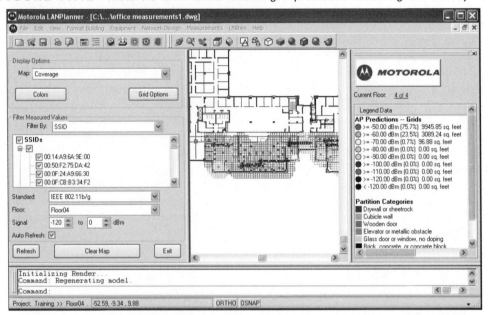

In Exercise 11.3, you will explore a predictive modeling site survey program.

EXERCISE 11.3

Installing RF3D WiFiPlanner2

In this exercise, you will install the RF3D WiFiPlanner2, a cost-effective, full 3D design tool for planning or upgrading wireless networks.

RF3D WiFiPlanner2 system requirements:

Software:

- Windows 7/Vista
- Windows XP SP2 or
- Windows 2000 SP3

- Internet Explorer 5.01 or later (for online licensing)
- Microsoft .NET Framework 4.0 (free download from Microsoft)

Hardware:

- Processor: Intel Pentium 2.0 GHz or faster
- Display: 1024 ×768 or more
- RAM:
  - 1 GB for small and medium plans (<50 APs)
  - 2 GB recommended for larger plans

The RF3D WiFiPlanner2 demo version is available from Psiber (www.psiber.com).

1. Download the RF3D Demo Version from the Psiber website. As of this writing, the name of the compressed file is RF3D2.0.1.8DemoPackage.zip.

2. Extract the files to a folder on your computer.

3. Browse to the folder containing the extracted files and open the readme.txt file to read the contents.

4. Start the setup process by executing the RF3DWifiPlanner2_Installer_Demo.exe program. Depending on the version of the Microsoft OS you are using, you may see a User Account Control dialog box. Click the Yes button to continue. The Installing RF3D WiFiPlanner2 dialog box appears.

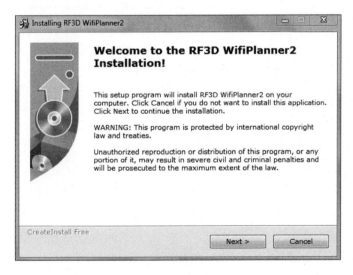

5. Click Next to start the installation process. The Destination Folder screen will appear. Click Next to accept the default location.

6. A screen that says "The RF3D WiFiPlanner2 has been successfully installed!" will appear.

7. Click Finish to complete the installation. The program will start and the RF3D WiFi-Planner2 home screen will appear. The program is now ready to use.

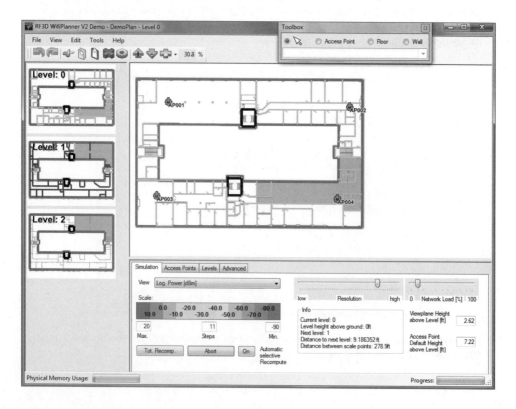

8. Click the Access Point radio button in the Toolbox dialog box.

9. Click within the floor plan image to place a few access points.

10. Click the Wall radio button in the Toolbox dialog box. Click on the drop-down box to view the options for the building material and their attenuation values.

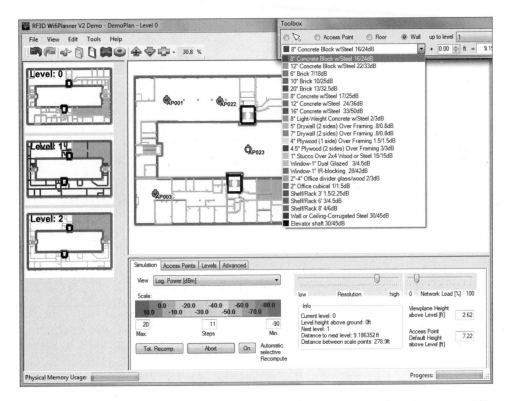

11. Click on the floor plan images on the left side of the screen to view the various RF propagation heatmaps.

12. Experiment by trying some of the various options, such as adding, moving, and deleting access points and drawing walls and doors. Notice that the heatmaps change as you make changes to the environment.

13. To see their options, click the Access Points, Levels, and Advanced tabs near the bottom of the screen.

14. Click File and Exit to close the program.

15. Uninstall the program using the Control Panel when you are finished using it. You can also purchase a license online.

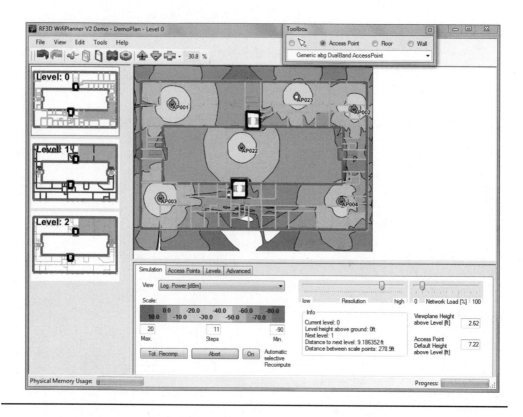

There are many different site survey programs to choose from, both commercial and freeware or shareware. You should compare the programs and determine which would be best suited for your environment based on features, cost, and capabilities. Here are many common standalone programs for predictive modeling or manual site surveys that are available on the market today:

Site survey software program	Website
AirMagnet Survey/Planner	www.airmagnet.com
AirTight Networks	www.airtightnetworks.com
Berkeley Varitronics Systems (BV Systems) Swarm	www.bvsystems.com
Ekahau Site Survey	www.Ekahau.com
Fluke Networks InterpretAir	www.flukenetworks.com
Motorola LANPlanner	www.motorola.com
Motorola SiteScanner	www.motorola.com

Site survey software program	Website
Psiber RF3D WiFiPlanner	www.psiber.com
TamoGraph Site Survey	www.tamos.com
VisiWave – AZO Technologies	www.visiwave.com
InSSIDer (freeware)	www.metageek.net
NetStumbler (donationware)	www.netstumbler.com

Some enterprise wireless client adapter utilities can also be used in manual RF wireless LAN site surveys to provide basic information such as signal strength and signal-to-noise ratio.

Internet-Based Predictive Modeling Site Survey

Some manufacturers of wireless LAN equipment have Internet or web-based predictive modeling wireless site survey programs available. This type of program is based on the assumption that you will be using their equipment in your wireless LAN deployment. The Aerohive "Wi-Fi Planning" tool is robust and free to access. You can also access free online training on its use. The process in using these tools is fairly straightforward. You need to request access or create an account on their website. You will then be able to log in and upload a floor plan map to the website program.

Site survey Internet-based	Website
Aerohive Wi-Fi Planner	www.aerohive.com/planner
Meraki WiFi Mapper	www.meraki.com

Protocol Analysis

Wireless LAN protocol analyzers are becoming a common tool, and many network administrators will have one as part of their wireless LAN toolkit. A *protocol analyzer* allows a network administrator or engineer to view all wireless frames that are traversing across the air in the hearing range of the analysis device. At one time protocol analysis was a specialty role, and without extensive training few people had the skills to perform this task. Along with the evolution of wireless LAN technology in recent years, protocol analyzers are becoming more mainstream, affordable, and easier to use. Many variations of analyzers are available in the market today. Listed here are some of the manufacturers and their products:

Manufacturer	Product	Website
AirMagnet	WiFi Analyzer	www.airmagnet.com
BV Systems	Yellowjacket	www.bvsystems.com
Motorola	AirDefense Mobile	www.airdefense.net
MetaGeek	Eye P.A.	www.metageek.net
NetScout	Sniffer	www.netscout.com
Network Instruments	Observer	www.networkinstruments.com
TamoSoft	CommView for WiFi	www.tamos.com
WildPackets	OmniPeek	www.wildpackets.com

Most wireless protocol analyzers require the use of certain network adapters and in many cases a special device driver. I recommend that you verify you have access to an adapter supported by the protocol analyzer's manufacturer.

Protocol analyzers are available in software programs that can be installed on a notebook computer and are also available in specialty dedicated handheld devices. In addition to performing protocol analysis or frame decoding, many analyzers are feature-rich, with the capability to view security information, perform legislative compliance analysis and reporting, and generate a variety of reports. Figure 11.13 shows an example of a wireless LAN protocol analyzer.

The main goals of a wireless LAN analyzer, or any protocol analyzer, are to troubleshoot network problems, gather information about security issues, and optimize the network's performance. When it comes to wireless LAN site surveys, a protocol analyzer is a valuable tool for evaluating which wireless LAN devices are currently in the same RF space where the proposed wireless LAN will be deployed. They can also be used to view the signal strength, security implementations, network name or SSID, and which channels access points and other devices are currently operating on. An analyzer will show not only access points but any wireless LAN device that may have an impact on the site survey and deployment. Some of the devices an analyzer is able to locate and identify include:

- Access points
- Ad hoc networks
- Wireless bridges
- Mesh networks
- Client devices

FIGURE 11.13   OmniPeek by WildPackets identifies nearby wireless networks.

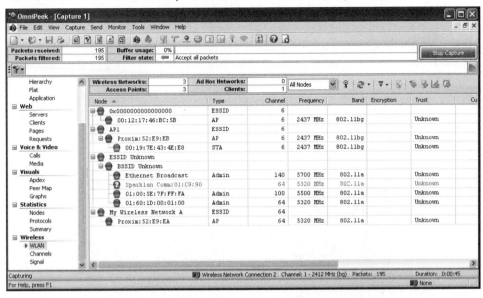

In Exercise 11.4, you will explore a protocol analyzer.

EXERCISE 11.4

Installing a Protocol Analyzer

In this exercise you will install the CommView for WiFi protocol analyzer by TamoSoft. This protocol analyzer demo program is available from the TamoSoft site at www.tamos.com. or at the download page for this book, www.sybex.com/go/cwts2e

System Requirements:

- A compatible wireless adapter. For the up-to-date list, visit www.tamos.com/products/commwifi.

- Pentium 4 or higher.

- Windows XP/2003/Vista/2008/7 (both 32- and 64-bit versions).

- 10 MB of free disk space.

Microsoft Windows 7 Professional was used for this exercise. The steps may vary slightly depending on the version of the operating system used.

1. Download the CommView for WiFi setup program from the TamoSoft website at www.tamos.com. or at the download page for this book, www.sybex.com/go/cwts2e. As of this writing, the name of the compressed file is ca6.zip.

2. Extract the files to a folder on your computer.

3. Browse to the folder containing the extracted files and open the readme.txt file to read the contents.

4. Start the setup process by executing the setup.exe program. Depending on the version of the Microsoft OS you are using, you may see a User Account Control dialog box. Click the Yes button to continue. The CommView for WiFi Setup Wizard will appear on the screen.

5. Click Next to start the installation process.

6. The license agreement will appear. Read the license agreement, select the "I accept the terms in this license agreement" radio button, and click Next. The Select License Type screen will appear.

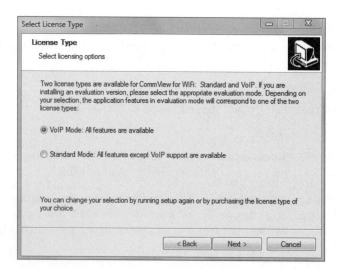

7. Click Next to continue.

8. The Destination Location screen will appear. Click Next to accept the default location.

9. The Additional Settings screen will appear. Select the appropriate language and deselect the "Launch CommView for WiFi once the installation has been completed" checkbox.

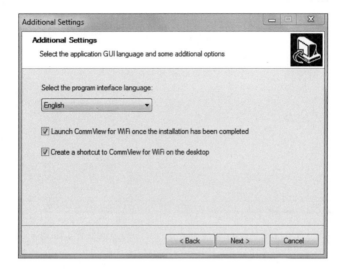

10. Click Next; the Ready To Install screen will appear. Click Next to start the installation.

11. After the installation is complete, the CommView For WiFi screen will appear. Click Finish to complete the installation.

12. Click the CommView for WiFi icon on your desktop to start the program. Depending on the version of the Microsoft OS you are using, you may see a User Account Control dialog box. Click the Yes button to continue. The CommView for Wi-Fi dialog box will appear for the driver installation.

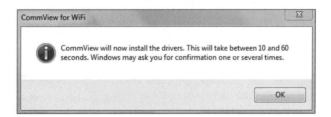

13. Click OK. Depending on the version of the Microsoft OS you are using, you may see a Windows Security dialog box appear. Click the Install button to continue if you choose to continue with the installation. The program will attempt to install the device driver for your supported wireless network adapter. After the device driver is installed the CommView for Wi-Fi program will start and the home screen will appear.

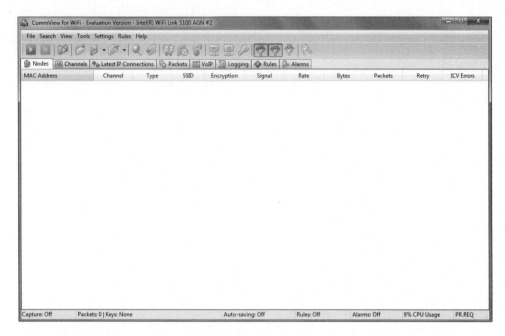

14. Click on the arrow in the upper-left corner of the program window or click the File drop-down box and select Start Capture to start a capture with the program. The Scanner dialog box will appear.

15. Select the channel you wish to view or click the Start Scanning button. Then click Capture.

    The screen will show all wireless LAN devices captured on the channel scanning.

16. Click various buttons to see the features associated with this program. When finished with the demonstration, exit the program by clicking the File drop-down menu and choosing Exit.

17. A "Thank you for trying this evaluation version" dialog box will appear. Click OK to close the program.

18. If necessary, using Device Manager, restore the original device driver for the wireless network adapter used with this demonstration.

After you have completed the exercise, you can remove the software from your computer or continue to use it for the remainder of the evaluation period. You can purchase a license online if you choose to continue using the program after the evaluation period has ended.

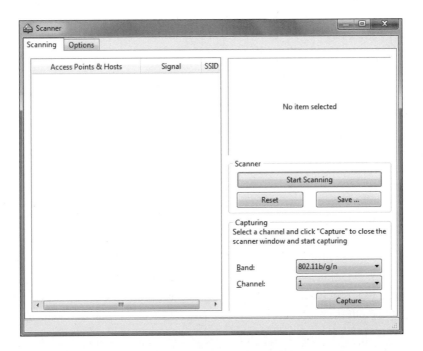

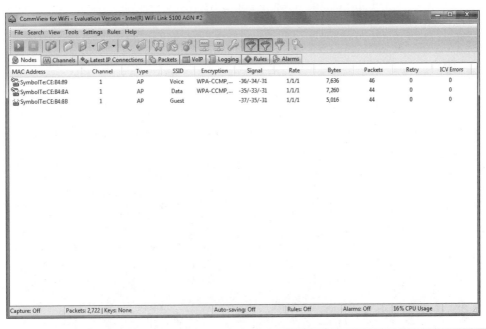

Documenting Existing Network Characteristics

Existing wireless networks can play a big role in a new wireless LAN deployment. Understanding the current location of infrastructure and other wireless LAN devices is an important part of a wireless LAN site survey. One way to see devices that are part of a wireless network is to use a protocol analyzer. Other programs will also be able to view existing wireless networks, such as NetStumbler and InSSIDer, and in some cases these programs may be adequate based on the complexity and size of the site survey. But these typically do not have the extensive feature set that many protocol analyzer packages have.

Some of the questions that you should take into consideration when performing a wireless LAN site survey are:

- What frequency range will the new wireless LAN operate in?

- Are there any existing IEEE 802.11 wireless LANs in the same RF space?

- Will all or part of the existing wireless LAN be utilized in the new deployment?

- What effect will the neighboring wireless networks have on this deployment?

Ignoring existing IEEE 802.11 wireless networks may have a significant impact on how the wireless LAN will operate and result in poor performance for the clients or devices that will be connecting.

Figure 11.14 shows an example of a software tool that will identify existing wireless networks.

FIGURE 11.14 InSSIDer by MetaGeek can identify IEEE 802.11 wireless networks.

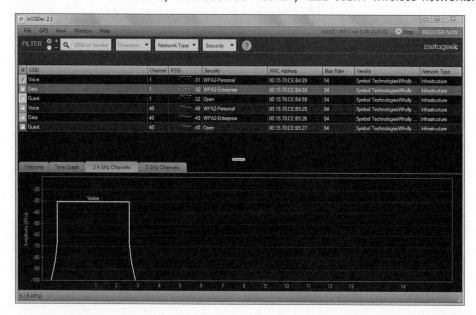

RF Coverage Requirements

As mentioned previously, one of the main goals of a wireless LAN site survey is to determine areas of RF interference and RF coverage. The details of the required coverage and capacity in any wireless network are part of the wireless LAN design, which involves determining the need, use, and business requirements of the network. This was discussed in Chapter 10. Some of the factors that need to be taken into consideration during a physical site survey are:

- Size of the physical location
- Number of users and wireless devices, including bring your own device (BYOD)
- Obstacles that may impact RF signal propagation
- Radio frequency range
- Bandwidth requirements of applications to be used
- Selected radio frequency of wireless LAN hardware

The planning process will provide some of the answers whereas a site visit and on-site testing will determine others, such as obstacles, signal propagation, and RF range.

Infrastructure Hardware Selection and Placement

In addition to identifying areas of RF coverage and interference, a site survey will determine the best locations for wireless access points and other infrastructure devices. The correct placement of these devices is important in order to allow clients and devices to benefit fully from the deployment of wireless LAN. The location of these devices is traditionally based on the following criteria:

- Desired RF coverage
- Required bandwidth
- Aesthetics requirements
- Applications both hardware and software
- RF cell overlap
- Channel reuse patterns

Mapping out the infrastructure device placement is considered part of the planning and design process. Manual, software-assisted, or predictive modeling site survey processes will help identify the proper locations based on the items mentioned above. In most cases, a preliminary visit to the location is highly recommended regardless of the size and the site survey method that will be used. Knowing the physical location will benefit the entire site survey process because it will help identify areas of concern.

Infrastructure Connectivity and Power Requirements

Even though the main objectives of this book are all about wireless networking, it is still important to understand that infrastructure devices require some sort of wired connectivity for data and electrical power. Data access will usually come by way of an Ethernet connection from a wired network infrastructure or backbone. As stated in the IEEE 802.3 Ethernet standard, the maximum length for unshielded twisted-pair Ethernet cable is 328 feet or 100 meters. This limitation may have an impact on how and where access points and other infrastructure devices are placed.

During the wireless site survey process, the surveyor will need access to wiring closets. This will allow the surveyor to evaluate and perform a survey of the wired network infrastructure as well.

Another consideration is electrical power requirements. Infrastructure devices need electrical power as well as data connectivity to operate. If the electrical power is decentralized and located at each device, an electrician will need to evaluate and determine the requirements.

An option for supplying electrical power to infrastructure devices is Power over Ethernet (PoE). This technology is now very common and is supported by all enterprise device manufacturers. A survey of the wired infrastructure and devices is almost always required to determine if the infrastructure will be capable of handling the new PoE devices that will be installed. Keep in mind that zoning and building regulations, electrical contractors, and labor union requirements may add to the overall cost of wireless LAN deployment. PoE was discussed in Chapter 3, "Wireless LAN Infrastructure Devices."

Received Signal Strength

The main objective of a wireless network is to provide access to computer network resources and services for wireless devices that are connected to the network. This means it is essential for wireless client devices to have reliable connectivity to the wireless network infrastructure. To provide this connectivity, the wireless site survey process should include testing to verify that the received signal is adequate for the application of the device.

Devices that communicate wirelessly require two-way communications in order to operate correctly. This means the receiver must be able to receive enough of the signal in order to determine the data that was sent from the transmitter. Wireless LAN client devices use what is known as the *received signal strength* to show the amount of power received from a transmission. Figure 11.15 shows a client utility that displays specifics regarding the received signal.

FIGURE 11.15   Broadcom Wireless Utility shows signal, noise, and data rate.

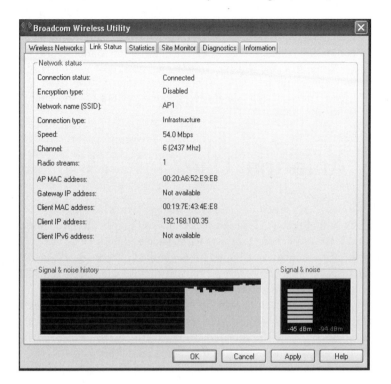

The amount of received signal strength required will be determined by the type or application of the wireless device as well as the amount of radio frequency noise in the area. RF noise consists of extraneous undesired radio signals in the area emitted by a variety of devices other than the transmitter. You should check with the device manufacturer to determine the minimum amount of received signal that is acceptable for a specific application. Some applications will require more received signal than others. For example, the manufacturer of a voice handset may recommend a minimum of −65 dBm to −67, dBm whereas a computer network card may require a minimum of −70 dBm.

The *signal-to-noise ratio* (SNR) is the difference between the received signal and the noise floor. For example, if the received signal is −65 dBm and the noise floor is −95 dBm, then the signal-to-noise ratio will be 30 dB. This value is calculated by subtracting the received signal from the noise. In this case −65 dBm − (−95 dBm) = 30 dB.

The recommended signal-to-noise ratio (SNR) for most wireless LAN systems is a minimum of 20 to 25 dB.

In IEEE 802.11 wireless LAN technology, the received signal strength indicator (RSSI) value is an arbitrary number assigned by the device manufacturer. There is no standard for this value, and it will not be comparable between devices from different manufacturers. When performing a site survey, whenever possible it is beneficial to survey with the same network adapter model that will be used in the deployment. This will provide more accurate results for the client devices using the network.

Testing Antenna Use

In Chapter 7, "Wireless LAN Antennas and Accessories," we looked at various types of antennas, including omnidirectional, semidirectional, and highly directional models. The characteristics and features of these antennas were discussed, as well as the best use for each based on a specific scenario. In Chapter 10 we looked in more detail at the most common scenarios and the antenna choices they typically dictate. Here we'll consider how best to conduct antenna testing in a wireless LAN site survey

As part of a manual site survey, it may be necessary to test different antennas to determine the best RF coverage. This usually requires the surveyor to connect and temporarily mount various types of antennas to access points in order to determine the proper radiation pattern and to verify RF coverage within the desired area. Some predictive modeling site survey programs will allow you to change different antennas so you can see how that will change the RF propagation pattern. A temporary antenna mounting example is shown in Figure 11.16.

FIGURE 11.16 Expandable light pole used for temporary mounting and testing of Yagi and Patch antennas

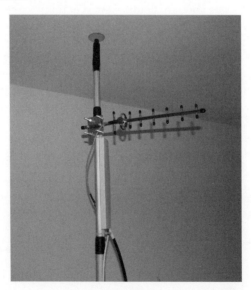

Testing Multiple Antenna Types

If different antennas will be used in the deployment, it is important for the surveyor to have several types of antennas as part of the site survey kit. Some organizations that deploy wireless networks are extremely concerned about aesthetics; they will allow only specific types of antennas to be used. For example, if access points with removable antennas are used, in many cases the only type allowed will be omnidirectional antennas that are attached directly to the access point with a gain of about 2 or 3 dBi. Other deployments may use access points in which antennas are permanently part of the access point and cannot be removed or changed.

Keep in mind that polarization of antennas must be taken into consideration during a manual site survey. Polarization of antennas for infrastructure devices is critical, and tests should mimic as closely as possible what will actually be installed. With the variety of wireless client devices that may be used in a wireless network, it is a challenge to predict the polarization of all the devices that might be used. However, it is advisable for the surveyor to take this into consideration during the site survey.

Choosing the Correct Antennas

Choosing the correct antenna to be used in a specific deployment is part of the wireless design and site survey process. Many factors play a role in determining which antenna will be best for the application. Some locations have strict requirements about the type of antenna that may be used. Therefore, the surveyor may have to work with specific antennas to ensure proper RF coverage. Take the following factors into consideration when choosing antennas:

Manufacturer's Recommendations   The manufacturer of an access point may recommend only a specific type of antenna. If this is the case, it is important to perform the site survey with the same type of antenna.

Customer Requirements   A customer may require only specific types of antennas to be used. In this case, the survey should be performed with the type of antenna required by the customer. For example, a deployment consisting of walled offices may require the use of thin access points. Usually this type of access point uses an omnidirectional internal antenna.

Environmental Conditions   The environment where the wireless network is installed may also determine the type of antenna to be used. If the location is a factory with harsh environmental conditions, that could have an impact on the type of antenna and may also call for an enclosure for the access point.

Aesthetics   Many organizations are sensitive to the type of devices that are seen by customers and clients. Therefore aesthetically pleasing antennas may be required by the customer in order to be a good fit for the location in which they will be used. Figure 11.17 shows an example of this type of antenna.

FIGURE 11.17   Ceiling mount antenna from L-com

Image provided by: www.L-com.com.

Required Coverage   The required RF coverage will also affect the choice of antenna as well as the gain of the antenna. For example, a large office area may require the use of omnidirectional antennas that are physically attached to access points. A manufacturing facility may require semidirectional antennas to cover areas of the manufacturing floor. Keep in mind that in addition to being passive bidirectional amplifiers, antennas shape the coverage by either an increase or decrease in antenna gain.

Number of Wireless Access Points   The number of access points to be installed in a location will also be a determining factor in the type of antenna to be used. An office building with a combination of walled offices and cubicles may have a dense deployment of access points with a limited number of users connecting to any particular access point. Omnidirectional antennas connected directly to the access point may be an adequate solution for this type of deployment.

Physical Geometry of Location   The attributes of the physical location will have an effect on the type of antenna to be installed and therefore should be tested during the site survey. This includes propagation of the signal and attenuation of obstacles. In the case where a building has long hallways or corridors, a Yagi antenna would be a good candidate for a solution.

Regulatory Agency and Local Codes   When selecting antennas, both indoors and outdoors, it is important to become familiar with and completely understand any radio frequency limits or regulations that apply from the governing body, regulatory agency, or any local codes that exist. In addition to the radio frequency codes, these may include, for example, height limitations and proximity to airports. Violations of any of the above may result in large fines or other penalties.

Wireless Channel Architectures

There are two common types of channel architectures available today that pertain to IEEE 802.11 wireless LAN technology. In wireless LAN technology, channel architecture is the design, layout, or channel plan in use. In the 2.4 GHz band, for example, the use of non-overlapping channels 1, 6, and 11 is a channel architecture. The CWNP program defines these two wireless LAN architectures as multiple-channel architecture (MCA) and single-channel architecture (SCA).

Multiple-Channel Architecture

Most wireless LAN deployments today use *multiple-channel architecture* (MCA). This type of installation will use access points set to different RF channels in order to avoid overlapping channel interference, as shown in Figure 11.18. A channel plan may be used with access points set to specific channels, or in many cases automatic channel selection allows the devices to choose the best channel to operate on. Until recently this is how all wireless LAN access points were deployed.

FIGURE 11.18   An example of multiple-channel architecture deployment

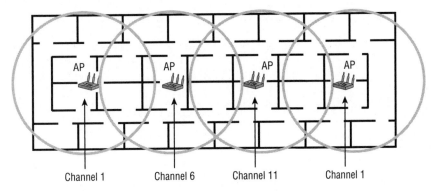

Channel 1   Channel 6   Channel 11   Channel 1

Single-Channel Architecture

Single-channel architecture (SCA) is a wireless networking technology available from only one manufacturer. SCA allows all access points to communicate on the same RF channel. The controller that the access points are connected to manages these access points and avoids co-channel interference. In single-channel deployments, not all access points are transmitting at the same time. The controller will determine which access points can transmit simultaneously based on the wireless devices that are in a specific area. A wireless LAN site survey for SCA equates to providing radio frequency coverage based on the access point placements as the wireless LAN controller manages all the radio frequency.

There are a few terms you should know with respect to single-channel architecture: stacking, spanning, and blanketing. They all refer to a means of managing coverage in a single-channel architecture.

For example, let's look at a three-story building. Each floor in the building may be assigned a channel to use; with SCA architecture this is known as *stacking*. The first floor would be set to channel 1, the second floor would be set to channel 6, and the third floor would be set to channel 11. Since all access points on the same floor are set to the same RF channel, co-channel interference or overlapping channel interference is not a significant issue because of how the SCA technology works.

Using single-channel architecture may help save some time when it comes to the site survey. It is best to follow the manufacturer's recommendations for deployment for this type of system. Figure 11.19 shows an example of single-channel architecture.

FIGURE 11.19   An example of single-channel architecture deployment

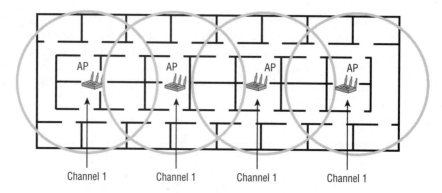

Channel 1   Channel 1   Channel 1   Channel 1

Wireless Device Installation Limitations

The installation limitations of any device that will be installed and used on the wireless network need to be evaluated. Sometimes things look great on paper, but when it comes time to actually perform the task it may be a little different. The installation limitations of various wireless devices include the following:

Wireless Access Points   An installer may run into limitations when it comes to mounting access points or other infrastructure devices. For this reason the surveyor must pay close attention to the intended location where these devices will be mounted. The type of ceiling and mounting hardware need to be considered. A wireless site survey should include a physical walkthrough evaluation of the proposed mounting locations to observe any issues that may affect where access points, bridges, or repeaters can be mounted.

Antennas   If antennas other than those that are designed to be connected directly to an access point are used, special circumstances may need to be taken into account, including:

- Mounting issues
- Cabling issues
- Aesthetics
- Height restrictions

Ethernet/PoE   As mentioned earlier in this chapter, the maximum distance an Ethernet unshielded twisted pair cable can run is 328 feet or 100 meters, per the IEEE 802.3

standard. Part of the wireless site survey process includes verification of the distance infrastructure devices will be mounted from the wiring closet to be certain they do not exceed the maximum. The capabilities of the Ethernet system must also be evaluated to verify the capacity of the wiring system. This will ensure that there is adequate connectivity for the new wireless infrastructure devices.

If PoE will be used, it is important to verify that the infrastructure will be able to support the number of devices that require DC power from the PoE infrastructure devices. If the current wired infrastructure is not PoE compliant, the infrastructure may need to be upgraded prior to wireless deployment. If an upgrade is not feasible, an alternate solution such as single port power injectors or patch panels may be required.

Local Code Restrictions   In some cases, places like elevator shafts and stairwells have become areas where local codes or regulations will not allow devices to be installed. This must be identified up front for expectation purposes, especially where voice over wireless LAN is used so the users are aware of the limitations that may be beyond the surveyor or installer's control. Also, it is important to be aware of the fact that some fire codes may require plenum rated (fire-retardant) cable and devices in certain places where wireless LANs will be installed.

Site Survey Report

The survey report should be a complete document itemizing all components of the wireless site survey. This includes the business aspects of the wireless site survey as discussed in Chapter 10 as well as the physical aspects of the wireless site survey as discussed in this chapter. This report should include but not be limited to notes, charts, graphs, photos, test results, and any other pertinent data that will have an effect on the wireless LAN deployment. Most reports will be of a custom nature based on the individual needs and requirements of the customer. Most commercial site survey application programs have built-in reporting features that can be included in the site survey report. Figure 11.20 shows a sample page from a commercial site survey application with report generation features.

The main content of the site survey report should include:

- Customer requirement analysis
- Radio frequency interference source analysis
- Radio frequency coverage analysis
- Device capacity and application analysis
- Infrastructure device placement and configuration information

As I mentioned in the earlier section "The Physical Radio Frequency Site Survey Process," the RF dynamics of many environments are constantly changing as more devices using radio frequency for communications become a part of the wireless LAN or share the same RF space. It is a wireless network engineer's responsibility to understand that site requirements may also be constantly changing. Therefore the RF site survey is becoming an ongoing process, and the site survey report can be seen as a living document. You can download a sample site survey report from Ekahau at this book's companion website: www .sybex.com/go/cwts2e.

FIGURE 11.20 Ekahau site survey built-in reporting features

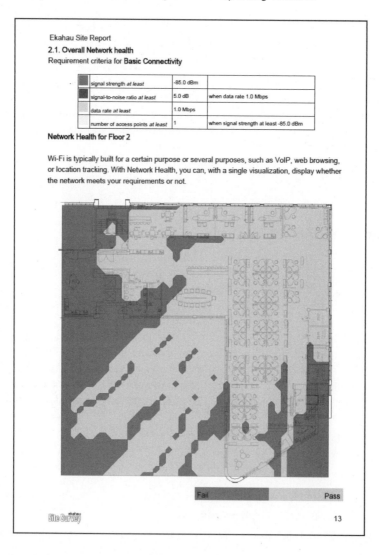

Ekahau Site Report

2.1. Overall Network health
Requirement criteria for **Basic Connectivity**

	signal strength *at least*	-85.0 dBm	
	signal-to-noise ratio *at least*	5.0 dB	when data rate 1.0 Mbps
	data rate *at least*	1.0 Mbps	
	number of access points *at least*	1	when signal strength at least -85.0 dBm

Network Health for Floor 2

Wi-Fi is typically built for a certain purpose or several purposes, such as VoIP, web browsing, or location tracking. With Network Health, you can, with a single visualization, display whether the network meets your requirements or not.

Fail   Pass

Site Survey   13

Summary

In this chapter, you learned about the wireless LAN site survey process. This process is one of the most important components of a successful wireless LAN deployment. Many areas need to be considered, including an RF spectrum analysis to determine RF interference sources that may affect the wireless deployment. Although a spectrum analysis can be considered optional, it is advisable to complete one whenever possible. Keep in mind the spectrum analysis is based on a walkthrough of a facility and recording data at an instant in time. The results of this type of spectrum analysis can change once the surveyor has left the area. Spectrum analyzers are available in various types, consisting of instrumentation devices, PC card–based, USB adapters, and now may be part of the wireless access point.

In this chapter we compared Wi-Fi and non-Wi-Fi sources of interference, both which can have an effect on the performance of a wireless LAN installation. It is important to understand the various sources of interference, such as:

- Microwave ovens
- Bluetooth devices
- Radar systems
- Devices that operate in the ISM band
- Devices that operate in the UNII band
- Other IEEE 802.11 wireless LANs

We looked at the various types of wireless site surveys that can be performed, including manual and predictive modeling. We also explored the two types of manual site surveys, passive and active. Passive surveys see all RF from access points in the hearing range of the survey device. An active survey requires an association to a specific access point. Manual site surveys typically require a walkthrough of the entire area. Predictive modeling site surveys perform a simulated analysis of the proposed space where the wireless LAN will be deployed. The accuracy of a predictive survey is dependent on the information input to the program. Both manual and predictive site surveys can be simplified by using a variety of software programs made specifically for this function.

We discussed some of the items that may be included in a survey toolkit as well as temporary mounting examples for access points and antennas. We looked at the use of a protocol analyzer in a wireless site survey and how one could be used to identify existing wireless networks in the area of concern.

Finally, you learned about both multiple-channel architecture (MCA) and single-channel architecture (SCA) and the differences between them. Best practices for hardware placement were also reviewed, including access points and antennas as well as some of the limitations that may be encountered during the wireless LAN site survey process.

Exam Essentials

Understand the need for an RF spectrum analysis and how to locate sources of interference. Know that an RF spectrum analysis will allow you to "see" RF in an area proposed for a wireless LAN. Identify different types of RF interference that can have an effect on a wireless network.

Know the differences between manual and predictive modeling site surveys. Know that a manual site survey typically requires a complete walkthrough and testing throughout the proposed area where a wireless LAN will be deployed. A predictive modeling site survey may require minimal time on-site and is a software-based analysis solution.

Identify two different types of manual site surveys. Know that manual site surveys can be passive or active and understand the differences between each.

Know how a protocol analyzer can be used as part of wireless LAN site survey. Explain how a wireless protocol analyzer can be used to help identify existing wireless networks and how they may have an impact on the site survey.

Understand the importance of identifying existing wireless networks. Know the importance of existing wireless networks and how they may have an effect on a new wireless LAN deployment.

Be familiar with the limitations of placement regarding wireless infrastructure devices. Explain some of the limitations regarding placement of wireless LAN devices, including access points, bridges, and antennas.

Understand the factors regarding proper antenna use. Identify the different uses of antennas based on the customer requirements and characteristics of the environment.

Review Questions

1. A main objective of a wireless LAN site survey is to determine _____ and _____. (Choose the best two options.)

   A. Areas of RF interference

   B. Applications to be used

   C. Access point locations

   D. Wiring closet locations

   E. Security implementations

2. You are a network engineer tasked with performing a site survey for a multiple-channel architecture (MCA) system in a three-story building. Which characteristic must be considered while performing a site survey?

   A. All omnidirectional antennas should be vertically polarized.

   B. Multiple floors require the same channel.

   C. Each floor should be treated as an individual site survey.

   D. The channel plan should take all three floors into consideration.

3. What devices, tools, or programs can be used in a manual site survey? (Choose two.)

   A. Spectrum analyzer

   B. Passive scanning utility

   C. Predictive site analyzer

   D. Association analyzer

   E. Authentication analyzer

4. The manual site survey consists of which possible methods? (Choose two.)

   A. Passive

   B. Scanning

   C. Active

   D. Spectrum

   E. Packet

5. Non-Wi-Fi interference for an 802.11g network can be caused by _____ and _____. (Choose two.)

   A. AM radios

   B. Microwave ovens

   C. 802.11b networks

   D. Cordless phones

   E. Radar systems

   F. Digital TV systems

6. You are a network consultant hired to perform a manual site survey for a small office building. The wireless network to be installed will use data and voice. For backward compatibility, the customer needs to support 2.4 GHz equipment. To provide the highest quality of service for the voice application, you recommend that the received signal strength be a minimum of _____ for a data rate of 54 mbps.

   A. −20 dBm

   B. −25 dBm

   C. −67 dBm

   D. −76 dBm

7. A type of site survey that is software-based, requires minimum time on-site, and takes into consideration the attenuation value of materials such as the type of walls and doors is _____.

   A. Active

   B. Passive

   C. Predictive

   D. Optional

8. You are performing a protocol analysis in order to determine potential interference from other wireless LANs in the immediate area of the site survey. You discover several wireless LANs that can potentially cause interference with the proposed installation. Which technology in use would *not* have an impact on the 802.11g wireless network you are surveying for?

   A. FHSS

   B. OFDM

   C. DSSS

   D. ERP-OFDM

   E. PBCC

9. You are using a wireless client adapter with a site survey utility and a notebook computer to perform a manual site survey in a very small office building. Which values are important to record to verify proper RF coverage for the location? (Choose two.)

   A. Signal strength

   B. SNR

   C. Packet retries

   D. Signal loss

   E. Propagation loss

10. You have been hired by a company to perform a manual site survey. When explaining the difference between a manual and predictive modeling site survey, you let the customer know the advantages and disadvantages of each. A manual site survey has which advantage?

   A. Speed

   B. No hardware required

   C. Accuracy

   D. Facility access not required

11. A spectrum analyzer can be used to view what?

   A. Radio frequency

   B. Wireless packets

   C. Data rates

   D. Association frames

12. You have been hired by a company to perform a wireless LAN site survey in a multitenant building. You discover numerous access points on channels 1, 6, and 11. To optimize the new deployment, what recommendation could you make to the customer? Assume that all new hardware will be purchased and backward compatibility is not required.

   A. Configure the access points to automatic channel selection for the 2.4 GHz ISM band.

   B. Configure the access points to operate in the 5 GHz band.

   C. Perform a spectrum analysis to find space in the 2.4 GHz band.

   D. Perform a predictive modeling site survey to determine which channels to use.

13. Which of the following is true of a predictive modeling survey?

   A. It takes more time than a passive survey to get accurate results.

   B. It takes less time than a passive survey to get accurate results.

   C. It finds areas of interference from neighboring wireless LANs.

   D. It helps you choose the manufacturer's equipment to be used for the wireless LAN.

14. When using a predictive modeling site survey approach, which of the following is true about manual verification?

   A. Manual verification never has to be performed.

   B. Manual verification is always required.

   C. Manual verification should be performed only at the customer's request.

   D. Manual verification should be performed, but it is not required.

15. When performing a manual site survey, choose the best way to identify areas that lack RF coverage.

   A. Mark them with tape so they can be located at a later time.

   B. Use a camera to take a photograph and document it in the report.

   C. Show the site manager the areas that lack coverage.

   D. Document on the floor plans or blueprints.

16. When a device associates to an access point during a site survey, it is performing what type of survey?

   A. Predictive

   B. Active

   C. Passive

   D. Required

17. When considering the use of antennas for wireless LAN deployment during a site survey, which antenna could be tested to verify proper coverage for a long hallway or corridor?

   A. High-gain omnidirectional

   B. Low-gain omnidirectional

   C. Parabolic dish

   D. Yagi

18. You need to perform a site survey for a small real estate office that currently has no wireless network. Which factors must be considered as part of the site survey?

   A. Spectrum analysis

   B. Packet analysis

   C. Environmental conditions

   D. Correct antenna selection

19. Co-channel interference is caused by access points on _____.

   A. Channels 1 and 1

   B. Channels 1 and 2

   C. Channels 1 and 6

   D. Channels 1, 6, and 11

20. Which guidelines are recommended when performing a manual site survey? (Choose two.)

   A. Walkthrough of location

   B. Predictive analysis

   C. Equipment purchase

   D. Client device configuration

   E. Spectrum analysis

Chapter
12

Troubleshooting and Maintaining IEEE 802.11 Wireless Local Area Networks

---

THE FOLLOWING CWTS EXAM OBJECTIVES ARE COVERED IN THIS CHAPTER:

✓ **5.2 Recognize common problems associated with wireless networks and their symptoms, and identify steps to isolate and troubleshoot the problem. Given a problem situation, interpret the symptoms and the most likely cause.**

  ▪ Throughput problems

  ▪ Connectivity problems

  ▪ RF coverage or capacity problems

  ▪ Interference from Wi-Fi or non-Wi-Fi sources

  ▪ Application performance problems

  ▪ RF performance problems, such as multipath and hidden nodes

✓ **5.3 Identify procedures to optimize wireless networks**

  ▪ Infrastructure hardware selection and placement

  ▪ Identifying, locating, and removing sources of interference.

  ▪ Client-load-balancing and infrastructure redundancy

  ▪ Analyzing infrastructure capacity and utilization

Troubleshooting and maintenance are important parts of a successful IEEE 802.11 wireless LAN deployment. Wireless networks, like most areas of technology, do require support and maintenance. The extent of this will depend on the size and complexity of the network. Troubleshooting problems is a key component in the maintenance, reliability, and operation of an IEEE 802.11 wireless network. A wireless LAN technical support engineer will encounter all the same problems that occur with regular networking as well as additional problems because this technology uses radio frequency for communication and to exchange information.

In this chapter, you will learn about common problems associated with standards-based IEEE 802.11 wireless networking, how to identify problems based on the symptoms, and how to determine whether they are global (affecting many) or isolated (affecting an individual). These problems range in complexity and magnitude and many times are associated with the following:

- Wireless connectivity

- Radio frequency received signal strength

- Wireless LAN throughput

- Wireless infrastructure and client device upgrades

Troubleshooting is not something that can be learned overnight or from reading a book. Troubleshooting is an acquired skill that requires many hours of hard work and the "school of hard knocks." This is true with any type of troubleshooting, not just computer networking. Becoming a good mechanic, for example, takes years of working with automobiles to learn how to diagnose and perform the necessary repairs.

The steps involved in troubleshooting a wireless networking problem will vary, and they depend on the complexity of the network and the environment. In this chapter, we will discuss causes and solutions associated with throughput, connectivity, signal strength, and upgrades. We will also explore procedures used for optimizing a wireless network. Some of these topics may sound familiar because they are also related to site surveys; however, you may have to make changes to accommodate physical environment conditions that have an impact on a wireless LAN installation. Finally, we will review multipath and the effect it has on an IEEE 802.11 wireless LAN, and look at different types of hidden node problems.

Identifying Wireless LAN Problems

A first step in troubleshooting wireless LAN problems is to identify whether an issue is global or isolated. Global issues often include wired and wireless infrastructure devices and components. A global problem usually involves many client devices or groups of devices. Some of the wireless devices that can be related to a global problem include:

- Wireless access points

- Wireless bridges

- Wireless LAN controllers

- Wired infrastructure devices

In addition to wireless infrastructure devices like access points, wired infrastructure components like Ethernet switches or Layer 3 routers can also be a potential source of global problems. Keep in mind that wireless client devices nearly always require a wired infrastructure in order to pass information between infrastructure devices or outside the wireless network. Devices and components that can contribute to wired infrastructure problems include:

- Ethernet cabling

- Ethernet switches

- Layer 3 routers

- Wide area network (WAN) connectivity ·

As shown in Figure 12.1, there are many components that can be the source of problems associated with wireless networking.

FIGURE 12.1 Many components, whether wired or wireless, can be the source of or contribute to wireless LAN problems.

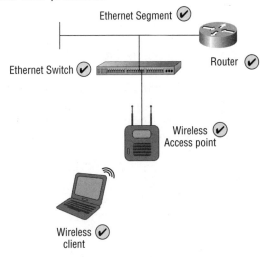

Once it has been determined whether the problem is global or isolated, appropriate steps are necessary to determine the solution. But before we look at common problems associated with IEEE 802.11 wireless networking, it is important to understand a little more detail about how wireless LAN technology functions. This includes understanding the components used to send and receive radio frequency information and is accomplished by two main components:

- Radio frequency transmitter
- Radio frequency receiver

Radio Frequency Transmitters and Receivers

As discussed in previous chapters, IEEE 802.11 wireless networks use radio frequency to send and receive data. This is possible because all wireless devices have transmitter and/or receiver capability. Unlike a television or FM radio you may have in your home, both of which are only receivers, all IEEE 802.11 wireless LAN devices have the capability to act as either a transmitter or a receiver (also known as a transceiver). The following sections explain transmitter and receiver functionality in order to provide the groundwork necessary to diagnose and resolve IEEE 802.11 wireless networking problems.

Radio Transmitter

In wireless networking, a *transmitter* combines binary digital computer data (all of the 1s and 0s) with high-frequency alternating current (AC) signals to prepare it to be sent across the air. This is known as *modulation*. The connected antenna then transforms this signal into radio waves and propagates them through the air. The frequency of the signal depends on the technology in use. With IEEE 802.11 standards-based wireless networking, there are a few select frequency ranges.

Radio Receiver

A *receiver* collects the propagated signal from the air using an antenna and reverses the process by transforming the received signal back into an alternating current signal. Through the use of a demodulation process, the digital data is recovered. The modulation/demodulation technology used depends on the wireless standard or amendment with which the device is compliant. For example, an IEEE 802.11g wireless LAN will use 64QAM (quadrature amplitude modulation) when transmitting data at 54 Mbps. Figure 12.2 illustrates this entire process. Keep in mind that wireless LAN devices are transceivers, so they have the capability of performing either task. In this figure, the access point is the transmitter and the client device is the receiver. The details of modulation technologies are beyond the scope of the CWTS exam objectives and are not covered in this book.

Figure 12.2 sums up the entire process of IEEE 802.11 wireless LAN communications discussed throughout this book and is an introduction to understanding the process of troubleshooting.

FIGURE 12.2 A wireless access point (transmitter) and wireless client device (receiver) with computer data traversing the air using radio frequency

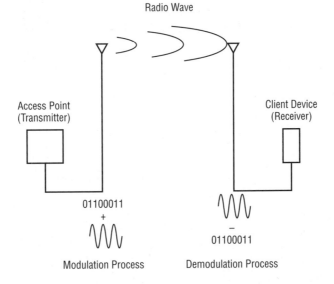

Wireless LAN Connectivity—Coverage and Capacity Problems

Many factors can cause connectivity problems in IEEE 802.11 wireless LANs. Wired computer networks use physical cabling to connect devices. This bounded medium is less likely to have connection issues unless the physical medium (cable) is damaged or broken. With wireless communications there is no bounded medium, because the air is what's used to carry the data using radio frequency.

No Wireless Connectivity

Several components of a network can cause connectivity issues with wireless networking. Keep in mind that wireless networks are not bound by a physical medium such as Ethernet cable; therefore, issues other than wiring may result in either no connectivity or intermittent connection problems.

Let's review some of the OSI model information discussed in Chapter 1, "Introduction to Computer Networking." The Physical layer provides the medium for connectivity (the air) in a wireless network and is used to carry radio frequency information that contains the computer data. This layer also includes components such as network adapter cards, which provide an interface to the wireless computer or other wireless device. Layer 1 connectivity provides the capability to transfer information that is sent between devices. Figure 12.3 illustrates the Physical layer and wireless connectivity.

FIGURE 12.3   The lower two layers of the OSI model are responsible for the operation of wireless networks. The Physical layer provides a connection between devices.

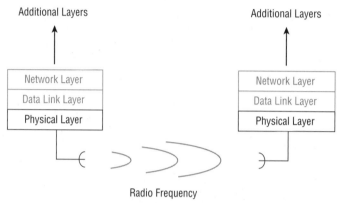

No Wireless Connectivity on the Client Side

IEEE 802.11 wireless networks require Physical layer connectivity in order to provide successful communications. This section describes some potential connectivity issues associated with client-side wireless devices. In many cases, no connectivity on the client side is an isolated issue that will not affect a large number of devices or users. Problems that can cause client-side lack of connectivity include:

- Disabled radio or wireless network adapter

- Misconfigured wireless client utility

- Microsoft Windows 7 AutoConfig service or the Windows XP Wireless Zero Configuration (WZC) not running or not configured

- Protective supplicants (wireless client device side) that can disable the radio in response to specific policy violations

A disabled radio or client adapter in a wireless client device can cause a lack of connectivity. Many devices, such as notebook computers, have physical switches or a combination of keys that can disable a radio. In many cases, a user does not even realize they turned off the physical switch for the wireless LAN radio. A disabled radio cannot provide RF communication between the client device and the wireless infrastructure, such as an access point. Figure 12.4 shows the icon for a disabled wireless adapter and the window explaining that the Microsoft WZC service is not started on a notebook computer with Microsoft Windows XP.

With the newer Microsoft Windows 7 operating system there are built-in diagnostics and troubleshooting that may help with some wireless LAN connectivity issues. Figure 12.5

shows the wireless connection dialog box as "Not connected." If you click the Troubleshoot link, Windows 7 will go through a series of steps to try to resolve the issue. In this case the Windows wireless service was not running, and Microsoft was able to determine this and identified the problem.

If a client utility is misconfigured—for example, an incorrect SSID is specified—it would cause a lack of connectivity for the wireless client device. Client utilities have the capability to specify the SSID as a parameter. If the client does not see an access point with the specified SSID, it will not be able to connect to the IEEE 802.11 wireless LAN. This feature in a client device is often set by a selection to connect to a preferred SSID only by using a specific profile.

Remember that the service set identifier (SSID) is case-sensitive and has a maximum length of 32 characters or 32 octets as defined in the IEEE 802.11 standard. Incorrect use of case in the SSID can lead to a lack of connectivity, because the SSID will not match. Uppercase and lowercase letters are different ASCII characters. This can also lead to unnecessary help desk calls. Client devices will not connect to the wireless LAN if they have an incorrect SSID specified in the wireless client utility profile. This could be unintentional (accidental) or in some cases intentional, such as for the purpose of getting around a firewall or other SSID restriction.

FIGURE 12.4   Disabled wireless LAN adapter and Microsoft Windows WZC service not running

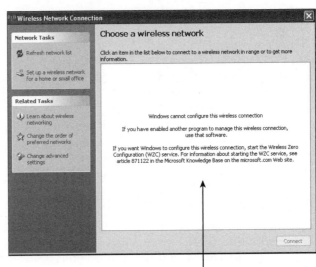

Icon showing wireless network is disabled

Microsoft WZC service not started

FIGURE 12.5   Microsoft Windows 7 wireless service not running and resolution using the built-in troubleshooting feature

View the wireless connections.

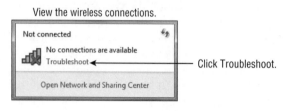

Click Troubleshoot.

Microsoft Windows will diagnose the problem and ask to repair.

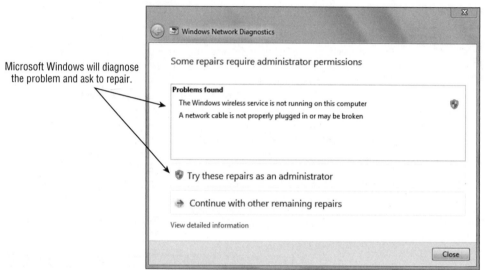

The Windows built-in wireless client utility is a popular client utility for connecting to IEEE 802.11 wireless networks. The Windows wireless service (Microsoft Windows 7 AutoConfig service or Wireless Zero Configuration [WZC] for Windows XP) runs as a service or background process in the Microsoft Windows operating systems. If this service is not running or if the client device is not configured correctly to use Windows wireless services, the wireless client device will not be able to connect to the wireless network unless a third-party client utility from the adapter manufacturer is used. Figure 12.6 illustrates some of these potential issues from a wireless client device that may cause a lack of connectivity to the wireless network infrastructure.

Other Wireless Connectivity Issues

Connectivity issues can also arise if a misconfigured client utility has incorrect wireless LAN security settings or client IP address issues. Both will prevent a wireless client device from successfully completing the connection process and will prevent the transfer of computer data. Even though the Physical layer (Layer 1) and Data Link layer (Layer 2) connection may have been successful, the Layer 3 process would not be complete, and therefore data would not be transferred.

FIGURE 12.6 Devices and components that make up a wireless LAN showing potential wireless client-side issues

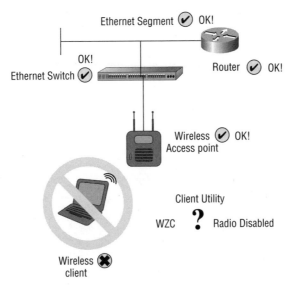

Before we discuss incorrect security settings further, it is important to have a better understanding of how an IP address (a logical address for a network interface) may have an impact on a successful connection and some of the issues associated with TCP/IP.

IP Address Connectivity Issues

Although wireless networks operate at Layer 1 and Layer 2 of the OSI model, Layer 3 and IP addressing also play a role because TCP/IP is used in most of today's computer networks. (Feel free to refer back to the discussion of the seven layers of the OSI model in Chapter 1.) Not long ago computer networks used various proprietary protocols to communicate with one another, such as Novell's IPX/SPX or Microsoft's NetBEUI. (A *protocol* is a set of rules that defines data communication between devices.) With the growth of local area networks, expanding to wide area networks and the World Wide Web (WWW) service, TCP/IP has become the standard protocol used in virtually all computer networks. Remember that Layer 3 and Layer 4 of the OSI model are responsible for addressing and routing both information and the session connection using the TCP/IP protocol. Figure 12.7 illustrates the two layers responsible for the TCP/IP protocol and the function of each.

Misconfigured IP address information can cause connectivity issues in an IEEE 802.11 wireless LAN. Most wireless networks, both SOHO and enterprise, have the capability to use *Dynamic Host Configuration Protocol* (DHCP). DHCP is a service that issues IP addresses and other TCP/IP parameters to connected computer network client devices. This service eliminates the need to manually assign logical Layer 3 IP addresses to all devices on the network. In IEEE 802.11 wireless networking, this DHCP service is provided directly from an access point, a wireless router, and a wireless LAN controller or from a server running DHCP services on the wired LAN. Many client device issues related to Layer 3 or above can cause failure to obtain a valid IP address. But this problem is often blamed on the wireless network even though a successful IEEE 802.11 authentication and association have occurred. Figure 12.8 shows an example of DHCP services using a wireless residential gateway/router.

FIGURE 12.7   Layers 3 and 4 of the OSI model are responsible for the addressing and routing of information as well as the session connection between devices.

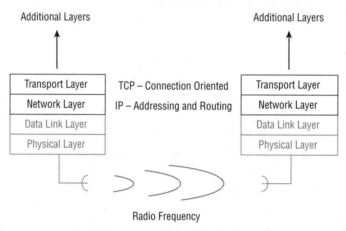

FIGURE 12.8   DHCP and IP address information from the ISP to the wireless client device

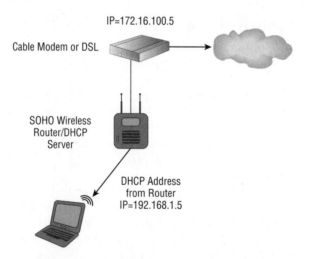

A cable or digital subscriber line (DSL) modem device connected to the ISP service will receive a DHCP address from the ISP. This modem will then issue IP addresses to wireless client devices or intermediary devices such as the IEEE 802.11 wireless router. If DHCP services are not running or are not operating correctly on the wireless router, the connected wireless client devices will not be able to obtain a valid IP address and will not be able to communicate above Layer 2.

The computer operating system in use will determine what action the client device takes if an IP address cannot be obtained from a DHCP server. Windows uses a service that became available starting way back with Windows 98 and is now available in all versions of Windows, called *Automatic Private IP Addressing (APIPA)*. APIPA is designed to provide an IP address automatically to any computer network device requesting one that is connected to a common LAN. APIPA does not require the use of a DHCP server. It also eliminates the need for users to manually set up IP addressing on all the devices. An APIPA address will be in the 169.254.X.X range. For example, a device such as a notebook computer may have an APIPA such as 169.254.100.20. If DHCP services are running on the LAN and a device cannot obtain an address from the server, or if DHCP services are not available, an APIPA will be issued. Figure 12.9 shows the ipconfig command displaying an IP address from Microsoft's APIPA.

FIGURE 12.9 Microsoft Windows APIPA

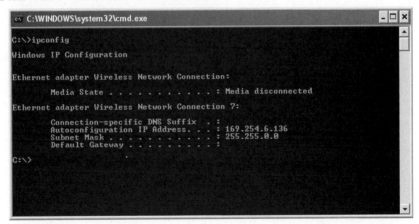

If a wireless access point or wireless router is connected to an IP subnet other than the one that uses automatic addresses, the wireless client device will require a valid IP address from the DHCP service in order to complete a network connection. If a valid IP address cannot be obtained from the DHCP service, the client will not have a valid TCP/IP connection to the access point or wireless router and instead will obtain an IP address from the 169.254.X.X range. This was much easier to identify in the Windows XP operating system. If this is the case, the wireless connection icon will show a "Limited or no connectivity" message and exclamation point, as shown in Figure 12.10.

FIGURE 12.10 Limited or no connectivity as the result of an IP address not being obtained from a DHCP server

No valid IP address received
from a DHCP server

With the newer Windows 7 operating system you would need to look a little further to make the determination, as shown in Figure 12.11.

FIGURE 12.11   Windows 7 on a notebook computer with no IP address

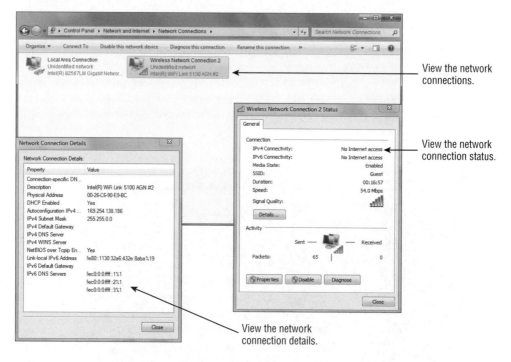

View the network connections.

View the network connection status.

View the network connection details.

 NOTE   It is always a good idea to simply restart the wireless client network adapter, which will often correct some wireless client device connectivity issues.

Wireless Security Settings

Incorrect security settings can also cause connectivity issues. Although you may get a physical Layer 2 wireless connection to the access point even with incorrect security settings on a wireless client device, you will not get a valid Layer 3 TCP/IP address from the DHCP server. For example, assume an access point is using WPA 2.0 personal mode for security. If a wireless client device has the wrong passphrase or preshared key entered, it will not complete the additional authentication that occurs after the IEEE 802.11 authentication and association process and will not have a valid Layer 3 TCP/IP address. In this case with the Windows XP operating system, the network adapter would stay in the "Acquiring network address" state; it would not be able to complete the Layer 2 connection process and would not receive a valid Layer 3 IP address. In the Windows 7 operating system the network adapter would show "Attempting to authenticate" in the network adapter status.

Figure 12.12 shows an example of a wireless network adapter with the wrong passphrase set using the Windows 7 client utility.

FIGURE 12.12   The Windows 7 wireless adapter shows "Attempting to authenticate" when a wrong WPA passphrase is entered.

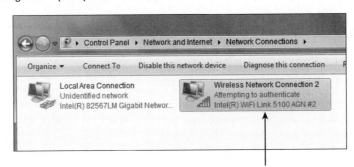

Windows 7 wireless service shows
"Attempting to authenticate" because
an incorrect passphrase was entered.

Intermittent Wireless Connectivity Problems

Intermittent problems of any type are often the most difficult to diagnose and repair. You may have had the experience of an intermittent problem with your car. For example, at a stoplight the car may start to idle roughly and stall. There is not really any rhyme or reason as to when this happens—it could be in the morning; it could be in the afternoon. You take your car to the mechanic for repair and of course the problem does not occur. Therefore the mechanic may have to keep your car for a period of time to try to duplicate the problem.

Intermittent problems with computers and networking are no different—they are difficult to diagnose if they can't be reliably reproduced. In many cases using a protocol analyzer to capture frames is invaluable. Frame traces will allow you to see what is happening between the wireless transmitter and the receiver. You learned about protocol analyzers for IEEE 802.11 wireless networks and their use in Chapter 11, "Performing an RF Wireless LAN Site Survey."

Most intermittent connectivity issues in IEEE 802.11 wireless LANs are associated with the amount of received signal strength. If nothing else has changed (for example, a security setting or any type of device upgrade) and the wireless client device was working before, there is a good possibility the problem is associated with the amount of received signal.

Understanding the Received Signal Strength

One of the main concerns associated with IEEE 802.11 wireless networking is how much of the transmitted signal is identified as usable signal by the wireless client device. As mentioned in Chapter 11, this is known as the received signal strength indicator (RSSI) value. RSSI is an arbitrary number assigned by the device manufacturer. There is no standard for this value, and it will not be comparable between devices from different manufacturers. The calculation of the RSSI value is done in a proprietary manner, and a wireless device from one manufacturer may indicate a different received signal strength than that indicated by another, even though they both are receiving the exact same signal and at the same actual signal strength. This value is a key determinant of how well the wireless LAN device will perform. How the device is used with the network will determine the required levels of signal for optimal connectivity. Two wireless LAN client devices that are equal distance from the access point may display different RSSI values. Some client software utilities display this information in signal level bars to represent the amount of signal received. The more bars, the better the signal, whereas others may show the value in dBm. Wireless network engineers and support personnel should be able to know what the bars or numbers reveal and what they do not.

The actual recommended signal strength will vary based on the manufacturer, but some general numbers do exist. For example, in the 2.4 GHz ISM band, in order to get the maximum data rate, and depending on the application (either voice or data), some manufacturers recommend a range of −65 dBm to −67 dBm of received signal strength. Keep in mind, the closer the number is to zero, the better the received signal, and −65 dBm is closer to zero than −67 dBm. Figure 12.13 shows an example of an access point with an output power of 100 mW and the wireless client receiving a fraction of that amount, or 0.000001 mW. Although the wireless client device is receiving only a fraction of the transmitted power output, it is still able to move data at the highest data rate. Amazing!

FIGURE 12.13   Wireless client device receiving a fraction of the amount of power output by the access point

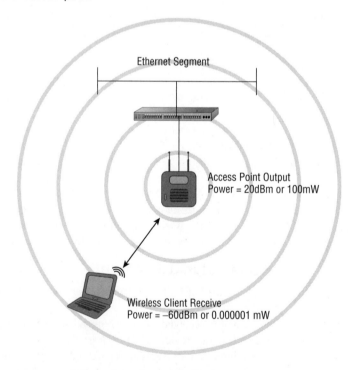

Testing the Received Signal Strength

So what does this mean? It means the lower the amount of radio frequency signal that is received by the receiver, the lower the data rate will be. As mentioned in Chapter 11, several tools are available that will allow a technical support specialist to see the received signal strength. These tools include:

- InSSIDer (free download)
- NetStumbler (free download)
- Wireless network adapter client utilities
- Spectrum analyzer utility

Any of these tools can be used to check the received signal strength by a wireless client device or at an end user's location to determine how much signal is being received, which will relate to the rate they should be transferring computer data.

Figure 12.14 shows the Windows wireless service utility with bars representing the amount of received signal strength and the current data transfer rate.

 The Windows Wireless client does not contain any specialized utilities that show signal strength or signal-to-noise ratio values. However, this utility will display bar values representing the received signal strength.

FIGURE 12.14 Representation of received signal strength (signal quality) and data rate using the Microsoft Windows wireless client utility

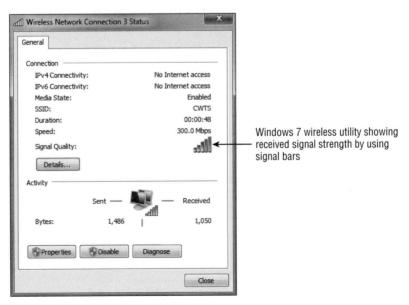

Weak, Low, or No Radio Frequency Signal

Weak, low, or no radio frequency signal is typically an indication that the wireless LAN client device is too far away from a wireless access point or it is experiencing some level of RF interference. This could also be the result of some obstruction either blocking or severely attenuating the radio frequency signal. This is most often the result of a poor or nonexistent wireless LAN site survey or significant environmental changes. You learned about performing a wireless LAN site survey in Chapter 11. In order for a client device to operate correctly, the signal will need to be strong enough to connect to an access point and maintain the connection. A wireless client device will have a difficult time distinguishing between the RF signal and the RF noise if the signal level is too close to the noise floor.

To review, the signal-to-noise ratio is the difference between the amount of received signal and the noise floor level in the area where the wireless client device is located. Chapter 11 discussed the noise floor and signal-to-noise ratio in more detail. Figure 12.15 shows the Windows 7 wireless utility and several wireless access points in the vicinity. Notice that the client device shows different received signal levels for the access points, as indicated by each one's number of bars. The Guest and CWTS SSIDs show a high received signal, but Data and Voice show only two bars, which represents lower received signal strength.

FIGURE 12.15   Microsoft Windows wireless client displays signal strength difference between nearby wireless access points.

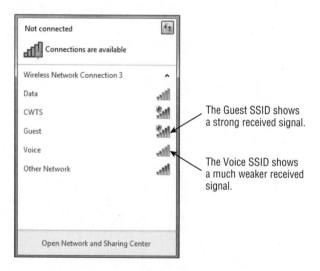

Other wireless client utilities may show a more elaborate view of the signal strength and the noise level in an area. These are represented by dBm values rather than bar levels. In addition to client utilities, third-party utilities such as NetStumbler or InSSIDer will show received signal strength or noise levels, or possibly both.

Wireless LAN Throughput

Papa User says, "Someone's been taking my throughput!" Mama User says, "Someone's been taking my throughput!" Baby User says, "Someone's been taking my throughput and that someone still is!" Sound familiar? Receiving and maintaining enough throughput can be a tough chore in today's world of IEEE 802.11 wireless networking. Users just can't seem to have enough.

It is important to understand the difference between data rate and throughput. *Throughput* is the rate at which data is being transferred. It seems there is never enough to go around. When it comes to throughput, expectations are a key factor. It is important for users to realize that the actual throughput will always be lower than the advertised data rate. For example, in an IEEE 802.11n MIMO network the maximum data rate is theoretically 600 Mbps, but the actual throughput will be between 30 and 120 Mbps, much less than half of the advertised data rate. Keep in mind that these numbers will vary based on many factors, including the environment and the IEEE 802.11n technology features that are enabled.

Maximizing throughput is part of overall network design. A well-designed wireless LAN and site survey will yield excellent results. However, several factors may affect the throughput the users are receiving, including these:

- The wireless client device distance from an access point
- The radio frequency transmit output power of an access point
- The number of wireless devices associated to the access point

The Wireless Client Device Distance from an Access Point

As we discussed earlier, as the wireless client's distance from an access point increases, the radio frequency received signal strength will decrease, thereby providing less average overall throughput. The type of wireless client device in use—computer, VoIP handset, handheld device, tablet, or barcode scanner—will determine the acceptable levels of data throughput. Most wireless client utilities will show that the expected data rate is based on the received signal strength. It is important to remember that the expected data rate is not actual throughput. Figure 12.16 illustrates this point by showing two different throughput sessions, both connected to the same access point. Session 1 is in close proximity, about 15 to 20 feet from the access point. Session 2 shows the throughput at a greater distance, about 45 feet from the access point.

FIGURE 12.16 Two FTP file transfer sessions showing the difference in throughput based on distance from an access point

FTP file transfer shows 19.4 mbps at close range to access point.

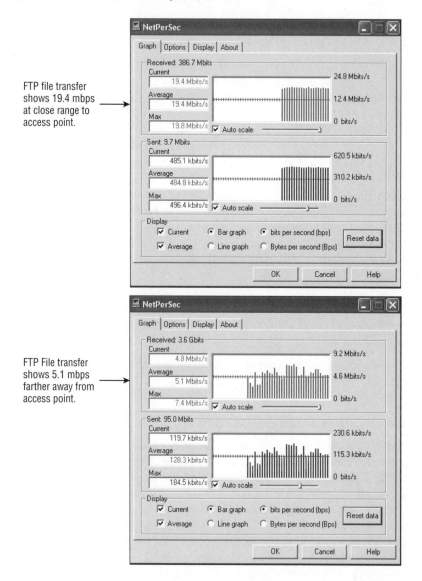

FTP File transfer shows 5.1 mbps farther away from access point.

The Radio Frequency Transmit Output Power of an Access Point

The amount of radio frequency transmit output power being sent from the wireless access point will also determine RF signal strength for the connected wireless client devices. This is because the higher the RF power, the farther an RF signal will travel or propagate. If a wireless client device is receiving a low RF signal and adding an additional access point is not an option, increasing the output power of the access point may do the trick. However, keep in mind that this needs to be evaluated closely.

If a physical wireless RF site survey is performed, I recommend that you have the access points set to less than the full available transmit output power. What the transmit output power level is set to during a site survey will depend on the engineer who performs the survey or the manufacturer recommendations. If an access point is not set to full power, it will be possible to make adjustments to compensate and potentially correct problems such as a wireless client device experiencing low throughput because of a low received signal strength value.

The Number of Wireless Devices Associated to the Access Point

Because wireless LANs use the air as a shared medium, the more wireless client devices that associate to the wireless access point, the less throughput each device will be able to receive. The type of hardware can also affect the throughput based on the number of associated users. For example, if 25 users are associated to an access point using wireless barcode scanners that typically transfer small amounts of information, they may have better performance than 5 users using bandwidth-intensive applications such as CAD/CAM on notebook computers. Load balancing of devices between access points can help limit the number of associated wireless client devices. Co-channel interference can cause the same issue, because wireless devices on the same or a close channel, associated or not, are part of the same contention domain.

Solutions to Low Wireless LAN Throughput

There are several possible solutions to low throughput problems clients may be experiencing. The appropriate solution will depend on the specific situation. If an RF site survey was performed correctly and thoroughly, additional access points should not be needed unless there have been environmental or capacity changes in the area since the original survey was performed. Solutions to low-throughput problems include the following:

- Adding more access points
- Increasing output power of access points
- Increasing antenna gain
- Enabling load-balancing solutions on access points

One or more of these solutions may help increase the throughput for users connected to a wireless network. Figure 12.17 shows a before-and-after scenario based on output power of an access point.

Of the solutions just discussed, none is always better than the others. Which solution you choose is going to depend on several factors, including the number of wireless client devices, the number of access points, budget constraints, and potential interference issues.

FIGURE 12.17   Increasing the output power of an access point will provide higher received signal strength for the client, resulting in better overall throughput.

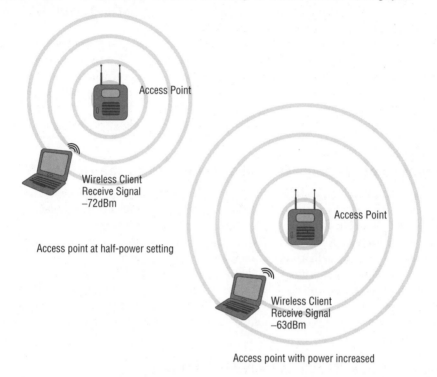

Keep in mind that increasing the output power of an access point will also increase the cell size and potentially allow for more wireless client devices to associate. This will in turn increase the load or number of associated devices on the access point and may contribute to interference in other areas. It may also lead to an increase in the hidden node problem (discussed later in this chapter). More power is not always a good choice. If the budget allows, adding more access points as needed to reduce collision domain size (RF cell) is usually a better solution.

Application Performance Problems

As you now know, IEEE 802.11 wireless networks are a major part of every computer network in all industries and homes. Many different types of applications, both software and hardware, want to take advantage of the wireless network capabilities. Therefore it is important to understand the various types of applications your IEEE 802.11 wireless LAN may use and how to prevent problems that can arise from the use of these applications. Some of the common applications that are used via wireless LANs are:

- Application servers for user software, such as word processing
- Databases
- Engineering applications, such as computer-aided design
- File servers for storing data
- Barcode scanners
- Printers
- Voice handsets

This is not a complete list, but for the most part every resource or application that is used in the wired network is also a candidate for the wireless network. Many of the problems that you experience with a wired network will be even more common on a wireless network. We have all the same potential problems as we do in a wired network, but more because it is wireless. Remember that IEEE 802.11 wireless LANs use a shared medium (the air) and are contention based, which will create both interference and capacity problems. Using the appropriate tools such as a wireless packet analyzer and radio frequency spectrum analyzer will help to identify and resolve these problems. The following sections describe how to identify and resolve these problems.

Wireless Device Software and Hardware Upgrades

Software and hardware upgrades play a role in the maintenance and support of any wireless LAN deployment. Having the latest device drivers or software client utilities will help improve performance and solve problems associated with software-related issues. Firmware also needs to be updated periodically to ensure the latest and greatest fixes, and new features are applied to the devices such as access points or wireless LAN controllers.

Client Device Software Upgrades

Upgrading the software related to wireless LAN technology has many benefits that may help resolve performance or operation issues. Technical support or network engineers should find time to stay up-to-date with the latest software versions available for the hardware in their network. This can be done by looking at the manufacturer's website or subscribing to a service that will announce changes and updates. Software upgrades for wireless networks commonly fall under three areas:

- Device drivers
- Client device adapter utilities
- Device firmware

Software upgrades on any of these components will help enhance the performance of the client devices. These upgrades can come as a fix for a problem with the software or potentially provide new features for a client device. In Chapter 4, "Wireless LAN Client

Devices," you learned about some of the software components required that will enable a client device to connect to an IEEE 802.11 wireless network. This section focuses on the process of upgrading the software associated with these devices.

Device Drivers

Device drivers are the software components that allow a hardware device to function with a computer operating system. This is accomplished by the software providing an instruction set for all devices that connect to a computer, tablet, handheld, or any other device that runs with an operating system. The following list is a sampling of the devices that will require a software device driver:

- Hard drive
- Video card
- Keyboard
- Mouse
- USB ports
- Network adapters

With wireless networking, the device driver that is of most concern is the one used for the wireless network adapter. This adapter is what allows a computer or other client device to connect to a wireless network in either infrastructure or ad hoc mode. Figure 12.18 shows an example of viewing the device driver properties for a wireless network adapter in the Windows 7 operating system.

FIGURE 12.18   Device driver information in Windows 7 for an ORiNOCO   IEEE 802.11a/b/g/n USB wireless network adapter

In addition to causing intermittent connectivity problems, device drivers may become corrupt and prevent the device from starting up correctly. They can even cause operating system startup problems. With today's sophisticated computer operating systems and features, such as plug-and-play, having to worry about the physical settings of a device is less common than it was a few years ago. Upgrading or replacing a device driver in Windows operating systems is a fairly straightforward process. Exercise 12.1 will step you through upgrading a device driver for your wireless network adapter.

EXERCISE 12.1

Upgrading a Device Driver

In this exercise, we will look at the process of upgrading a device driver for a wireless network adapter. This process is based on using the Broadcom 802.11g Network Adapter.

Downloading a Driver Package from a Website

1. With the help of a web browser, connect to the appropriate website to search for the latest version of the device driver, in this case www.broadcom.com.

2. In most cases, you will look for either a Support or Downloads link to find the location for software such as drivers. The current link on this site is Downloads & Support. Click the appropriate link.

3. You should be able to search by model number for the driver you will need. Download the correct device driver. This may come in the form of an individual file or possibly an entire software client utility program.

4. In this case, an update for this wireless adapter is not available from the adapter manufacturer, and because the adapter is integrated into a notebook computer, it will be necessary to visit the website for the computer in which this adapter is installed. It is important to note that for client devices with integrated adapters it is best to visit the website of the manufacturer for the device. In this case, the website is www.lenovo.com.

5. This website has links for support and downloads. Click the Support and Downloads links (http://support.lenovo.com/en_US/).

6. Browse for the correct driver based on the installed adapter.

7. In this case, you will have to download an entire package. This one is approximately 78 Mb. Run the downloaded program to install the latest device driver file.

Manually Upgrading a Driver

These next steps show how you would manually upgrade a device driver using an individual file:

1. Click Start and the Control Panel icon. Double-click the System icon and the System Properties dialog box appears.

2. Select the Hardware tab and then click the Device Manager button. The Device Manager dialog box appears.

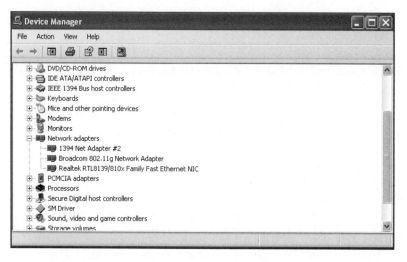

3. Expand the Network Adapters menu and double-click on the correct network adapter. The Network Adapter Properties dialog box appears.

4. Select the Driver tab and then click the Update Driver button. The Hardware Update Wizard launches. Select the Install From A List Or Specific Location (Advanced) radio button. A new screen (called Please choose your search and installation options) appears.

5. Click the Don't Search, I Will Choose The Driver To Install radio button. Then click Next.

6. Click the Have Disk button and browse to the folder where the driver is located. Select the driver, and then click Open. At the Install From Disk screen, click OK. The Select Network Adapter screen appears.

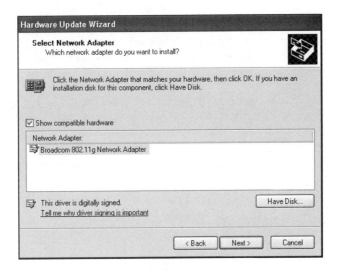

7. Click Next to continue. The update will process. Click Finish to complete the device driver upgrade.

Automatically Upgrading a Driver

Some manufacturers are making it easy to upgrade a device driver for your wireless network adapters. They do this by creating an executable program that does everything for you automatically. All you need to do is download a file from the manufacturer's website and execute the program. Everything from that point is automatic.

Client Device Adapter Utilities

Client adapter utilities may need to be upgraded occasionally. By upgrading the client adapter utility, you will usually add new features or settings to enhance the performance and function of the utility.

The Windows wireless utility is usually upgraded either from a service pack or a hotfix available from the Microsoft website.

Device Firmware

Device firmware is the instruction set that allows hardware to operate based on its design. *Firmware* is simply software that remains in memory when the power is removed. Firmware tends to be hardware oriented, but not all firmware involves the control of hardware. Many Layer 7 user interfaces and agents are implemented as firmware burned into read-only memory devices (ROMs).

Conversely, there are many examples of software directly controlling hardware. Most drivers for hardware devices are software (loaded into volatile memory only when power is present) and not firmware (always resident in static memory regardless of power). Firmware upgrades are common support tasks that need to be done periodically, either to fix issues with the way the hardware is operating or to provide new features for the hardware.

All infrastructure devices, either SOHO-grade or enterprise-grade, allow you to upgrade the firmware. In enterprise environments, firmware upgrades can be performed either manually or automatically with the aid of a wireless LAN management system software or appliance.

 Many manufacturers of enterprise-grade equipment require you to purchase a support contact or service agreement in order to download firmware for wireless infrastructure devices.

Most infrastructure devices have several options for performing upgrades. These upgrade options include:

- Hypertext Transfer Protocol (HTTP)
- Trivial File Transfer Protocol (TFTP)
- File Transfer Protocol (FTP)

Figure 12.19 shows an example of a graphical user interface (GUI) screen where a firmware update is being processed.

 Real World Scenario

Upgrading Firmware Warning

It is imperative to follow the manufacturer's instructions when performing a firmware upgrade. Failure to do so may result in the device becoming unusable or needing to be returned to the manufacturer for repair. Several items are very important when you are performing a firmware upgrade on any device:

- Always verify that you have the correct firmware file for the device to be upgraded prior to performing the upgrade.
- Always read the release notes that come with the firmware.
- Never upgrade firmware on a device that is running on battery power.
- Never power down the device while the firmware upgrade is in process.

FIGURE 12.19 Motorola AP7131 wireless access point firmware update screen

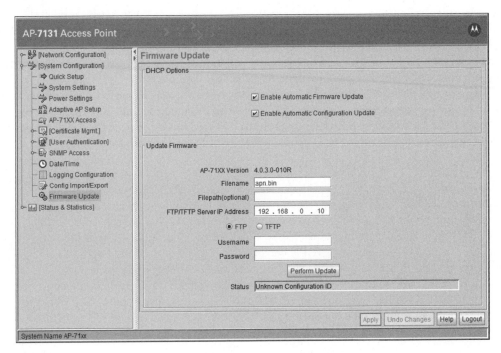

The firmware in enterprise-grade access points and wireless controllers can usually be upgraded using the command-line interface instead of the GUI if desired.

Wireless Infrastructure and Client Device Hardware Upgrades

There may be various reasons to upgrade hardware for both infrastructure and client-side devices. Hardware upgrades are a part of the ongoing maintenance process with all networking devices, including wireless LANs.

Wireless Infrastructure Devices

Upgrading wireless infrastructure devices can be an expensive and time-consuming task. Justifying these infrastructure device upgrades may require preparing reports that include performance of the wireless LAN infrastructure and client devices as well as documentation that shows how an upgrade will enhance the end-user performance and make users more productive in their job functions.

Upgrading wireless infrastructure devices such as access points can give an organization the ability to enhance the performance of the wireless network by increasing the speed or reliability of the wireless LAN. The hardware currently in use helps determine the extent of an upgrade. Some upgrades may only require the installation of a new or additional radio. Some access points are modular and provide this capability. One example of a wireless infrastructure upgrade is moving from IEEE 802.11b/g to IEEE 802.11n and MIMO technology.

Antennas

Unless the physical characteristics of the area where the wireless LAN is deployed have changed since the site survey, chances are that antennas will not need to be upgraded. If characteristics such as additional walls or types of furnishings or other physical attributes have changed, antennas with different propagation patterns or higher gain may be required. Another situation where antennas may need to be upgraded or changed is if the initial site survey was not performed thoroughly or correctly. In some cases where external antennas are used on an access point, they may have been struck and accidentally moved, changing the polarity. A physical inspection of the deployed infrastructure devices should be part of routine wireless LAN administration or support to locate and correct such issues.

Wireless Client Device Upgrades

Client device upgrades can be automatic if the technology refresh for devices has taken place. For example, if a company replaces 50 notebook computers with newer models, the new notebooks will probably have wireless LAN adapters that are capable of IEEE 802.11a/b/g/n. The capabilities of these new notebooks may be more advanced than the wireless infrastructure that is currently deployed.

Another situation where wireless client devices may need upgrading is one in which the infrastructure changes to different hardware or technology. If a company upgrades access points from IEEE 802.11b/g to IEEE 802.11n and the clients only support 802.11b/g, the client devices may need to be upgraded in order to take full advantage of the new IEEE 802.11n wireless infrastructure.

Optimizing Wireless Networks

Making changes to an IEEE 802.11 wireless LAN installation may be required in order to provide optimal performance for the devices that will be connecting. In some cases, a wireless LAN site survey is considered an ongoing process due to the dynamics of radio frequency and changes in technology. This being the case, an existing wireless LAN deployment may have to be resurveyed to provide optimal performance for the users. Here are some of the factors that you need to consider when *optimizing* a wireless LAN:

- Wireless infrastructure hardware selection and placement
- Radio frequency interference sources
- Client device load balancing
- Access point capacity and utilization
- Minimizing multipath
- Understanding hidden node problems

Wireless Infrastructure Hardware Selection and Placement

Wireless infrastructure hardware selection and placement are typically part of the wireless LAN site survey process. However, occasionally you may need to reevaluate after the wireless LAN has been installed. Although the objective of a site survey is to design the network, find locations and sources of interference, and decide on locations for infrastructure devices, you may have to make some adjustments to allow for optimal performance. These adjustments may include minor relocation of access points as well as radio frequency adjustments, including channel and output power settings. These adjustments would ensure that clients have maximum signal strength, throughput, and roaming capabilities. Applications—both hardware and software—and user requirements could also change, requiring an optimization or resurvey of the wireless network.

Identifying, Locating, and Removing Sources of Wi-Fi and Non-Wi-Fi Interference

In Chapter 11, we discussed how to identify areas of radio frequency coverage and Wi-Fi and non-Wi-Fi interference. This usually is part of the wireless LAN site survey process. The best way to identify sources of interference is with a spectrum analyzer. This could be in the form of an instrumentation device or a PC card–based spectrum analyzer designed specifically for wireless networking.

During this wireless site survey process, interference sources should be identified. However, changes to the environment may introduce new sources of RF interference. Also, keep in mind that a walkthrough spectrum analysis of an area will only record the RF it sees at that instant in time. If a new piece of equipment is introduced into an area, it may cause interference with the wireless network that would not have been present during the RF site survey spectrum analysis process. Businesses or organizations that use wireless LANs where this could be a factor include:

- Healthcare deployments
- Warehouse/retail deployments
- Manufacturing deployments
- Industrial deployments

Therefore, an ongoing spectrum analysis may be required to identify and if possible remove the sources of interference. If these new sources of interference are there to stay, it will be necessary to make appropriate adjustments for the network to operate as designed. The number one source of interference in a wireless network is other wireless devices.

Newer access points contain spectrum analysis capabilities integrated with the access point. This allows an administrator or network engineer to connect to the access point and view the radio frequency in the area without having to visit the location.

Figure 12.20 shows an example of a PC card spectrum analyzer that can be used to perform a spectrum analysis to help locate new sources of RF interference after a wireless LAN has been deployed.

FIGURE 12.20   AirMagnet Spectrum Analyzer showing devices that may cause RF interference

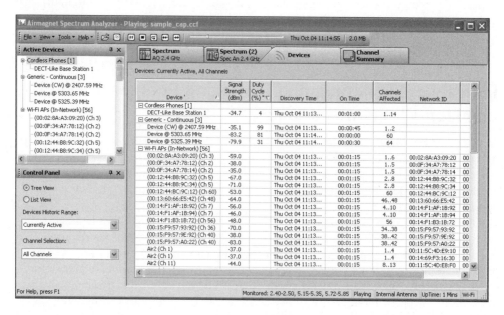

Wireless Client Device Load Balancing and Infrastructure Device Redundancy

Client *load balancing* is a mechanism that prevents wireless client devices from associating to an access point that has already reached the maximum number of client devices for optimal performance. There are a variety of ways this can be accomplished, typically proprietary to the manufacturer. Parameters for load balancing can be set on the access points, wireless LAN management software, or wireless LAN controllers. Load balancing will allow optimal use of all access points in a specific area by preventing too many devices from connecting to a single access point and overloading the access point, which in turn would cause poor performance for all associated devices. Band steering in now implemented by many wireless equipment manufacturers. Band steering will attempt to get wireless client devices that are 5 GHz capable to use the 5 GHz band rather than the 2.4 GHz band. Figure 12.21 illustrates the load-balancing process for wireless LAN access points.

FIGURE 12.21   Load balancing ensures optimal performance for connected wireless client devices.

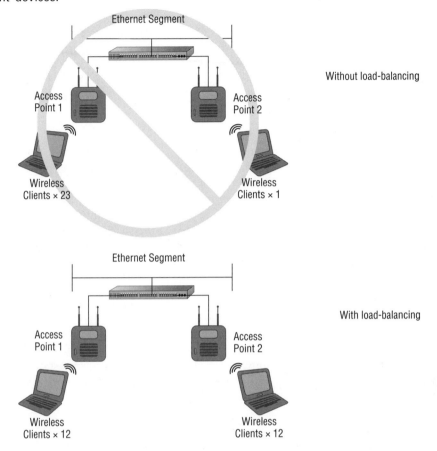

The ways in which load balancing is implemented depend on the manufacturer of the wireless LAN equipment. One solution is a settable parameter in an access point specifying a maximum number of devices allowed to connect at any one time. Once the access point has reached its capacity, a client device wanting to associate will be presented with an error message and will not be allowed to complete the process. Some manufacturers will direct the wireless client device to an access point that will be able to accept the connection rather than deny the connection.

Wireless Infrastructure Device Redundancy

Designing for wireless LAN redundancy is an important factor in most enterprise wireless LAN deployments. In both wireless LAN controller-based implementations and wireless access points implementations, it is critical to eliminate any potential single point of failure in the wireless LAN.

Wireless LAN Controller Redundancy If you were to have only a single wireless LAN controller and that controller failed, the entire wireless network would be down for any controller-based access point. Therefore a redundant controller should be considered to eliminate the single point of failure. Some manufacturers offer zero license controllers at a decent price that would only be used in the event of a wireless infrastructure controller failure. For example, if you have 24 controller-based access points, that would require 24 access point licenses. You would have two controllers of 24 ports each for a total of 48 ports. However, this would only allow for 24 licensed access points to be used at any one time. The second zero license controller would be for failover purposes only.

Autonomous or Cooperative Access Point Redundancy As you learned in Chapter 3, "Wireless LAN Infrastructure Devices," autonomous and cooperative access points do not require a wireless LAN controller to operate. An autonomous access point operates as a standalone device, requiring each device to be managed individually or with the help of wireless LAN management software solutions. Cooperative access points are cloud based and do not require the use of a wireless LAN controller, as they have their own management software that does not rely on a dedicated controller. If one of these access points was to fail, only those wireless client devices that were part of that basic service area might lose a connection to the network.

Depending on the design of the wireless LAN, the surrounding autonomous or cooperative access points may be able to increase their radio frequency power to compensate for the failed access point, allowing the wireless client devices that were connected to it to still maintain a connection to the network. This should only be a temporary solution, and the failed access point should be replaced immediately. In a single-access-point installation, if the access point did fail that would be a single point of failure. For both enterprise and SOHO deployments I recommend a spare access point be kept on hand in the event of a failure.

Analyzing Wireless Infrastructure Capacity and Utilization

It is important to have a baseline for the performance of your wireless LAN. This baseline will show the average utilization and capacity of the connected infrastructure devices at various times during the company's business hours. Continuous monitoring of the wireless network is similar to that of a wired network. Performance metrics will be needed to gauge the use of the wireless LAN and infrastructure devices and show how well the system performs. These metrics will also show areas that are lacking in performance, including bottlenecks or overutilized access points. Using these performance metrics will show which infrastructure devices need attention. This may include moving or adding access points for additional capacity or to allow for higher utilization. Changes to the environment, such as the addition of users, may justify the need for additional access points.

Using IEEE 802.11e or WMM-compliant devices combined with the corresponding QoS settings can improve overall performance in such an environment.

Radio Frequency Performance Problems: Multipath

With IEEE 802.11 a/b/g systems, poor throughput can be the result of corrupted data, which may be caused by multipath. Multipath is various radio frequency wavefronts of the same signal being received at slightly different times. Multipath is caused by RF reflections based on the physical attributes where an access point is placed. As discussed in Chapter 7, "Wireless LAN Antennas and Accessories," antenna diversity will help minimize the problems for IEEE 802.11a/b/g systems caused by multipath.

It is important to understand that although multipath is a hindrance in most IEEE 802.11a/b/g wireless LAN implementations, it is beneficial for IEEE 802.11n systems. MIMO technology used with 802.11n is designed to take advantage of multipath and increase throughput by using the effects of multipath as an advantage. You learned in Chapter 5, "Physical Layer Access Methods and Spread-Spectrum Technology," that unlike IEEE 802.11a/b/g SISO systems, IEEE 802.11n MIMO access points use multiple radios with multiple antennas. The multiple radio chains and some additional intelligence are what give 802.11n MIMO access points the capability to process reflected signals. Since MIMO works with both the 2.4 GHz ISM and 5 GHz UNII bands, a dual-band IEEE 802.11n MIMO access point will have up to six radio chains—three for 2.4 GHz and three for 5 GHz—and six antennas (one for each radio) for data rates of up to 450 Mbps. IEEE 802.11n MIMO technology allows for up to four radio chains, which in turn would provide up to 600 Mbps. However, very few manufacturers are providing four radio chains.

If you are experiencing performance problems where multipath may be a potential issue, you will need to evaluate your environment to determine if this is contributing to the issues. Using the proper diversity technology for IEEE 802.11a/b/g systems and upgrading to IEEE 802.11n systems are some of the options. If you are using diversity-capable access points with integrated antennas, spacing between antennas will be correct. If you are using external antennas, keep in mind that the spacing between the antennas should be in multiples of the wavelength for the frequency that is used. Check with the manufacturer of the access points you are using to determine how diversity antennas should be installed.

Radio Frequency Performance Problems: Hidden Node

More IEEE 802.11 wireless LAN installations experience hidden node problems than you would probably imagine. *Hidden node* is the result of wireless client devices connected to an access point and not able to "hear" each other prior to starting a transmission. This will result in collisions at the access point and the loss of data. As discussed in Chapter 5, the CSMA/CA process is designed to avoid collisions between devices sharing the same medium. This process includes the use of a mechanism called *clear channel assessment (CCA)*. CCA detects radio frequency energy from other IEEE 802.11 wireless client devices in the same RF space and understands that the medium is busy. Therefore, that wireless client device will not attempt to transmit until it detects the medium is clear.

Three causes of the hidden node problem are:

- Hidden node obstacle (obstructions)

- Hidden node distance (signal strength)

- Hidden node technology (signaling methods)

There are both hardware solutions and software solutions to resolving hidden node problems. The following sections describe hidden node problems and solutions in more detail.

Hidden Node Obstacle or Obstruction

Hidden node obstacle is caused by two or more client devices connecting to an access point in which access point–to–client device RF communication is clear but client device–to–client device RF communication is blocked. Figure 12.22 illustrates an example of hidden node obstacle.

FIGURE 12.22 · Hidden node caused by an obstacle or obstruction

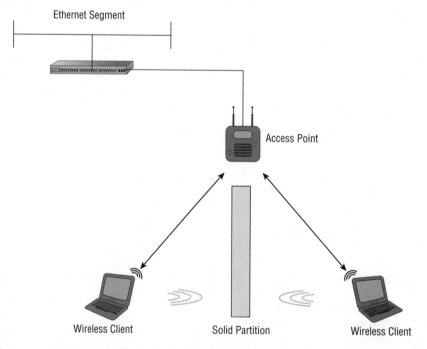

There are several physical solutions to the hidden node obstacle problem. Any of these solutions should allow for the correct RF communication between access points and wireless client devices. Some of the physical solutions to hidden node obstacle include the following:

Removing the Obstacle   Removing any obstacles that do not allow for clear RF communication between client devices will solve the hidden node problem. However, in most cases removing obstacles is not feasible. If this type of hidden node problem does exist, a good reason could be poor network design or an inadequate wireless LAN site survey.

Adding Access Points   Adding more access points will help resolve issues caused by hidden node where obstacles are a factor. This will allow for clear RF communication between access points and clients as well as between client devices connected to the same access point. Keep in mind, however, that careful planning must be taken into consideration when adding access points. Too many access points or access points that are too close together can cause other problems, like co-channel interference. This is where a software-assisted wireless LAN site survey program comes in handy. You can use a program like this to perform a passive RF site survey by walking the area and gathering RF data. We discussed various manufacturers of software-assisted wireless LAN site survey programs and you learned about passive site surveys in Chapter 11.

Hidden Node Distance or Signal Strength

With hidden node distance or hidden node signal strength problems, client device–to–client device RF communication cannot occur because the client devices are too far apart and not in radio range of each other. However, access point–to–client device RF communication does take place, because these devices are within radio range. Figure 12.23 shows an example of hidden node distance.

FIGURE 12.23   Hidden node as a result of distance between wireless client devices

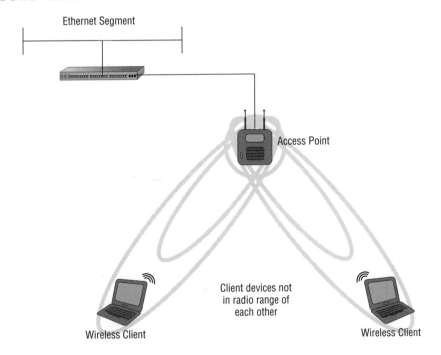

Just as in hidden node obstacle problems, physical solutions exist for the hidden node distance problem. These physical solutions provide adequate RF communication for access point–to–wireless client device and for client device–to–client device. The following are examples of solutions for hidden node distance:

Increasing the Output Power of Client Devices   Increasing the RF output power of client devices allows them a larger radio range. This enables wireless client devices to hear each other and therefore know whether the medium is clear prior to starting a transmission.

Moving the Client Devices Closer Together   Moving the wireless client devices closer together allows the devices to hear the RF communication between each other. In this situation they are able to detect whether the RF medium is clear prior to starting a transmission to the access point. This is a better solution than increasing the transmit power.

Adding More Access Points   Another solution would be to add more access points. This would allow wireless client devices to detect a clear RF medium. More access points mean a smaller basic service area for each access point on the network. This allows client devices to associate with an access point in close range, and they will not be required to contend for the same access point with other wireless devices at a distance. As mentioned earlier, adding more access points needs to be carefully considered.

Hidden Node Physical Layer Technology or Signaling Methods

Hidden node technology problems occur when access points experience excessive collisions because of different spread spectrum or Physical layer communication technologies that are sharing the same RF medium. This can happen when, for example, an access point has to share transmissions between 802.11b (HR/DSSS) and 802.11g (ERP-OFDM) client devices. Figure 12.24 illustrates the hidden node problem due to different Physical layer technologies in use.

In this example the only physical solution to the hidden node technology problem is to allow either 802.11b or 802.11g devices to communicate with the access point but not both. In most cases, this is not a realistic solution, because allowing only one of the technologies to communicate with an access point prevents devices using the other technology from using the network. In other words, giving only 802.11g (ERP-OFDM) devices the capability to use the network would prevent 802.11b (HR/DSSS) devices from using the network resources, or vice versa.

IEEE 802.11n, the newest communication amendment and now part of the IEEE 802.11-2012 standard, consists of four protection modes. The same potential hidden node problems will exist with 802.11n devices but even more so because 802.11n is capable of operating in both the 2.4 GHz ISM and 5 GHz UNII bands. These modes are known as High Throughput (HT) protection modes and are a set of rules client devices and access points will use for backward compatibility. You learned in Chapter 8, "Wireless LAN Terminology and Technology," that these modes are constantly changing based on the RF environment and associated wireless client devices.

FIGURE 12.24   Hidden node based on technology types such as HR/DSSS and ERP-OFDM

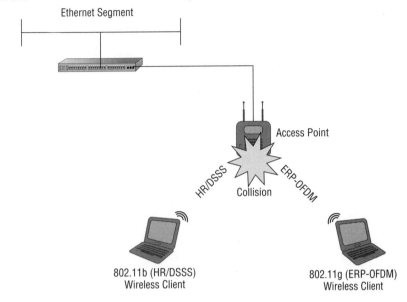

The Software Solution to Hidden Node Problems

There is a software configuration solution for all of the hidden node problems just described. This software configuration solution is known as a process called request to send (RTS), clear to send (CTS), or RTS/CTS. The RTS/CTS process allows devices to reserve the medium for a specified period of time, enabling a device to complete a frame exchange and avoid collisions. RTS/CTS frames are also used with protection mechanisms to allow different IEEE 802.11a/b/g/n technologies to interoperate. You learned about protection mechanisms and Mixed Mode in Chapter 8. The RTS/CTS process was discussed briefly in Chapter 8 but is beyond the scope of the CWTS exam objectives and therefore is not discussed in detail.

Summary

In this chapter, we looked at troubleshooting and maintenance concerns that may involve wireless networking. This included identifying wireless LAN problems as both global (many) and isolated (individual) and the process for troubleshooting these problems. Global problems may include wireless infrastructure devices, such as:

- Wireless access points
- Wireless bridges
- Wireless LAN controllers

Isolated problems usually include a single wireless LAN client device or computer that could be experiencing connectivity or data transfer issues. We also looked at basic radio frequency communications using a transmitter and receiver and how these devices operate in a wireless LAN. We examined connectivity issues, including no connectivity or weak connectivity, and the problems that can be associated with connectivity issues. No connectivity on the client side could be something as simple as a network adapter not enabled or could be related to something more in depth, including:

- Upper layer TCP/IP issues
- Security configurations

In this chapter, you learned about received signal strength and the difference between a strong signal and a weak signal, as well as some of the reasons why a wireless client device may experience weak or no signal. Throughput is another area we explored that involves client-side performance. We discussed some of the factors that could cause low throughput and how to solve these issues.

Upgrading software is another area that needs be taken into consideration with wireless LANs from the client side, upgrading device drivers or client software utilities, as well as the infrastructure side, which includes upgrading firmware. All of these areas are important parts of wireless LAN maintenance and support.

Finally, you saw how to optimize wireless networks and some of the areas that should be considered for this optimization, which may include making the necessary adjustments from the original wireless site survey. These adjustments could be a result of changes to the environment such as walls, doors, windows, or other physical attributes of the location. Other important factors include client load balancing, multipath, and hidden node issues.

Exam Essentials

Identify the symptoms of common problems associated with wireless networks.   Know what may cause poor throughput or connectivity issues with wireless LAN infrastructure and client devices.

Understand common troubleshooting techniques and procedures to help resolve issues associated with wireless networking.   Know how to isolate problems based on symptoms and be able to correct using a suitable resolution.

Be familiar with the effects radio frequency issues may have on a wireless network. Understand received signal strength and how a weak signal could affect the performance of a wireless client device.

Understand the importance of correct placement of wireless infrastructure devices.   Know that load balancing prevents infrastructure devices from becoming overloaded by allowing too many client associations. Understand the hidden node problems, what can cause them, and their solutions. Be familiar with what causes multipath, the solutions for it, and where it can be beneficial.

Review Questions

1. In wireless networking, multipath is the result of what RF behavior?

    A. Refraction

    B. Diffraction

    C. Absorption

    D. Reflection

2. A wireless client device is showing a low receive signal strength value. What option could improve this situation?

    A. Upgrade the client device

    B. Add another access point

    C. Upgrade firmware on devices

    D. Eliminate multipath

3. You recently installed an IEEE 802.11g wireless network in a small office. One of the employees has been complaining of poor performance and mentioned her notebook computer runs very slowly because of the access point it connects to. What could cause this notebook computer to be performing poorly?

    A. The new 5.8 GHz cordless telephone in her office is interfering with the IEEE 802.11g wireless LAN.

    B. The access point is located at the opposite side of the building from the user's office separated by several walls.

    C. A media access control (MAC) filter is enabled on the notebook computer, causing excessive retries.

    D. You recently rolled out a new version of the access point's firmware to enable new features that became available.

4. The RF signal strength seen by a wireless client device from an IEEE 802.11n access point can be improved by _____.

    A. Increasing the output power on the access point

    B. Enabling load balancing

    C. Upgrading the ISP service

    D. Enabling WPA 2.0 on both the access point and the client

5. You are a help desk technician providing support for a wireless network. A user calls and complains he cannot access the Internet. The user tells you he has good signal strength, but the network connection states "acquiring network address" and the IP address is all zeros. What could cause this problem?

    A. The client device has a static IP address.

    B. The client has an 802.11a network adapter.

    C. There is an incorrect WPA passphrase on the client device.

    D. A computer virus has infected the client device.

6. You provide consulting services for various companies and receive a call from one of your clients that their notebook computers suddenly started experiencing slow data transfers from the wireless LAN. This company is located in a multitenant building. What could cause a sudden change in performance for the notebook computers?

    A. A firmware upgrade was recently performed on the access point.

    B. The access point for a new tenant in the building is set to the same RF channel.

    C. The access point shows a low received signal strength.

    D. Someone activated the diversity antennas on the access point.

7. What can solve a hidden node problem caused by an obstacle or obstruction on an IEEE 802.11g wireless network?

    A. Adding another access point

    B. Setting the access point to Mixed Mode

    C. Increasing the distance between the access point and the clients

    D. Adjusting the received signal strength on the client

8. Weak signal strength would have an impact on what device?

    A. Infrastructure device

    B. Client device

    C. Multipath device

    D. Transmitter device

9. An incorrect passphrase set on a client device will result in a different preshared key that is generated for a device using WPA 2.0 as a security solution. What will be the result of a mismatched passphrase between the client device and an access point?

    A. Association is established and terminated and no valid IP address

    B. Invalid association and valid IP address

    C. A deauthentication

    D. A disassociation

10. The throughput of a wireless LAN can be affected by _____ or _____.

    A. Distance from access point, IP address

    B. Distance from access point, MAC address

    C. Distance from access point, output power of access point

    D. Distance from access point, output power of client device

11. The device driver of a wireless network adapter card is _____.

    A. Required

    B. Optional

    C. Used with security

    D. Another name for SSID

12. What is a valid solution to a hidden node problem caused by different technology types?

    A. Mixed Mode technology

    B. Additional access point

    C. Increasing output power

    D. Removing an obstacle

13. You are a network administrator and receive a call from a user stating that she cannot access the wireless LAN. The office contains 50 other users, and nobody else is complaining about the network. What could be a potential problem that would keep this user from connecting to the access point?

    A. The connection to the Internet has been terminated.

    B. The access point needs to be upgraded.

    C. Incorrect firmware was installed on the access point.

    D. The wireless client device has a corrupt device driver.

14. Lack of RF connectivity on a wireless client could be caused by which layer of the OSI model?

    A. Layer 1

    B. Layer 3

    C. Layer 4

    D. Layer 7

15. What address would be considered a Windows Automatic Private IP Address, assigned when no DHCP server is available on the LAN?

    A. 192.168.0.1

    B. 172.168.0.1

    C. 169.254.0.1

    D. 10.1.0.1

16. Weak or no signal at a wireless client device can be the result of _____.

    A. Distance from an access point

    B. Distance from other client devices

    C. Distance from the wiring closet

    D. Distance from Ethernet switch

17. What does the signal-to-noise ratio represent?

    A. The difference between output power and noise floor

    B. The difference between received signal and noise floor

    C. The difference between access point output power and received client power

    D. The difference between client output power and noise generated by the access point

18. What can IEEE 802.11n MIMO technology use to provide higher throughput to wireless client devices that 802.11g cannot?

    A. Hidden node

    B. Received signal strength

    C. DHCP

    D. Multipath

19. The throughput of a wireless LAN client device can be increased by performing which task?

    A. Adding access points

    B. Upgrading the client software to full-duplex mode

    C. Increasing the RF noise

    D. Hiding the SSID

20. The received signal strength of a wireless client could be increased by _____.

    A. Upgrading the wireless client device

    B. Enabling load-balancing features on the access point

    C. Increasing the gain of the antenna on the access point

    D. Installing the Microsoft Wireless Zero Configuration utility

Appendix
A

Answers to Review Questions

Chapter 1: Introduction to Computer Networking

1. C, E. Wireless LAN technology operates at Layers 1 (Physical) and 2 (Data Link) of the OSI model. The Session layer opens, closes, and manages sessions between end-user application processes. The Network layer is responsible for addressing and routing functions of data and the Application layer is the interface to the user.

2. C. The bus topology is also known as a high-speed linear bus and was commonly used with early IEEE 802.3 networks. The ring topology is rarely used with LANs today but is still widely used by Internet service providers (ISPs) for high-speed, resilient backhaul connections over fiber-optic links. In a mesh topology, each device in the mesh network has one or more connections to other devices. The star topology consists of multiple devices connected by a central connection device and is the most commonly used method of connecting devices on a LAN today.

3. B. The Physical layer is the lowest layer in the OSI model and consists of bit-level data streams and computer network hardware connecting the devices together. The Data Link layer is responsible for organizing bit-level data for communication between devices on a network, and the Network layer is responsible for addressing and routing functions of data.

4. B. The logical address is an IP address. The Layer 2 address is the hardware address or physical address on the network adapter.

5. D. The Data Link layer is responsible for organizing bit-level data for communication between devices on a network and detecting and correcting Physical layer errors. The Physical layer consists of bit-level data streams and computer network hardware connecting the devices together. The Application layer provides an interface to the user and the Transport layer is for connection-oriented and connectionless communications.

6. B. The Network layer is responsible for addressing and routing of information. The Physical layer consists of bit-level data streams and computer network hardware connecting the devices together. The Transport layer is for connection-oriented and connectionless communications. The Application layer provides an interface to the user, and the Transport layer is for connection-oriented and connectionless communications.

7. C. Encapsulation allows for Application layer data communication between two stations using lower layers as a support system. Logical addressing is the Layer 3 or IP

address, and physical addressing is the hardware or media access control address. Data encryption scrambles the data, and point-to-point communications may be used to connect LANs together.

8. A. The ring topology may use a token passing access method. The bus topology is also known as a high-speed linear bus and was commonly used with early IEEE 802.3 networks. A mesh topology is where each device in the mesh network has one or more connections to other devices. The star topology consists of multiple devices connected by a central connection device and is the most commonly used method of connecting devices on a LAN today.

9. D. The Application layer provides an interface to the user. The Physical layer consists of bit-level data streams and computer network hardware connecting the devices together. The Data Link layer is responsible for organizing bit-level data for communication between devices on a network. The Presentation layer provides delivery and formatting of information for processing and display, and the Transport layer is for connection-oriented and connectionless communications.

10. A. The media access control (MAC) address is a unique address of the network adapter. The logical address is an IP address as well as the Layer 3 address.

11. D. Encapsulation is adding header and trailer information to a frame. The MAC address is a physical address assigned by the device manufacturer. The IP address is the logical address assigned to a device and the topology is the physical arrangement of devices in a network.

12. A, C. Peer communication is a logical or "horizontal" link between devices. The vertical link would be equivalent to the encapsulation between layers. The physical link is related to addressing.

13. B. The physical address of a network device determines the actual hardware address and is used to identify the source and destination of a frame. The routing information is part of the logical addressing process as well as the logical location.

14. B. The Data Link layer of the OSI model is responsible for compiling or packaging bits into frames. The Physical layer allows frames to be sent and received across a medium. The Transport layer is responsible for connection-oriented or connectionless protocols. The Network layer is responsible for addressing and routing of frames, and the Application layer is the interface to the user.

15. D. TCP is a connection-oriented protocol that uses acknowledgments. UDP is a connectionless protocol and does not guarantee delivery. IP is used for addressing and routing. ARP is used to resolve physical addresses to logical addresses, and HTTP is an Application layer protocol.

16. A. Internet Protocol (IP) is used for addressing and routing functions and operates at Layer 3 of the OSI model. TCP is a connection-oriented delivery protocol. UDP is a connectionless protocol and ARP is used to resolve addresses.

17. D. The Network layer is responsible for translating physical (MAC) addresses into logical (IP) addresses. The Application layer is where the user sends data to the OSI

model. The Session layer opens, closes, and manages sessions, and the Transport layer is for session delivery.

18. B. The Data Link layer consists of two sublayers the LLC and the MAC. The PLCP and PMD are at the Physical layer. TCP and UDP are Transport layer protocols, and HTTP and FTP are Application layer protocols.

19. A. The Physical layer of the OSI model is used to deliver data to a destination. The Data Link layer is responsible for organizing bit-level data for communication between devices on a network. The Network layer is responsible for addressing and routing functions of data, and the Transport layer is responsible for connections.

20. B. 192.168.200.1 is a valid logical IP address. 255.255.0.0 is an example of a subnet mask. Both AB.CD.EF12.34.56 and 12.34.56.AB.CD.EF would represent physical (MAC) addresses.

Chapter 2: Introduction to Wireless Local Area Networking

1. A, C. Semidirectional and highly directional antennas are used for point-to-point links. Omnidirectional antennas are for point-to-multipoint links. Long-range omnidirectional antennas do not exist.

2. B. Point-to-multipoint links typically have three or more connections.

3. A. MIMO can use reflections due to the multiple radio chain technology. Reflections will hurt throughput in a single-input single-output (SISO) technology. Antenna diversity is used with SISO to lessen the effects of reflections.

4. D. The FCC is the local regulatory authority responsible for frequency regulation in the United States. ETSI is a European standards organization responsible for producing standards for information and communications technologies. The Wi-Fi Alliance is an interoperability testing organization. The IEEE creates standards, and WPA is a pre-802.11 certification by the Wi-Fi Alliance.

5. D. 802.11g LANs operate in the 2.4–2.5 GHz ISM band. 900 MHz is not used with 802.11 wireless LANs, and 5 GHz is for 802.11a.

6. E. The Wi-Fi Alliance performs interoperability testing and verifies standards compliance. The FCC is the local regulatory authority responsible for frequency regulation in the United States. ETSI is a European standards organization responsible for producing standards for information and communications technologies. The IEEE creates standards and WPA2 is a post-802.11 certification by the Wi-Fi Alliance.

7. C. 802.11a uses OFDM; ERP-OFDM is used in 802.11g. HR/DSSS is used with 802.11b and 802.11g. FHSS is specified in the original IEEE 802.11 standard and is obsolete with respect to modern Wi-Fi technology.

8. A, C, D. 802.11b can use 1, 2, 5.5, and 11 Mbps. 6 and 12 Mbps are OFDM data rates and used in 802.11a and 802.11g networks.

9. A, D. 802.11g is backward compatible with DSSS and HR/DSSS. 802.11a OFDM operates in the 5 GHz band. ERP-OFDM is not used in 802.11a technology and 802.3af is for Power over Ethernet (PoE).

10. A. The UNII-3 band can be used indoors or outdoors, but was at one time mainly used outdoors only.

11. C. 802.11i addresses security. 802.11e addresses quality of service. DSSS is a PHY technology defined in the IEEE 802.11 standard, and MIMO (multiple-input multiple-output) is used with IEEE 802.11n technology.

12. B. Wi-Fi Alliance performs interoperability testing for IEEE 802.11 wireless LAN standards-based equipment. The IEEE creates standards. The FCC is the local regulatory authority responsible for frequency regulation in the United States and ETSI is a European standards organization responsible for producing standards for information and communications technologies.

13. D. WMM is a proactive Wi-Fi Alliance certification for quality of service. WPA and WPA are certifications that address wireless security. IEEE 802.11w is for protection of management frames and IEEE 802.11r is for Fast Transition (FT); neither currently has an associated Wi-Fi Alliance certification.

14. A. Wi-Fi Protected Setup was designed with SOHO users in mind. Enterprise organizations use IEEE 802.11i, WPA, and WPA2 certifications. The FCC is the local regulatory authority responsible for frequency regulation in the United States.

15. C, D. 802.11g can use ERP-OFDM and DSSS. The 802.11 standard specifies FHSS for 1 and 2 Mbps. OFDM is used with 802.11a devices, and MIMO (multiple-input multiple-output) is used with 802.11n technology.

16. D. WPA was designed as a pre-802.11i solution for wireless security and intended as an interim certification. 802.11a, 802.11n, and 802.11g are communication amendments, and the 802.11e amendment specifies quality of service.

17. D. 802.11e is a specific function amendment addressing quality of service. 802.11e can operate in either the 5 GHz frequency range or the 2.4 GHz frequency range. 802.11i addresses wireless security, and 802.11e can work with all data rates, not only 1, 2, 5.5, and 11 Mbps.

18. D. The IEEE requires 6, 12, and 24 Mbps for 802.11a. The data rates of 1, 2, 5.5, and 11 Mbps are for the 2.4 GHz band and 802.11b/g.

19. B, C. WPA 2.0 Personal and WPS are both designed with the small business in mind. Wired Equivalent Privacy (WEP) is legacy and not secure. Wi-Fi Multimedia (WMM) addresses QoS, and WPA 2.0 enterprise is designed for larger organizations.

20. A, D. WPA 2.0 consists of personal mode using passphrase and enterprise mode using 802.1X/EAP.

Chapter 3: Wireless LAN Infrastructure Devices

1. D. In computer terminology, half duplex is two-way communication but only one way at a time. Full duplex is two-way communication in both directions simultaneously.

2. C. An autonomous access point is an intelligent, self-contained network infrastructure device. Controller-based access points (also called thin access points) work with a wireless LAN controller.

3. A, C, D. SOHO access points typically are managed from a web browser and do not have a command-line interface feature.

4. B, C. Bridges must be on the same RF channel and have the same SSID in order to communicate.

5. B, E. Wireless repeaters do extend the cell size and will potentially allow more users to connect. However, using a wireless repeater will decrease throughput.

6. B. A wireless LAN controller uses centralized administration, not distributed administration.

7. B. Many SOHO access points use 15 dBm or 32 mW for transmit output power.

8. C. The PoE standard specifies 48 VDC as nominal. The range is 32–57 VDC.

9. A. A midspan device will inject power into an Ethernet cable. Endpoint power is delivered directly from a switch or controller.

10. B. Layer 2 is the Data Link layer. A MAC address is a unique identifier of the network card.

11. A, C. SOHO uses HTTP or HTTPS for configuration. Enterprise can also use CLI. SMTP is Simple Mail Transfer Protocol.

12. B. An administrator should avoid configuring an access point from the wireless side of the network unless absolutely necessary.

13. A, B. Depending on the specific function, APs operate at Layers 1 and 2. Repeaters function only at Layer 1.

14. A, B, D. Enterprise access points have adjustable output power. Power sourcing equipment is used in PoE to deliver power and data.

15. B. VLANs involve logical separation of ports.

16. A. A controller-based access point connected to a port on the switch is considered to have direct connectivity.

17. B. PSE delivers DC power, not RF power. The DC power is delivered to an end device such as an access point.

18. C. Root access point is the default mode in most cases. An access point in root access point mode allows users to connect to the network.

19. A, B. Single-port and multiport injectors combine power and data in the same cable. Endpoint power is out of the switch port. There is no such thing as an endspan injector.

20. A, B, D. Wireless LAN controllers may contain many advanced features, including centralized administration, captive portal, and built-in RADIUS services. Network Address Translation (NAT) and IP routing are common in wireless residential gateway devices.

Chapter 4: Wireless LAN Client Devices

1. D. Wireless USB adapters connect through a USB port in the notebook computer. Virtually all notebook computers have USB ports. PCI adapters are for desktop computers and are installed in an available PCI slot on the motherboard. Wireless Full Mini-PCIe is internal to the device and would require an available interface.

2. C. PCMCIA cards are available in three types. The only difference in the three types is the thickness. PCI adapters are for desktop computers and are installed in an available PCI slot on the motherboard. A wireless Half Mini-PCIe adapter is internal to the device and would require an available interface. An ISA (Industry Standard Architecture) adapter is a legacy interface within a desktop computer.

3. D. SDIO cards were originally designed for flash memory storage used in digital cameras and evolved to be used in IEEE 802.11 wireless devices. PCMCIA cards are available in three types. The only difference in the three types is the thickness. Because of advancements in technology, both PCMCIA and SD cards are not as popular as they once were but are still available and used. PCI adapters are for desktop computers and are installed in an available PCI slot on the motherboard. An ISA (Industry Standard Architecture) adapter is a legacy interface within a desktop computer. It would be rare to find a wireless adapter that uses an ISA slot.

4. B. A PCI adapter is a 32-bit card that requires a PCI slot inside a desktop computer. Notebook computers, tablets, and barcode scanners with either have built-in wireless capabilities or a port for an external adapter interface.

5. A. A device driver is a required component for the USB adapter to function with the operating system. Installation of client utility software may not be required when using a device that has the wireless client software built into the operating system, such as

Windows Wireless Zero Configuration. Profiles are typically a function of the client utility software.

6. B. A USB 2.0 adapter can be connected to a port on the outside of the computer. Mini-PCI and Half Mini-PCIe are typically used in notebook computers and other portable devices and require some level of disassembly. PCMCIA cards can be used in desktop computers only if an internal PCI adapter is used, which will require disassembly of the computer case.

7. C. A wireless workgroup bridge will connect an Ethernet segment to a wireless network, allowing all devices connected to a common physical layer boundary to communicate wirelessly. A PCMCIA adapter is used to connect a single device such as a notebook computer to a wireless network. An Ethernet bridge is not a wireless device and is used to connect Ethernet segments together.

8. B. The original USB standard was intended to replace serial and parallel ports. A PCI slot is found on the motherboard in a desktop computer. ISA (Industry Standard Architecture) and EISA (Extended ISA Industry Standard Architecture) are also slots that would be found on some motherboards in a desktop computer.

9. A. Serial communication transmits one bit at a time. Parallel transmits several bits at a time.

10. D. A Mini-PCI card may be mounted in a notebook computer motherboard by removing a panel within the computer case. PCI adapters are for desktop computers and are installed in an available PCI slot on the motherboard, and PCMCIA, another name for PC Card, will use an external interface on a notebook computer.

11. B. Most manufacturers recommend installing a wireless USB adapter at a specific point. This is usually after the device driver has been copied to the computer during the setup process. In order for the device drivers to load, the device must be powered on. USB and other adapters are capable of being inserted or removed while a device is powered on. Technical support should be called when the user has exhausted other troubleshooting steps.

12. D. Enterprise client utilities have more advanced features such as a site survey utility. PCI configuration includes physical settings prior to installation. A spectrum analyzer is a separate product used to analyze radio frequency. A setup wizard can be a part of a SOHO-grade adapter as well as an enterprise-grade adapter.

13. B. Device drivers are required in order for the network adapter to communicate with the operating system. A Mini-PCI card is used to allow a device to connect to a network. Third-party and enterprise client utilities are used to configure the settings for a wireless network.

14. B. A wireless workgroup bridge acting as a client device will connect an Ethernet segment to an access point, eliminating the need to install wireless adapters in all of the Ethernet computers. Two wireless NICs connected together are said to be in ad hoc mode. Connecting two client bridges together is not common practice.

15. C. CF cards are identical in length and width. Type I is 3.3mm thick and Type II is 5.0mm thick. The other characteristics are the same.

16. B, C. PCMCIA and USB devices connect to an interface external to the computer and no disassembly is required. PCI, PCIe, and Mini-PCI adapters all require some type of disassembly of the computer device.

17. D. Pocket PCs have SD slots and can use SDIO cards. Access points may use a Mini-PCI adapter or have a surface mount radio adapter. Not all desktop computers or notebook computers have interfaces for SDIO cards.

18. A. Wireless network cards require device drivers in order for the card to work with the computer operating system. The OS (operating system) uses the device driver to control the wireless network adapter or other device that is installed.

19. A. Wireless workgroup bridges can connect wired devices to a wireless LAN. Mini-PCI adapter and PCI adapters are standalone adapters used to connect a device to a wireless network.

20. B. Device drivers are required. A third-party client utility is optional because manufacturers usually include a utility with the device.

Chapter 5: Physical Layer Access Methods and Spread-Spectrum Technology

1.   C. IEEE wireless LAN devices use half-duplex communication. Half duplex is defined as two-way communication only one way at a time. Wired LANs can use full-duplex communication, which is two-way communication transmitting in both directions simultaneously. An example of duplex is to combine signals from two different frequencies into a single transmitter/receiver.

2.   A. DSSS devices operate in the 2.4 to 2.5 GHz ISM band. OFDM devices operate in the 5 GHz UNII bands.

3.   B. 802.11g operates in the 2.4 GHz ISM band. A total of three access points can be co-located before interference becomes an issue.

4.   D. The IEEE 802.11n amendment devices use MIMO, multiple radio chains, and antennas to operate. 802.11a/b/g devices use one radio and may use multiple antennas for diversity.

5.   C. Spread-spectrum technology sends data over many subcarrier frequencies. Narrowband technology is not used in IEEE-based WLANs but is used in other technology such as radio and TV. Wireless broadband provides high-speed wireless data communications and wireless Internet over a wide area network. Wideband uses a wide range of frequencies, and spectral mask refers to the signal levels of the radio frequency.

6.   B, C, D. 802.11b channels need to be separated by at least five channels or 25 MHz to be considered non-overlapping. Channels 3 and 9 are separated by six channels, channels 6 and 11 are separated by five channels, and channels 2 and 8 are separated by six channels. All of these scenarios are nonoverlapping channels.

7. A. CSMA/CA uses collision avoidance. CSMA/CD uses collision detection. CSMA/CR and CSMA/DSSS do not exist.

8. A. DSSS uses Barker code at 1 Mbps. CCK is for 5.5 Mbps. DBPSK and DQPSK are modulation technologies, not spreading codes.

9. A. FM radio stations use narrowband communication, which is high power and narrow frequency. WLANs use spread-spectrum technology, which is low power and wide frequency.

10. C. HR/DSSS channels are 22 MHz wide. FHSS uses 1 MHz subcarrier frequencies. OFDM, ERP-OFDM, and HT-OFDM use 20 MHz–wide channels, and HT-OFDM can also use 40 MHz–wide channels.

11. D. Bluetooth operates in the 2.4 GHz band and can cause interference with WLAN devices that operate in the 2.4 GHz band, including FHSS, DSSS, and OFDM.

12. D. OFDM can be used in 802.11a or ERP-OFDM used in 802.11g and supports a maximum data rate of 54 Mbps. 802.11b supports a maximum data rate of 11 Mbps. OFDM is also used with 802.11n devices, but the maximum data rate is 600 Mbps.

13. C. HT-OFDM used in IEEE 802.11n can support data rates as high as 600 Mbps, OFDM used in 802.11a supports a maximum of 54 Mbps, and DSSS supports a maximum of 11 Mbps. Ethernet is not a wireless LAN technology.

14. C, D. IEEE 802.11a wireless LANs operate in the 5 GHz UNII bands. 802.11b/g wireless LANs operate in the 2.4 GHz ISM band.

15. D. IEEE 802.11b and 802.11g amendments are interoperable. 802.11a networks operate in the 5 GHz UNII bands and therefore are incompatible with 802.11b/g.

16. D. 802.11b operates in the 2.4 GHz ISM band and will allow for 14 channels. The channels that can be used will depend on where the wireless LAN is located.

17. A. FHSS uses 1 MHz subcarrier frequencies to transfer data. 20 MHz–wide, 22 MHz–wide, and 40 MHz–wide channels are used with other technologies.

18. B. The IEEE 802.11b amendment specifies data rates of 5.5 and 11 Mbps. OFDM allows for data rates up to 54 Mbps and is used in IEEE 802.11a and IEEE 802.11g amendments.

19. C. FHSS constantly changes frequencies while transmitting data in a WLAN. DSSS, OFDM, and MIMO use set channels and frequencies to transmit data.

20. D. Current MIMO technology allows for up to 600 Mbps. One way this is accomplished is by using multipath as a benefit rather than a hindrance.

Chapter 6: Radio Frequency Fundamentals for Wireless LAN Technology

1. B. Frequency is the number of times in one second a signal will oscillate. Phase is a shift, amplitude is height, and wavelength is a distance of one cycle.

2. B. There are three nonoverlapping channels in the 2.4 GHz ISM band. Fourteen channels are available in this band. The locale will determine which channels can be used.

3. A, D. The capacity of an access point is dependent upon the number of users and software applications in use. Too many users or too many bandwidth-intensive applications will affect the performance of an access point.

4. A. Refraction occurs when a signal changes speed and bends when passing between mediums of different densities. Reflection bounces off a smooth surface, diffraction will pass around, and scattering bounces off an uneven surface.

5. A, E. RF communications require a transmitter and receiver. A transistor is an electronic component; a reactor does not exist in RF.

6. B, D. dB and dBi are relative measures of RF power. mW, dBm, and watt are absolute measures of RF power.

7. C. 25 MHz is required for channels to be considered nonoverlapping. 22 MHz is the width of a DSSS channel in the 2.4 GHz band.

8. A, C. Amplitude and phase are two characteristics of RF signals. Reflection, refraction, and diffraction are behaviors of RF.

9. B. UNII-1 band has four channels available for wireless LAN use. Eleven channels are available in UNII-2e.

10. A, C. Watt and mW are absolute measures of RF power. dB, dBi, and dBd are relative measures.

11. A. Channels 1 and 6 are nonoverlapping. There must be a separation of five channels (with the exception of channel 14) to be considered nonoverlapping in the 2.4 GHz band.

12. D. There are 14 channels available in the unlicensed 2.4 GHz ISM band. The channels used are determined by the locale.

13. B. The wavelength is the measurement of one complete cycle of an RF signal. The higher the frequency, the shorter the wavelength; therefore the shorter the range.

Frequency is the number of times an RF signal cycles in one second, amplitude is the height from a 2D perspective, and phase is a shift.

14. B. Obstacles affect the RF line of sight. Phase and amplitude are characteristics of radio frequency, and interference affects the throughput.

15. C. There are 11 channels available for wireless LAN use in the unlicensed UNII-2e band. The other three 5 GHz bands have only 4 channels each.

16. A. The amplitude is the height of an RF signal. The length of one cycle is the wavelength, the shift is phase, and width is not a valid factor.

17. B. A 2.4 GHz 802.11b signal is 22 MHz wide. 25 MHz is the distance required to be considered nonoverlapping.

18. B. An RF signal that bounces off a smooth surface is reflection. Refraction passes through, diffraction bends around, and scattering bounces off a non-smooth surface.

19. C. The gain of an antenna is measured in dBi. This is a relative measure of power.

20. D. Diffraction passes or bends around an obstacle. Reflection bounces off a smooth surface, refraction passes through, and scattering bounces off an uneven surface.

Chapter 7: Wireless LAN Antennas and Accessories

1. D. Omnidirectional antennas have a horizontal beamwidth of 360°. The vertical beamwidth will vary depending on the design and the gain of the antenna.

2. B. Antennas provide an increase in RF coverage by means of passive gain. Passive gain occurs when isotropic RF energy is focused into a specific radiation pattern. Active gain requires the use of an external power source.

3. A. Horizontal beamwidth is parallel to the earth's surface. This is based on how the E-field propagates away from the antenna element. Vertical beamwidth is perpendicular to the earth's surface.

4. B. An access point will require two antennas for diversity. Although there are two antennas, a single input/single output access point will have only one radio. The access point provides additional intelligence to determine which antenna to use. Other wireless LAN technologies such as MIMO may use up to three antennas.

5. B. A lightning arrestor is used to protect a wireless LAN system from an indirect lightning strike. A lightning arrestor will direct transient or induced electrical current to earth ground as a result of a lightning strike.

6. A. Active gain requires an external power source to provide an increase in signal strength. An amplifier is an example of a device that uses active gain. Antennas provide an increase in strength by using passive gain.

7. C. Highly directional antennas are typically used for long-range point-to-point connectivity such as bridge links. Omnidirectional antennas are used as part of an access point system or to provide point-to-multipoint links.

8. A. Changing the orientation of a device or antenna will change the polarization and affect the received signal strength. The signal strength may either increase or decrease depending on how the polarization is changed from the original position. Wavelength, frequency, and phase are characteristics of radio frequency.

9. A, C. Point-to-point and point-to-multipoint both require RF line of sight to be able to effectively communicate. Scattering, reflection, and refraction are all behaviors of radio frequency.

10. C, D. Cables and connectors can both result in a loss of signal strength. Antennas and amplifiers will add gain or increase signal strength. A transmitter outputs an absolute amount of power.

11. A. 802.11g access points require only one antenna to function. Systems that support antenna diversity will require two antennas to correctly operate.

12. B. 802.11a access points can use antenna diversity. Gain and polarization are considered RF concepts.

13. A. The image is an example of an omnidirectional antenna. This type of antenna provides a horizontal radiation pattern of 360°.

14. C. Of the answers listed, wind would have the biggest impact on a wireless LAN system. Rain, snow, and hail do not affect wireless transmission unless the weather is severe. In this case, the collection of the elements may have an impact on the wireless LAN signal transmitted or received.

15. C. Wireless LAN cables and devices are rated at 50 ohms impedance. Cable and satellite television is rated at 75 ohms.

16. B. The curvature of the earth or earth bulge will have an impact on a wireless LAN signal after seven miles. If the signal needs to travel farther than seven miles, the antenna will have to be installed in a higher location.

17. A. A patch antenna provides semidirectional coverage. The amount of coverage depends on the design and gain of the antenna. Parabolic dishes are highly directional.

18. B. The horizontal RF radiation pattern of an antenna is displayed using an azimuth chart. The vertical radiation pattern is displayed using an elevation chart.

19. D. It is recommended that at least 60 percent of the Fresnel zone be free of obstruction in order to have acceptable RF line of sight. Up to 40 percent of the zone can be

blocked by obstructions without affecting the signal.

20. D. The image shows a patch antenna. This is an example of a semidirectional antenna.

Chapter 8: Wireless LAN Terminology and Technology

1. B. When a wireless client device listens for beacons, it is performing passive scanning. Active scanning is sending a probe request. Authentication occurs after the probe phase. Power save puts the device into a low power state.

2. C. Dynamic rate switching (also called dynamic rate selection) allows a wireless LAN device to adjust data rates based on received signal. Dynamic frequency selection allows an access point to pick the best frequency to operate on based on the environment. Transmit power control automatically adjusts output power. Transmit save mode does not exist.

3. A. An IBSS uses no access points and is also known as peer-to-peer or ad hoc networking. A BSS uses one access point.

4. C. If a device is part of a peer-to-peer network, it will connect to other like devices. An access point and a wireless switch are both infrastructure networking devices and will be part of either a BSS or ESS.

5. A. The data rate decreases as a wireless LAN device moves away from an access point. The data rates increase as a wireless LAN device moves closer to one access point. The output power does not change based on the location of the wireless device in the radio range of the access point.

6. C. An SSID can be a maximum of 32 characters or octets and is also case-sensitive.

7. B. If access points on the same distribution system are set with different SSIDs, the client will lose the connection while roaming unless all SSIDs are set in the client utility. The channel is set by the access point, and the BSSID is the MAC address of the AP radio.

8. C. Beacons are management frames and are used in the passive scanning process. Data frames carry data payload. Control frames reserve the medium and acknowledgment frames. Detail frames do not exist.

9. B. The client must authenticate to an access point before it can associate. After both authentication and association have been completed, the client is considered to be part of the BSS.

10. B. Moving throughout a location will cause a wireless client to roam from one access point to another. As part of the roaming process a client sometimes, but not always, needs to reauthenticate.

11. A, C. To successfully set up an ad hoc network, a user must know two parameters, the SSID and the RF channel it will be operating on. The BSSID is automatically generated in an ad hoc network. The BSSID is the MAC address of an AP radio; APs are not used in ad hoc networks. Protection mode does not apply to the situation.

12. B. Open system authentication uses two frames. The first frame is from the client to the access point and the second frame is from the access point back to the client. Shared-key authentication uses four frames.

13. C. In 802.11b/g and mixed mode environments, throughput will be affected because of ERP protection mechanisms. Association and authentication are normal frames exchanged and do not affect throughput. HT protection mode is for 802.11n.

14. A, C. An SSID has a maximum of 32 characters or octets. SSIDs are case-sensitive.

15. A. The BSSID is the unique identifying MAC address of the access point's radio network adapter. This abbreviation is sometimes confused with SSID, which is a network name. The other MAC addresses are used in networking but are not representative of the BSSID.

16. B. A network consisting only of wireless client stations is an independent basic service set (IBSS). Other terms for this type of network are ad hoc and peer-to-peer. Infrastructure mode is a term used with a basic service set that consists of a single access point. Active and passive are scanning modes in which wireless devices connect to a wireless network.

17. C. Because the computer is almost always plugged into an AC power source, it is unnecessary to have the device perform power save functions. Therefore, active mode (sometimes referred to as continuous aware mode) is the best solution. Power save mode would work well for a device that is on battery power and will help extend the battery life. Association and passive mode do not pertain to power save.

18. A. An ESS as stated in the IEEE 802.11 standard is one or more interconnected basic service sets.

19. A. In order for a wireless client to become part of a basic service set, it must first authenticate and then associate. The distribution system is the network in which the access point is physically connected. Deauthentication and reauthentication occur when a client either logs off the wireless network or roams from one access point to another.

20. B. A BSS consists of only one access point. An IBSS has zero access points. A network with more than one access point would be considered an ESS.

Chapter 9: Wireless LAN Security Basics

1. A, B, E. WPA Enterprise, WEP, and MAC filtering can all be used to secure 802.11g access points. PPTP is a Layer 3 security solution that consists of both tunneling and encryption. IPSec is a Layer 3 VPN encryption mechanism. RBAC stands for role-based access control and is a way of restricting access to only authorized users.

2. A, D. Both WPA2 Personal and WEP support shared key security. The WPA2 Personal algorithm creates a 256-bit preshared key. WEP can be used with either a 64-bit or 128-bit key. WPA Enterprise, 802.1X/EAP, and WPA2 Enterprise all use the 802.1X process to create a key.

3. B. Passphrases are available for use with WPA Personal or WPA2 Personal and are capable of providing strong security for the home user or small office. SSID hiding should not be used for security because the SSID can be found in frames other than beacons. MAC filters are considered legacy solutions and can be easily spoofed using software downloadable from the Internet. 128-bit WEP can be cracked very quickly using software tools and is therefore not a secure solution.

4. C. In order to provide a secure connection between your laptop and the office network, a Layer 3 VPN solution would be the best choice. Passphrase security and WEP require the access point to be configured, and this typically is not the case in public hotspots. 802.1X/EAP is enterprise security and usually does not apply to public hotspots.

5. E. A MAC filter is used to allow or deny wireless LAN devices access to a wireless access point. WEP is a shared key security mechanism. IPSec encryption is used in Layer 3 VPNs. SSIDs are used as a network name and for segmentation. RF is radio frequency and cannot be filtered.

6. B. The IEEE 802.11i amendment to the standard requires CCMP. WEP is an optional authentication/encryption method defined in the original 802.11 standard. TKIP is an enhancement to WEP that usually was accomplished as a firmware upgrade for older equipment. PPTP and VPN are both Layer 3 solutions and not defined in any IEEE wireless amendment.

7. A. A virtual private network (VPN) is a Layer 3 security solution that provides secure data transmissions over a public network infrastructure such as the Internet. WEP, WPA, 802.1X/EAP, and WPA 2.0 are examples of Layer 2 security solutions.

8. A. Role-based access control (RBAC) is a method used to restrict access only to authorized users. RBAC assigns permissions or access to roles to which users can be added.

9. D. If the SSID of the wireless network is hidden, the user will need knowledge of the SSID in order to connect to the wireless network. The SSID broadcast is only enabled

on an access point or wireless LAN controller/switch. Getting a new password from the help desk will not provide the SSID of the wireless network. Entering a username and password is user-based authentication.

10. C. RADIUS is a centralized authentication method that is used to authenticate users on a wireless network. Accessing a corporate network using a modem is a function of remote access services. Making a call to the help desk and requesting a username and password is not a function of RADIUS; however, the help desk may be able to assist with username and password issues. Requesting remote assistance to help solve a software problem is more related to troubleshooting and not a function of RADIUS.

11. B. In 802.1X networking, the access point is also known as the authenticator. The supplicant is another term for the client device, and the authentication server can be a RADIUS or AAA authentication source.

12. D. The original IEEE 802.11 standard identifies WEP as an optional authentication/encryption method. AES and CCMP are addressed in the 802.11i amendment to the standard. TKIP is an enhancement to WEP and not identified in the original standard. EAP provides an authentication process and is used with 802.1X networks.

13. A, C. Higher levels of RF activity reported by an intrusion prevention system could mean an RF denial-of-service attack is underway or could be misrepresented as interference from a neighboring access point. A deauthentication storm or encryption attack would be identified differently in a wireless intrusion prevention system. A misconfigured client workstation would not cause this type of alert.

14. C. WEP is typically 64-bit or 128-bit encryption. The numbers 5, 10, 13, and 26 are related to the number of characters the WEP key can be in either ASCII or hexadecimal.

15. B. PIN-based security is mandatory for both access points and client devices in order to be considered Wi-Fi Protected Setup certified. PBC or push-button configuration is optional for client devices in this certification. WPA is a pre-802.11i certification that addresses TKIP and is used in either SOHO or enterprise-based wireless networks. Wi-Fi Protected Setup is not intended for enterprise WLAN deployments.

16. B. A wireless intrusion prevention system will automatically monitor the network for signatures that match potential intrusion techniques. An intrusion prevention system has the capability to automatically shut down a rogue access point. An intrusion detection system requires a manual shutdown. A WIPS will not notify a network administrator of a recent firmware upgrade.

17. B. If WEP must be used on a wireless network, the devices that use WEP should be separated using VLANs. This will protect the rest of the network from being compromised. Voice transmissions can be seen with the correct tools. CCMP/AES is available in newer devices that support the latest wireless security methods but is not available in older devices.

18. B. An intruder can spoof a MAC address in order to circumvent the MAC filter and gain access to the wireless network. Encryption cracking is a different form of intrusion that

also could possibly allow an intruder to steal a user's authentication credentials. An RF denial-of-service attack is caused by transmitting high-energy RF to prevent access to the wireless network.

19. C. PIN-based security is usually used with SOHO brand wireless devices that support Wi-Fi Protected Setup certification (WPS). The devices are typically used in small office/home office installations or by home-based users. WPA 2.0 solutions can use either passphrase or 802.1X/EAP.

20. A. Layer 2 Tunneling Protocol (L2TP) commonly uses IPSec for encryption. PPTP is another VPN method that uses MPPE 128-bit encryption. AES and WEP are used with Layer 2 802.11-based wireless networks.

Chapter 10: Wireless LAN Site Survey Basics

1. A, C. The purpose of a wireless site survey is to find areas of RF coverage and interference and to determine placement of equipment such as access points and bridges. The cost of equipment and selection of manufacturer also play a role but are not part of the site survey objective.

2. A. The number of required access points is a good gauge whether a site survey is required. The geographic location of the business, number of wiring closets, and the number of servers do not determine if a site survey is required.

3. C. Typically the first step of a wireless LAN site survey is to gather the necessary business requirements. Interviewing managers and users is the next step, followed by determining RF coverage and documenting existing networks. Installing access points is one of the final steps.

4. A. Enterprise wireless LAN deployments typically use omnidirectional antennas connected directly to an access point. Other antenna types may be used but are not as common in this type of deployment.

5. D. Manufacturing environments typically use equipment that interferes with devices in the 2.4 GHz ISM band. Wireless 3G and cellular telephones work in other frequency ranges and do not affect wireless LANs. 900 MHz is not used by IEEE 802.11 wireless networks. CB radios work at a different frequency range.

6. C. Healthcare locations typically have equipment that works in the 2.4 GHz ISM band. These devices could potentially cause interference with a wireless network that operates in this band. Office, government, and education installations will not have as much ISM equipment.

7. C. The type of applications—either hardware or software—that will be used on the wireless network will have a large impact on the final deployment. This is an important question to ask end users. The other questions also need to be answered, but they should be asked of managers and IT staff.

8. A, C. Physical and data security requirements are part of a wireless LAN site survey. These requirements may have an impact on the number of access points or other devices required for the network. Access point, device, and infrastructure security also plays a role but is typically not considered part of an initial site survey.

9. C. Of all the devices listed, the voice handset would be the best candidate that would use roaming features of a wireless network, mostly because of mobility and features. Notebook computers and tablet devices may have roaming capabilities, but these devices are not as sensitive to latency. Wireless cameras are usually stationary devices.

10. B. The number of devices is an important determining factor in the number of access points required for a wireless LAN deployment. The type and manufacturer of devices are not concerns. The antenna in a client device will help with providing and maintaining device connectivity.

11. A. Interviewing managers and users will help determine the performance expectations of the wireless LAN because they are the ones who will be using it and they have the best understanding of the needs of an organization. Locations of RF interference and access points are part of the network design stage, which takes place after the gathering of information stage. In most cases, creating floor plans is not a primary responsibility of a site survey; however, obtaining floor plans is significant.

12. D. Floor plans of facilities can sometimes be imported into site survey software programs. This helps in determining the RF propagation by placing access points in a simulated environment. Access point models as well as cost estimates are required at a later time in a site survey.

13. D. Storage of paint and other liquids in large quantities can cause RF to be absorbed.

14. A, F. The business requirements and purpose of the wireless LAN are two areas that would be discussed at an initial meeting regarding a site survey. The other topics will be discussed at a later time.

15. C. An RF jamming attack would fall under physical security. Access point security, infrastructure security, and wiring closet security do not involve RF jamming. Data security is a separate issue.

16. B. The aesthetic requirements are usually discussed with hotel management since they are the ones responsible for the appearance of the hotel. PoE requirements and RF coverage and interference would be questions for a different group, which in some cases may be an outside provider.

17. A. The applications used will determine the number of access points in a wireless LAN deployment. Bandwidth-intensive applications may require more access points. Security requirements are important but typically do not strongly affect the number of access points required. Ceiling height is a factor when determining the RF coverage, not necessarily the number of infrastructure devices.

18. B. Access point output power is a determining factor in what type of coverage the AP will provide. Wiring closet locations and electrical power requirements are more related to wired infrastructure connectivity. Floor plans and blueprints will be used to note access point locations.

19. D. The initial gathering of information includes number of users, applications and their use, and other wireless networks in the area. The cost of the proposed equipment is not usually addressed at this point.

20. C. Office building deployments commonly use omnidirectional antennas that are mounted directly to an access point. Manufacturing, warehousing, and sports arena deployments more often use a combination of omnidirectional, semidirectional, and sometimes highly directional antennas.

Chapter 11: Performing an RF Wireless LAN Site Survey

1. A, C. The main objectives of a wireless site survey are to determine areas of RF interference and RF coverage as well as locations of access points and other infrastructure devices. The applications used have more to do with capacity planning. Wiring closet locations and security implantations are factors that need to be taken into account but are not the main objectives.

2. D. Because of RF propagation, site surveys are really three-dimensional. Therefore in a three-story building all floors need to be taken into consideration. Omnidirectional antennas may be polarized either vertically or horizontally. Single-channel architectures use the same channel for multiple floors.

3. A, B. A spectrum analyzer and a tool that passively scans for wireless networks such as NetStumbler can be used for a manual site survey. The other options' association and authentication can be viewed using a protocol analyzer and are not "standalone" tools.

4. A, C. Manual site surveys can be either passive or active. Scanning is a method of locating wireless LANs. A spectrum analyzer will allow you to see the RF. A packet is information that carries computer data from one device to another.

5. B, D. Non-Wi-Fi interference is interference by anything other than wireless LANs that operates in the same frequency range. AM radios and digital TV systems do not operate in the license-free bands. 802.11b interference is wireless LAN interference. Radar systems operate in the 5 GHz UNII band.

6. C. Recommended received signal strength for voice applications in the 2.4 GHz ISM band at a data rate of 54 mbps is about −67 dBm. A recommended signal-to-noise ratio is more than 20 to 25 dB.

7. C. A predictive modeling site survey is software-based and takes the attenuation values of the building and other materials into consideration. Active and passive are forms of manual site surveys and record actual information about the site.

8. B. OFDM networks operate in the 5 GHz UNII band and would not affect an 802.11g network that operates in the 2.4 GHz ISM band. FHSS, DSSS, and ERP-OFDM all operate in the 2.4 GHz ISM band and could cause interference with an 802.11g network.

9. A, B. The signal strength and SNR are two important values to record during the manual site survey process. Signal loss and propagation loss have different effects, and packet retries are more of an issue with dynamic rate selection.

10. C. Manual site surveys can be very accurate because actual readings are taken at the site using test access points and a wireless client. This can take quite some time to complete depending on the size of the location. Wireless hardware is required to perform the site survey, and access to the whole facility is required.

11. A. A spectrum analyzer can be used to view radio frequency. Wireless packets, data rates, and association frames can be viewed with a protocol analyzer.

12. B. Since new hardware will be purchased and backward compatibility is not required, you could recommend using wireless network hardware that works in the 5 GHz band. This will eliminate interference from the other tenants that are using the 2.4 GHz ISM band. Automatic channel selection, spectrum analysis, and predictive modeling site survey will not help because surrounding access points already use the entire band.

13. B. A predictive modeling site survey will take less time than a passive survey because a passive survey requires a manual analysis. On-site protocol analysis or scanning utility will determine areas of RF interference from wireless LANs. The predictive modeling survey does not help you choose manufacturers' equipment to be used in a deployment.

14. D. A verification of the predictive survey should be performed to verify that the survey meets the customer's requirements. Although not required, it should be considered.

15. D. Dead spots (areas that lack RF coverage) should be identified on floor plans or blueprints. This is part of standard documentation practices. Marking them with tape, taking a photograph, and showing the site manager in person are not the best ways to document dead spots.

16. B. An active site survey requires the survey device to associate to an access point. A passive site survey monitors all access points in the area. A predictive modeling site survey does not involve associating to an access point. Associating to an access point is not a required part of manual testing.

17. D. A semidirectional antenna such as a Yagi is a good choice for an application requiring coverage down a long hallway or corridor. Low- or high-gain omnidirectional

antennas will provide 360-degree horizontal coverage. Parabolic dish antennas are typically used for outdoor long-range bridging.

18. D. In this situation, correct antenna selection is important to provide optimal coverage as well as proper aesthetics. In this example, a spectrum analysis or protocol analysis could be performed but is not required. Environmental conditions are typically not an issue in a small office deployment.

19. A. Co-channel interference is caused by two access points operating on the same radio frequency channel. Access points operating on channels 1 and 2 may cause adjacent channel interference. Channels 1, 6, and 11 are nonoverlapping channels and will not interfere with one another.

20. A, E. A walkthrough of the location and spectrum analysis are both recommended guidelines when performing a manual site survey. Equipment purchase and client device configuration are additional factors to consider but are not part of the manual site survey. A predictive analysis is a software-based site survey solution that does not require manual testing.

Chapter 12: Troubleshooting and Maintaining IEEE 802.11 Wireless Local Area Networks

1. D. Multipath is caused by reflected signals arriving at the receiver at slightly different times (delay spread). Refraction is an RF behavior caused by passing through an object of different density, resulting in a change of the signal strength. Absorption is the result of a signal not reflecting or bending or passing around an obstacle.

2. B. A wireless client device showing a low received signal strength value could be too far away from an access point. Of the answers listed, an additional access point would be the best solution. Upgrading the client device or the firmware would not help the situation. Multipath is caused by reflections and cannot be eliminated.

3. B. A user experiencing a slow connection could be too far away from an access point to get a strong enough signal to move data at the highest rate. A 5.8 GHz phone is operating at a different frequency and would not cause interference with an 802.11g wireless LAN. A MAC filter is set on an access point and will either allow or disallow a client connection. If a firmware upgrade was causing a problem for an access point, it would affect all users.

4. A. Increasing the output power of the access point will result in a higher received signal at the wireless client device. Enabling load balancing will not improve signal strength but will limit the number of devices that associate with an access point and may improve throughput. Upgrading the ISP service to faster data rates will not improve signal strength for the wireless client. Enabling security such as WPA 2.0 will not increase the signal strength seen by the client but is recommended to secure the transmission.

5. C. Incorrect security parameters such as a WPA passphrase will prevent a wireless client device from completing a Layer 2 connection and obtaining an IP address from a DHCP service. If the client device is different technology like 802.11a, the device would not have been able to connect. If a static IP address is used, it will not display all zeros. Although a computer virus can create problems for the client device, it would not prevent the device from obtaining an IP address after connecting to the wireless network.

6. B. A sudden change in performance might occur if an access point for a new tenant is set to the same RF channel as your client's access point. This could cause interference, which would degrade performance. A firmware upgrade on the access point usually fixes problems or provides enhancements. Received signal strength is typically an issue based on distance from an access point. Diversity antennas would help minimize the problems associated with multipath and in most cases would improve performance rather than degrade it.

7. A. A hidden node problem caused by obstacles or obstructions could be resolved by adding another access point so wireless client devices would not be subject to clear channel assessment issues. Setting an access point to Mixed Mode will allow both 802.11b and 802.11g clients to connect to the network. Increasing the distance between the access point and the clients will not improve the situation but will actually make it worse. Adjusting the received signal strength on the client would improve performance for that client but would not necessarily solve the hidden node problem.

8. B. The wireless LAN client device would be mostly affected by weak signal strength. An infrastructure device such as an access point generates the signal received by the client. Multipath is a phenomenon that is a result of several wavefronts of the same signal reaching a receiver at different times. A transmitter device is responsible for sending an RF signal.

9. A. A passphrase or preshared key will be validated after an 802.11 authentication and association. In order for the client device to get a valid IP address, a successful authentication, association, and passphrase would have to occur. A deauthentication will end the authentication state, and a disassociation will no longer allow a device to pass traffic across the access point.

10. C. Two factors that may have an impact on throughput in a wireless LAN are distance from the access point or the output power level of an access point. The IP address and MAC address identify the device on the network and would not affect throughput. The output power of the client device has more to do with its transmitting capabilities than the receiver's capabilities.

11. A. The device driver is a required component that allows the wireless network adapter card to interface with the operating system. A device driver does not provide security nor does it identify the network.

12. **A.** Hidden node caused by different technology types is the result of the access point not being able to differentiate between spread-spectrum technologies. An access point set to Mixed Mode will understand both HR/DSSS and ERP-OFDM, which will solve the problem. Adding another access point or increasing output power would not solve the problem, although that would be a solution for other hidden node scenarios. Removing an obstacle is a valid solution for a different hidden node problem.

13. **D.** A corrupt device driver may cause the network adapter card in a wireless client device to operate incorrectly or to malfunction. A terminated Internet connection would be a global problem and would affect all users. An upgrade or incorrect firmware would not cause the problem only for a single user.

14. **A.** Layer 1 provides the physical connectivity between devices, which use the air as the medium to carry the radio frequency. Layers 3 and 4 are responsible for TCP/IP. Layer 7 is the interface to the user, also known as the Application layer.

15. **C.** Windows 98 and later are designed to use the Automatic Private IP Address service. This service will provide an IP address to client devices in the range of 169.254.*x.x*. This will allow local connectivity for any devices that are connected to a common LAN.

16. **A.** The distance from an access point could affect the received signal strength for a wireless client device. The distance from other clients has no impact on devices that are connected to an access point. The distance from an Ethernet switch or from the wiring closet has no impact on a wireless client.

17. **B.** The signal-to-noise ratio represents the difference between the received signal strength and the level of the noise floor. A good signal-to-noise ratio will give a client the ability to distinguish between signal and noise and allow it to recover data that was transmitted.

18. **D.** 802.11n takes advantage of multipath, which is typically a problem for other wireless LAN technologies. By using multipath, 802.11n devices will have better throughput than 802.11g devices. Received signal strength means the same thing across technologies. DHCP is a service that provides IP addresses automatically. Hidden node is a problem that may degrade throughput for connected devices.

19. **A.** Adding access points can help increase the throughput for a wireless LAN client device. This is possible because additional access points would allow for load-balancing features and therefore provide less contention at that access point. Upgrading the client software to full-duplex mode is not an option, and if the RF noise was increased, throughput would be less. Hiding the SSID has no impact on throughput.

20. **C.** Increasing the gain of an antenna will provide a larger RF coverage cell, thereby providing more received signal at the same distance for a wireless client device. Upgrading the wireless client will not improve the received signal strength. Load balancing will help with throughput, and Microsoft WZC is an example of a built-in client utility.

Appendix

B

About the Additional Study Tools

IN THIS APPENDIX:

✓ Additional study tools

✓ System requirements

✓ Using the study tools

✓ Troubleshooting

Additional Study Tools

The following sections are arranged by category and summarize the software and other goodies you'll find from the companion website. If you need help with installing the items, refer to the installation instructions in the "Using the Study Tools" section of this appendix.

> **NOTE** The additional study tools can be found at www.sybex.com/go/cwts2e. Here, you will get instructions on how to download the files to your hard drive.

Sybex Test Engine

The files contain the Sybex test engine, which includes two bonus practice exams, as well as the Assessment Test and the Chapter Review Questions, which are also included in the book itself.

Electronic Flashcards

These handy electronic flashcards are just what they sound like. One side contains a question, and the other side shows the answer.

Bonus Content

We have included additional bonus content, including demo software, and a white paper on site surveying and a video.

Demo Software The author has included numbers demo versions of popular wireless software products you might be using in your day to day activities.

> **TamoSoft CommView® for WiFi v.6.3** This is a network monitor and analyzer for 802.11 a/b/g/n networks that displays important information such as the list of access points and stations, per-node and per-channel statistics, signal strength, a list of packets and network connections, protocol distribution charts, etc. Look for file ca6.zip on the study tools directory. For more information on this product visit www.tamos.com.

> **TamoGraph® Site Survey 3.0** This is a wireless site survey software tool for collecting, visualizing, and analyzing 802.11 a/b/g/n WiFi data. Wireless network deployment and maintenance requires the use of a professional RF site survey tool that facilitates otherwise time-consuming and very complex tasks, such as ongoing analysis and reporting of signal

strength, noise and interference, channel allocation, data rates, etc. Look for file `tg3.zip` on the study tools directory. For more information on this product visit `www.tamos.com`.

TamoSoft® Throughput Test   This is a utility for testing the performance of a wireless or wired network. This utility continuously sends TCP and UDP data streams across your network and computes important metrics, such as upstream and downstream throughput values, packet loss, and round-trip time, and displays the results in both numeric and chart formats. Look for file `tt1.zip` on the study tools directory. For more information on this product visit `www.tamos.com`.

MetaGeek Chanalyzer v4   Chanalyzer turns data collected from a Wi-Spy into highly interactive charts and graphs, allowing users to visualize their wireless landscape. Look for file `Chanalyzer-4-Installer.msi` on the study tools directory. For more information on this product visit `www.metageek.net`.

MetaGeek inSSIDer   inSSIDer is an open source WiFi scanner that allows you to scan settings of nearby access points, inspect security and channel selection and measure signal strength. Look for file `inSSIDer-Installer-2.1.5.1393.msi` on the study tools directory. For more information on this product visit `www.metageek.net`.

White Papers   The author has included the Ekahua Sample Site Survey Report white paper. This is a sample report that was generated from Ekahau Site Survey, a WiFi planning, site survey, and troubleshooting Tool. For more information on this product visit `www.ekahau.com`.

Videos   The author has include a video from TamoSoft showing how to use their TamoGraph Site Survey 3.0 product.

PDF of Glossary of Terms

We have included an electronic version of the Glossary in `.pdf` format. You can view the electronic version of the Glossary with Adobe Reader.

Adobe Reader

We've also included a copy of Adobe Reader so you can view PDF files that accompany the book's content. For more information on Adobe Reader or to check for a newer version, visit Adobe's website at `www.adobe.com/products/reader/`.

System Requirements

Make sure your computer meets the minimum system requirements shown in the following list. If your computer doesn't match up to most of these requirements, you may have problems using the software and files. For the latest and greatest information, please refer to the ReadMe file located in the downloads.

- A PC running Microsoft Windows 98, Windows 2000, Windows NT4 (with SP4 or later), Windows Me, Windows XP, Windows Vista, or Windows 7

- An Internet connection

Using the Study Tools

To install the items, follow these steps:

1. Download the .ZIP file to your hard drive, and unzip to an appropriate location. Instructions on where to download this file can be found here: www.sybex.com/go/cwts2e.

2. Click the Start.EXE file to open up the study tools file.

3. Read the license agreement, and then click the Accept button if you want to use the study tools.

The main interface appears. The interface allows you to access the content with just one or two clicks.

Troubleshooting

Wiley has attempted to provide programs that work on most computers with the minimum system requirements. Alas, your computer may differ, and some programs may not work properly for some reason.

The two likeliest problems are that you don't have enough memory (RAM) for the programs you want to use or you have other programs running that are affecting installation or running of a program. If you get an error message such as "Not enough memory" or "Setup cannot continue," try one or more of the following suggestions and then try using the software again:

Turn off any antivirus software running on your computer. Installation programs sometimes mimic virus activity and may make your computer incorrectly believe that it's being infected by a virus.

Close all running programs. The more programs you have running, the less memory is available to other programs. Installation programs typically update files and programs; so if you keep other programs running, installation may not work properly.

Have your local computer store add more RAM to your computer. This is, admittedly, a drastic and somewhat expensive step. However, adding more memory can really help the speed of your computer and allow more programs to run at the same time.

Customer Care

If you have trouble with the book's companion study tools, please call the Wiley Product Technical Support phone number at (800) 762-2974, or email them at http://sybex.custhelp.com/.

Index

Note to the Reader: Throughout this index **boldfaced** page numbers indicate primary discussions of a topic. *Italicized* page numbers indicate illustrations.

T

Free Online Study Tools

Register on Sybex.com to gain access to a complete set of study tools to help you prepare for your CWTS Exam.

Comprehensive Study Tool Package Includes:

- **Assessment Test** to help you focus your study to specific objectives

- **Chapter Review Questions** for each chapter of the book

- **Two Full-Length Practice Exams** to test your knowledge of the material

- **Electronic Flashcards** to reinforce your learning and give you that last-minute test prep before the exam

- **Searchable Glossary** gives you instant access to the key terms you'll need to know for the exam

- **Additional Resources** including White Papers

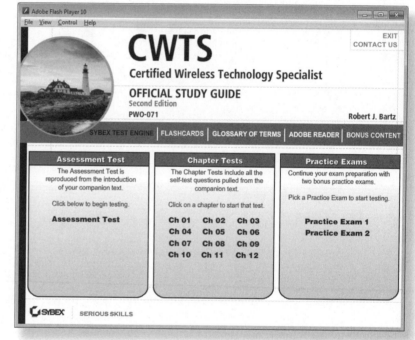

Go to www.sybex.com/go/cwts2e to register and gain access to this comprehensive study tool package.